LEGAL GUIDELINES for the CLINICAL LABORATORY

LEGAL GUIDELINES for the CLINICAL LABORATORY

Edited by Robert J. Fitzgibbon

Medical Economics Company
Book Division
Oradell, New Jersey 07649

Library of Congress Cataloging in Publication Data

Main entry under title:

Legal guidelines for the clinical laboratory.

Includes index.

1. Medical laboratories – Law and legislation – United States. I. Fitzgibbon, Robert.

KF3826.L3L43 344.73'041 80-22470

ISBN 0-87489-243-0

Cover design by Elaine Kilcullen

ISBN 0-87489-243-0

Medical Economics Company
Oradell, New Jersey 07649

Printed in the United States of America

Contents

Contributors

Christopher J. Bale is *MLO's* Washington correspondent.

Jackie Blakeney, MT(ASCP), is now clinical chemistry supervisor at Pathology Laboratories, Ltd., Hattiesburg, Miss.

Marlene A. Brownson, CLA(ASCP), is a certified laboratory assistant at Saginaw Osteopathic Hospital, Saginaw, Mich.

David N. Buhr, MT(ASCP), was a medical technologist at the VA Hospital in Iowa City, Iowa.

Lyle L. Bulgrin, MT(ASCP), is chief medical technologist at Pekin Memorial Hospital, Pekin, Ill.

Richard Conniff was senior associate editor of *MLO*.

John Davidson is chief technologist at Wentworth-Douglass Hospital, Dover, N.H.

Robert M. Dews was supervisor of the forensic section, laboratories division, Idaho Department of Health and Welfare, Boise.

Harold L. Engel, M.D., J.D., is associate clinical professor of anesthesiology at the University of Southern California School of Medicine in Los Angeles. He is also president of Mid-Valley College of Law in Van Nuys and practices law with Bonne, Jones, Bridges, Mueller & O'Keefe in Los Angeles.

Gretchen Evenson, MT(ASCP), was evening supervisor at Mt. Sinai Medical Center, Milwaukee.

Joyce Fisher is chemistry supervisor at St. Vincent's Medical Center of Richmond, Staten Island, N.Y.

Patricia A. Flury, MT, is administrative technologist at Memorial Hospital, Hollywood, Fla.

Mary E. Gaskin, MT(ASCP), was chief technologist at Medical Arts Group, Cadillac, Mich.

Barbara E. Goergen, MT(ASCP), is assistant chief technologist at Badger Red Cross Blood Center, Madison, Wis.

Edward S. Graff is now laboratory manager at Community Hospital of Brooklyn, N.Y.

Frank Greaves, MT(ASCP), is the pseudonym of an assistant laboratory manager at a large urban hospital.

Michael Guarnieri, Ph.D., M.P.H., is laboratory director of Chemical Determinations for Medicine Inc., Baltimore.

S.R. Guarnieri, M.D., M.P.H., is director of clinical services for the Baltimore City Health Department.

Howard C. Hay, J.D., is a partner in the law firm of Paul, Hastings, Janofsky, & Walker, Costa Mesa, Calif.

Neal M. Hoffman, M.P.A., is assistant to the president for affirmative action, State University of New York, Upstate Medical Center, Syracuse.

Pamela Krueger, MT(ASCP), was a technologist at Mt. Sinai Medical Center, Milwaukee.

David J. Kull is senior editor of *MLO*.

Peggy Leverton, MT, is laboratory supervisor at Holvey & Derwin Medical Corp., Los Angeles.

Robert J. Loder, M.A., MT(ASCP), is administrative technologist at Loma Linda University Medical Center, Loma Linda, Calif.

Carl W. Mantey, M.H.A., is now assistant administrator at Huntsville Memorial Hospital, Huntsville, Tex.

Bettina G. Martin, M.S., HT(ASCP), is administrative technologist and professor of medical technology at State University of New York, Upstate Medical Center, Syracuse.

Joseph Meier, MT(ASCP), is a technologist at St. Joseph Hospital and Health Care Center, Lancaster, Pa.

Don Harper Mills, M.D., J.D., is clinical professor of pathology at the University of Southern California, Los Angeles.

Paul Moffett, MT(ASCP), is now administrative technologist at Christian Northeast Hospital, St. Louis.

Jane C. Monaghan is managing editor of *MLO*.

Michael X. Morrell, J.D., is a partner in Sonnenreich & Morrell, P.C., Washington, D.C.

Robert B. Nichols, M.D., J.D., is on the board of directors of Hollywood Presbyterian Medical Center and is a clinical instructor in orthopedics at the University of Southern California School of Medicine, Los Angeles.

Kay M. Oesterreicher, CLA(ASCP), is a laboratory assistant at Riverview Hospital, Wisconsin Rapids, Wis.

Charles S. Petty, M.D., is director, Southwestern Institute of Forensic Sciences, Dallas.

Lawrence A. Reynolds Jr., is now quality assurance manager at Syva Co. Cupertino, Calif.

Alvin M. Ring, M.D., is director of laboratories, Holy Cross Hospital, Chicago.

V. Beverly Rogers, MT(ASCP)SBB, is blood bank supervisor, Cottonwood Hospital, Murray, Utah.

Vicki Salmon, MT(ASCP), is blood bank supervisor at Mary Lanning Memorial Hospital, Hastings, Neb.

Vincent Scicchitano is assistant personnel director at State University of New York, Upstate Medical Center, Syracuse.

Walter L. Scott, Ph.D., is now with the FDA's Bureau of Medical Devices, Silver Spring, Md.

Kathleen Crowley Sheedy, MT(ASCP)SBB, is blood bank supervisor and instructor in medical technology at State University of New York, Upstate Medical Center, Syracuse.

Henry B. Soloway, M.D., is with Associated Pathologists in Las Vegas and is adjunct professor of biology at the University of Nevada.

Josephine Soublet, MT(ASCP), is a medical technologist at Kaiser Foundation Hospital, Oakland, Calif.

Larry A. Stanifer, M.P.H., is laboratory administrative assistant at East Tennessee Baptist Hospital, Knoxville, Tenn.

Ted Street, M.B.A., is administrative assistant of laboratories at Wesley Medical Center, Wichita, Kan.

James A. Terzian, M.D., is now assistant pathologist, Cayuga County Laboratory, Auburn, N.Y.

Pam Troyer, MT(ASCP)SBB, is education coordinator at Badger Red Cross Blood Center, Madison, Wis.

William O. Umiker, M.D., is director of laboratories at St. Joseph Hospital and Health Care Center, Lancaster, Pa.

Marian Wolfson is senior editor of *MLO*.

Christine Woodrum, RT, CNMT, is managerial technologist, department of nuclear medicine, Bradford Hospital, Bradford, Pa.

Joyce Yeast, Ph.D., is now field representative with the Joint Commission on Accreditation of Hospitals, Chicago.

Foreword

As an attorney whose firm specializes in the health-care field, I can sympathize with the plight of laboratorians on legal matters. First of all, they face the ever-present threat of becoming involved in medical malpractice suits. And that threat is not diminishing.

Then they face a growing body of legislation and regulation promulgated at all levels—Federal, state, and local. Since CLIA 1967 was enacted, consider just some of the regulatory agencies that now impact directly on the clinical laboratory: HHS (formerly HEW), FDA, CDC, HFCA, OSHA, BMD, HSA, SHPDA, NRC, NLRB, EEOC, NCHCA, EPA. The alphabet-soup list could go on and on, and even the most knowledgeable laboratorian might be hard-pressed to identify each agency and how it affects the clinical laboratory.

That's the point of this book. Drawing on the hundreds of management articles *MLO/Medical Laboratory Observer* has published, Editor Bob Fitzgibbon has selected the most pertinent and useful ones to comprise this legal handbook for the clinical laboratory. Each article has been reviewed, revised, and updated where necessary, and the whole has been organized under 11 subject headings. The wise laboratory manager should be versed in each of these areas.

I can't guarantee that this book will keep you and your lab out of legal predicaments, but it will authoritatively guide you in avoiding them. And having it at hand for ready reference will surely add to your legal peace of mind.

Michael X. Morrell, J.D.
Member, *MLO* Editorial Advisory Board
Partner, Sonnenreich & Morrell, P.C.
Washington, D.C.

MALPRACTICE LIABILITY

1

Laboratory Malpractice Risks

Don Harper Mills, M.D., J.D.

Most injuries involved in medical malpractice litigation arise as direct complications of medical, surgical, or laboratory procedures. In this context, ''injury'' means the continuation of the patient's original disease process because of a delay in diagnosis (perhaps induced by laboratory error) and the performance of unnecessary therapeutic procedures as a result of misdiagnosis of the patient's condition (perhaps caused by laboratory error).

Laboratories, therefore, may be liable for indirect injuries to patients they have never seen. The laboratory-patient relationship is established, in these instances, when specimens are received for examination or analysis.

Liability for an injury to a patient exists only if that injury was caused by some type of misconduct by the laboratory. Misconduct encompasses a broad range of activities, explained better by examples than by legalistic verbiage. However, as we pass through the various phases of potential laboratory liability, keep the following questions in mind:

If the patient suffered an injury from a direct laboratory complication or from an error in laboratory analysis relied on by the attending physician, why did the error or complication occur? Was it the result of negligence? Was the laboratory or its employee competent to perform the procedure from which the error or complication arose? Should the possibility of this type of error or complication have been anticipated? If so, was anything done to try to prevent it? Once it occurred, was it handled properly?

Those are the searching questions that must be answered to the jury's satisfaction. No one in court is expected to be better versed on them than members of the defendant laboratory. This is their field. Therefore, if they cannot establish their own defense, it is unlikely outside experts can.

Laboratories are sued less often than clinicians. The procedures laboratories perform, while not risk-free, are less apt to cause major calamities. Injuries caused *directly* by laboratory activity are less frequent and less severe than those caused by attending physicians and surgeons.

Laboratories can cause injuries *indirectly* by producing incorrect test results upon which the attending physicians may rely to their patients' detriment. However, before a laboratory can be held liable for causing this type of injury, someone has to produce evidence that the physician had the right to rely upon the incorrect laboratory report. Though the physician's "right to rely" depends upon the facts of each case, the existence of this intermediate issue–reliance–insulates laboratories, to some extent, from malpractice liability. Laboratories will continue to risk less than attending physicians and surgeons; however, there is no reason for complacency. The risk is still significant. Let's look at these risks in detail, starting with *direct* injuries:

Extraction of specimen. Venipuncture is the most likely source of injury. Though it can induce many types of complications, real injury is rare. So venipuncture is not a significant source of liability for laboratories. Some claims involve multiple, unsuccessful attempts to obtain venous blood specimens, usually because of inexperienced technicians. They must be taught when to call for help.

Arterial puncture poses a greater risk. It demands considerable expertise, as well as adequate follow-up evaluation of the patient's extremity to assure continued arterial sufficiency. Medical standards requiring increased use of blood-gas determinations may precipitate a number of lawsuits alleging improper arterial extraction technique.

Some laboratories perform spinal taps to obtain CSF specimens for requested examinations. In some cases, these taps are performed by pathologists with limited expertise in this procedure. In one case, the pathologist made five attempts to secure a specimen before he finally gave up. In the meantime, because of actual nerve root injury or, possibly, anxiety, the patient complained of persistent back pain. A claim was made and settled with minimal payment. But this underrepresents the medicolegal dangers involved. Unless laboratory personnel are efficient in lumbar punctures, someone who is should be given the responsibility for securing these specimens.

Protection of the patient. Fainting associated with venipuncture is so well known that all patients deserve some form of protection. Ideally, if the patient is not recumbent during and shortly after extraction, he should be given three-sided support in a proper chair. Having a patient sit on a stool without such support invites potential liability should he faint, fall, and hurt himself. Fortunately, most such injuries are minor. But catastrophe can occur.

One case involved a patient who, unknown to the venipuncturist, was on an anticoagulant. He fainted and fell, suffering a minor scalp bruise. The technician dismissed him without instructions for follow-up observation. Twenty-four hours later, the patient was brought to the emergency department in coma as a result of a subdural hematoma. He survived, but suffered permanent brain damage.

The resulting lawsuit dealt not only with the issue of lack of protection of the patient during the extraction of the venous blood specimen, but also with the lack of proper evaluation once the original injury occurred. Anyone suffering even a slight head injury under potential liability circumstances should be questioned about anticoagulant therapy, followed by appropriate medical attention when indicated.

Some patients have known fainting tendencies. Each patient should be questioned routinely so that increased precautions can be undertaken when indicated. For every patient, a record should be made that a question about fainting tendencies was asked and answered (e.g., the lab test requisition could be stamped: "Denies fainting tendency"). Such a record shows that the question was asked and a negative answer received. This piece of evidence may be extremely important in the event a patient who did faint and injure himself brings a lawsuit alleging that the technician failed to inquire.

Injecting foreign substances. Laboratories are frequently asked to perform tests requiring the injection of foreign substances, such as bromsulphalein (BSP). This substance is capable of inducing both systemic reactions and serious local tissue destruction (when it infiltrates into extravenous tissue). Lawsuits involving such injuries raise several issues: Who, among laboratory personnel, has the legal right to administer these substances to patients? Must it be a physician, or can it be a technologist? This depends upon local state law. And, assuming someone other than a physician can legally administer this substance intravenously, would he be wise to do so without available medical help? If we accept the proposition that there is a calculated risk of systemic reaction from this substance, a laboratory without the facility or personnel for immediate care of such a reaction is exposing itself to additional liability.

Most test substances given to patients are sent to laboratories with brochures or package inserts outlining the manufacturers' recommendations for use. These inserts are required by the Food and Drug Administration. When relevant to the issues of a lawsuit, they are admissible as evidence against the defendant laboratory.

If, for instance, the manufacturer recommends a certain type of sensitivity testing prior to full use of the substance, the jury will be told about it if the laboratory failed to do the preliminary testing. The value of such sensitivity testing is still a subject of scientific dispute, and, of course, that argument is used for the defense of the laboratory. However, it is not always successful in the face of clear-cut recommendations by the manufacturer, approved by the FDA. Each laboratory should evaluate such recommendations and establish definite policy positions as to whether specific recommendations will be followed or not.

Consent. Consent is a problem for laboratories only when there is direct contact with the patient, accompanied by the possibility of inducing a direct injury. Laboratories must understand the consent laws of their own states. More often than not, this particular problem involves minors. Many states have lowered the age of majority, but such legislative action has not been uniform. The definition of minority and majority varies from state to state. So also does the definition of an emancipated minor. Finally, some states have laws allowing certain minors to consent to certain procedures (e.g., tests for V.D. or pregnancy).

Whether or not disclosure of risks must be made by laboratory personnel also varies from state to state. Laboratories should understand the application of rules of disclosure in their own states. Generally speaking, however, courts do not require major disclosure of potential risks for routine extraction procedures.

In actual practice, consent issues have been a minor liability risk for laboratories. This may change, but laboratories will probably never be confronted with the magnitude of consent cases faced by attending physicians and surgeons.

Misidentification. Performing a laboratory procedure on the wrong patient is rarely defensible, yet it happens often enough to require a review of procedures to assure proper identification. Whether in the hospital or in an outpatient setting, spoken identification alone is not enough. Inpatients should be identified by wristband. Outpatients must be identified by a driver's license or other written document that includes the bearer's name.

Ordinarily, the injury is minimal, such as performing a venipuncture on a patient who does not require that procedure. However, the injury could be major. One such case involved the extraction of venous blood from the wrong patient without subsequent precautions in the face of active anticoagulation, resulting in major hemorrhage before the problem was appreciated.

The most common injury associated with misidentification is administering a blood transfusion to the wrong patient. This is most likely to happen to inpatients in settings where the responsibility for administering the transfusion rests more with hospital personnel than with laboratory technologists. If, on the other hand, the misidentification is the result of mislabeling the bottle of blood by the laboratory, the resulting injury is an indirect one. Let's now consider in detail that and other *indirect* injuries.

Mislabeling. A primary laboratory function is to induce others to rely upon issued products and reports. Otherwise, laboratories would serve no useful purpose in the chain of patient care. Therefore, episodes of mislabeling by laboratory personnel are rarely defensible. Occasionally, mislabeling involves blood used for transfusion. If a nurse or attending physician, relying on the label, administers the blood to the wrong patient, serious injury to that patient can occur and probable liability for the laboratory will result.

Mislabeling reports of laboratory tests can be just as dangerous. In one case, the laboratory mislabeled a blood-type report on an obstetrical patient, listing her as Rh positive rather than Rh negative. Consequently, the physician did not investigate potential Rh incompatibility prior to or after delivery of the woman's first child. The error was not discovered until repeat testing was done with the second pregnancy less than a year later. By that time she had already developed high titers.

Sloppy reports. Assume a patient has a serious infection requiring proper antibiotic guidance and for which the laboratory has issued a report of culture and sensitivity testing. Assume that the report is filled in by hand by a laboratory employee who was rushed by the load of his duties. Assume further that the checkmarks under "sensitive" and "resistant" tended to cross beyond the spaces where they were intended to be. If the sloppiness is borderline, the physician may proceed, unaware that he is administering a drug that was not properly indicated for his patient. This happened in one case involving the administration of kanamycin, resulting in ototoxicity and deafness. While the physician was held liable for relying upon a document about which there was a question of clarity, so also was the laboratory for issuing it.

Miscalculation. Many chemistry tests require individual calculations by laboratory personnel, and errors occur now and then. In several cases involving hemolytic disease of the newborn, laboratories miscalculated and reported incorrect results of serum bilirubin tests. In each instance, the test result showed a level significantly less than 20 mg%, whereas the actual reading should have been greater than 20 mg%. The error induced a delay in the performance of exchange transfusion of the infant, resulting in brain damage from kernicterus. Suits on behalf of these infants against the laboratories were successful. Fortunately, the likelihood of miscalculation is declining because many laboratories now use automated testing devices with built-in quality-control systems.

Improper test performance. Automation has reduced potential error in this area as well. However, there are still a number of procedures that have not yet been automated. For instance, special procedures in toxicology are frequently performed by hand, requiring close observation of technique and the quality of reagents.

In one case, a girl was brought into the hospital with suspected aspirin intoxication, and the laboratory was asked to determine her salicylate level. This test had not been done in that laboratory for quite a while, and the reagent had deteriorated, a fact not appreciated by the technologist. An abnormally high test result was reported in error. Fortunately, the child did not exhibit clinical symptoms in keeping with the laboratory result. When the director of the laboratory arrived the next morning and was asked by the attending physician for another test, the problem was discovered and corrected. While the child sustained no injury other than an overnight stay in the hospital, the potential of real damage existed.

Lost specimen. Busy laboratories sometimes lose specimens. Fortunately, most specimens can be taken again, but the risk of liability is real. Three malpractice cases involved the loss of excisional biopsies of skin lesions that were suspected to be melanomas. It takes little imagination to see that real damages can ensue if safeguards are not taken against the loss of specimens.

The inadequate specimen. It is the duty of the laboratory to evaluate the adequacy of specimens submitted for examination or analysis. If the specimen is considered inadequate for proper examination, the clinician deserves a timely notice. In one case involving difficulty in diagnosing a patient's heart attack, a clinician entered the following note in the progress record of the patient's chart: ''It is a pity that the laboratory did not report 'Q.N.S.' for CPK and HBD on the day blood was drawn, as this may have been the day that these tests were abnormal.'' This lawsuit did involve aggravation of the patient's heart condition because of a delay in diagnosis. Whether the clinician was right or wrong, the laboratory is going to have to defend itself for a lack of prompt notice concerning the inadequacy of the specimen.

Interpretation of tissue specimens. Pathological examinations of tissue specimens, like all other human endeavors, are subject to error. The pathologist sits in an uncomfortable position because the specimens that he interprets are retained for posterity. If he interprets a lesion as benign and it turns out malignant, the slides in his possession can be reviewed subsequently by other pathologists to uncover errors.

The defense may claim that it was an ''honest mistake.'' But is this really a defense? Honesty is material to a malpractice case only if it is absent. The great majority of malpractice cases involving mistakes are colored with total honesty. The issue is the presence or absence of negligence. In the case of tissue slides, the failure to see disease that is seen by most other pathologists on the same slides raises a strong inference that the defendant pathologist was careless.

Not infrequently, good pathologists entertain doubt about their own interpretation of specific slides, whereupon they submit these slides to other pathologists. Occasionally, if the count comes back four to two in favor of cancer, the pathologist reports it to the clinician as cancer without qualification. The clinician is left with no suspicion of doubt. Herein lies the seed of potential malpractice liability. Whatever doubt exists should be passed on to the clinician to assist him in determining the future course of treatment. In many cases, doubt may be unimportant. In some, it might, and it is these cases that cause concern.

A word about circumstantial evidence is in order. Most people feel that a person injured by someone else's misconduct should receive compensation. They also feel that those who cause injuries in the absence of misconduct should avoid liability. Therefore, the determination of fault is critical to malpractice litigation.

When the specimen is preserved (e.g., a tissue slide), the opportunity to evaluate prior conduct is available. If, on re-examination, the evidence indicates no error, or if error is discovered and the evidence indicates justification, the lawsuit deserves a full defense. On the other hand, if it is discovered there was an error that should not have occurred, the case merits settlement, provided it can be accomplished within reason. In suits such as these, the evaluation of prior conduct is based on direct evidence (the specimen itself).

When a specimen is consumed during or discarded after the original test and report, direct evidence for re-evaluation no longer exists. The suit then turns on inferences derived from indirect or circumstantial evidence, a situation that often favors the patient more than the lab. In such cases, the attending physician is frequently put into a defensive position in order to justify his misdiagnosis or mistreatment. As a result, he might blame laboratory error as a cause of his conduct.

If, in any manner, the specter of probable laboratory error enters the picture, the practical burden shifts to the laboratory to prove—if it can—the absence of error or misconduct. Such proof might come from two sources: records that trace the proper performance of the particular test involved in the lawsuit and records of adequate quality control. Since the former are rarely available, evidence of quality control becomes extremely important. These records may be the only mechanism by which the laboratory can establish that it was doing as much as it could to avoid error. Quality control, therefore, helps to avoid inferences of error as well as errors themselves.

2

Liability in the Laboratory: An Overview

Walter L. Scott, Ph.D.

Malpractice. That word strikes alarm in the minds of physicians, hospital administrators, and just about everyone in the health-care field. Fortunately, laboratorians as a group have been less hard hit with malpractice suits than other health-care providers. But that does not mean there are *no* legal risks associated with lab medicine or that laboratorians are *never* involved in malpractice suits. There are, and they can be.

For these reasons, then, and because malpractice is an important health-care issue, laboratorians should know what constitutes malpractice, where potential trouble spots lie, what legal doctrines are common in malpractice cases, and what they can do to protect themselves and their laboratories from suit.

First, let's consider what malpractice is: Legally speaking, it is a failure to provide the standard of care that is due a patient. More succinctly, malpractice is professional negligence. But, in order for malpractice to be proved against a physician, a hospital, or a hospital employee, three distinct elements must be present:

- The patient must have sustained measurable injury.
- The court must find negligence on the part of the defendant—that professional standards of care were not followed.

- There must be proof that the negligent action was the cause—the legal term is proximate cause—of the patient's injury.

To illustrate these points, let's look at a malpractice case involving a laboratory. In June 1964, a baby was born to Rh-incompatible parents in a small Iowa town. Laboratory tests done at the local hospital showed a rapidly rising bilirubin level, and the baby displayed clinical symptoms that suggested the possibility of imminent brain damage. Concerned by both the symptoms and the test results, the family physician referred the baby to a pediatrician at a large hospital in a nearby city. This physician ignored the clinical symptoms and the local laboratory's test results and relied solely on test results from his own hospital, which indicated a low bilirubin level.

Unfortunately for everyone concerned, those test results were incorrect. The city hospital's laboratory, which was managed under a contract with two pathologists, had no regular quality-control procedure to check the reliability of its test results. The expiration date for the reagent used in the bilirubin test had, in fact, passed. The test results were wrong, and the infant suffered permanent brain damage.

The parents brought suit, and when the case was finally decided in 1974, the court found that the pediatrician, the city hospital, and the two pathologists who provided its laboratory service were all liable. Each had to contribute to a judgment of more than $900,000 in favor of the child and his parents.

Now, let's see how this case fills the three requirements for malpractice. First, there was unquestionable injury to the child—the court, in fact, described it as catastrophic. Next, on the question of negligence, the court found the pediatrician negligent for relying only on the test results from his own hospital in the face of the baby's clinical symptoms and of conflicting reports from another hospital. It also found the pathologists negligent for failing to maintain quality control and for the extent and duration of the erroneous results, and it found the hospital vicariously liable for the laboratory's errors. As for the proximate—or direct—cause of the child's injury, the court found both the lab's consistently erroneous test results and the physician's exclusive reliance on those tests to be at fault.

This case shows that a lab can be found negligent on grounds of poor quality control and incorrect test results. Courts do not hold laboratories to a standard of perfection—they recognize that test results cannot *always* be accurate—but in this case, the extent of the errors was considerable. "This was not an isolated fluke in a single test," the court ruled. "For this patient alone, the laboratory ran not one but several faulty tests . . . [and] they were completely wrong."

All this, in the court's opinion, increased the laboratory's liability.

Many other areas of potential negligence exist in the lab. Let's examine some of them:

Misidentification and mislabeling. This is one area that's commonly recognized as a source of medicolegal problems, and most labs stress the need for scrupulous attention to identification and labeling procedures. These cannot be sometime things: They require ongoing effort from everyone to avoid mistakes and to follow sound identification procedures without deviation.

Instrument failure. As we've seen, poor quality control can have drastic legal consequences. So can inadequate instrument maintenance. Failure to standardize equipment, a jammed key on an automatic printout device, misplaced decimal points, or inversion of numeric values can all spell medicolegal trouble.

Specimen validity. Here's a lesser-known trouble spot, perhaps, but one with definite malpractice potential. Unless proper collection and transportation techniques are used to assure the integrity of the specimen, the tests run on it may be worthless. In the case of pregnancy tests, for example, false positives that may have been caused by unsuitable specimens have led to unnecessary surgery, which, in turn, has given rise to malpractice suits.

Venipuncture. This everyday, routine procedure is fraught with hazards. Phlebotomists must be skilled and able to provide good patient care when they draw specimens, for both inpatients and outpatients. Problems that can arise include hematoma, abscess, and cellulitis at the puncture site, and the possibility that the patient may faint, fall, and injure himself after or during the phlebotomy.

Intravenous substances. Reactions to and complications from administering intravenous substances for diagnostic tests are still another area ripe for suit.

This listing by no means exhausts the possibilities of what can cause medicolegal problems for a laboratory, but it should give an idea of the kinds of occurrences—both expected and unexpected—to beware of. One comforting thought here is that even if a mishap occurs, it isn't malpractice until proved to be the result of negligence.

And proving negligence in the courtroom means showing that the defendant departed from a professional standard of care. Since a lay jury cannot be expected to know what the professional standard of care should be, expert witnesses are called to define it. From their testimony, the jury can then decide whether or not the standard of care was met. The issue then becomes: Would a reasonable laboratorian, in accordance with the accepted standard of care under similar circumstances, do what the defendant did?

Expert testimony is thus a crucial factor in establishing negligence. But what if a "conspiracy of silence" kept professionals from testifying against each other? Years ago, that's exactly what plaintiffs' attorneys said was happening. They couldn't find physicians to appear as expert witnesses against their colleagues, so they looked for another way to prove negligence. They found it in a legal doctrine called *res ipsa loquitur*. Translated from the Latin, the phrase means "the thing speaks for itself," which in turn means that the very fact that the injury occurred is proof of negligence.

As the doctrine has been tested in court over the years, it hasn't always—or even usually—worked out as the plaintiffs' attorneys had hoped. Here's a case in point:

A patient in a Utah hospital had an ovarian cyst removed and received two units of blood during and after the procedure. During the second transfusion, she showed symptoms suggesting a hemolytic transfusion reaction: distress, perspiring, and shaking as from chills. Her treatment continued in the hospital, but she died 10 days later. The cause of death was determined to be kidney failure, and her survivors sued the hospital for negligence.

They based their suit on *res ipsa loquitur,* claiming that the reaction itself was proof enough that the hospital was negligent. The court disagreed. It said that blood transfusion is a recognized therapy, its techniques standardized, and its hazards well known. Evidence showed that the hospital had followed all procedures correctly, and its records of testing and retesting the blood showed that the transfused blood was compatible. Further, the defense gave evidence that even in the best of circumstances, hemolytic reactions will occur in a small number of cases, and fatalities in a small percentage of those. The court found no negligence.

Cases like this have made some medicolegal experts feel that the power of *res ipsa loquitur* has been overestimated. It certainly hasn't proved to be the bonanza that plaintiffs' attorneys had hoped for.

Another concept that has drawn much medicolegal attention in the past few years is informed consent. The idea is that the patient has the right to know what he's getting into, as well as the right of self-determination—deciding whether or not he wants to go ahead with a certain procedure. Without the patient's consent, a physician or hospital runs the risk of being liable for battery, or unauthorized touching. If the consent is invalid because the physician failed to disclose a particular risk, and if this nondisclosure results in injury to the patient, a charge of negligence may also be brought against the defendant.

Fortunately, a patient's consent need not always be written—or even spoken. Implied consent for many routine procedures is given by the patient's own actions—walking into a doctor's office, sitting on an examining table, or rolling up a sleeve for a venipuncture. With more complex procedures, however, and with those that carry greater risks to the patient, the duty of the physician or hospital increases to describe those risks to the patient and get his informed consent to the procedure.

At that point, it becomes a matter of *how much should be disclosed*. In today's atmosphere emphasizing individual rights, courts are ruling more and more in favor of full disclosure. This means the physician should tell the patient what the procedure is, its attendant risks, and alternative methods of treatment. When the patient understands these things, he can then make an intelligent, informed decision as to whether he wants to undergo the procedure. And he's fully within his rights to refuse it.

Physicians have been understandably jittery about informed consent because the doctrine is still being tested in the courts. Until the early 1970s, the scope of disclosure was determined by the "standard of practice" formula. In other words, physicians had a duty to tell their patients only as much as "reasonably careful medical practitioners" in similar circumstances revealed.

Two landmark decisions in 1972 have done a lot to change that. Both indicate that the scope of disclosure should not be determined by the standards of the medical community, but rather by the patient's need.

And that need is described as "all the information material to his decision." Particular emphasis is placed on risks of death or serious injury and on risks associated with unusual procedures or treatments.

Here's an example of a consent case involving a blood transfusion: A patient who received 500 cc of blood during a D&C contracted hepatitis. She sued, claiming that the doctor had failed to inform her of the risks involved in a blood transfusion. The court dismissed her claim. It found that the risk of hepatitis is insignificant in comparison with the risk of shock if a transfusion is needed and not given. Nor, apparently, did the court believe the plaintiff when she said she wouldn't have consented to the procedure if she had been aware of the attendant risks.

Consent forms are one way physicians and hospitals have tried to solve this medicolegal problem, but they are not suit-proof. Unless someone actually explains the procedure and the attendant risks to the patient (and preferably to another member of his family as well) and unless the physician also describes alternative modes of treatment, the consent form itself is next to worthless.

Special consideration, of course, must be given when it's a matter of consent for children or for those who are incompetent. The general rule with minors is to obtain consent from a parent or guardian; with the mentally incompetent, from a legal guardian.

Autopsy consent forms are of particular concern to pathologists. In most cases, consent must be obtained from a surviving spouse or next of kin. Autopsy statutes govern the details in all but a few states, and they vary considerably, so most pathologists are careful to check with state or local authorities if there is any doubt.

Still another concept of medicolegal importance to laboratories is *respondeat superior*. Literally translated, "Let the master answer," this means that an employer (usually the hospital or independent lab) is responsible—and liable—for the acts of its employees as they discharge their duties. Also known as vicarious liability, this doctrine puts the major burden of insuring against and defending negligence suits on the hospital or laboratory and not on its employees.

And where does the pathologist fit into this picture? Technically, *respondeat superior,* which is also called the captain-of-the-ship doctrine, could apply to the pathologist or laboratory director as well as to the hospital. Technically, the pathologist could be held directly responsible and liable for the acts of the technologists in his laboratory. But that seldom happens today. Over the years, and most recently in some landmark cases, the captain-of-the-ship doctrine has lost much of its malpractice clout. Almost always now, the hospital as employer, not the physician as captain of the ship, is being found liable for employees' acts of negligence.

Then what about the technologist's personal liability? And should technologists carry liability insurance? Pathologists, of course, *must* carry professional liability insurance, but it's generally considered optional for technologists to do so. Though liability coverage is available for technologists for a modest annual premium (about $30), technologists are rarely named in suits. In fact, a 1973 article in *MLO* pointed out that during a 20-year period, in only two cases did technologists have to pay even part of a malpractice settlement.

Now that we've seen what can go into a case to prove a laboratory's negligence, let's consider briefly what a lab can do to defend itself.

The best defense, obviously, is prevention. Laboratories should go all out to guard against mistakes in the first place. They should develop sound procedures for everything from collecting specimens through reporting out the results, and they must adhere to them meticulously. This requires care and constant vigilance by every member of the laboratory staff.

One especially important part of these procedures is record keeping. Careful, properly maintained records are vital and have provided the most powerful defense in many malpractice cases. If records show that standard and accepted procedures have been followed, they can go a long way toward relieving a laboratory's liability when an untoward event does occur.

3

My Testimony in a Malpractice Trial

Mary E. Gaskin, MT(ASCP)

I was terrified. The lab procedures at my clinic had been questioned, and now I was in court, subpoenaed to testify for the defense in a malpractice trial. What in the world am I doing here? I asked myself.

I looked at the jury. Here were 12 nonmedical people who had no idea of what goes on in a laboratory. They certainly wouldn't appreciate the anxieties and concerns that any good technologist feels about patients and patient testing. Could I make them understand?

My attention was suddenly brought back to the present. "Mary, will you please tell the court what your profession is?" our attorney asked me. "And will you then tell the court what your qualifications for your profession are?"

I took a deep breath. "I am a registered medical technologist," I replied. Then I listed my qualifications: three years of college and a one-year internship in an accredited hospital; a bachelor of science degree in medical technology; and an ASCP registry, which I had kept current for 21 years. I concluded by explaining what an ASCP registry is, adding that I had been continually employed in hospital laboratories or in group practice labs for the past 21 years.

As I waited for the lawyer's next questions, I recalled the events that had brought me into court. It had all started two years ago, when one of the doctors at our clinic asked me to check a patient's semen for a sperm count. The doctor explained that the patient had had a vasectomy several years earlier. "The patient's wife became pregnant two months after the vasectomy," the doctor added.

I did the sperm count after the patient emerged from the laboratory rest room and handed me his specimen. I looked at a drop of concentrated semen on the microscope slide, and I discovered sperm present. These sperm were 95 percent motile. On dilution, the sperm count was 14 million.

When I placed this report in the patient's chart, I discovered that I had also done this patient's first sperm count—six weeks after his vasectomy. My first report said that no sperm had been seen. This notation was not unusual, and I felt no immediate cause for concern.

Later that day, however, the doctor in charge of the case told me that the patient and his wife were suing him *and* the medical group for malpractice. These two plaintiffs were asking for $28,000, plus unspecified damages sustained by the patient's wife for the pain and anxiety caused by an unwanted pregnancy.

An insurance adjuster representing our clinic questioned me several days later. The adjuster asked me to describe the method of semen analysis that I had used on the patient's first specimen. The adjuster specifically asked me if this first specimen could have been mixed up with someone else's specimen.

I checked my records and discovered that only one semen specimen had been received in the lab on the date in question. A mix-up would have been impossible. But if the patient had not followed the instructions which he had been given for the collection of that first specimen, I told the adjuster, the test results could be misleading.

I heard no more about the case for almost two years. Then our business manager suddenly told me that I would have to go to court and testify for the clinic. Although I was not a defendant, just the thought of testifying scared me.

Never, in my long career, had my test results ever been questioned. Sure, I'd had doctors ask me to recheck a patient's abnormal test results if the results weren't compatible with their original diagnosis. I'd always done these rechecks, and they had always been correct. Now, for the first time, I was being questioned *in court* about my test results.

Another question from our lawyer jerked me back to reality. "Mary, how long have you been employed by your medical group?" After I told him that I had been employed there for four and a half years, he asked me to describe our group's procedure for doing sperm counts—in detail.

I took a deep breath. "Sperm counts are treated as a priority test in our laboratory," I said. "In other words, when a sperm count is brought into the laboratory, that count is done right away. This can be most important in fertility counts because of sperm motility.

"Since most of our patients travel 20 to 30 miles to our office, I tell them to keep the specimen warm by placing it inside their clothing. This helps keep the specimen at body temperature. I also tell them to bring the specimen into the laboratory within one hour of collection."

As the jury watched me, I explained that the patient registers at the reception desk when he arrives at the clinic. He leaves the specimen with the receptionist. The receptionist has instructions to bring the specimen and the registration slip directly to the laboratory.

"When I receive the specimen," I told the court, "I call on the intercom for the patient's chart to be brought in from the record room. Then I make out a requisition slip and immediately begin to examine the specimen.

"First, I measure and record the amount, color, and appearance of the specimen. Then I examine the undiluted semen on a slide, and note the motility and morphology of the sperm.

"Next, I make the proper dilution in a white blood cell pipette. I put the pipette on the shaker and plate the count on the counting chamber. After the solution settles, I do the count and multiply the number of sperm counted by the factor of one million."

I explained that since vasectomy surgeries have become routine there are usually very few, if any, sperm to be seen in postoperative specimens. Nevertheless, I always carefully scan several drops of both the mixed *and* undiluted semen under the high-power objective of the microscope. Sometimes I see only one dead sperm in the fluid. Even this sperm would be reported to the doctor. By using undiluted semen, I testified, I have a 50 times better chance of seeing even one sperm.

"I then sign the report, cut off the laboratory copy, and glue the doctor's copy to the patient's chart," I said. "This chart is then given to the patient's physician."

Our attorney asked me if I had any doubts about the procedure that I had used for the specimen that had brought me into court—the first of the two. After I said No, he asked if I had followed my regular procedure for sperm specimens in this disputed case. I replied that I had never varied my procedure during my employment at the clinic. I concluded by stating that I had seen no sperm in the patient's first specimen.

Our lawyer sat down. The plaintiff's lawyer got up and started to cross-examine me. He put me through living hell. "Was there anyone else working in the laboratory with you?" he asked.

I explained that I worked with an assistant whom I had trained. "But she isn't trained to do sperm counts," I added. "I perform them by myself."

"How can you be sure that the receptionist actually brought the plaintiff's specimen directly to you?" he shot back.

I replied that all of the receptionists have written instructions to deliver semen specimens directly to the laboratory. From my personal experience, I knew that no queasy-stomached receptionist would ever leave any kind of specimen at her desk any longer than necessary.

"This would also apply to urine and stool specimens," I told the plaintiff's lawyer. "The receptionists have always promptly delivered these specimens."

The plaintiff's lawyer had other questions. He asked me whether or not I had ever made a mistake. How long did a specimen sit before I examined it? He asked if the specimen could be kept warm in a paper bag. "Would that bag be sufficient insulation?" he asked.

I replied that I was not an insulation expert and did not know if the insulation properties of a paper bag would be sufficient.

He kept pounding me on the point that, although I could not remember this particular semen specimen, I was positive that I had handled it the same way that I handled all the others that I'd received over the years.

"Have you ever found a patient's sperm count to be negative one time and positive the next?" he asked.

I replied that I had seen this happen before, but I was unable to recall a specific case at that moment. He found this portion of my testimony unacceptable, and he tried to discredit it. He rambled on and on, asking the same questions over and over. He was trying to confuse me, trying to destroy my credibility as a witness.

Finally, it was over. I was asked to step down. Breathing a sigh of relief, which I'm sure everyone could hear, I asked our attorney if I could go back to work. He gave me permission to leave the courtroom, adding that he didn't think that I would have to testify again.

On the following morning, the business manager at the clinic told me that the judge had dismissed the malpractice charges against the physician who had performed the vasectomy. The surgery had been performed correctly, the judge ruled. The plaintiff had been rendered sterile, even though his second sperm count was 14 million. The judge ruled that this count was far below the normal sperm count of from 60 million to 300 million.

Unfortunately, there were still charges pending. The matter of the possibility of error in the plaintiff's first sperm count still had to be decided. The business manager asked me to return to court for the attorneys' final arguments to the jury. My heart sank.

I returned to court that morning and sat beside our attorney. Fortunately, I didn't have to take the stand again. I listened while the lawyers for both sides summed up their cases to the jury. Then the judge gave the jury their instructions. He told the jurors that there was no precedent for this case. The judge said that their verdict would go down in legal history.

The judge ordered the jury to weigh all the facts that had been presented in court, and then to find for either the defendants or the plaintiffs. If the jury decided for the plaintiffs, the judge said, they were then to decide on the amount of money that they felt would compensate the patient and his wife for the injuries caused to them.

I searched the faces of the jurors for some hint of what they were thinking. There was no sign of emotion. I wondered if this group of nonmedical people had really understood any of the things that I had tried so hard to explain.

Did they understand the medical terminology that I had used? I had described a procedure involving a dilution of 1:50, and a counting chamber with squares marked off on it. Would it make sense to them? Did they understand how conscientious and careful a good technologist must be? Did they believe that *I* was a good technologist?

The judge finished his instructions, and the jury left the courtroom to begin their deliberations. Each minute seemed like an eternity.

The jury returned after deliberating for only 10 minutes. I held my breath. What would their verdict be? The judge asked the foreman to rise and read the verdict. The foreman got to his feet. "Your honor, we find in favor of the defendants," he said in a very quiet voice.

I could have shouted with joy! They understood. The jury had really understood everything that I had said. The judgment of that jury restored my faith in myself, in human nature, and in the legal processes of our country.

4

How to Prevent Transfusion Crises

Kathleen Crowley Sheedy, MT(ASCP)SBB

One of our patients experienced what every blood bank hopes it will never see—a hemolytic transfusion reaction. We were particularly shaken by the incident because we pride ourselves on how careful we are. We take precautions against just that sort of accident, and yet it happened to us. How? Let me tell you the story.

On Tuesday, Sept. 30, 1975, Mary Foley (not her real name) was admitted to the hospital for a total hip replacement. On admission, blood was drawn for a routine CBC, glucose, and BUN. The surgery was scheduled for Thursday, so at 7 o'clock Wednesday morning, blood was drawn for type, group, and crossmatch. The phlebotomist was a technician in our hematology section who routinely draws blood in our outpatient department.

When the blood bank got the specimen, which was properly labeled with the date and the patient's full name and hospital number, a technologist typed and crossmatched the blood. The patient was typed A positive, and we crossmatched four units of blood for her for the following day. On Thursday afternoon, the patient received those four units of blood.

Later that afternoon, the anesthesiologist on Mrs. Foley's case came into the blood bank with a urine specimen that looked like Coca-Cola and a freshly drawn tube of blood for a workup on a transfusion reaction and a type and crossmatch for two more units of blood.

It was after 5 o'clock, and one of our troubleshooting techs was called in to handle the problem. She spent the next four hours trying to solve it. She recrossmatched the four units of blood the patient had received and found that they were, indeed, incompatible with the newly drawn specimen. Yet, both pre- and post-transfusion specimens typed A positive. We had 40 units of A positive blood on hand, and the technologist tested each one for compatibility with the patient's specimen. Two of the 40 units appeared to be compatible and were sent to the floor. The patient's condition didn't improve.

The patient was experiencing a classic hemolytic transfusion reaction, but we couldn't find a reason for it. Special studies of elutions and panels for antibody identification were done, and they, too, showed negative results.

At this point, the blood bank technologist had exhausted her supply of pretransfusion specimen, and she asked the chemistry section if any serum from the patient's admission blood work was left. There was, so the technologist was able to do reverse grouping on the specimen. That was how we finally found out that the patient was group O, accounting for the hemolytic transfusion reaction. How was it that her post-transfusion specimen was group A? She had received so much of the A positive blood that she appeared to type as group A.

Where had the mixup occurred? By working back, checking the blood request form, and calling the technologist who drew the blood and signed the requisition, we discovered what had happened:

Mary Foley was in a semi-private room. The phlebotomist checked the names on the door and saw that Mrs. Foley was in the bed next to the window. She approached that bed, saw Mary Foley's chart by the bed, and asked the patient if she was Mary Foley. When the patient answered yes, the technologist drew the blood specimen. Unfortunately, the real Mary Foley was asleep in the next bed.

What the technologist did may sound all right, but it wasn't. Our procedure demands that a phlebotomist check the patient's armband for identification, not ask the patient what his name is. As we all know, hospital patients may be disoriented, or even delirious, and respond incorrectly to any question. If the patient doesn't have an armband (and this one didn't), the technologist must not draw the specimen, but check with the nursing staff and ascertain the patient's identity.

If this identification procedure is correctly followed, there won't be any mixups. In this case, the technologist knew the protocol, knew she shouldn't draw a patient without an armband, but drew the specimen anyway—with nearly tragic results and what could very easily turn into a malpractice nightmare.

As soon as we correctly grouped the patient, we gave her two units of frozen O negative blood. That, along with medical treatment to overcome the transfusion reaction, got her past the crisis, and she recovered. Once that immediate, technical problem was solved, we had to turn our attention to the ramifications of the incident: Why the patient who was drawn didn't have an armband; why the technologist didn't positively identify the patient; and most important of all, how to keep such an incident from happening again.

I reviewed all our procedures, and I'm still convinced they're sound. The main lesson we learned, I think, is that even with the best procedures and the best intentions in the world, we can never be complacent, never relax, never forget that an accident in the blood bank can be fatal.

As I listed our procedures for my own review, it occurred to me that our checklist of essential safeguards in the blood bank might prove helpful to others. Perhaps the following tips, grouped in various categories, will prevent you from making a tragic mistake.

Identification. Probably the greatest source of transfusion mishaps is misidentification—as it was, indeed, in this case. The wrong patient is drawn, or a tube is mislabeled, or the wrong bag of blood is pulled for the wrong patient. The way to avoid such errors is to insist that protocol be rigidly followed. Be sure your blood bank demands that each patient's specimen be labeled with the patient's full name and hospital number, the date, and the phlebotomist's signature on the requisition. Don't accept specimens that are incorrectly labeled.

But proper labeling isn't enough. In the case of Mary Foley, we received a properly labeled specimen and signed requisition—but it came from the wrong patient. Each patient must be identified with an armband with his full name and hospital number. This band must be attached to the patient's arm or leg—not to his bed, I.V. pole, or other object. If both patients in Mary Foley's room had been correctly armbanded, and if the phlebotomist had positively identified her patient, this particular accident would have been avoided. You must insist that your phlebotomists positively identify the patient before drawing his blood.

Education. Everyone involved with blood transfusion must be made aware of its seriousness. This applies not only to technologists, but to any clerical, nursing, and house staff who may be involved. All of these people must be taught the importance of proper patient identification and specimen labeling.

Our education program consists of yearly lectures for house staff and nursing personnel and weekly lectures for all of us in the blood bank. For nurses and house staff, we explain how we draw bloods, how they must be labeled, and which tubes to use for various situations. For medical technology students, we set aside a week on correct techniques for phlebotomy and patient identification, and for our own staff, we schedule weekly lectures by me, my assistant, or one of our pathologists. We try to keep these short, snappy, and to the point, placing particular emphasis on the latest developments in blood banking and related topics.

I can't emphasize too strongly the need for continuing education in the blood bank. It's one of the primary duties of any blood bank supervisor.

Updating procedures. Keep blood banking procedures up to date by following AABB standards. Federal and state requirements also change from time to time, and you have to stay abreast of those changes, too. Whenever AABB standards change, we revise and update our procedures manual. Not all procedures will change, of course, but it's essential to be aware of the latest developments.

Coverage. As a supervisor, you must make sure that each shift is adequately covered. In our blood bank, we have full coverage 24 hours a day, seven days a week. In addition, five of us rotate being on call for any problems that may arise, any time of the day or night.

Quality control. Among the daily quality control procedures in the blood bank are: testing reagents, doing titers and avidity testing on them, checking cells to make sure they're the right blood groups, as well as keeping incubators, water baths, and refrigerators at the correct temperatures.

Records. It's up to each blood bank to know how long it must keep its records, as the requirements vary from state to state. In New York, we have to keep records for seven years, although Federal and AABB requirements say they must be kept for only five.

We keep daily primary worksheets and also separate patient records, showing each patient's blood type and group and what units and derivatives of blood each receives.

We also keep a patient's pretransfusion specimen and a specimen from all crossmatched units that the patient receives for one week, just in case there is a transfusion reaction. After a week, all of the specimens are thrown out.

Incident reports. These are essential in the event of a malpractice suit. Whenever an accident occurs in the blood bank (or any other department, for that matter), it must be written up and safely filed away.

Our resident wrote up the incident involving Mary Foley after he investigated the entire matter. The report has been filed in our laboratory director's office, along with all the worksheets and other laboratory records relating to the patient.

Even minor incidents should be written up. For example, if your blood bank draws donors, you should write it up if a donor leaves before the allotted time after drawing blood or if he gets a large hematoma.

None of this procedure is easy, nor can it be set up overnight. And once it is established, it requires constant vigilance to keep it working right. But if everybody involved in blood transfusion is made aware, kept aware, and is reminded of the patient on the other end of that tube of blood, incidents like ours can be prevented.

5

Minimizing Transfusion Reactions

Henry B. Soloway, M.D.

In 1976, Taft B. Schreiber, a prominent businessman, political fund raiser, and benefactor of the University of California at Los Angeles, entered U.C.L.A. Hospital for urologic surgery. He expired 10 days after surgery, apparently as the result of an acute hemolytic transfusion reaction. Mr. Schreiber's untimely death underscores the hazard associated with the transfusion process, a hazard learned—only to be learned and learned again—ever since physicians first attempted to transfer blood from one living being to another.

Hemolytic transfusion reactions are not a 20th-century invention. Dr. Chester A. Zmijewski's history of transfusion reveals that Pope Innocent VIII died of an apparent hemolytic blood transfusion reaction in 1492, 10 weeks before Columbus's discovery of the New World. The Pontiff's case was even more tragic than Mr. Schreiber's, in that all three of the donors selected for the transfusion died too.

No more fortunate than Pope Innocent was an unnamed patient who succumbed nearly 200 years later to a hemolytic transfusion reaction after being transfused with sheep's blood. In this case, Dr. Jean Denys, physician to Louis XIV, precipitated what was probably the first medical malpractice action for wrongful death from a transfusion reaction. After a long legal battle, Dr. Denys was exonerated of murder (lucky for him his royal patient hadn't received the transfusion!), but was forbidden by court order to perform subsequent transfusions unless specifically sanctioned by the Faculty of Medicine in Paris.

At the turn of the 20th century, Karl Landsteiner discovered the ABO blood group system, which at last clarified the immunology of human-to-human hemolytic transfusion reactions. His studies held out the promise that a new era of safe transfusion therapy was about to dawn. But even now, hemolytic transfusion reactions continue to plague transfusion services. Despite our improved Coombs serum (with gobs of anticomplementary activity), modern temperature-alarm systems, quality control on centrifuges and heating blocks, automated cell washers, and what have you, hemolytic transfusion reactions remain with us. They occur from coast to coast, at good hospitals and at bad. They injure and kill the meek and the mighty—and they are almost 100 percent preventable. Acute hemolytic transfusion reactions are preventable because they occur, not as the result of random technical error or instrument malfunction, but as the result of human error, and more specifically, human error in patient or specimen identification.

If we confine our discussion to hemolytic transfusion reactions resulting from misidentification, we find that such errors can occur at four separate steps in the combined laboratory and nursing processes relating to blood transfusion.

Patient identification. The first is in the initial identification of the patient for whom type and crossmatch has been ordered. This identification carries the greatest potential for human error, for two important reasons: First, the patients are not personally known to hospital personnel when they are originally encountered, and second, the highest rate of laboratory personnel turnover is usually among laboratory assistants—those most likely to make that initial contact.

As we all know, many patients will answer Yes to almost any question. This is particularly true of elderly patients who are either hard-of-hearing or bewildered by the hospital setting. Because of this phenomenon, it is essential to ask the patient, "What is your name, please?" and not, "Are you so-and-so?"

Once the patient has stated his name (or even better, spelled it), the phlebotomist must then examine his wristband, confirm the first and last names, and make sure that the identification number on the requisition and wristband agree. If first and last names, requisition data, and wristband identification all agree, a sample may be drawn for type and crossmatch. If this information does not agree, no sample should be drawn until the discrepancy has been cleared up. Finally, let me emphasize that no blood sample should *ever* be drawn from a patient without a wristband!

On occasion, phlebotomists may feel pressured into drawing patients who have not yet been wristbanded—as when one or more exsanguinating patients are brought to the emergency room in the aftermath of an automobile accident. To prevent compounding the disaster, phlebotomists must stand their ground, and probably should take even greater care than usual, since car accidents often involve several members of the same family—with, of course, the same last name. The main problem here is that hospital personnel are often lulled into a false sense of security when a patient has a unique last name, such as Belliveau or von Schoonhoven. Unfortunately, a unique last name does not mean unique—and compatible—blood, and if four exsanguinating von Schoonhovens were brought to the hospital, the statistical probabilities are that two will be group O and two, group A. The disastrous conclusion to this scenario is self-evident.

When a sample has been drawn, AABB standards require it to be labeled immediately by the phlebotomist with at least the patient's first and last names, identification number, and date. Only if this label—firmly attached to a stoppered tube—agrees with the information on the type-and-crossmatch requisition, should blood bank personnel proceed with blood grouping and compatibility testing on that sample.

Many hospitals employ a set of blood bank control numbers as a double check on the initial patient identification. A set of gummed labels with identical numbers is carried on the phlebotomist's tray. After drawing a sample, the phlebotomist affixes one of the labels to the patient's hospital wristband (or to a separate blood bank wristband), another to the test tube containing the sample, a third to the requisition slip, and a fourth to the transfusion service log sheet. This double check acts to insure that if a misidentification has occurred, it can be discovered before hanging a unit of blood.

Switching samples. The second possible source of misidentification that can result in hemolytic transfusion reaction is switching sample tubes within the laboratory. This occurs much less frequently than errors in patient identification because someone must copy identification data directly from the test tube to the log sheet. This positive action in itself acts as a fail-safe mechanism.

Also, personnel entrusted with crossmatching are more likely to be senior technologists, selected for such traits as attentiveness, ability to work under pressure, and knowledge of the hazards of the transfusion. Additionally, many laboratories require that two technologists separately determine the ABO group and Rh type of the intended recipient and that at least one technologist verify that the blood unit itself has been properly identified by checking the group and type of the integral segments attached to it. Such thoroughness is rarely devoted to initial patient identification. If it were, many hemolytic transfusion reactions resulting from misidentification would quietly self-abort before reaching the courtrooms, newspapers, and medical magazines.

Releasing the unit. The third potential source of error in identification arises when a unit of blood is released by the transfusion service to be administered—usually by the nursing service. When blood is released, the laboratory technologist selects the proper unit from the blood bank refrigerator, checks the unit number and ABO and Rh types against the information listed on the compatibility testing log sheets, and hands the unit to the nurse. The nurse, in turn, rechecks the same information against the "request for issue of blood" slip that she brings with her from the nursing station. This slip must contain the recipient's first and last names, hospital identification number, attending physician's name, date, and ABO and Rh types. In hospitals using special blood bank control numbers, the nurse usually is required to copy the four-digit control number onto the "request for issue of blood" slip as still another safeguard that the laboratory and nursing services both intend to transfuse the same patient.

This brings us to Kaplan's Law. Dr. Harold S. Kaplan, a blood banking maven from New York City and an astute observer of medical laboratorians, advises that "whenever a double-check or triple-check system is instituted to eliminate a potential source of serious error, you had better be damn sure that the first check catches all the mistakes."

From a mathematical standpoint, if the chance of error in performing a specific function is 1/100 and if a second person rechecks the first person's work, then the chance of error is lessened to 1/10,000 (1/100 × 1/100). Similarly, if a third person is assigned to recheck the work of the previous two, the chance of error should drop to 1/1,000,000.

From a practical standpoint, however, human proficiency in detecting errors is inversely proportional to the number of persons who have previously performed the same task and the subconscious assessment of their competency in doing it. In other words, when a nurse with a requisition slip for issuing a unit of blood rechecks the paperwork done by the senior blood bank technologist, she frequently assumes that everything must be in order and signs the consignment sheet without carefully checking the data. Laboratorians should be flattered by such confidence in their performance, but patients would be better served with more skepticism and less flattery. As Kaplan has observed, it better be right the first time around!

Transfusing the blood. The fourth, and final, potential source of misidentification arises when the intended recipient is reidentified, and the unit of blood is transfused. There appear to be specific circumstances at this point in the process that predispose to misidentification—the common denominator, of course, being failure to compare the information on the patient's wristband with that on the paperwork accompanying the unit and with the number on the unit itself. Among the more common circumstances leading to misidentification at this point are these:

1. Transfusions administered to patients with unique and unusual last names may result in error because personnel are not aware that more than one member of a family may require transfusion simultaneously. Such occurrences often transpire in busy emergency rooms stressed beyond their capacities as the result of common disasters.

2. Transfusions administered on the evening or graveyard shifts are also more apt to be complicated by human error. Not only are these shifts smaller, but they are also frequently staffed by newer employees who are less familiar with the laboratory and its protocol.

3. Patients with common names like Paul Smith or John Brown may also be more likely to receive incompatible blood because more than one patient with the same name may be hospitalized at the same time. Many hospitals place warning notes on the blood bank refrigerator door when two patients with identical or near-identical names are simultaneously hospitalized, as a double check against mishaps.

4. VIPs who require transfusions are also at increased risk, as Mr. Schreiber's case illustrates. When a VIP is hospitalized, unusual things happen. The chief laboratory technologist may be assigned to draw his blood—a chore he or she perhaps can't do as well as someone lower down the pecking order who performs that same chore 40 times a day. Frequently, a pathologist gets into the act, and that always compromises laboratory protocol. Perhaps the most dangerous thing of all is to let the chairman of a medical school anesthesiology department put a VIP to sleep and then transfuse him. All such variations from standard operating procedure increase the likelihood of something going wrong. When Dr. Albert Starr (co-inventor of the Starr-Edwards valve) wrote about his own coronary artery bypass surgery, he noted that he refused offers of special postoperative VIP treatment because he feared it might, in fact, result in more harm than good.

How then can we keep transfusion reactions to an irreducible minimum? First, it's important to have an adequate patient- and specimen-identification system, preferably one using a separate blood bank control number, as I have described here. It is also important to tell hospital personnel why the system is designed as it is. They must be taught the logic of the system and the consequences that can follow when its integrity is violated. Hospital personnel policies should insure adequate staffing and minimize personnel turnover.

Continuing education is essential. Give all nursing and laboratory personnel periodic reviews and updates relative to the transfusion process. During such sessions, discuss all incident reports, especially those on "near misses." At the physician level, emphasize that transfusions should be avoided when there are alternatives for treating anemia. If transfusions must be given, autotransfusion is the safest route. When the patient requires a homologous transfusion, it should be done, if feasible, during the day shift, with the patient awake.

Forgiving may be divine, but a hemolytic transfusion reaction resulting from human error is more apt to be litigated than forgiven.

6

Avoiding Problems in Phlebotomy

Paul Moffett, MT(ASCP)

In the days when phlebotomy was used therapeutically, treatment often ended with the patient bleeding to death. Today's drawing of small quantities of blood for diagnostic purposes does not have that danger. Still, phlebotomy is one of the most important—and inherently dangerous—duties performed by laboratorians. If it is not done properly, it can lead to critical complications for the patient and malpractice liability.

To make the procedure as safe and trouble-free as possible, the phlebotomist should keep these five principles in mind:

- The patient must be identified properly, and the specimen labeled correctly.
- The experience should be untraumatic as well as safe for the patient.
- An appropriate amount of blood should be drawn.
- Specimens must be in satisfactory condition for testing.
- Specimens must be delivered to the laboratory at the proper time and place.

These principles sound simple, but following them all consistently is far from easy. Let's look at each point to see where the pitfalls are—and how they can be avoided.

Correct identification, proper labeling. Any blood bank will tell you that most hemolytic transfusion reactions occur because a misidentified specimen is used for crossmatching. This can happen when the phlebotomist takes the blood from the wrong patient, or mixes up the labeling on specimens taken from the right patients. In either case, an incorrect crossmatch can result in serious complications or even death for the patient.

When an incorrect specimen is used for other tests, the consequences are often no less drastic. Misleading results can cause incorrect diagnosis and treatment of the patient. At best, the results can be so confusing and inappropriate that the clinician questions their validity. The laboratory then becomes defensive and shows the doctor pages of computer printouts proving that the test was done correctly. The doctor will be unhappy, the laboratory insulted. The mystery will be solved only when someone remembers to check the patient identification as well as the quality control.

Identifying the patient is not always easy, particularly if he is unable to communicate. The following rules should help:

1. Upon meeting the patient, ask for his full name. *Do not* ask, ''Are you James Jones?'' If the patient is hard of hearing or confused, he may answer Yes to anything you ask. When the patient gives his name, check it against the one on the requisition.

2. If the patient cannot communicate, have a nurse or family member make the identification.

3. Always check identification bracelets. Inpatients must have I.D.s attached when they are admitted. Check to see that the information on the bracelet corresponds with that on your requisition. Make sure the names are spelled the same on both. Do not rely on name tags on beds or other items, such as thermometer stands. Patients are often moved, and these tags can be left behind.

4. Do not identify by name only. The requisition may say James Jones, but the patient says James Johns. If the phlebotomist is not alert, the difference may slip by. It's important to check some unusual item, such as a birthdate or patient identification number—something that requires special thought. All of us, at one time or another in our work, are victims of habit and routine. This double check on identification is a good defense against lack of concentration at such times. And the hospital can help by having a policy to keep patients with similar names as far apart from each other as possible.

Mistakes in labeling also can be avoided through use of proper procedures. Here are some guidelines:

1. Handle requisition slips with care. All slips except the one you are currently working with should be kept in a secure place. It's easy for a phlebotomist to place a pile of requisitions on a bedside table while drawing the next specimen. It's also easy for one of the slips to be blown to the floor, or for the pile to be shuffled by a cleaning person. The error is completed when you take the labeling information from the top requisition—the wrong one. To be absolutely sure that you are not working with the wrong requisition slip, take your labeling information directly from the patient's identification bracelet and check it against the requisition.

2. Never prelabel tubes. Do the labeling immediately after taking the specimen.

3. Always put enough information on the tube so that the laboratory can be sure the patient has been identified correctly. Minimum information is the patient's full name, identification number, the date and time, and your initials. Blood banks may require more information and have written standards for labeling. If a label is incomplete, the laboratory must discard the specimen and obtain another.

Maximum safety, minimum trauma. When drawing blood, your primary concerns should be for the patient's psychological and physical well-being. A phlebotomist does not need a degree in psychology to recognize an apprehensive patient and to take steps to lessen his fears. Show your concern for the patient, but be as confident and professional as possible. Explain that the physician has requested the sample, and that the needle may hurt a bit. Most patients will calm down once they understand the importance and the need for the procedure. But remember that the patient does have the right to refuse the test and may not be forced to submit to it. Your hospital should have a written procedure to follow in such instances.

The patient's safety is the most important consideration. Some commonsense rules will help minimize the few risks inherent in the drawing procedure itself: Be sure the patient is in a secure position, preferably lying down, to avoid a fall from fainting; see that the bleeding has stopped before you leave; and keep a watchful eye on the patient who has had special preparation for tests, such as glucose tolerance, which might cause a reaction.

Draw enough the first time. How many times have you had to restick a patient because an insufficient sample was obtained the first time? This happens frequently. It's time-consuming for the phlebotomist and an inconvenience for the patient. Avoiding the problem is largely a matter of technique.

Before drawing blood, examine both arms for a suitable puncture site. Often, an exhaustive search will turn up only a small vein. This might be satisfactory for a small sample, but may not hold up for several tubes. In those cases, you should consider using a syringe rather than an evacuated tube. You can control a syringe so there is less negative pressure on the vein than with an evacuated tube. The lower the negative pressure, the less likely it is that the vein will collapse before you've gotten a sufficient sample. You should always have a supply of syringes—in several sizes—for use in these difficult cases.

In some instances, the phlebotomist can save time and avoid a restick by collecting an extra tube. For example, if a Stat hemoglobin and hematocrit are ordered, there is a good possibility that a transfusion will be necessary. A small clot for the blood bank's crossmatching can be taken at the same time as the sample for the tests. Or if a patient is difficult to stick, it's a good idea to take some extra blood when you can get it—if his condition allows. Then you have saved time and trouble if a tube breaks in centrifugation, or the physician orders additional tests later in the day.

Sometimes it will be impossible to obtain enough blood for testing. When that happens, the phlebotomist should follow the established procedure for such cases—usually tell the chief tech or pathologist, who can alert the attending physician to take alternative action.

Watch the quality. The quality of a specimen is as important as its quantity. One of the most common problems is hemolysis. Hemolyzed specimens are unsatisfactory for most chemistry tests because elements released by the damaged red cells affect the results. These samples are also inappropriate for most colorimetric analysis.

If you are not sure about a hemolyzed sample's usefulness for an ordered test, discard it and try again. You can usually avoid hemolysis on a second attempt by increasing the size of the needle you are using on the evacuated tube, or by changing to a syringe. If after several attempts the specimen is still hemolyzed, the reason for the hemolysis itself should be investigated.

Lipemic specimens also cause problems in most colorimetric analysis. Lipemic samples usually can be avoided by having the patient fast for 12 to 14 hours before the blood is taken. If after that time the specimen is still lipemic, a physiological cause should be suspected.

Another problem specimen is one that has clotted when it shouldn't have. Be sure that all tubes with anticoagulant are thoroughly mixed as soon after venipuncture as possible. If the withdrawal is a lengthy one, tissue thromboplastin may cause clotting before you can do the mixing. If you suspect that this has happened, check the sample with a wooden applicator stick to be sure there is no small clot.

Complete the job—on time. As laboratories have grown in size and become departmentalized, the chance of a specimen being lost or misplaced has increased. It's up to the phlebotomist to make sure that samples are delivered to the right person or place. Equally important, he must deliver the samples on time. Many tests are run in batches only once a day. If a deadline is missed, it could mean a delay of up to 24 hours. Other tests, such as blood gases and pro times, measure unstable qualities of the blood. Specimens for these kinds of tests become useless if their analysis is delayed.

Delivering specimens should be the easiest part of the phlebotomy procedure. That's why you should be wary of the complacency that can stem from habit and routine. The best phlebotomy in the world will be wasted if the blood doesn't make it to—or through—the test.

7

Laboratory Liability Pitfalls

Robert J. Loder, M.A., MT(ASCP)

The malpractice crisis has become an ever-present and at times painful reality to all of us in the medical field. Malpractice headlines assault us, statistics are spewed out and analyzed ad infinitum, and lawyers and medicolegal experts expound learnedly on the causes of the problem.

What bothers me as a chief tech is that much of what the experts say about malpractice seems so remote from the everyday happenings in the laboratory. And yet, that's exactly where malpractice suits often start: Somebody makes a mistake in a routine procedure, the patient suffers an untoward result, and bam—you've got a malpractice suit on your hands.

The concept I try to make everyone in the lab aware of is that malpractice suits grow from little things and often in unexpected places. When techs are hired, I tell them the kinds of problems I want them to look out for, and I spell out procedures I want followed in legally sensitive areas. Here are examples of what I mean:

Did you know that wrongful disclosure of patient records can lead to a lawsuit? Patients are entitled to strict confidentiality. Before a hospital can release any patient information—even to insurance companies or to other doctors or hospitals—the patient must sign a form authorizing the release. Certain data, such as births, deaths, the incidence of communicable disease, and injuries of a criminal nature, must, by law, be reported to the Bureau of Vital Statistics. But even that information may not be given to anybody else. I tell my staff that requests for patient records, other than from people who are directly connected with that patient's care, must be referred to the hospital's medical records department.

Loose talk—a poor relation of wrongful disclosure—can also bring on a suit. Even in our lab, where I stress the necessity of confidentiality, incidents occur. Take this one, for example: A clerical worker who was sorting laboratory reports noticed that one of her neighbors was a patient. She looked at the chart, saw that the neighbor was having cosmetic surgery, and proceeded to spread the news around the neighborhood. Needless to say, the patient was infuriated.

She came to me with her complaint and threatened to sue the hospital. There's not much I can do in a situation like that but listen and offer sincere apologies. I assured her that I sympathized with her predicament and that such an incident wouldn't happen again with that particular employee because I was going to dismiss her. My expressions of sympathy for her situation and the fact that I was doing something about it satisfied her, and she dropped the matter.

In such cases, corrective action must be taken. The employee should be reprimanded, if not fired, and a report entered in his personnel file. The patient must be shown tactful consideration for his embarrassment or discomfort. Otherwise, such an incident, coupled with a poor patient relationship, would almost surely precipitate a lawsuit.

Did you know that you shouldn't remove a mischarted report from a patient's record? If a patient sues, and it can be shown that something was removed from his hospital records, that could be very damaging to the defendant hospital or physician. The plaintiff's attorney would be sure to suggest that if something was removed from a chart, it was done in order to protect the doctor or hospital.

The correct procedure is to mark the report "mischarted" or "void," call the physician, tell him a report was mischarted in his patient's record, and check whether he ordered any tests or anything that would affect the patient's care. Then the report should be written up again in the lab, signed by the technologist who performed the test, and entered in the right patient's chart. In our hospital, laboratory personnel are directly responsible for entering lab reports in patient records, so I make a point of educating our staff in this procedure. I also talk to all nursing personnel during inservice education week and tell them about it. If they discover the mischarted data, they are supposed to call the lab immediately so we may handle it.

A lot of labs take the easy way out: They send the chart copy to the floor and expect the nursing service to post it in the patient's record. Then, if a record is lost or misfiled, the lab can jump on the nursing service about it. I think that's poor management, to say nothing of being unfair. The laboratory should take responsibility for posting its reports in patient charts.

Certain information should never appear in a patient's record. Incident reports, useful as they are to the hospital, can be damning evidence if they are presented in court. The purpose of incident reports is to help the administration correct undesirable conditions in the hospital. The reports are rightly made when an untoward accident occurs, and they're filed in the administrator's confidential files—never with patients' records where they might be subpoenaed as evidence in a malpractice case.

We had an "incident" recently, and I was careful to write it up for my own files, as well as for the administrator's. This occurrence involved a hospital employee who came into the lab to donate blood. The venipuncturist had trouble drawing blood from him; in fact, he couldn't get it out of one arm and went to the other arm. As it happened, a hematoma developed in the arm that was first punctured, and the man went to his doctor, telling him that his father had had a similar problem. The doctor put him in the hospital and kept him there for four or five days on anticoagulant therapy, treating him almost as if he had phlebitis. Afterward, the patient came to me and wanted restitution.

In this case, I can't say I had much sympathy for the man, but, to be on the safe side, I told him to send all his bills to the laboratory, and we'd see that they were taken care of. We got not only his hospital bills, but also bills for daily prothrombin tests he had run for a week after his hospitalization. All that for a hematoma!

Fortunately, we were able to smooth it over. We paid his bills—to the tune of about $1,300—and the patient pursued the matter no further. If he'd sued, and if his attorney had had access to the incident report, the case might have gone badly for us. As it is, we have the report and all related details, we've learned something from it, and the report itself couldn't be presented in court.

Did you know that the blood-donor release form isn't worth much more than the paper it's written on? That man with the hematoma signed the release form, but I couldn't say to him, "Sorry, but you signed the release, and there's nothing I can do for you." He could have gone right ahead and sued us anyhow—you can't sign away your inalienable right to seek redress.

All laboratories and blood banks should bear that in mind. If some kind of incident occurs after blood is drawn, the best preventive measure against suit is an honest attempt to help the person, to attend to any injury he may have suffered, and to pay for the medical care he receives as a result of it.

Remember, too, that a patient has the right to refuse to have blood drawn. A venipuncturist should never try to force the issue, but instead should refer any problem patients to the attending physician. I know of a case in which the venipuncturist locked the door and forcibly drew a young patient's blood. The child was so traumatized by the incident that he required psychiatric counseling, and the hospital, of course, had to pay for it.

Since you're probably already familiar with some of the more common sources of legal trouble in the lab, I haven't mentioned them yet. But they shouldn't be ignored. All laboratories encounter these problems from time to time, and all of the problems can be legally hazardous. Among these other potential trouble spots are mislabeled specimens or reports, incorrect patient identification, illegible handwriting, and lost or long-delayed specimens.

Care is nine-tenths of the cure in such cases. For example, our front-office people are instructed to check all outgoing lab reports for illegible handwriting. If they can't read a report, they send it back to the technologist who prepared it to write it up again.

Perhaps the best deterrent to carelessness and mishandling specimens is to remember that we're dealing with human beings, not hospital numbers. That's an old notion, but one we too easily forget when it should be uppermost in our minds. If a specimen is lost, it's not a matter of "drawing Room 300 again." It's a matter of subjecting a sick person to a second—and also unnecessary—

withdrawal of blood. If a report is delayed, it could mean that someone has to stay in the hospital longer than he needs to, with all the attendant expense and inconvenience.

We must not let laboratory routine lull us into complacency and carelessness. Attitudes such as these make it extremely easy for problems to develop—problems that can land us right in the middle of a malpractice suit.

FIGURE 7-1

Patient's Bill of Rights

Many hospitals have adopted the Patient's Bill of Rights, as promulgated by the American Hospital Association. Some states, such as Minnesota and California, have passed laws making the document mandatory. It's conceivable that the bill of rights could become the basis of a lawsuit if a patient feels his rights have been violated. But whether or not these rights are the basis of a suit, it's a good idea for laboratorians to know what they are, because they're certainly consistent with good hospital care. Here, in condensed form, are the basic patient rights endorsed by the AHA:

The patient has the right to:

- considerate and respectful care.
- information from his physician concerning his diagnosis, treatment, and prognosis in terms he can understand.
- information from his physician necessary for him to give informed consent to any procedure or treatment.
- refuse treatment.
- every consideration of privacy during his case discussion, consultation, examination, and treatment. Anyone not directly involved in his care must have his permission to be present.
- confidentiality of all communications and records pertaining to his care.
- a reasonable response by the hospital to his request for services.
- information about the relationship between his hospital and other institutions as far as his care is concerned, and information about the professional relationship among individuals treating him.
- be advised if the hospital intends to engage in human experimentation affecting his care. He may refuse to participate in experimentation of that sort.
- reasonable continuity of care.
- an explanation of his bill, regardless of the source of payment.
- know what hospital rules apply to his conduct as a patient.

8

Legal Liability in the Laboratory

Michael X. Morrell, J.D.

Unheralded, even stealthy, perhaps. But along with the emergence of clinical laboratories as an integral part of our health-care system have come many complex legal issues. So numerous and complex, in fact, that we can identify and discuss them only preliminarily.

Indeed, framing relevant legal issues is often more difficult and more important than finding *the* answer itself—especially in science and medicine, where today's answer may not work tomorrow because of technological and medical advances.

The underlying legal issues will not change, however, so it is important to define them to insure that the ensuing debate and pursuit of "right" answers will be effectively focused.

Professional standards. Before discussing any specific legal issues, a word of caution is in order: In deciding on an appropriate course of action in the laboratory, you should always follow your professional judgment, based on your training and experience. Because of the ever-increasing legislative and regulatory standards being applied to clinical laboratories, you may assume that they take precedence over your professional judgment. They do not. While deference must be given to legal standards, your responsibility is to the patient's interest.

There are several reasons for this. First, legal standards *per se* cannot even address, let alone answer, the many problems confronting laboratories every day. Nor do governmental authorities have the expertise to understand the technicalities of operating clinical laboratories. Second, legal standards are promulgated not in response to the majority, but to the improper activities of a tiny percentage of clinical laboratories that fail to conform to standards of professional conduct.

Let me emphasize that governmental intervention usually occurs when a profession fails to regulate its own members. Thus it is essential for the profession to develop and implement its own standards. This will insure that the standards are realistic, and at the same time, avoid the imposition of standards from an outside agency. In the past, this has occurred most often when there's a regulatory void regarding health-care procedures that are increasingly important for patients and costly to the general public.

Testing and liability. Like the rest of the health-care system, clinical laboratories are subject to conflicting forces that seek, on the one hand, to limit utilization of services and cut costs and, on the other, to provide quality care and simultaneously reduce potential liability for failing to do so. Laboratory tests to diagnose and treat a patient's disease are an integral part of that care. And cutting overutilization of laboratory testing is a major concern of third-party payers.

This concern is manifested by pressure from utilization review committees to reduce the number and types of tests. A still more graphic example of this philosophy is the legislative objective on the Federal level to limit all hospital cost increases to a fixed annual percentage, despite the fact that this will inevitably adversely affect the quality of patient care. This philosophy becomes even more troublesome for the professional because excluding or restricting laboratory tests may result in potential malpractice liability for failure to utilize "all tests."

This standard of liability is not merely speculative: Courts have already decided that if a physician does not use all the scientific means and facilities available to him for making a diagnosis, such an omission may be evidence of negligence.

If failure to abide by the "all tests" standard can result in the physician's liability, it isn't difficult to see why physicians practice defensive medicine and order every conceivable test they think they may need to make a diagnosis. They do so to meet their professional responsibility to their patients and to protect themselves from potential liability. Fortunately, physicians have resolved the cut-costs-or-cut-care dilemma in favor of their patients' interests, not those of the bureaucrats.

Let's consider two major pieces of legislation that have a big potential impact on laboratories. They are the certificate-of-need provisions of state laws and the Federal Health Planning Act, and the as-yet pending Clinical Laboratory Improvement Act.

Certificate-of-need laws. These laws are, of course, an effort to control capital expenditures for equipment and construction. They affect laboratories by mandating regulatory approval of all expenditures that exceed a fixed amount—in some cases as low as $10,000. In making its decisions, the regulatory agency considers need and utilization of the patient population within a defined geographic area. If a particularly sophisticated laboratory instrument, for example, is available at one hospital in the area, the agency might rule that others are unnecessary and deny other laboratories' requests for that instrument.

This entire certificate-of-need area is fraught with problems that raise serious questions about the hospital's and the laboratory's ability to provide quality care to patients. This will likely have an even greater restrictive effect on laboratories as more sophisticated, technologically advanced, and by its very nature, more expensive equipment is developed. Laboratories will need this equipment not only to provide quality patient care, but also to insure that the laboratory is not subject to potential malpractice liability because of the "all tests" standard. If it failed to perform "all tests" for a patient, the laboratory could face charges of negligence, even though it *could not* do the tests because it was denied the particular diagnostic equipment as not "needed."

The Clinical Laboratory Improvement Act. If this act becomes law, its impact will be tremendous. Laboratorians have already expressed concern over various sections of the law. Among them: mandatory licensure; national standards for quality, accuracy, and precision of laboratory testing; and uniform regulatory programs on the Federal level together with inspection, license revocation, and the imposition of civil or criminal penalties for violation.

But in my opinion, these are not the most significant aspects of the law. Rather, the most interesting feature is the opportunity for professional associations to develop standards and certification for their members in clinical laboratories. This is unique because the regulators are inviting the regulated—clinical professionals in clinical laboratories—to take the initiative to establish policy and standards that will be critical in determining the nature, scope, and direction of the law, as interpreted by the Department of Health and Human Services.

The realization of this concept of cooperative regulation requires the immediate attention of the various clinical laboratory associations. If they do not meet this challenge by developing their own standards and certification procedures, the Federal government will certainly fill the void. This would be unfortunate, since the Federal effort could not possibly be based on the same level of experience and expertise as that of the professional associations. It is therefore critical for the associations to address this issue without delay to insure that they will play an appropriate role in the forthcoming regulatory action.

So far, we have examined the legal issues that have been created in the laboratory by legislative and regulatory actions. Now let us go into the heart of the laboratory for a look at potential malpractice liability in the testing process itself.

Informed consent. When a physician orders laboratory tests, the first question is whether the patient gave his informed consent for those tests. Perhaps the easiest way for laboratories to be sure that patients give their consent for tests is to insert a reference to laboratory tests in the hospital's standard consent form. When the patient signs this form upon entering the hospital, it removes any doubt about his voluntary agreement to all tests necessary for his medical care. This is far less cumbersome administratively than using a separate consent form for all laboratory tests.

Certain aspects of informed consent are peculiar to laboratory testing. Does a patient's general consent, for example, cover tests other than those ordered by the physician? Not long ago, the FDA published a proposed regulation that if blood were used for other than ordered tests, specific consent for the other tests would be required. This proposal was withdrawn, but it is noteworthy because it reflects the attitude of a major Federal agency that specific consent is a prerequisite for any testing other than that ordered by the doctor. This view, of course, does not agree with the traditional, generally accepted standard that a patient's informed consent applies to all testing reasonable and necessary for his care.

A second example involves the sale of a patient's plasma after the completion of testing. This practice, employed when certain rare conditions are present, is potentially explosive, since patients are most likely to maintain that their consent did not give permission to sell their plasma. It is fair to assume that any court confronted with this issue would concur with the patient and rule against any laboratory engaged in this practice.

Rather than risking such an unfavorable outcome, laboratories should either stop the practice or justify it. The most reasonable justification is to point out that the plasma is of no use to the patient and will be destroyed if it is not sold. Nor should the sale result in personal profit. Any profit realized must be used to reduce the overall cost of laboratory operation or to improve the quality of patient care.

Standard hospital consent forms do not include authorization for the sale of plasma or other body fluids. This is either because of the inevitable public hue and cry over such an issue relating to personal property or because of the administrative difficulty of giving patients enough information to withstand challenges that the consent obtained was not truly informed. A better approach would be to adopt a written hospital policy outlining the approved manner of sale of any such materials and the approved utilization of any resulting income. (We'll discuss more about written policies later on.)

Although it is not legally mandated that informed consent be written, it is by far the safer course, especially considering the large population of hospital patients and the fact that litigation to resolve any consent issue will probably take years to come to trial.

Inappropriate testing. Now assume that the patient has given his informed consent and the physician has ordered certain laboratory tests. The next question is whether the proper tests have been ordered. First, let me emphasize again that, as professionals, you are an integral part of the health-care team. Consequently, even though you cannot initiate laboratory tests, this in no way lessens your responsibility to insure quality patient care.

Since you have not examined the patient and cannot know the symptoms he has displayed, how can you tell whether the physician has ordered the proper test? There is no simple response. But in obvious situations, such as when a physician orders full test panels three times a week for one patient, you are obligated to tell him that such utilization is inappropriate.

Realistically, most situations are not so obvious, but the basic principle is the same: When you become aware that inappropriate tests are being ordered, you must do what you can to stop it. Perhaps the best way to do this is by education through communication between professionals—clinical laboratorians and physicians. Tell physicians about new developments and applications that will help them in specific diagnoses. It's up to you to initiate this communication because you, more than the physician, are the experts in this field.

By way of further explanation, your relationship with the physician is much like that between a pharmacist and physician. When a pharmacist is given a patient's prescription, he may conclude that it is inappropriate. As a professional, the pharmacist is obligated to tell the physician so, and he, in turn, will either change the prescription or direct it to be filled as written. In the latter case, the pharmacist must comply with the order, but to protect himself from potential liability, he should ask for written confirmation from the physician or, at the very least, make his own written notation in his files.

Similarly, if you know that a physician has ordered an inappropriate test, you are obligated to tell him so. If he insists upon the test as ordered, you should write a note to that effect for the laboratory files. This should minimize the laboratory's liability if the patient were misdiagnosed and mistreated as a result of data from the inappropriate test.

Improper performance of tests. Liability can also occur if you perform tests improperly or if you perform follow-up tests that were not ordered by the physician. An interesting issue arises in the latter situation: When laboratories, as a matter of practice, perform tests as ordered and obtain certain results, those results may trigger follow-up tests that are not specifically ordered by a physician. Again, the validity of this practice depends on professional judgment. But when an ordered test generates data that demand follow-up tests, you must run those tests to maintain quality patient care. If you report results of the follow-up tests to the physician so that he can commence or modify treatment accordingly, you have fulfilled your professional obligation.

What happens if the follow-up tests are performed improperly so that the test results are wrong? If the physician relies on those results and if the patient is injured, the laboratory will be liable for negligence.

In light of this potential liability, you might conclude that the safest way to conduct your profession is to do only those tests that a physician orders. But we've already seen that it is your professional obligation to perform follow-up tests when necessary.

Written policy. The alternative and better approach is to develop a formal, written policy in the hospital that authorizes follow-up tests, even if not ordered by the physician, provided that certain standards and procedures are followed. A written policy, in and of itself, is neither law nor regulation as enacted by a governmental authority. But in this area in which standards are so undefined, courts rely on a written policy as the best existing standard against which to judge negligence.

A word of caution: Once a written policy is adopted, it must be followed. If not, the laboratory places itself in the classic position of failing to follow its own rules—and thereby subjects itself to liability.

Still another word of caution: As technology and knowledge advance, the policy should be correspondingly amended on a periodic basis. Failure to do so could result in the laboratory being measured by outdated standards. An injured patient, of course, will rely on the written standards to show that they were not met, and that constitutes *prima facie* evidence of negligence. Although evidence to the contrary can be presented to show that the standards had changed, it will be extremely difficult to overcome the court's reliance on the existing written standard to determine negligence.

A written policy can also be helpful with the issue of whether unordered follow-up tests are eligible for reimbursement. The written policy demonstrates that performing such tests, based on defined test results and done according to defined procedures, is standard practice among clinical laboratories. This also serves as justification for third-party payers that this policy is acceptable and reimbursement should be allowed.

Once the tests have been done, the next step is to report their results to the doctor. It is essential that you report them in such a way that the doctor can readily grasp their importance and proceed to treat his patient accordingly.

Again, communication from the laboratory to the physician is critical. Although it is legally sufficient merely to give the test report to the physician, it is better and more professional to highlight the key results. The laboratory, more than the physician, is familiar with the critical aspects of the testing and should report them so as to insure that the physician will be fully aware of their significance.

9

Legal Liability in the Laboratory: A Rebuttal

Henry B. Soloway, M.D.

In the preceding chapter, Michael X. Morrell, J.D., discussed the legal implications of laboratory testing. While most of what attorney Morrell said was appropriate, he raised a few points, which, if I interpret them correctly, could place laboratorians in serious legal jeopardy.

Frankly, I suspect that Morrell's representations in these areas are faulty—and are so because they are based on his misconceptions about how a clinical laboratory is organized. Further, I feel it is important to brand these concepts as erroneous lest they be perpetuated, first as points of law, then eventually as regulations or standards against which our laboratory performance is assessed.

To begin with, attorney Morrell asserted that when laboratorians become aware that inappropriate tests have been ordered, they must do what they can to intercede. I maintain that such intervention is clearly not the lab's function unless—or until—the attending physician *requests* the consultation of the pathologist.

Next, Morrell made no distinction among the various strata of personnel who work in the clinical laboratory, nor did he suggest that this intervention should be done, if at all, on a physician-to-physician basis. In fact, by comparing the laboratorian-physician relationship with the pharmacist-physician relationship, Morrell clearly implied that technologists, as well as pathologists, were under an obligation to intercede with the clinician.

I maintain that, with a few notable exceptions, nonphysician laboratory personnel are not trained or qualified to advise an attending physician that he ordered an inappropriate test. They do not have access to the patient's medical records; they are not privy to the physician's deductive logic; and they do not share his responsibility for the patient's treatment.

This is not to say—and here I agree with Morrell—that when an obvious ordering error has been made—such as ordering a Philadelphia chromosome determination on a child admitted for a routine tonsillectomy—nonphysician lab personnel should remain silent. But it does pertain to all gray areas of ordering practice.

If an attending physician feels that he needs lab data above and beyond that ordered by other practitioners, we must accept, though not necessarily respect, his judgment. Certainly, he could glean much valuable information by asking both physician and nonphysician laboratory personnel about certain procedures and results. But implying that lab techs have an obligation to tell physicians that their test orders are inappropriate is without legal merit or foundation.

Another reason this intercession is unnecessary is that there are already established mechanisms by which physicians who use laboratories improperly can be taught the error of their ways. One is the hospital utilization review committee, which continually reviews the quality of patient care. Another is the more subtle approach of cloakroom diplomacy, in which the pathologist-laboratory director buttonholes the offending physician and tactfully suggests changes in his ordering practices. If this were done by nonphysicians, it would be met with undisguised hostility.

In addition, most hospitals have medical audit committees, which have the authority to review any aspect of patient care. Audits that reveal that a particular physician is ordering laboratory tests inappropriately are forwarded to his department for review. If the department concurs with the audit committee, it advises the physician that his peers disagree with his practices and cites reasons for the disagreement.

Another notion of Morrell's that I found whimsical was his concept of "quality patient care." He equated it with ordering the proper test, then stated "in obvious situations, such as when a physician orders full test panels three times a week for one patient, you [he implies all lab personnel] are obligated to tell him that this is inappropriate."

For starters, quality patient care in the laboratory consists of reporting prompt and accurate results on the tests that physicians order for their patients. It does not consist of laboratory personnel accosting a physician and telling him that "even though I cannot initiate laboratory tests, I have a responsibility to tell you that ordering three full test panels in a week for one patient constitutes poor quality care." Indeed, anybody working in my laboratory who makes such a speech—even though he feels obligated to do so based on attorney Morrell's counsel—will be out of a job.

I also believe that Morrell's advice was faulty when he discussed the laboratory's liability for misdiagnosis as a result of an inappropriately ordered test. Let's assume again that a laboratorian has caught an erring physician and tells him he has ordered improperly. And let's suppose the physician responds, "It's my job to order the tests, and it's your job to do them. You keep your nose out of my business, and I'll keep my nose out of yours."

In such a case, Morrell suggested that the laboratorian write a note about the incident for the laboratory's files. This, he said, "should minimize the laboratory's liability if the patient were misdiagnosed and mistreated as a result of data from the inappropriate test."

Poppycock! The attending physician has the sole responsibility for diagnosing and treating a patient's illness—and for selecting such diagnostic modalities as the history and physical, X-rays, lab work, and consultation with other physicians.

In many court cases, a physician has been found negligent for failing to consult. But I know of no litigation that has found a would-be consultant negligent for failing to impose his opinion on another physician. And unless case law exists to disprove my position, I suggest that we all forget this very strange piece of advice.

Attorney Morrell's response. First, Dr. Soloway insists that laboratorians should not intervene with a physician who has ordered inappropriate tests unless the attending physician requests consultation. In response, by the very fact that the physician ordered tests, he has requested that consultation. Thus, the physician involves the laboratorian in the treatment process and imposes on him the professional obligation and legal duty to insure quality care.

Second, Dr. Soloway points out that I failed to distinguish among various strata of laboratory personnel and suggests that I must want chaos to prevail by allowing all laboratory personnel to communicate directly with physicians. Perhaps I was not as explicit as Dr. Soloway demands, but I am reasonably confident that laboratorians reading my article concluded that they should use established lines of communication. Thus someone at the supervisory or managerial level would be responsible for screening comments and relaying them to the physician involved. Needless to say, chaotic communication is not acceptable.

Third, Dr. Soloway states that the laboratory must accept, though not necessarily respect, a physician's demands for unnecessary or inappropriate tests. Nowhere did I deny a physician's right to order any tests he wants. Only after the tests are performed and shown to be inappropriate does the laboratorian have a duty to so inform the physician.

I can't believe that Dr. Soloway seriously believes that laboratorians have no responsibility to tell physicians when they have ordered inappropriately. The laboratorian's function is not limited to providing the physician with reliable data for diagnosis and treatment. If it were, this would raise a serious question about the laboratorian's role in the health-care system. Patient care must be the foremost consideration in the system. The fact that allied health professionals' involvement in the system may result in debate or a physician's anger is irrelevant.

Fourth, Dr. Soloway states that the laboratorian need not intercede with the physician because mechanisms to teach him the error of his ways already exist. He then cites various hospital committees and "cloakroom diplomacy." Indeed, I'm aware of these channels of communication. They in no way detract from, but rather support, a major point I made: The laboratorian is obligated to communicate with the physician.

It is imperative that the hospital utilization review and medical audit committees have representation from the clinical laboratory and review testing patterns. But the one drawback of these committees is that they meet periodically and cannot respond to immediate problems. For this reason, I recommended more flexible communication systems.

Fifth, Dr. Soloway makes the point that it is not the laboratorian's responsibility to accost physicians. Agreed. Physicians—and other members of the health-care team—should not be accosted. I seem to have greater faith in laboratorians than Dr. Soloway. I think they can communicate with physicians without accosting them.

I trust that Dr. Soloway at least concedes that laboratorians can be liable for injury that befalls a patient if his physician relies on inaccurate laboratory data and misdiagnoses or mistreats him. It is puzzling why Dr. Soloway can't make the leap to a situation in which the laboratorian finds that the physician has ordered an inappropriate test. In this case, the test data the physician relies on are just as unreliable as those from a test improperly performed or results inaccurately reported. In all these cases, the potential harm to the patient is the same. Dr. Soloway fails to recognize the fundamental legal principle that the same duty exists in all three situations: The laboratorian must exercise due care and professional judgment to insure that no harm comes to the patient from negligence.

Sixth, Dr. Soloway disagrees with my suggestion that if a physician refuses to change his test order as recommended by the laboratory, the laboratorian should write a note to that effect for the laboratory files. In fact, he calls it poppycock because the physician has sole responsibility for diagnosing and treating the patient.

It's true that where the physician requests no laboratory tests, he bears sole responsibility. But when the physician has ordered tests, he then bears the *primary* responsibility, and the laboratory bears part of the responsibility for the patient's care.

Seventh, Dr. Soloway correctly says that physicians have been found negligent for failure to consult, but that he knows of no cases finding a would-be consultant negligent for failing to impose his opinion on another physician. This is entirely misleading. At no point did I suggest that the laboratorian should impose his opinion on a physician. Rather, I said he has a legal duty to communicate with him. There's a vast difference between the two.

Finally, Dr. Soloway asks for case law to disprove his position. I'm happy to oblige and refer him to 51 American Law Reports 2d 947. It contains a full discussion supporting the legal principle that health professionals who operate under the guidance and instructions of attending physicians cannot escape liability for failure to fulfill their duty by merely stating they were following physicians' orders.

10

Medicolegal Problems in Laboratory Medicine

Harold L. Engel, M.D., J.D.

It's been said that the medical malpractice crisis peaked in the mid-'70s and that complaints against doctors have tapered off since then. I'd like to be able to report that this is true, but as a lawyer who defends physicians in malpractice cases, I haven't noticed any decline. The rate of increase may have slowed, although I'm not even sure of that because accurate figures are hard to come by.

Laboratories are involved in a number of these cases. The clinical laboratory is no longer the haven from malpractice suits it once was, although pathologists as a group are less likely to be sued than primary-care physicians.

The main reason for the large number of malpractice suits is that the whole country is more litigation-minded. More lawsuits of every kind are being filed each year. Doctors, along with everyone else, are more vulnerable to lawsuits now than they ever have been in the past. And because the trend in medical malpractice cases is toward spreading the blame, pathologists, as well as others in the laboratory, are being named in an increasing number of lawsuits.

In theory, if a doctor always follows a high standard of practice, it isn't likely that he will become involved in a malpractice suit. But doctors make mistakes, and even the best doctors are occasionally sued.

Malpractice is a term used to describe professional negligence. That is, every person has a duty to act toward other persons in a reasonable manner. When his action is unreasonable and causes injury to the other person, he's said to have been negligent. If he's a professional—such as a physician, attorney, or accountant—then his negligence is called malpractice.

Sometimes a doctor will attempt to justify his actions on the ground that he made an honest mistake. He'll say he did his best and didn't mean to make a mistake. This is no defense. All negligence is assumed to be caused by mistakes. No one accuses a doctor of doing something wrong deliberately. If he did, he wouldn't sue in the area of malpractice. He would sue in the area of intentional tort, or wrongdoing, which is an entirely different matter.

Community rule. The crucial question in every medical malpractice case is not whether the physician made a mistake, but whether he or she has practiced medicine according to the accepted standard in the community—the so-called "community rule." That is, did he handle the case the way other reputable doctors in the same community with the same training would have handled it? If he did—even though he made a mistake—a case may be made in his favor.

In recent years, the community rule has been enlarged to include any city or area of similar size or sophistication. That is, it's no longer a valid argument to say that in a laboratory everything is done the way it's done in other labs in the community if all the community's labs are below the standard of similar labs elsewhere in the country.

Today, with better medical information available and more opportunities for sharing it, medical professionals everywhere are expected to adhere to the same high standard of practice. The way a pathologist in Iowa is expected to handle a case is no different from the way a pathologist in New York City is expected to handle it.

Errors in diagnosis. Of malpractice suits involving the laboratory, by far the most arise from errors in diagnosis. And of these, the most serious involve tumors. Either the pathologist called a benign lesion malignant, and an organ was removed needlessly, or the lesion was diagnosed as benign, and the patient died or his condition deteriorated because he received no treatment. These misdiagnoses most often involve the breast. Bone lesions are also frequently misdiagnosed.

Not all errors in diagnosis can be prevented, but precautions can and should be taken to keep them to an absolute minimum. The most important precaution a pathologist can take is to get a second or third opinion when in doubt. But this in itself isn't enough. He should make sure the attending physician or surgeon is aware of these doubts.

We had one case in which a pathologist looked at a frozen section of a breast and diagnosed it as malignant, then showed it to a colleague, who said he thought it was benign. So he asked another pathologist, who agreed with him that it was malignant. He then went back and, without mentioning the dissenting opinion, told the surgeon that the tissue was malignant, and the surgeon removed the patient's breast. The next day the permanent section showed that the tumor was indeed benign.

The patient sued for malpractice, and during the trial, the surgeon stated that if he had known about the third pathologist's opinion, he would have postponed the surgery until he'd had a chance to see the results from the permanent section.

It's most important to keep careful records. Unless this is done, physicians who practice side by side at a hospital may become adversaries during a malpractice suit. If there's doubt about the accuracy of lab tests or if there's a difference of opinion in the diagnosis, it should go into the patient's record. If the pathologist is called to the operating room to look at a specimen that's still in the patient's body and asked for an opinion, he should make a note on the progress sheet as to when he was called in, what he was asked, and what he said. Then later, if the attending physician or surgeon forgets he ever got that information or denies that he got it, the record will prove that he did.

In making his diagnosis, a pathologist is obligated to call upon all the resources available to him. If his diagnosis will make the difference between a patient losing or keeping an organ, and he practices in a small town, he may be wise to consult with someone in another city—or a center that has a large collection of pathological materials to draw upon.

Sometimes a pathologist who has made a correct diagnosis will get into trouble because of the way he communicates this diagnosis: He tells either too little or too much.

A diagnosis that leaves out important information or only hints at a problem and thus leads the attending physician to administer the wrong therapeutic program can come back to haunt the pathologist.

On the other hand, a diagnosis that goes too far—that wanders into the gray area of speculation—can cause just as much trouble. In one case, a patient who had received a blood transfusion developed an extremely high fever that may or may not have been caused by the transfusion. But because a physician had written ''transfusion reaction'' on the patient's chart as the cause of death, the pathologist and the blood bank were held liable. If the physician had consulted the anesthesiologist before coming to his diagnostic conclusion, he might have come to an entirely different conclusion, such as a nonpreventable case of malignant hyperthermia.

Records and reports. Records should be as complete as possible, but they should stick to the facts. Physicians should be very reluctant to write diagnoses that place blame on anyone. In malpractice cases, these records are read to the jury, and jurors can hardly be blamed if they take the records at face value.

In general, reports should be made as soon as possible. They should show the date and the time when the report was dictated and whether the information was called directly to the attending physician. If abnormalities are present or if it's clear that the physician needs immediate notification, he should be called, and that fact noted in the report.

Only the person who dictates a report should sign it. No one else. I think it's dangerous to use a rubber stamp with a signature on it because this suggests that the report may not have been read. No one should send out a report over his name without reading it personally. Admittedly, this takes a lot of time, but it may not only save a lawsuit—it could save a patient's life.

Another area in which suits sometimes arise is in the laboratory's failure to communicate important information to the clinician. If a specimen that is inadequate comes into the lab and the report goes back, ''No abnormal cells seen in the specimen,'' without indicating that the specimen was inadequate, both the lab and the clinician can get into trouble.

Or the laboratory may fail to tell the clinician that he sent the wrong type of specimen for the test he wants. We had one case in which a patient's malignancy was overlooked because the clinician sent in a Pap smear instead of a biopsy. The pathologist was brought into the case because he failed to tell the clinician that he should have sent a biopsy specimen instead.

Any abnormality should be reported immediately. If the pathologist sees a piece of ureter in a hysterectomy specimen, for example, he should call the surgeon immediately and not wait until he dictates a report. It may be days before the report is typed up and the surgeon sees it, particularly over weekends.

Cases involving the lab. In most malpractice cases involving the laboratory, it's the pathologist who is sued. As the director of the lab, he may be considered the employer, and as such—along with the laboratory itself or the hospital—he is responsible for the actions of his employees. But this isn't to say that employees are not responsible for their own mistakes. Everyone—in the medical field as well as elsewhere—is liable for his own negligent acts. The employer usually pays the damages because he usually has the money or the insurance. But negligent employees are also named in suits. And if the employee has a house or other assets, he may have to pay monetary damages, too.

Furthermore, if an employer is held liable for damages caused by his negligent employee and has done nothing wrong himself, he may have a right to action against the employee. No one in a laboratory or anywhere else should feel that he can be negligent and harm someone and not be liable for payment.

We get a number of cases that have resulted from an employee's negligence. In the blood bank, for example, mistakes can be made all along the line, from the selection of the donors to the administration of the blood to the patient. If a blood donor isn't tested for hepatitis or syphilis, and because of that the patient is injured, the patient can bring a lawsuit. The whole area of blood donations—and whether to use paid or volunteer donors—is fraught with potential malpractice problems.

In general, blood banks are expected to conform to AABB guidelines or state regulations. This means that to stay out of trouble, they must take the necessary precautions in selecting and testing donors, in typing and crossmatching, and in transfusing the blood.

Another area that's extremely important is quality control. Any lab that wants to avoid suits must make quality control an ongoing process in which the work of technologists, pathologists, and everyone else in the laboratory is continually scrutinized. All rules, regulations, and governmental standards that apply to the laboratory must be followed, particularly the laboratory's own rules.

We had a case in which a technologist who worked in a lab during the day freelanced at night. She collected Pap smears from doctors' offices and read them at home. Of course, this practice was expressly forbidden in her laboratory's rules, but the pathologist was supposedly supervising her work. However, a malignancy slipped through, and the patient sued both the technologist and the pathologist. In a malpractice case, it's extremely difficult to defend a laboratory that has clearly flaunted its own rules and regulations.

Another way a laboratory gets into trouble is by failing to get a patient's informed consent. For most routine procedures like drawing blood or obtaining urine specimens, the hospital's standard consent form is probably adequate. But it's wise for the lab to have its own form for special procedures like bone marrow biopsies or injections of foreign substances that may cause a systemic reaction. Incidentally, this kind of procedure should always be done by a qualified professional, and a test dose should be injected before the total dose is administered.

In the final analysis, the best way for a laboratory to keep out of trouble is to set up efficient procedures and adhere to them. Of course, government rules and regulations must be followed, but I don't think more regulation is the answer. Most malpractice suits are brought against laboratories that had sufficient rules to prevent the mistake. The problem is that those guidelines weren't followed.

11

The Changing Malpractice Climate

Robert B. Nichols, M.D., J.D.

The country is still in the midst of a malpractice crisis, and medical professionals are still being sued in record numbers. But one thing has changed for the better: We are fighting back.

Instead of settling out of court, we're demanding trials more often. When we're exonerated, we're more inclined to countersue. We're even giving lawyers a taste of their own medicine by suing them for malpractice. And to bring the cost of insurance down to reasonable levels, we have formed our own insurance companies.

Of course, patients should have legal recourse when mistakes cause them injury. But one of the reasons for our current malpractice crisis is that, in the past, these suits have been filed indiscriminately. In California, until recently, any lawyer with a disgruntled client and a $53 filing fee could file suit. He wasn't required to appear in person. He wasn't even required to produce evidence of injury. All he had to do was send a law clerk down to the courthouse with the papers. Whether or not his client had a cause for action, there was nothing to dissuade him from filing suit.

On the contrary. He had every reason to feel encouraged. To file a malpractice suit was to make money. Working on a contingency fee basis—whereby the patient agreed to split any monies collected 60/40 or

50/50—he could start the wheels in motion for a negotiated settlement with a few telephone calls and some simple discovery procedures.

The defendant's insurance company was usually happy to settle out of court because it knew that mounting a successful defense would cost, say, $10,000 or $12,000. If it could settle for $5,000 or $6,000, it figured it was saving money. The doctor—pressured by his insurance carrier to settle and worried about the possibility of losing his insurance the following year—usually felt it was wise to go along rather than try to fight the case.

This scenario was played out thousands of times. Up until 1975, about 95 percent of the malpractice cases filed in California were handled this way. It proved to be so lucrative for attorneys that in the late '60s and early '70s, one of the most popular continuing-education courses for lawyers was how to handle malpractice cases. In California alone, it was offered six to eight times a year all over the state.

Excess litigation. By 1975, 90 percent of all the medical malpractice cases ever filed in California had been filed during the previous 10 years. Many of these cases never should have been filed. The attorneys themselves admitted this. In June 1978, the president of the Los Angeles County Bar Association, speaking to a group of doctors and lawyers, said, "We recognize there are a lot of claims that should not be brought." As a member of the claims review committee for a large doctors' cooperative, I've personally found that eight out of 10 claims are totally without merit.

The problems all this malpractice activity has caused are well known. Careers have been ruined. Innocent people have suffered embarrassment and lost standing in their communities. Malpractice insurance rates have shot up. Many doctors began practicing a costly and wasteful brand of defensive medicine. The clinical laboratory witnessed this in overutilization of services.

Eventually, these increased costs are passed along to the patient and the public in general. In the long run, everyone suffers except the lawyers. They are the only ones who really benefit from the current crisis. Even injured patients often end up with very little money after their legal fees and expenses are paid.

The situation is still dismal. In California, one out of every four doctors is currently being sued for malpractice. About 85 or 90 percent of the cases are still settled out of court. But things are changing. We medical professionals have begun to use some effective methods for stemming the malpractice tide.

For one thing, we're going to court more often. We've begun to resist efforts to settle claims that are over $3,000 if they are without merit. Doctors, hospitals, and insurance companies alike are beginning to see the light on this subject. Medical professionals realize that their inflated malpractice premiums are largely the result of uncontested settlements. And insurance companies, aware of the fact that the public has begun to see a relationship between high malpractice insurance rates and high doctors' fees, are backing these professionals when they ask to have their day in court.

Going to court. Fortunately, California has recently passed legislation that encourages doctors to go to court—and this could point the way to similar laws elsewhere, since California seems to lead the nation in malpractice litigation.

Any suit that is settled out of court for $3,000 or more must now be reported to the state's Board of Medical Quality Assurance, which then undertakes an investigation of the doctor. This applies subtle pressure on doctors to go to court when the merits of a case can be argued. Frequently, they can block a meritless case even before it gets off the ground. If the plaintiff's attorney has filed a claim but hasn't researched it or found a doctor to review it, the defendant's attorney can ask the judge to make a summary judgment; that is, the judge can rule that there is no case to decide.

This step may no longer be necessary in California, however, because a new state law makes it harder to file a malpractice claim. When a plaintiff's attorney files a claim, he must also file a certificate of merit showing that he has had a doctor review it and can substantiate that indeed there was medical negligence. This law is bound to cut down the number of suits.

When named in a suit, a defendant's first move is to notify his insurance carrier. This is usually stipulated in the insurance contract. The carrier then investigates the claim to decide what course of action to follow. If it finds that the suit is without merit and decides to go to court, its attorneys will represent the defendant. Sometimes the attorneys of several insurance carriers are involved.

Occasionally, a doctor hires his personal attorney to represent him as well, but I think this is a mistake. Malpractice law is a complex field, and lawyers who aren't involved in it on a regular basis can do more harm than good. Not long ago, when a doctor lost a malpractice case, he sued his own lawyer for malpractice and won.

Admittedly, going to court is a long, drawn-out process. Usually, three or four years are spent on the discovery procedure alone. This is the information-gathering process. During this time, if the case involves a laboratory, the lawyers for both sides collect laboratory slides, reports of test results, and testimony from everyone involved in order to build a case. It may be five years or more before the case ever reaches the trial stage.

But when doctors do go to court, they win about 90 percent of the time. If a defendant has done his best in a case—and other reputable professionals would have handled the situation the same way—juries are almost always favorably impressed. Recently, when a doctor won a verdict in California, the jury asked to meet him. Afterward, they explained that they wanted the doctor to know that they respected and appreciated what he and the medical profession were accomplishing.

Countersuits. Another method that's proving effective in helping to stem the malpractice tide is the countersuit. In the mid-1970s, virtually no one was filing countersuits. Many people felt it was a waste of time because these suits are very hard to win—and favorable decisions are often reversed on appeal. In 1978, by my own count, more than 100 countersuits were filed in the Los Angeles area. Many more medical professionals are now willing to fight this uphill battle.

When someone is wrongfully sued, he is put through a greal deal of agony. He doesn't have to be guilty to spend sleepless nights and suffer humiliation. Just being accused causes him considerable pain—and loss of professional reputation as well. He should have legal recourse against his accusers and, fortunately, in most states he does.

Here are some of the causes of action to consider in filing a countersuit against a plaintiff and his attorney who have filed a malpractice suit without merit: malicious prosecution; abuse of process; invasion of privacy; defamation of character; intentional infliction of emotional distress; prima facie tort (which recognizes the principle of guaranteeing every person a legal remedy for any injury to person, property, or reputation); violation of the barratry statute (which deals with inciting unwarranted litigation); and violation of the canons of professional responsibility. An attorney whose client is motivated by a desire to harass or vex (if, for example, he simply doesn't want to pay his bill) has a duty to withdraw from the case. If he doesn't, he is violating the canons of professional responsibility and can be countersued.

A countersuit can be filed anytime during the course of a malpractice case if it is based on any cause but malicious prosecution. To sue using malicious prosecution as a cause, a defendant must first be found innocent. But so many doctors are now going back to court to countersue after being exonerated that plaintiffs' lawyers have had to pull in their horns, particularly if they've been using the scattershot technique.

In the past, in an effort to spread the blame and thus tap funds from more than one insurance company, plaintiffs' attorneys have had a tendency to name as defendants everyone remotely connected with a case. Pathologists and laboratories have often been named in suits this way. Now plaintiffs' attorneys are picking and choosing defendants much more carefully. They have no desire to spend time and money defending themselves in a countersuit, nor do they want their own insurance premiums to go up—which happens when lawyers are sued, just as it does when doctors are sued.

Even though winning a countersuit is an uphill battle, more doctors are filing them every year. Even hospitals are filing them. In California, two hospitals are currently countersuing patients who originally brought suit against them. I believe these are the first hospital-initiated countersuits ever filed.

Most major medical societies help doctors with countersuits. The California Medical Association has reviewed more than 200 such suits and is currently supporting more than 20. Altogether, hundreds of cases have been filed across the country.

Doctor-owned insurance. Another way we medical professionals are easing the malpractice crisis is by forming our own insurance companies and cooperatives to make malpractice insurance affordable. There are already 19 insurance companies sponsored by state and local medical societies, and many more operate independently.

As an orthopedic surgeon in California, I'm a member of a doctor's cooperative. It's not an insurance company—in fact, we had to get special legislation passed by the state before we could begin to operate—but it provides us with the money (up to $1,000,000 per incident) we need to defend ourselves if we are sued. It works something like the farmers' cooperatives that were so popular in the '20s and '30s.

Our cooperative has about 1,500 members. Every member pays $500 a year in dues to the organization plus a fixed, one-time payment into our trust fund. For orthopedists, this payment amounts to about $22,000. The trust fund is held by a bank and pays interest. So with the dividends and interest, we are able to protect our members. We share the risk.

If in the future, our expenses ever exceed what we have in the fund and we have to raise money, we can do so easily because the cost is spread among so many people. With a membership of 1,500, each member pays $666 to raise $1,000,000, for example. If I had to pay a commercial insurance company for the same protection, it would cost me $30,000 to $35,000 every year. I figure I've already saved more than $100,000 as a member of our cooperative.

If a member has a patient experience with a bad result and the patient seems unhappy, he reports the incident to the cooperative, and we immediately try to avert any threat of a suit. The incident is evaluated by our claims review committee. If the committee decides that remedial measures should be taken, we contact the patient and invite him to see another specialist and start remedial treatment. Usually, these positive steps are enough to keep the problem from getting worse. We've even reoperated on a patient through our cooperative.

If for some reason a patient is still dissatisfied after we've taken remedial measures and decides to sue, he must—under another new California law—give the doctor 90 days' notice of his intention to sue. During this time, we once again try to resolve the problem ourselves. If this fails, we start the discovery process and handle the case as a commercial insurance carrier would.

Every doctors' organization works a bit differently, but the members all have one thing in common: They're trying to bring down the cost of malpractice insurance. Our own cooperative has been doing this so successfully that I believe this kind of organization is the coming thing. In my opinion, malpractice insurance will soon be a thing of the past.

The whole medical profession would benefit if we all became more involved in helping to solve our current malpractice problems. In California, it took a severe crisis to force us to find the solutions that are beginning to lead us back to sanity. I hope others can learn from our experience.

RECORDS AND REPORTS

12

Legal Aspects of Laboratory Records

Walter L. Scott, Ph.D.

Mere mention of laboratory records and record keeping is enough to send most laboratorians' blood pressure soaring. But despite the headaches they create, everyone knows how essential records are.

Not only are they required by law and various accrediting and regulatory agencies, but they are of prime importance in defending physicians, hospitals, laboratories, and laboratorians in malpractice suits.

The legal significance of laboratory records is what I want to explore in this chapter. Among the questions we'll try to answer are these: Which laboratory records are important from a legal standpoint? How long and in what form should lab records be kept? Who owns these records? Who has legal access to them? And when and where may the contents of these records be disclosed?

We'll also be looking at related issues and legal concepts. Among them are statutes of limitation, the discovery rule, patient-physician privilege, and confidentiality.

These last two, of course, are related to the accessibility of medical records, and this whole issue has recently been colored by the burgeoning patient-rights movement: Patients more and more believe that they have the right to see and copy their own medical records, a right that the health professionals have traditionally guarded as theirs alone.

Let's begin our investigation of these fascinating and complex practical matters.

Which records are legally important? That's an easy question to answer: Virtually all laboratory records have potential value in litigation. This includes technical and administrative procedure manuals, personnel qualifications, accession logs, quality-control manuals, proficiency-testing records, corrective- and preventive-maintenance logs, reagent records, notes on observations during testing, and, of course, records of patient test results and specimens, tissue blocks, and slides.

Some of these records, like test results, often become pivotal evidence in proving or disproving a physician's or laboratory's negligence.

Other records are used in court mainly to establish the reliability and quality of the laboratory's results. If a witness could point to a section in a procedure manual, say, that detailed the established procedure for handling unusual results, it would go a long way toward demonstrating laboratory reliability.

In a recent case in Colorado, for example, a pathologist testified in detail about the laboratory's quality-control procedures even though the tests in question had been performed five years past. Defense attorneys later told the pathologist that by showing that the physician used quality laboratory work in the care of his patient, this evidence was crucial in their successful defense.

Here's another example of how important accurate record keeping can be in a court case: In 1977, a New York trial court dismissed the evidence a hospital blood test offered because the records were incomplete. The test itself would have been admissible proof of intoxication in an auto accident case, but the records did not show who drew the specimen, what labeling procedure was followed, or what the chain of custody was from the person who drew the specimen to the one who performed the analysis.

How long should lab records be kept? From the foregoing discussion on the importance of medical records, you might conclude that a laboratory should keep all its records indefinitely. This is generally not recommended and certainly not practical.

Some records should be kept longer than others, and circumstances vary from one institution to another as well. A teaching hospital and medical center, for example, would doubtless want to keep certain case records and specimens longer than would a small community hospital that has no formal education program and only limited storage space.

Several considerations should go into any decision about how long to keep your laboratory records. A primary one, of course, is patient care. Records must be kept long enough to be consistent with quality care.

Another consideration is meeting requirements set by licensing and accrediting agencies. Both CLIA '67 and Medicare regulations set a retention period of at least two years on laboratory records. JCAH, which carefully spells out record-keeping guidelines in its accreditation manual, says that records should be kept as long as required by local, state, and Federal laws and also specifies a retention period of at least two years in most instances.

The CAP has also published guidelines on retaining laboratory materials in its "Guidelines for Pathologists: Professional Practices (1977)." Because of the general confusion surrounding the subject, these guidelines are reproduced here in Table 12-1.

Still another consideration in retaining lab records is that, in most hospitals, the medical records department becomes ultimately responsible for all patient records. Since that's the case, the laboratory should make sure that all pertinent lab reports are correctly included in the patient's chart. Duplicate copies that are kept in the lab—lab slips, for example—may safely be discarded long before it is safe to discard the patient record itself.

Finally, in any discussion of how long to keep laboratory records, we must consider statutes of limitations. These are laws that set a limit to the length of time after an incident that suit may be brought. If a suit isn't brought within the limit, the action is barred by law. All states have such laws.

These statutes were enacted to assure fairness to all parties in a suit. They solve the problems that can arise when witnesses die or move away or memories fade, making it more difficult to arrive at the facts in a case. The laws apply to all kinds of litigation; the length of time involved varies from state to state, though a typical period is two years, and also varies for the kind of suit involved. Some states have separate statutes for professional liability; others apply the general statutes of limitation to malpractice cases.

Over the years, courts and legislatures realized that strict application of a limitations statute could sometimes be unduly harsh. Take this case, for example: In New Mexico, several years after undergoing a mastectomy, a patient discovered that the diagnosis of malignancy had been in error. She filed suit, claiming that the operation was unnecessary and improperly performed. The court dismissed her claim because the statute of limitations had run out.

Some states have adopted certain rules that ameliorate such harshness. One such is the discovery rule, which says that a limitations statute does not start to run until the patient knows or should have known of the

TABLE 12-1

CAP Guidelines for the Preservation of Material and Reports in the Laboratory*

Material	Period of Retention	Comment
SURGICAL PATHOLOGY		
Wet tissue	For 2 weeks after the final report is issued	Inform surgeons of policy
Paraffin blocks	3 years	To correlate with reports
Slides	20 years	
Reports	3 years	Original on chart
Accession log	1 year	
CYTOLOGY		
Slides (negative and unsatisfactory)	3 years	Retain for statute of limitations
Slides (suspicious and positive)	3 years	Follow-up should be completed in 3 years
Reports	3 years	
Accession log	1 year	
AUTOPSY MATERIAL		
Wet tissue	Until final report is issued	
Paraffin blocks	2 years	
Slides	3 years	Retain for statute of limitations
Reports	3 years	Retain for statute of limitations
Accession log	1 year	

negligence. One common application of this rule is in cases in which a foreign body is left in the patient at the time of surgery. It's often impossible to detect these objects immediately, and they may not be discovered until years later.

In a classic example, a patient had an operation in 1958 and another in 1968. During the second procedure, the surgeon found that a forceps had been left in the patient's abdomen. The Ohio court held that the patient

Material	Period of Retention	Comment
CLINICAL PATHOLOGY—GENERAL		
Reports (inpatients)	30 days	Original on chart
Reports (outpatients)	3 years	Retain for statute of limitations
Log books	30 days**	Longer retention useful for fiscal control
Routine plasma and serum	7 days	
Quality control records	3 years	For triennial inspections
Maintenance logs	For life of the instrument	
HEMATOLOGY		
Bone marrow slides and reports	20 years	As for surgical pathology
Special blood smears and reports	20 years	As for surgical pathology
Routine blood smears	2 weeks	
BLOOD BANK		
Post-transfusion bags	2 days	
Serum and cell samples	7 days	AABB requirement

*Also refer to your state's statute of limitations.
**The author recommends retention for two years for legal purposes.

could sue, even though the time limit had run out on the first operation. It said that since evidence of negligence is so clear in such foreign-object cases, the statute of limitations did not begin to run until discovery.

Other courts have extended the discovery rule to include other cases of negligence—radiation burns, for example, or negligent surgery, as here: A patient had surgery on his spleen, and a much later second operation showed that his pancreas had been damaged. Applying the discovery rule, a New York court let the patient bring suit against the first surgeon.

Another rule that can mitigate the severity of limitations statutes is the fraudulent concealment rule. This means that the statute of limitations is interrupted when it can be proved that the defendant physician deliberately concealed the cause of action from the patient.

Here's a recent example: A patient claimed that she suffered a nerve injury as a result of a surgeon's negligence during surgery. After the operation, however, she said the surgeon told her that her pain and other problems would disappear if she had physiotherapy. After four years of such treatment, she was told by another surgeon that she had suffered nerve damage that could not be repaired. The patient sued, and a New York court ruled that the patient's reliance on the physician's misrepresentations was enough to bar the invocation of the three-year statute of limitations for malpractice.

A third ameliorating rule is the continuing negligence—or last treatment—rule. This holds that the statute of limitations doesn't begin to run until the termination of treatment or the end of the physician-patient relationship.

Here's how one court applied the rule: In 1974, a patient sued her physician for negligence in operating on her broken ankle in 1961 and for his continuing negligent treatment thereafter. The physician claimed that the statute of limitations, which he said should have run from the initial operation, barred the suit. The court disagreed and ruled that the cause of action accrues at the end of the treatment when the facts show continuing treatment for a particular illness or condition.

Not all court rulings on limitations statutes favor the patient, of course, but the intent of the rules we've discussed was generally to make it easier to bring suit against physicians. As a result of this and other factors, there developed what is commonly referred to as the malpractice crisis of the late '60s and early '70s.

During those years, million-dollar awards and settlements were making headlines, and physicians' and hospitals' malpractice insurance premiums were skyrocketing. Malpractice insurers, hit by the huge claims, were pulling out of states en masse, and in 1975 and 1976, state legislatures, which were concerned about severe cutbacks in medical services, started to enact reforms in malpractice laws.

Most of the legislative reforms sought to codify the exceptions to limitations statutes and to impose maximum time limits regardless of the circumstances of a particular case. The Florida law is an example. It states that a malpractice action must be brought within two years of the incident or discovery of the incident, but it also imposes a four-year maximum time limit for such actions. In addition, many reform statutes have sharply restricted the time period in which minors can bring a malpractice claim.

What all of this means for the laboratory is that you must establish record-retention policies in accordance with your state's limitations statute. You may decide to keep your records longer than the law requires, but on the other hand, you may find that you're keeping old records—and taking up valuable storage space—unnecessarily.

Here's a case in point: A shared-service organization for a group of hospitals in San Jose, Calif., recently studied the record-retention policies of its six member hospitals. The organization researched and reported on the state's legal requirements, the length of time each hospital's records were in use, and the length of time each of the hospitals kept various records.

The results were surprising—and probably typical of hospitals across the country. In almost every case, the hospitals were keeping records—and duplicates—longer than necessary; none of the hospitals had written record-retention policies; and department heads generally had no knowledge of legal requirements regarding record retention.

As a result, the hospitals adopted new retention policies that satisfied all legal and clinical requirements and realized a 50 percent reduction in storage space. The lessons are clear: Find out what the legal requirements are, promulgate written retention policies, get them approved by licensing and accrediting agencies, and abide by them.

Moving on to other matters of legal interest concerning medical records, let's look at some issues that recently gained prominence because of the consumer-rights movement.

Who owns a patient's medical records? The JCAH manual clearly states that the medical record is the property of the hospital. But even though it belongs physically to the hospital, case authority has shown that, with the exception of psychiatric patients in certain states, the patient has a right to the information in the record.

In addition, while hospitals have a duty to safeguard patients' records and their contents, they may not deny access to them to the patient or his authorized representative. Nor may they disclose that information, in most cases, to third parties without the patient's consent.

Who may have access to a patient's records? First, obviously, are those individuals who are involved in a patient's care while he is in the hospital. Patient information may also be used in patient-care-evaluation studies, in departmental review of work performance, for educational and research programs, and various other hospital programs.

Certain patient information may also be released to fulfill public health and statistical reporting requirements, such as for births, deaths, and cases of infectious disease.

All other release of patient information requires the patient's written consent. Only with consent, for example, may the hospital release information to a third-party payer. Most hospitals today routinely obtain that authorization when the patient is admitted or when he signs a consent form for surgical or medical procedures.

Most people willingly give their consent for third-party access to their medical records—after all, the insurance company is paying the patient's medical bills. Patients probably realize that much of this information goes into huge computer systems for data processing. But do they realize all the implications of this vast computer storage system? I doubt it.

According to a 1976 Government-sponsored study, "Computers, Health Records, and Citizen Rights," countless organizations that are not connected with health care in any way can gain access to an individual's medical data. Such organizations include life and automobile insurance companies, employers, law enforcement agencies, and credit bureaus, to name a few. Obviously, if sensitive medical information got into the wrong hands, it could be extremely detrimental to the individual. And it has been shown that abuses have occurred with these data banks.

Such erosion of privacy is one reason consumer groups have been clamoring for patient access to medical records. If outside agencies have access to them, it's not only reasonable but imperative for the individual to know what others are seeing—and do whatever he can to correct any mistakes or suppress any nonessential information that the records might contain.

Until recently, hospitals and physicians seldom—if ever—let patients see their medical records. The reasons usually given for this were that the patients wouldn't understand them and might even be upset by some of the information. The trend today, though, is toward greater patient access—and in fact, 15 states now have laws that guarantee patients direct access to at least part of their medical records.

What legislators and administrators must realize is that as they provide wider access to medical records, they must also develop guidelines to assure confidentiality of those records. We'll consider the confidentiality issue in answering our final question:

When and where may the contents of medical records be disclosed? Physicians and hospitals are caught on the horns of the access-confidentiality dilemma. On the one hand, they're pressured to release enough information to satisfy third parties that care was appropriate and thus reimbursable.

On the other hand, they're concerned about maintaining the traditional physician-patient relationship that relies on strict confidentiality. Without it, a patient might withhold information from the physician, and his treatment might suffer as a result.

Confidentiality is thus an essential ingredient of medical care, and one that is protected by law. If a physician or hospital wrongfully discloses confidential information and the patient is injured by the disclosure, he has grounds for suit.

Confidential—or privileged—information may even be withheld in court in those states that recognize physician-patient privilege. What this means is that in the 38 states that have laws recognizing the physician-patient relationship as privileged, a physician or hospital may not disclose confidential information in court without the patient's consent.

With the patient's consent, of course, a physician or hospital representative may testify, and the hospital records may be entered as evidence in litigation.

Let's look at what these issues of privacy and confidentiality mean in terms of daily laboratory routine. For one thing, lab personnel must remember—and perhaps be reminded from time to time—that patient information and test results are confidential. They must not discuss such information with outsiders. And they must be particularly wary of supplying patient information over the telephone unless they know the caller or he can offer proof of his identity.

I hope this chapter has helped clarify questions you may have had about laboratory records. Let me summarize what I consider the most important points: Determine which records you should keep; find out how long you must keep them to comply with Federal and state laws, statutes of limitations, and agency requirements; formulate a written policy on record retention; and make sure that access to those records is limited to authorized persons.

General References

''Accreditation Manual for Hospitals,'' 1979 Edition. Joint Commission on Accreditation of Hospitals, Chicago, 1978

Annas, G.J. *The Rights of Hospital Patients*. New York: Avon, 1975

Domanico, L., and Leverette, T. Shared project studies, revises hospital record retention policies. *Hospitals* 52 (1978): 133-136

Feegel, J.R. *Legal Aspects of Laboratory Medicine*. Boston: Little, Brown, 1973

''Guidelines for Pathologists: Professional Practices.'' Skokie, Ill.: College of American Pathologists, 1977

Halper, H.R., and Foster, H.S. *Laboratory Regulation Manual*. Germantown, Md.: Aspen, 1976

Health Law Center. *Problems in Hospital Law*. Rockville, Md.: Aspen, 1974

Hirsch, D.J. (ed). *Defense of Medical Malpractice Cases*. Milwaukee: Defense Research Institute, 1977

Westin, A.F. ''Computers, Health Records, and Citizen Rights.'' Washington, D.C.: National Bureau of Standards, 1976

13

Keeping Records and Specimens

Alvin M. Ring, M.D.

"How long do you keep lab records and specimens?" That was the question asked in an article and detailed questionnaire in the May 1976 issue of *MLO*. A total of 117 laboratories from every section of the country responded.

Their answers demonstrate widely differing retention policies—mostly because laboratorians simply don't know how long they *should* keep records and specimens.

Evidence of their confusion comes from responses to a question about the bases for their retention policies. Half to as many as three-fourths were unable to answer in various categories—presumably, they know of no adequate guidelines. Of the remainder, more than half rely mainly on their own hospital or lab standards. The exception to this is blood banking, where about two-thirds follow AABB guidelines. In the area of quality-control records, 21.3 percent named the CAP as the source for their policies.

The actual length of time those surveyed report keeping records and specimens further illustrates the confusion that exists over guidelines. Surgical pathology wet-tissue specimens, for example, are kept anywhere from less than a month (25.6 percent) to forever (3.3 percent). The same variations exist in every other category. (For specific informa-

TABLE 13-1

How Long Various Records and Specimens Are Kept

RECORD OR SPECIMEN	LESS THAN 1 MONTH	1-11 MONTHS	1-2 YEARS	3-5 YEARS	6-9 YEARS	10-14 YEARS	15-19 YEARS	20-29 YEARS	30 OR MORE YEARS	FOREVER	OTHER
SURGICAL PATHOLOGY											
Wet tissue	25.6%	53.3%	7.8%	2.2%	3.3%	1.1%	—	—	—	3.3%	6.7%
Slides	—	—	2.2	6.7	1.1	4.4	1.1%	8.9%	—	75.6	—
Paraffin blocks	—	2.3	3.4	10.2	4.5	14.8	2.3	6.8	—	54.6	1.1
Register	—	—	2.3	8.2	—	5.9	1.2	7.1	—	75.3	—
Reports (file copy)	—	1.1	3.2	4.3	3.2	4.3	1.1	5.4	1.1%	76.3	—
Reports (chart copy)	—	—	—	2.6	5.1	1.3	1.3	8.9	2.6	76.9	1.3
CLINICAL PATHOLOGY—GENERAL											
Requisitions (file copy)	6.1	24.4	36.6	13.4	12.2	1.2	1.2	—	—	4.9	—
Requisitions (chart copy)	3.5	1.7	1.7	8.8	8.8	1.7	1.8	7.0	—	63.2	1.8
Inpatient reports (file copy)	1.1	17.6	41.7	16.5	6.6	—	—	—	—	16.5	—
Inpatient reports (chart copy)	—	—	1.2	6.0	2.4	2.4	1.2	9.7	1.2	74.7	1.2
Outpatient reports (file copy)	—	9.6	37.2	19.2	10.6	—	—	—	—	23.4	—
Outpatient reports (chart copy)	—	—	1.5	7.4	4.5	1.5	1.5	6.0	—	50.7	26.9
Logbooks	—	5.4	37.6	16.1	4.3	4.3	1.1	—	—	31.2	—
Quality control records	—	2.2	45.6	28.3	3.3	—	—	—	—	20.6	—
Statistics logs	—	1.2	40.0	25.0	2.5	3.8	3.8	—	—	23.7	—
Serum or plasma	92.5	5.4	—	—	—	—	—	—	—	—	2.1
CYTOLOGY											
Slides (negative)	—	1.2	19.8	27.9	4.6	2.3	2.3	1.2	—	40.7	—
Slides (suspicious and positive)	—	—	3.4	12.6	2.3	3.5	2.3	1.2	—	74.7	—

CYTOLOGY (cont.)											
Register	—	—	6.6	7.9	2.7	2.6	1.3	2.6	—	76.3	—
Reports (file copy)	—	1.1	9.0	15.7	6.8	4.5	1.1	3.4	—	58.4	—
Reports (chart copy)	—	—	—	2.7	4.0	1.3	1.3	8.0	1.3	77.4	4.0
AUTOPSY											
Wet tissue	1.1	21.6	34.1	12.5	4.5	3.4	1.1	—	1.1	10.2	17.0
Paraffin blocks	—	2.3	5.7	11.4	4.6	12.5	1.1	4.5	—	56.8	1.1
Slides	—	—	1.2	4.7	1.2	3.5	3.5	4.7	—	80.0	1.1
Register	—	1.3	5.0	3.8	1.3	2.5	1.3	5.1	—	79.7	—
Reports (file copy)	—	1.1	1.1	2.3	2.3	3.4	—	6.9	—	83.9	—
Reports (chart copy)	—	—	—	4.0	4.0	1.3	1.3	10.7	1.3	74.7	2.7
HEMATOLOGY											
Bone marrow slides	—	1.2	4.7	8.3	1.2	2.4	1.2	3.6	—	76.2	1.2
Bone marrow reports (file copy)	—	3.7	9.9	7.4	1.2	4.9	1.2	3.7	—	69.1	—
Bone marrow reports (chart copy)	—	—	1.4	2.8	2.8	1.4	1.4	9.9	1.4	81.7	—
Routine smears	45.9	36.7	11.2	2.0	1.0	—	—	—	—	4.1	—
Unusual cases	4.4	4.4	5.6	3.3	—	1.1	—	—	—	78.9	6.7
BLOOD BANK											
Post-transfusion bags	97.4	1.3	—	1.3	—	—	—	—	—	—	—
Serum and cell samples	96.7	2.2	—	1.1	—	—	—	—	—	—	—
Donor logs	—	1.5	1.5	23.2	10.1	7.2	1.5	1.4	—	53.6	—
Reaction reports (file copy)	—	—	7.0	17.4	7.0	4.6	—	1.2	—	62.8	—
Reaction reports (chart copy)	—	—	—	7.5	1.2	2.5	—	8.8	1.2	78.8	—

(Totals may be more than 100 percent because of multiple responses.)

tion on how long respondents reported keeping various records and specimens, see Table 13-1.)

Although most respondents have no specific suggestions for improving their own policies on the length of time they keep records and specimens, a vast majority (86 percent) answered Yes to the question "Do you feel the need for more clear-cut guidelines regarding the length of time records and specimens should be kept?" Almost the same number complained that their state statutes on the subject are inadequate or nonexistent. Here's what some of them had to say:

Lab director, Illinois: "State requirements for retention of records are very vague."

R&D technologist, Maryland: "Guidelines for surgical pathology seem vague. Clinical lab reports statutes seem reasonable at this point."

Lab supervisor, New York: "Slide retention for 20 years is O.K. Wet-tissue storage is a problem, and there are no guidelines for it."

Pathologist, Florida: "Two-year storage on duplicate reports and records. No specimen guidelines."

When asked who they thought should issue uniform national guidelines, the majority (54 percent) named the CAP, with the rest about evenly divided between Federal (22 percent) and state (25 percent) government. A number of respondents suggested a joint effort by the CAP and government to set realistic guidelines that would also conform to legal requirements.

Unfortunately, state laws vary and, in many cases, are so vague as to be almost useless. And, along with the escalation in the volume of malpractice suits and the amounts of claims, the courts are extending the period for filing suits under statutes of limitations.

All this uncertainty leaves labs pretty much up in the air. Confusion and fear of legal problems make them wary of discarding any data. A pathologist from Connecticut summed up the feelings of many respondents when he said: "I heard of one lab that saved chemistry slips and records indefinitely—even though the state requirement was only two years. They were hit with a suit for a result that had been reported seven years before. Fortunately, they still had the records. I'd hate to be held responsible for a technologist who might no longer be here or for circumstances that one can't remember or verify because of the long time element."

Despite these concerns, only one laboratorian reported running into legal trouble because her lab hadn't kept results long enough: Four years after the fact, the lab was called upon to provide its (discarded) records on a rape case. Clearly, there is a need to identify potential medicolegal material and store it separately for a longer period than routine information is stored.

We also need to cut down on duplication of records. Many labs keep copies of test reports out of fear that the chart copy of a report will be lost. They also retain logbooks and worksheets with duplicate information. They keep copies of reports they send to physicians because they don't know what the physician does with his copy of the report. Redundancy is overwhelming.

TABLE 13-2

Problems in Record Retention

Does your laboratory have a space problem regarding record and specimen storage?

Yes	88%
No	12%

Does your laboratory have a record retrieval problem?

Yes	20%
No	53%

Does your state have clear statutes governing the retention of laboratory records and specimens?

Yes	20%
No	80%

Do you feel the need for more clear-cut guidelines regarding the length of time records and specimens should be kept?

Yes	86%
No	14%

Who should set such standards?

Federal government	22%
State government	25%
Hospital	15%
CAP	54%
Other	10%

(Total adds up to more than 100 percent due to multiple responses.)

All these factors—legitimate retention of records and specimens, keeping records out of fear of lawsuits, and duplication of material—create a serious storage problem. Indeed, 88 percent of respondents reported difficulties in storing records and specimens. The space shortage creates another problem—retrieval. Following are some typical comments:

Chief technologist, New Mexico: "Records are all over the place. You need a map to find them, but there just isn't any one place with adequate space. This is a small hospital that was built 20 years ago. No one anticipated such a tremendous increase in suits and red tape."

Pathologist, Alabama: "Unable to get reports more than three years old without a lot of effort. Fortunately, they are rarely needed."

Chemistry supervisor, New York: "Retrieval system is informal—it involves getting to the right storeroom and finding the right cardboard box!"

Pathologist, Ohio: "Access to records is quite difficult."

Chief technologist, California: "We box everything over two years old. Retrieving these things—like logbooks—is a headache."

Administrative assistant, Illinois: "Loss of productive time. Due to lack of space, things are crammed together and take hours to find."

Lab director, Pennsylvania: "Reports one year old or more are stored in a warehouse. They're difficult to retrieve. Requests for old reports often do not have correct spelling of patient name or approximate test date."

There's a crying need for someone—anyone—to establish uniform guidelines for record and specimen retention. Many laboratorians, wary as they are of Federal intervention, would even welcome comprehensive, uniform government standards, but most feel the limits should be established within their own profession. Unless someone does something—fast—labs will be buried in paper and paraffin blocks, and retrieval will be impossible. The responsibility for solving this problem lies with those organizations concerned with and representative of laboratories. They must come up with an answer.

14

Our System for Correcting Erroneous Reports

Kay M. Oesterreicher, CLA(ASCP)

It can happen in any lab—and from time to time it does. The lab reports an erroneous test result, and it's entered in the patient's chart, where the mistake could cause medical complications for the patient and legal problems for both the hospital and the lab.

Why do these incidents happen? We all know how important it is to report results accurately. But no matter how efficient or experienced we are, we occasionally make mistakes. While it is crucial to keep trying to prevent errors, we should also know what to do when and if we make an incorrect report.

Anticipating such mishaps in our 150-bed hospital, our director of laboratories drew up a set of guidelines for correcting all types of erroneous test reports, no matter how significant or insignificant the error might be.

When we discover that we have sent out an incorrect test result, our first obligation is to the patient. His health is our primary concern. Finding out who was responsible for the mistake is always a secondary consideration.

The first step after discovering a mistake is to notify the physician. In case of an emergency, or if the doctor cannot be reached, we call the hospital floor directly, tell the nurse what happened, and ask her to check the patient. If we have the correct result, we also give that information over the phone. If not, we tell the person when we expect to have the correct results.

The next step is to notify the section supervisor, who then reports the situation to the lab director. Their knowledge of the incident helps protect the lab from possible malpractice suits. The better informed the supervisor is, the better he can explain the lab's position in any problem resulting from the incident. And the director or supervisor may offer suggestions about how to handle the problem.

The lab's mistake must not only be acknowledged orally, but also documented with a supplemental lab slip. Once we know the correct result, we fill out a new slip, writing the words "corrected report" in red ink in the comments space on the form. The lab technologist making out this new slip initials the comment.

We hand-carry the corrected slip to the hospital floor. When we find the erroneous lab slip, we cross out the incorrect result by drawing a single line through the value and then cross out the entire results column with red ink. In the comments box, we write "error" in red and initial it.

We then make sure that both the corrected report and the erroneous report are attached to the patient's chart. This is the preferred record-keeping procedure to follow for legal purposes, and it also insures that the clinician will see the correction.

Besides helping laboratorians handle these difficult situations, our policy demonstrates to the hospital and physicians that we are willing to acknowledge and correct our mistakes, which enhances our professional image within the hospital. And by assuring that a discovered error is corrected immediately, these guidelines help protect both the patient from medical complications and the laboratory from legal action.

Let's see how our correction system worked with an incident that happened not long ago. A GI bleeder was given several units of blood over a period of a few days. While logging the transfusion information in the patient's files, we noticed that he had irregular antibodies in the screenings for his previous transfusions. Even though these antibodies were not evident in our more recent antibody screening, it was still possible that the patient could experience a serious transfusion reaction.

We immediately phoned the floor and told the nurses to stop the transfusion. We then called the physician and told him what had happened. He was grateful for the information even though the transfusion could have put his patient in serious condition.

Fortunately, the transfusion did not harm the patient. In many respects we were just plain lucky, but our correction system certainly helped us handle the situation. The incident gave us confidence in the system and also made everyone realize the importance of checking old files when crossmatching a patient for a blood transfusion.

What if we report an incorrect glucose level on a diabetic? Or because of a typographical problem with our gamma counter, we report a digoxin level of 0.5 ng on a cardiac patient when the real result is 2.5 ng? In a case like that, the physician, reading the normal value of 0.5 ng, might administer another dose. Since anything over 2.4 ng is toxic, this could be fatal. What then? We've found that no matter how severe the danger, our system helps us avoid panicking and promotes a safe, sensible method to handle such emergencies.

Of course, most lab errors aren't as dramatic as the ones I've mentioned here. But even with less critical situations, our policy outlines a practical system for correcting mistakes. Let's look at a typical problem.

While performing a subculture, suppose we find an organism that should have come out in the original culture. *Staphylococcus* coagulase positive, for example, is found a few days after we make a final bacteriology report on a throat culture as normal flora.

In this case, an immediate call to the doctor is not absolutely necessary, but it's good procedure. The physician may find the information helpful. We would then send a supplemental report to the doctor, confirming the additional growth. Since this report is made out in red ink, it catches the physician's attention as the corrected report. Susceptibility testing on the new organism would then follow within the next 24 to 48 hours.

In our lab, erroneous reports are corrected quickly and openly. They can't be corrected secretively. Everyone concerned learns of the error as soon as possible. The purpose of our system is not to fix the blame, but far more important, to correct the error—and this is for the good of the patient and the lab.

ments. As an example of the differences between the state and the CAP methods, the state regulations call for a reporting breakdown by all clinical services, such as pediatrics, medical-surgical, and ICU, not just inpatient and outpatient, as the CAP recommends.

But the majority of the hospitals were not doing workload recording at all. Statewide estimates, in fact, put the figure anywhere from 60 to 90 percent. These institutions were faced with several alternatives: A small, well-organized laboratory could actually keep workload statistics and prepare the necessary reports manually. Big hospital laboratories, on the other hand, almost certainly needed some kind of computer capability—either an in-house computer or a service bureau that gets the workload information from the laboratory and prepares the reports according to specifications.

In any event, the state requirements mean that laboratorians have to keep an accurate count of all the work they do, including quality control, repeats, and dilutions. And this brings up another major problem created by the regulations: Whenever you have to institute a new laboratory routine, you have to combat people's natural resistance to change—which is probably intensified when the change is imposed by an outside agency like the government. "We can't possibly do that." Or, "They don't know what they're talking about." And, "We don't do anything like this." These are typical comments people make when confronted by new regulations.

The best way to lower such resistance is to offer full explanations as to what the new system is all about. We recommend a laboratory-wide meeting to explain the CAP workload recording method (if it's an unknown quantity) and to tell why it must be implemented and how it will affect everyday routine. In most cases, we've found it takes technologists no more than a matter of minutes each day to compile the necessary data.

As an added—and quite unexpected—bonus, once the technologists become accustomed to workload recording, they like it. Why? Because these statistics supply concrete documentation of the work they accomplish each day.

Finally, and most important, we've learned that the best way to cope with requirements like these is to be prepared. And our advice is to start now. Get the latest edition of the workload recording manual from the CAP (7400 N. Skokie Blvd., Skokie, Ill. 60076). Read up on it. Pass it around the lab. You and your techs should be familiar with the system because sooner or later your laboratory will be going that way, too. And if you understand or, better yet, implement the CAP method, any variations or modifications imposed by your state will be much easier to handle.

III
CERTIFICATE OF NEED

16

The Law, the Lab, and Certificates of Need

Jane C. Monaghan

A sleeper. That's what you might call the National Health Planning and Resources Development Act of 1974. It sneaked through Congress in the waning hours of the session in December 1974 and was signed into law Jan. 4, 1975. Medical leaders have called it the most sweeping (and some, the most dangerous) piece of health legislation of the decade.

Senator Edward M. Kennedy called the health-planning law a prerequisite to the comprehensive national health insurance he was proposing. But the law isn't important only as a stepping stone to such programs. It is of immediate significance to hospitals and laboratories.

Why? Because this law has created a big new bureaucracy in the Department of Health, Education, and Welfare—now called the Department of Health and Human Services (HHS)—that is spreading a health-planning network across the country. It has also put sharp regulatory teeth into area-wide health-planning and state certificate-of-need (CON) programs. It gives local agencies the power to *implement* plans, not just propose them, and to approve and disapprove the use of certain Federal monies. The law also requires states to administer CON programs—or lose Federal funds.

What exactly does this mean to a hospital or laboratory? It means that a state regulatory agency decides, based largely on the recommendation

Federal Certificate-of-Need Regulations

On Jan. 21, 1977, HEW published final regulations on the certificate-of-need (CON) portions of the health-planning law. These regulations detail the criteria and procedures that HSAs and state agencies must follow in their CON reviews. Defining exactly which "health-care facilities" are covered by the law and which are not, the rules then get down to the essentials of describing which "new institutional health services" (the language of the law) are subject to review.

Here's how the regulations define those services and, in so doing, establish minimum thresholds for CON review. Any one of them can trigger a review. They include:

- the construction, development, or other establishment of a new health-care facility or health maintenance organization;
- any capital expenditure exceeding $150,000;
- any change in bed capacity that increases, relocates, or redistributes more than 10 beds or more than 10 percent of the total, whichever is less over a two-year period; and
- any newly offered health service (one not offered on a regular basis in that health-care facility during the preceding 12-month period).

The regulations make clear that these are minimum standards, and that states may impose more stringent criteria of their own—so long as they are "not inconsistent" with the Federal law or regulations.

The regulations also require state agencies to enforce CON programs by providing sanctions "such as the denial or revocation of a license to operate, civil or criminal penalties, or injunctive relief" for noncompliance with the law.

The Federal health-planning bureau and the states themselves are now seeing how they fit in with the Federal standards. Some of the states with legislation have stricter criteria than those in the Federal law. Some, of course, have had to beef up their criteria to meet Federal approval.

Other states have been performing reviews similar to CON under Section 1122 of the Social Security Act. They, too, have to make their standards conform to the new legislation and its regulations by the mandated deadline — the end of fiscal 1980 — or lose Federal public health service funds.

of a local health-planning agency, whether or not a hospital can add a new wing. Or renovate its laboratory facilities. Or buy a new highly automated laboratory instrument.

P.L. 93-641. Let's take a look at the law itself, its purpose, its history, the agencies it has created, and how far along it is to being fully implemented.

Congress enacted P.L. 93-641 "to facilitate . . . a national health-planning policy, to augment area-wide and state planning for health services, manpower, and facilities, and to authorize financial assistance for the development of resources to further that policy."

Despite massive injections of Federal money into the existing health-care system, says the law, many people still do not have access to good medical care. The lawmakers believe that careful planning will improve the health-care system and the distribution of health-care services, as well as restrain rising costs by eliminating unnecessary and costly duplication.

This law is the culmination of 30 years of Federal legislative efforts to encourage local health planning. Sometimes linking planning with funding for health-facility construction, like the Hill-Burton program, and sometimes legislating planning for planning's sake, like the Comprehensive Health Planning Law, earlier legislation didn't do the job.

P.L. 93-641, however, is expected to succeed where others failed for this simple reason: It makes *funding* contingent on planning. If states don't plan and monitor health-care expenditures, they'll lose Federal money.

The law establishes a Federal, state, and local health-planning hierarchy and spells out the roles of agencies at each level. Because of the importance the law attaches to local planning, the basic—and key—element in the program is the Health Systems Agency, a group of consumers and health-care providers from a geographically defined area. Although these HSAs are primarily advisory bodies, they also have some regulatory functions, like CON review, that worry health professionals who wonder how much power they will come to wield. Indeed, recommendations from HSAs carry considerable clout and can be crucial in a state's final decision on a CON application.

Among the responsibilities the law assigns to HSAs are: to gather and analyze data; to develop a comprehensive area Health Systems Plan (HSP) and Annual Implementation Plan (AIP); to make recommendations to the state on CON applications; to make recommendations to the state as to the "appropriateness" of existing health-care services (another function that worries health professionals); to coordinate its activities with the area Professional Standards Review Organization; and to approve or disapprove expenditures of certain Federal monies.

The geographic regions served by HSAs are called Health Service Areas. These areas were delineated by the state governors and approved by HEW, and each is based on such criteria as population (between 500,000 and 3,000,000 is the norm) and the availability of health services. Although local politics occasionally made the governors' jobs difficult (and even meant going to court in some cases), most of the 212 Health Service Areas were marked out by September 1975.

Agencies. When the Health Service Areas were defined, HEW began accepting applications from groups for designation as Health Systems Agencies. This, too, prompted some local battles, but by April 1976, the first 100 HSAs had received conditional designation. Latest count shows that all but a handful have been so designated.

The law provides for two agencies at the state level. One is the State Health Planning and Development Agency, which implements the health-planning activities of the state and, more important, administers the state CON program. This agency must also enforce the program by imposing sanctions, such as loss of licensure or civil or criminal penalties, for noncompliance.

The other state agency is an advisory board, the Statewide Health Coordinating Council. Its membership, like that of an HSA, is composed of consumers and health-care providers, and its main functions are to advise and review other health-planning bodies in the state. It must also prepare an annual state health plan.

Finally, at the national level, the law establishes a National Council on Health Planning and Development. Its duties are to advise, consult with, and make recommendations to the Secretary of HEW (HHS) on the implementation and development of the law. Among its 15 members must be members of local Health Systems Agencies and Statewide Health Coordinating Councils, again pointing up the importance HEW attached to local input on health-planning matters.

Responsible for the actual implementation of the law and for formulating its regulations is the Bureau of Health Planning and Resources Development, a part of the Health Resources Administration.

So there you have a very brief introduction to P.L. 93-641 and its organizational lineup. Like most Federal efforts, it has created a bewildering array of alphabetical entities—HSAs, HSPs, AIPs, SHPDAs, and SHCCs, to name a few. The accompanying glossary should prove useful in keeping them all straight.

An HSA in action. As for what it means to the daily working life of your laboratory, let's now consider the experience of one Health Systems Agency, how it arrives at its CON recommendations to the state agency, and the effect it has had on health-care institutions in its area.

Federal health planners refer to New Jersey as one of the leaders in state CON programs. Its law, enacted in 1971, is one of the older ones, as well as one of the most stringent. Since the Federal law sets only minimum thresholds for CON review, states are free to impose their own stricter criteria. New Jersey's law does this with a vengeance, setting lower thresholds in almost every category—beds, change of service, and dollar amounts— that can trigger the review process.

The Hospital and Health Council of Metropolitan New Jersey is the designated HSA serving the state's Health Service Area II, a five-county area that includes the Newark metropolitan area. I spoke at length with its senior planning associate for facilities, Martin Parker, to find out just what happens when a hospital or laboratory decides to update, replace, modernize—in short, change—its laboratory facilities.

New Jersey's law states that "No health-care facility shall be constructed or expanded, and no new health-care services shall be instituted except upon application for and receipt of a certificate of need."

Guidelines issued by the State Department of Health further detail the CON procedure and the criteria that mandate CON applications. Among the criteria are these: any building construction; any land acquisition that costs more than $100,000; any increase or decrease in bed capacity; any change in service; and certain dollar expenditures for equipment and modernization. For example, any expenditure on "major movable equipment" above $60,000 for hospitals or $10,000 for other health-care facilities requires a CON. Even lower expenditures require what is called an administrative review, a somewhat faster process, but still a careful review of whether or not something is really needed.

When an institution decides it should renovate its laboratory facilities—or even buy a new cell counter or chemistry analyzer—it must start thinking about justifying its acquisition.

The CON form requires a narrative description of why the purchase is necessary, how it relates to the institution's long-range health plan, and how it might affect other nearby institutions. All this, plus detailed information on how the purchase will be financed, the institution's overall financial picture, and the utilization patterns of the department involved in the acquisition must be spelled out on the form. The institution must prepare seven copies of the form—six for the state agency and one for the local HSA.

For major institutional renovations, the form becomes still more complex and detailed—and is probably more closely scrutinized because of the amount of money that is involved. Here's the case history of one such CON application, as Martin Parker of the N.J. Region II HSA describes it:

A Glossary of Health Planning Act Terms

Annual Implementation Plan (AIP)
A detailed statement developed annually by a Health Systems Agency. The statement describes short-range objectives to achieve the goals of the Health Systems Plan. It also sets priorities among those objectives with a view to what can be accomplished during that year.

Health Service Area
A geographic region approved by state and Federal governments and appropriate for effective planning and development of health services. These areas are based on such factors as population and the availability of health services and may, in fact, cross state lines. Ten states have single, statewide areas.

Health Systems Agency (HSA)
The Federally designated local or regional health-planning agency—and the key element in the planning network established by P.L. 93-641. A majority (but not more than 60 percent) of its members must be area residents who are health-care consumers; the remainder, resident health-care providers. The HSA must prepare and implement a Health Systems Plan (HSP) and AIP and perform certain regulatory duties, including review and recommendation to the state on certificate-of-need applications and the "appropriateness" of area health-care facilities. HSA operating expenses are funded by HEW (HHS).

"I guess this is a classic example of a certificate-of-need review, and I like it because it shows that the planning process really works—and isn't the enemy of the providers.

"A 160-bed, quasi-rural hospital in our area came in for a major renovation and construction project for its clinical laboratory. When we first looked over the application and saw the estimated cost—around $1.5 million—it seemed like a lot of money for a small hospital to be spending on laboratory facilities.

"At that point, since we don't pretend to have the technical expertise to judge the adequacy of clinical laboratory facilities, we called on an expert clinical pathologist to serve as our consultant. He reviewed the plan, and then he spoke with the hospital administrator and pathologist and visited their lab. He quite agreed that the facilities were inadequate

Health Systems Plan (HSP)
A detailed statement developed by an HSA of long-range goals for improving the health of area residents and increasing the accessibility, continuity, and quality of health-care services, while restraining costs. The HSP should be useful to area residents as a guide to how their health systems will develop and should also be a planning and communication bridge with other HSAs and state health-planning agencies.

National Council on Health Planning and Resources Development
A 15-member advisory board to consult with the Secretary of HEW (HHS) on the development of national health-planning policy and implementation of the health-planning law. Members must include providers and representatives from HSAs and SHCCs (see below), among others.

Statewide Health Coordinating Council (SHCC)
A state-wide advisory body. Its membership, of at least 16 gubernatorial appointees, must include representatives of all HSAs in the state. The council prepares a state health plan, reviews and coordinates HSPs and AIPs, reviews HSA budgets, and advises the state agency.

State Health Planning and Development Agency (SHPDA)
Also known as the state agency. Designated by the governor of each state and approved by HEW, this agency carries much of the regulatory authority of the health-planning law. It must implement the state health plan and administer and enforce the state certificate-of-need program. It must also, at least every five years, review and publish its findings as to the "appropriateness" of all health-care facilities in the state.

and had to be replaced, but after careful consideration, he thought there was a better—and cheaper—way. An open lab, he felt, would be more suitable and give them a flexibility to make future changes that the proposed set-room plan lacked.

"Accordingly, we told the applicant that we couldn't accept the plans as they stood, but we would reconsider them if they made certain recommended changes. Our consultant met with the applicant and his architect, they made significant changes in the plans—at a savings of about $300,000—and both our agency and the state approved the revised application."

As Parker says, this seems like a classic case—the CON process saved a significant amount of money, and the hospital ended up with a better facility. Another important point this story makes is that this HSA consults with experts in technical matters.

Here's another case history from the Region II HSA. This one involves applications for three separate instruments from two neighboring hospitals. The smaller of the two hospitals had no automated laboratory equipment at all, and since it had experienced a recent rapid increase in laboratory utilization, it wanted to buy both a cell counter and a discrete chemistry analyzer at a total cost of $125,000. The larger hospital was applying for approval of a replacement chemistry analyzer capable of performing 24 discrete analyses.

The HSA questioned the need for all three instruments in two hospitals a mile or so apart. Again it consulted its expert pathologist who concluded that all three requests were justifiable. He did, however, suggest that the larger hospital closely monitor the performance of the 24-channel analyzer, a relatively new instrument at the time, to ascertain whether it was doing all it was expected to do. Further, he recommended that the two hospitals share testing capabilities to effect maximum utilization of both analyzers. With these qualifications, then, the HSA and the state agency approved both applications.

One point open to interpretation in the New Jersey CON legislation is whether commercial labs are covered by the laws and regulations. (They are *not* covered by the Federal regulations.) It's quite clear that labs in hospitals are covered, but do commercial labs fall into the category of health facility? To answer that, Parker says, "According to the way the law has been interpreted to us, commercial labs must apply for certificates of need. And we have, in fact, reviewed applications from commercial labs in our area."

Not all CON applications receive favorable decisions, of course. But neither does the process always stir up the bitterness you read about in newspaper accounts of highly specialized services and equipment like burn centers and brain and whole-body scanners being denied certificates of need. Those are the stories that make headlines. CON approvals generally don't.

As for the impact of the CON law in operation, Martin Parker puts it this way: "What it has done is stop a lot of institutions from making purchases at the whim of one or two physicians. Now administrators are more reluctant to rubber-stamp departmental requests. They evaluate them much more closely, even before they get to the point of making a certificate-of-need application." And that, presumably, is what the law is all about.

Your state may not be as far along in its health-planning and CON programs as New Jersey, but despite legal challenges to the constitutionality of the planning law, it most likely will stand, and all states had to be in compliance by the end of fiscal 1980.

In any event, cutting health-care costs has a high priority in Washington, as proposed hospital cost-containment legislation makes clear. And any existing system to put a cap on costs is likely to gain power, not lose it. Health-care planning and its CON running mate are here to stay.

17

HSAs Getting Tougher

Christopher J. Bale

It came as a jolt to the pathology department at Valley Hospital in Ridgewood, N.J.

After earlier amicable dealings with the local Bergen-Passaic Health Systems Agency (HSA), Valley found its most recent certificate-of-need (CON) request—for an ACA III—flatly rejected.

"We made what we thought was a thoroughly reasonable request," said Laboratory Director Dr. Lawrence Wilkinson. "We wanted to replace our old ACA, which cost $50,000 about five years ago, with a new one that lists for $130,000. The manufacturer was offering us $45,000 for the old machine, plus a reduction in the new equipment's retail price if we bought it in 1979.

"But the HSA turned us down. It obviously wasn't impressed by the fact that next year this machine will cost us $50,000 more. Nor was it impressed by arguments of the potential benefits to patients or the fact that we would be able to do more tests, faster. One member of the capital expenditures committee said that the benefit of doing more tests simply would be to boost the pathologists' income."

According to Joseph Noon, project review director for the Bergen-Passaic HSA, what persuaded the committee to deny the Valley request was primarily a question of staffing.

"The machine Valley wanted had several special automated features, which they explained would save a great deal of time," he said. "And the committee replied, 'Great. Now where's the reduction in staff to go along with it?' They had no answer except to say their lab wouldn't have to hire any more staff.

"That answer might have been good enough a couple of years ago, but not today."

The HSA's denial of Valley's request "horrified" Dr. Wilkinson's colleagues throughout the county and state, he said. "There has always been a general feeling that HSAs would clear any sensible CON request. This really surprised people."

Indeed, there have been relatively few such "surprises" since the Health Planning Act of 1974 mandated all states to enact certificate-of-need programs through a hierarchy of local, county, and state review panels.

The operational CON programs have been busy, and generally generous. A sampling by the National Research Council's committee on technology and health care found that of 459 applications for either medical equipment or services, 436 were approved. HEW officials concurred with that estimate of the approval rate.

Does that amount to success or failure for CON programs and HSAs thus far? The views differ sharply. In its published report, the National Research Council complained that the "history of CON and capital expenditures review . . . is discouraging. Not only have few projects been disallowed, but CON appears to have no effect on the overall level of spending by hospitals."

Meanwhile, HEW predictably defended the CON process. "It's unfair to judge CON by disapprovals," one official staunchly contended. "The real story, and unfortunately there are no figures to substantiate it, is the number of requests that never get submitted because hospitals or labs speak with their local HSA in advance and decide their chances for acceptance are low to zero."

The official also pointed to a study conducted by the American Health Planning Association (AHPA). It shows that for the two years ending in August 1978, HSAs reviewed proposals valued at $12 billion and disapproved, or "saved," $3.4 billion in expenditures from the national health bill.

Just what percentage of the "savings" came at the expense of laboratories isn't known. But pathologists at a national leadership conference sponsored by the College of American Pathologists were put on notice that they must become "agents of planning" and "agents of change" where certificate-of-need legislation is concerned.

Gerry Gallwas, a Beckman Instruments executive, warned that "eyes are upon us. The increasing sentiment is that new processes and services are raising the cost of health care—and with little concern for cost benefit and cost effectiveness." The subliminal message is that new technology "is the real culprit," he said.

Thus far, "CON requests haven't stopped the acquisition of equipment or facilities," he went on. "But they have delayed acquisition."

Undoubtedly, HSAs have added an element of postponement, simply because there are several stages of approval for each CON request, stretching from the local HSA to the state planning council. But providers have resigned themselves to these holdups.

Most CON applications bump along the network for about three months before approval, a waiting period even Valley's Dr. Wilkinson admits can be relatively painless. "We wanted to get an SMA 12 with a Vickers computer and had the entire thing taken care of in two and one-half months."

But what worries Dr. Wilkinson, Gallwas, and others in the lab field is that, in Dr. Wilkinson's words, "HSAs are going to start looking for a much stronger pitch from those of us who must buy expensive equipment. They now mean business."

In comments that would make the National Research Council's technology and health-care committee members smile with satisfaction, Bergen-Passaic HSA's Joseph Noon confirms those suspicions.

"Yes, the time is here for a more hard-nosed approach to reviewing CON requests," he said. "If a potential buyer comes in and stresses that the new machine is heavily automated and will enable them to do more tests over a shorter period of time, we're going to demand to see their plans for staff reduction.

"The capital expenditures committee is also influenced by the cost-containment environment," Noon continued. "We will be looking to see that the purchase will bring hard savings, not just help out on what we call 'cost avoidance.'"

Noon claims this evolving philosophy is not unique, at least in New Jersey. "This is the way HSAs are headed throughout our state. Technology gets more sophisticated all the time. So, too, have the HSAs with experience.

"There was a time not long ago when physicians could come before a committee and dazzle them with the capabilities of a new machine," he explained. "Just the fact that a machine represented an improvement in technology weighed heavily in favor of approval. Now, however, it's going to get harder and harder to persuade committee members of a machine's value without also demonstrating likely dollar savings directly related to use."

In line with this thinking, he said, HSA panels will be less easily convinced that machines should be considered obsolete simply because a new model with esoteric features comes along.

"Maybe those features aren't really necessary," he said. "We have reached the point where we believe the average machine should accommodate a department for seven years."

That won't necessarily mean an increase in the number of CON rejections. More likely, it will mean fewer CON applications. And Noon believes the "system is working. I get more calls now from hospitals for preapplication meetings, sometimes by administrators who want me to convince the medical staff that equipment isn't easy to get. I think, overall, there's more cooperation among all parties."

18

Certificate of Need: A Review

David J. Kull

The document weighs almost five pounds, measures two inches thick, and crams its 357 pages with small print and column after column of numbers. The title isn't very catchy: "Memorial Hospital Medical Center, Long Beach, Certificate of Need Application No. 78-012."

No, it's not best-seller material, yet a great deal of money rides on its success or failure. It is, in fact, a key to the California hospital's new $5 million computerized information system—in large part involving test requisitions and reporting. Without government acceptance of the justifications in the application, the eight-year project could not begin. That objective, to sway absolute power, infuses the document with considerable importance.

There's much at stake, and certificate-of-need procedures are attracting considerable attention throughout the health-care field. The National Health Planning and Resource Development Act of 1974, which was signed into law in January 1975, mandated that all states set up certificate-of-need programs to screen major purchases, physical expansion, or increases in services proposed by health-care facilities. Health Systems Agencies, made up of health-care consumers and providers, were to review plans and recommend to state health departments whether or not a CON should be approved. In 1977, HEW published minimum requirements for the kinds of expenditures or plans that the state programs would have to approve—any capital expenditure exceeding $150,000, for example. (See Chapter 16.)

Since states have taken a variety of approaches to the reviews within these Federal guidelines, and since some CON programs have been slow getting started, the impact of the planning legislation has not been easy to assess. But, as of this writing, the last of the states are in the process of implementing the Federal law, and the pioneer programs have been in operation for several years. The act's effects on laboratory medicine are becoming clearer, though not all are easily measurable, and the situation is by no means static.

CON programs and the HSAs have not become the governmental takeover of medicine that some early critics predicted. Indeed, cases in which the law has directly affected laboratories—the labs have had to forgo instruments they wanted or had to alter plans in order to obtain approval—are difficult to find. Few states call for review of capital expenditures below the $150,000 standard.

There are some notable exceptions, such as New Jersey, where in some cases purchases as low as $40,000 are subject to review. But in general, most laboratory purchases have been exempt from the planning process. In most cases, only computer systems and the large automated analyzers have required certificates.

Laboratory involvement. But several trends are now heightening the importance of CON programs for the laboratorian. Increasing automation and computerization are making more big-ticket items available to and necessary for even smaller labs. And there are indications that HSAs are beginning to take a harder line with the laboratory requests they do receive. Some observers attribute this to cost-containment pressures and greater agency sophistication about the planning process itself.

In addition, laboratories can become deeply involved in CON applications for hospital-wide projects. That's the case with Memorial Hospital's information system, which, as noted, includes computerization of test requests and results. More broadly, in a state like Connecticut, HSAs review a hospital's total annual budget, so the laboratory is automatically drawn into the process.

The laboratorian's role in the review process is primarily as a provider of information about the proposal—either directly to an HSA or through an administrator responsible for coordinating applications. What information must the labs provide? What kind of presentation is most effective? How can a laboratorian increase his chances of receiving approval?

Dollar savings. According to most of the laboratorians, administrators, lawyers, and other experts we asked, the most convincing argument for a CON proposal is that it will result in savings. You may feel you need an instrument in order to improve patient care or keep pace with advances in medical practice. But don't count on those points carrying much weight with the HSA or state health department that rules on your application.

Lawrence Wilkinson, M.D., laboratory director at Valley Hospital in Ridgewood, N.J. (whose difficulties in obtaining HSA approval for a chemistry analyzer are detailed in Chapter 17), knows that savings are the overriding concern. "We were able to show the review committee that with the analyzer we would avoid future costs by not having to hire additional staff," Dr. Wilkinson said. "That wasn't good enough. They wanted to know how much we were going to save right now."

Valley Hospital resubmitted the application for the analyzer, along with additional evidence of the cost-effectiveness of the acquisition. This time, the HSA approved the plan unanimously.

N. Kent Demuth, director of information processing at Memorial Hospital in Long Beach, and the person who helped prepare the CON application for the medical center's computer system, is blunt about the attitude of regulators:

"The name of the game when working with the government agencies is, 'Don't tell us about improved patient care. That doesn't mean a thing. Tell us how many dollars you'll save.'" The center's application, therefore, concentrated on that very point.

"We focused very heavily on the cost justification," Demuth said. "We detailed what we were doing, what we expected to do, and what the savings would be. We went position by position. 'This person is doing this job now. The computer will do the job in the future, so the position will be eliminated.' That approach satisfied the cost-containment aspect of the process. It was also a logical way of presenting the project to laymen."

How much would the $5 million information system save? Over eight years, a projected $4.2 million. Not incidentally, much of the economy would come from eliminating 14 full-time technical and clerical positions in the laboratory.

Despite the strength of its economic argument, Memorial Hospital took no chances with the application. The group that prepared the justification followed the required procedure exactly and tried to answer every question in the format, whether or not it seemed applicable to the project.

"We even went out and got an environmental-impact statement from an architect," Demuth said. "The information system won't have any environmental impact except to use some electricity. But we tried to answer the question as best we could."

Community support. Another aspect of Memorial's presentation was community support for the project. A vice president of the local college, a city councilwoman, and other leaders testified on behalf of the hospital at the two public hearings on the CON request. These speakers discussed the importance of the hospital to the community and to their own particular constituents.

Michael X. Morrell, J.D., an attorney specializing in the health-care field, emphasizes the value of such testimony: "Basically you're dealing with a political process. It's a question of bringing pressures to bear, and one of the most important pressures you can bring is community support. You have to play a political game."

Internal politics also comes into play, as various departments compete for scarce resources. The laboratory may have an advantage here and in the CON process generally, because the financial benefits of its purchases can be quantified more easily than in some other hospital areas.

Manufacturers' involvement. One obvious source of assistance in putting together evidence of an instrument's value is the company that's trying to sell it. Manufacturers have become more expert at helping their clients deal with CON applications. The manufacturer's representative should be able to give you advice on how to make a case for an acquisition. He should also provide technical and cost information and evidence of the instrument's performance in other laboratories.

In some cases, manufacturers have also offered acquisition plans that avoided CON requirements. The applicable rule may cover purchases of $150,000 or more, but not extend to leasing arrangements, for example. Or the seller might discount the price of an instrument to bring it below the review threshold, then make up the difference through contracts for reagents at inflated prices.

According to Morrell, such maneuvers are becoming more difficult to justify legally as states and HSAs have become more sophisticated in their review procedures. Many states have plugged loopholes that allowed such arrangements, and President Carter recently signed into law amendments to the Health Planning Act that close other loopholes. In addition, most HSAs are becoming adept at assessing the true nature of an acquisition.

"Under the income tax law, the IRS looks at the substance, not the form, of income," Morrell said. "I think it's fair to say the state agencies are similarly looking at the substance of an acquisition, not the form. If you've acquired the equipment and the effect is equivalent to a capital expenditure, it doesn't matter how you treat it for bookkeeping. You're going to have to go through the review process. It's not nearly as easy as it was two or three years ago to avoid it."

HSAs' members and staff. One potential difficulty in the CON process for laboratorians is having to explain complex professional details to laymen. By Federal law, consumers must make up a majority of an HSA's membership. These members may have little understanding of instrument capabilities, quality control, sensitivity, specificity, and other factors behind instrument selection.

You could deal with this problem as Kent Demuth of Long Beach did with his application for the information system: by minimizing technical matters and focusing on the savings, by playing up what the instrument will do and avoiding the question of how it will do it.

William Lafferty Jr., assistant to the director for planning at Harrisburg Hospital in Pennsylvania, offers another suggestion for handling this issue: When you submit the application, try to work as closely as possible with the HSA's technical staff.

Most HSAs and state health departments have technical aides, who generally perform an advisory role. But their opinions can carry a lot of weight.

In Pennsylvania, Lafferty reports, HSAs assign such personnel to write objective reviews of all proposals. "You can write an 'objective' review that's slanted to the negative or positive. It's important that the individual who writes this analysis understand what you want to do." Carefully go over your plans with these staff people—even invite them to your lab for a firsthand look at your current operation and how the proposed changes would fit in.

Are CONs effective? When CON programs were set up, the theory was that they would force health-care providers to plan more thoroughly and utilize resources more efficiently than they would if left alone. Now theory has given way to practice, and we can look at the effects. First, have hospitals and laboratories improved their planning procedures in order to comply with the law? And second, has the review process screened out ill-considered purchases or expensive, inefficient changes in service?

Kent Demuth's answer to the first question is a definite No. Mapping the Memorial Hospital information system, senior-level managers from all departments met regularly for more than a year just to outline the project's general characteristics. They spent another year on the details.

"Every bit of this planning, with the exception of the effort that went into the application itself, was something that had to be done anyway," Demuth said. "Certificate-of-need requirements didn't make us come up with cost justifications. We don't do anything in this organization unless it's cost-justified."

Nor did the hospital modify its plan in any way to make approval more likely. "The only thing we modified was the timing of the plan," Demuth said. "Instead of getting started in the fall of 1977, we wouldn't be able to start until the fall of '78."

Other laboratorians and hospital administrators we interviewed also claimed the programs have had no real effect on their planning and justification procedures other than the negative ones of delay and extra paperwork. William Lafferty said Harrisburg Hospital personnel put in about 700 man-hours planning for the purchase of a chemistry analyzer to replace an obsolete model. About half that time represented the institution's normal planning procedure. The other half was devoted to meeting government regulations, he said.

The second point about the impact of the CON programs, the question of whether they've helped avoid unnecessary expenditures, might be fairly easy to examine—if we assumed that the denied CON applications in fact covered projects that would have been wasteful. Then we could total up their costs and say at least that much was saved.

According to a survey by the American Health Planning Association, over a two-year period ending August 1978, HSAs reviewed proposals valued at $12 billion and disapproved projects totaling $3.4 billion. Impressive savings? Maybe, but attorney Morrell approaches the statistics with caution.

''Those figures are somewhat misleading because programs that have been turned down are often modified and approved at a later date,'' he said. ''They also fail to consider the added costs of the CON process: the time and labor, the legal costs, and so on. If you start multiplying those expenses by the number of proceedings, I think you'll find the certificates of need aren't saving any money at all. They're probably costing money.''

CON programs are not without their defenders among health-care professionals. Robert J. O'Brien, senior vice president of Wesley Medical Center in Wichita, Kan., is one of them.

''We should be careful not to get too tied up in won-lost records,'' O'Brien said. ''Let's say an HSA has reviewed 10 applications. They've all been good, well-documented plans; all met the criteria. And they've all been approved. You can't say the score is agency '0,' providers '10,' and the agency isn't doing any good. Maybe 20 other hospitals were forced to take a closer look at their ideas and decided not to go ahead with them at all.''

He pointed out that hospitals don't drop their plans merely because of the difficulty in obtaining CON approval. They drop them after realizing that the proposals were not actually in line with the institution's best interests. The CON examination puts a damper of reality on initial, unrealistic enthusiasm.

''Is my gut reaction that I need this $150,000 piece of equipment ultimately correct?'' O'Brien said. ''What problems are we facing? What are the alternative solutions? The review process makes us more cautious when we consider expenditures. I see absolutely nothing wrong with that.''

CON and the future. Morrell believes the trend toward tighter government control of the planning process may be slowing. That's certainly apparent from the new amendments to the law that grant full exemption from the CON process to qualified HMOs.

Morrell also points to the concern voiced by President Carter and other leaders about America's lag in developing new technology. The review programs can be seen as a drag on progress in that manufacturers may shy from developing new instruments that hospitals and laboratories will have difficulty acquiring.

''The government will come to realize that advances in medical technology can bring a more efficient medical-care system, a better medical-care system, and maybe even a less expensive system,'' Morrell said.

He also thinks more emphasis will be placed on qualitative benefits of medical expenditures. He notes, for example, that the National Council on Health Planning Guidelines, a Federal advisory group, based original recommendations on the appropriateness of CAT scanner acquisitions strictly on the number of scans the instrument would perform. Unless a hospital uses the device 2,500 times a year, the guidelines said, it should not have it. More recently, though, the council modified its recommendation to include some qualitative criteria, such as special needs for accessibility or timeliness of scans.

In the future, laboratories' similar qualitative arguments about their diagnostic services may pull more weight with the HSAs. And laboratories may score more tellingly with the argument that early and accurate diagnosis saves money because it allows for the efficient use of other medical resources.

Morrell believes the cost-effectiveness of the CON process itself will come increasingly into question. ``When we spend more money on the gamesmanship of the procedure than we do on the health care itself, it becomes a case of the tail wagging the dog,'' he said.

It seems clear the review process is settling in for an extended stay as part of the nation's health-care system. That means laboratorians and other health-care professionals must not only learn to live with the process, but try to shape the way it develops. The most direct way to influence an HSA is by becoming a member of it, which is exactly what Wesley Medical Center's O'Brien suggests.

``It's difficult to second-guess decisions when you should have had a hand in formulating them,'' he said.

So much for the future. What about the decision on Memorial Hospital's information system? Did the 357-page application have a happy ending?

``We never had any doubts that the certificate-of-need application would be approved,'' said Kent Demuth. ``We just had to go through the effort to make it happen.''

The State of California approved application No. 78-012 without incident.

IV
FORENSIC MEDICINE

19

The Clinical Laboratory as a Forensic Tool

Charles S. Petty, M.D.

Clinical lab personnel traditionally avoid involvement with forensic problems. Indeed, many pathologists and technologists seem terrified when forensic pathology is mentioned even conversationally. The words conjure up visions of medical malpractice cases and court appearances. However, more forensic autopsies are done by clinical pathologists in clinical labs than by forensic pathologists working in labs designed especially for forensic studies. Indeed, the backbone of the medicolegal investigative system in this country is the ordinary pathologist working with nonforensic technologists in a hospital or private laboratory.

Nevertheless, clinical pathologists and technologists are frightened of the forensic case. Why? It seems that the term "forensic" is synonymous with "strange" and "unknown," and fear of the unknown is truly a part of us all. This chapter attempts to make the unknown area of forensics a little less forbidding, somewhat less amorphous, and perhaps more understandable.

The term "forensic" as used in medicine means " in relationship to the law." Thus, forensic pathology is the relationship of the medical specialty of pathology to the resolution of problems at law. A forensic technologist is one who works on laboratory problems that have legal ramifications.

The forensic pathologist spends time in the courtroom. There he testifies first as an ordinary witness, telling the court what he saw at the autopsy, and then serves as an expert witness to interpret the autopsy findings for the benefit of the jury and the entire court. The medical technologist may appear in court to testify as to the nature and details of the analyses performed.

To insure the admissibility in court of the information developed by laboratory analysis, the forensic team must develop a provable chain of evidence from the time the specimen is collected. This means that B, who received the specimen from A, must receipt, time, and date the transfer and, in a like manner, substantiate the transfer to C. At a later date, there can be no question as to who collected, transported, analyzed, and reported, and whether the specimen being discussed is provably the same as the specimen that was collected. This procedure is essential if the information is to be usable in the courtroom.

The very introduction of lab results in a trial record depends on the existence of a chain of evidence. For example, I remember an instance when a woman died and the pathologist performing the autopsy couldn't determine the cause of death. Later, someone suspected arsenic poisoning. The pathologist still had the liver, so we analyzed it for arsenic. There was no doubt that the woman had been given large doses of poison, so the case was prepared for trial. However, our report was inadmissible, because it could not be proved that the information we had developed was related to the case! The pathologist who first autopsied the body had stored the specimens in an unlocked area of the lab where everyone had access to them. There was no way of proving that the liver we had analyzed was, in fact, the liver that had come out of the woman's body. The result was that the body had to be exhumed, and we had to start all over again—this time properly.

This brings up another area of forensics that is intimidating to some clinical laboratorians: Forensic specimens are often quite different in character from clinical specimens. To begin with, the specimen frequently comes from a dead body, not a living patient. Substances such as bile are often collected in greater quantity than is usual in the clinical lab.

Samples also differ because there is no further need to preserve a patient's equanimity. Thus, hair specimens may include roots, for example. In addition, the site of collection is usually not one sampled in the living: middle ear cultures, brain tissue for viral study, vitreous humor for chemical analysis, and fingernail scrapings and clippings for blood grouping and examination of foreign substances, to name just a few of the collection sites.

Because many of the specimens are obtained at autopsy, they are sampled in a different way than those of the living. Urine may come directly from the bladder, blood from the heart.

After death, an inexorable set of changes takes place in the body. The blood stops circulating and settles in those blood vessels near the lowest part of the body. Clotting may take place. These clots may liquefy within a very few minutes of death, with a decrease or ultimate absence of fibrinogen in the sample collected and analyzed afterward. Bacteria invade the body, progressing from the outside, the gut, skin, air passages, etc. The cells of various tissues both dying and dead lose their ability to retain certain electrolytes. Thus, serum potassium levels rapidly increase. Blood glucose levels may drop rapidly—or perhaps progress in the opposite direction. Blood pH rapidly changes to the acid side. Blood pO_2 and pCO_2 may alter greatly and rapidly. Decomposition of the body begins, and if not halted by cooling or embalming, it will rapidly change even the external body appearance, with the corpse eventually bloating and stinking.

All of these differences pose problems for laboratory personnel. The very specimens may be repugnant to technologists because of appearance and odor. Clots may be arbitrarily used as an excuse for discarding blood specimens. Vitreous humor samples are so different from normal that the automated chemistry analyzer operator may not want to include the sample as part of the run, not knowing what to expect: Will the recorder be driven against the stops? Should the specimen be diluted? Does it really contain glucose? Does the expected result fail to meet—or overrun—usual standards?

Furthermore, laboratory analytical priorities must be considered. After all, the subject from whom the specimens were collected is dead, and the analytical results are not necessary for treatment. Cannot these strange specimens, collected in unusual ways, be left until the end of the line? If they are forgotten, perhaps they will go away or the pathologist will change his mind and retract his requests for analyses!

Despite postmortem changes, there are many routine clinical analytical procedures that can be applied to specimens collected during the forensic autopsy. In general, the procedures can be undertaken in any reasonably well-equipped clinical laboratory. Even minor modifications of equipment are usually unnecessary. All that is needed is a sample, properly collected, preserved, and submitted for analysis. Let's examine some situations in which clinical labs may be called upon to perform forensic analyses:

The victim with diabetes. There are two laboratory approaches to the investigation of a dead person who is suspected of having had diabetes mellitus, the object being to find out if he died of a diabetic coma or an insulin overdose. The first approach is the determination of glucose levels in the vitreous humor of the eye. And the second approach is to analyze the blood insulin level, making use of radioimmunoanalytic equipment.

Glucose levels in the blood change rapidly after death. Indeed, a prolonged agonal period with extreme physiologic stress can cause many alterations of blood components. But the fluid within the eye is shielded from rapid physiologic change, and postmortem analysis of the vitreous humor can reveal the approximate premortem concentration of glucose as well as certain other substances. Thus, death due to acute diabetic coma may be proved by finding very high glucose levels in the vitreous humor. Similar determinations of blood glucose levels obtained in the postmortem state would yield results of no value. If an automated chemistry analyzer is available, the vitreous humor, undiluted, may be run exactly as an ordinary blood sample would be. Values can be extremely high, and a second run using a diluted sample may be necessary for quantitation.

The radioimmunoassay determination of blood insulin is carried out in the same manner as if the sample were collected from a living patient. Overdoses that confirm other evidence of suicide or homicide can be proved by such analyses.

These two analytical approaches, well within the capability of most clinical laboratories, may thus be used to resolve problems of great forensic importance.

The rape victim. The victim may be alive or dead, but the value of detailed analytical procedures is great in either instance. There are several useful methods to be employed. It is important to keep in mind that a female sexual assault victim may have been attacked sexually other than per vaginam. Assaults by way of the oral cavity or anus are not unusual. Therefore, these areas must be examined just as carefully as the vagina.

Smears taken from the three significant areas are examined in two major ways: Stained smears are microscopically searched for sperm, and unstained smears are checked for certain blood group substances. Many different staining techniques are available. However, the nuclear fast red-picroindigocarmine stain[1] is the one we use: The sperm heads stain red and the tails green and red. The staining procedure is easy to do and fairly foolproof.

Smears can also identify the blood type of the rapist. An air-dried slide preparation with the smear fixed with a cytological fixative can be checked for ABO (A,B,H) blood group substances. Should such immunohematologic typing procedures be necessary, an additional step is essential to properly interpret the findings. The ABO type of the victim must be determined, and whether or not the victim secretes blood group substances into the various body fluids must be ascertained. A check of the saliva for secreted blood group substances may be conducted if the victim is living. Bile is a good substance to examine if the victim is dead. The gallbladder can be entered with a very small-gauge needle, and uncontaminated bile can thus be obtained for immunohematologic analysis.

If the victim is a secretor, and the seminal fluid contains blood group substances of the same type as the victim, then the assailant was either a nonsecretor or a secretor of the same ABO group as the victim. If the victim is of one blood group and the seminal fluid of another, there is no doubt about the blood group and secretor status of the assailant.

The clinical laboratory can provide further evidence in a rape case through acid phosphatase determinations. Usually, such determinations are quantitated and reported in terms of amount of the acid phosphatase present per unit volume of blood. Quantitation of the enzyme in the swab taken of the vaginal vault is not necessary and, indeed, may be misleading. The collection of the vaginal fluids by swab (or by any other technique) is not a quantitative procedure, and a true aliquot cannot be obtained.

Therefore, extensive laboratory quantitation of the specimen is not of value. What *is* desired is proof of the presence of acid phosphatase and, secondarily, proof of the prostatic origin of that enzyme. Seminal fluid contains a large amount of acid phosphatase of prostatic origin; a small amount of acid phosphatase of vaginal or female origin can be demonstrated in vaginal aspirates from women who have not had sexual intercourse for long periods of time.

The procedure for the determination of acid phosphatase is not difficult and requires only standard lab equipment and a few easily obtained chemicals. (Details have been published elsewhere and are readily available.[2]) The same techniques can be used to examine stains on clothing for clues to the blood type and secretor status of the assailant. The electrophoretic procedure used to distinguish between acid phosphatase of male and female origin is not much different from acrylamide-gel procedures used in the clinical laboratory for the separation and identification of other substances.[3]

The most frequently encountered problems in forensic investigation of rape cases are those of sample collection and preservation, and the creation of a reasonable chain of evidence. Much evidence is destroyed in the hospital emergency room if personnel fail to understand the importance of preserving the victim's clothes and taking prompt and proper smears. Often, in their haste to treat an assault victim, E.R. personnel overlook these medicolegal considerations.

The gunshot wound victim. In recent years, the investigation of the gunshot wound victim has changed from a fairly routine autopsy examination into a sophisticated autopsy *and* laboratory investigation. To be completely successful, such a dual approach must necessarily include a complete interchange of information about lab results and autopsy room findings.

There are three primary ways a modern lab can aid in the investigation of shooting victims. The first is through handwashings to find firearm residues—either on the victim (if considered a suicide) or on a possible assailant. Attempts to detect small traces of powder or residues of cartridge primers on the skin of a person who recently discharged a firearm carry the generic name "paraffin test," because molten paraffin brushed on the hands has been used as one method of collecting residues.

There are many variations, such as chemical color tests. However, these are unreliable for several reasons. They're too insensitive for finding minute amounts of primer residue, and interfering substances often yield false positives. This is particularly true in the search for nitrates—nitrates are nearly everywhere, in urine, fertilizer, etc. Other potential difficulties include unfamiliarity with the exact position of the weapon when the gun was fired, leading to confusion about whether there should be any residues, and unfamiliarity with the weapon that was employed.

Some of the unreliability of these older paraffin tests was corrected when neutron activation analysis was introduced. This technique is based on the removal of materials from the hands, either by washing with dilute acid or by using the paraffin procedure. The material is then subjected to radiation in a neutron source. The secondary radioactivity in the sample is then analyzed in a counter, and highly accurate determinations of the quantity of metal characteristic of primer residues (antimony, barium) can be made.

The technique is useful, but there are two major disadvantages: A lab must have access to a nuclear reactor and counting equipment, and the procedure is extremely sensitive, with a high degree of hazard in analyzing contaminants. Very few forensic centers use this technique.

A third technique, simpler and highly sensitive, is now available: atomic absorption. The instrumentation is found in many clinical laboratories. To be sure, special lamps are needed to permit analysis for lead, barium, and antimony, the metals in firearm residues. Here's how it works: The hands are washed with swabs moistened in a dilute solution of acid. The washing is then analyzed. The expected metals can be demonstrated on the hands of 25 to 30 percent of those who discharge a firearm.

An essential part of the examination of a firearms victim, and one that is often neglected, is analysis of his clothing. The pattern and amount of powder and primer residues on clothing can indicate the distance from which the victim was shot.

Probably the easiest way to accomplish this is examination through a dissecting microscope. Powder particles and tiny bullet fragments overlooked with the naked eye are visible. Particles suspected to be powder can be readily ignited with a hot wire loop, a simple but destructive method of proof. Protection of the victim's clothing (to prevent contamination and possible loss of the powder particles) is necessary at all stages, from the discovery of the victim until the articles arrive in the laboratory.

Skin and subcutaneous tissue can yield further information about a gunshot wound victim. Powder particles may be recognized in sections stained with hematoxylin and eosin combination. However, for the pathologist who does not have frequent opportunities to search sections for powder particles, a stain for nitrate can be most useful. The stain we use is a standard one.[4] With it, nitrate particles appear as a deep blue on a brown-yellow-red background. This stain is most useful in determining whether the gunshot wound (especially with small caliber weapons) is of contact or long-range nature. For example, a large quantity of nitrate-positive particles in the dermis and subcutaneous tissue would indicate that the gun was discharged with the muzzle in contact with the skin.

The hyperthyroid subject. In this age of thyroid suppressant drugs and "safe" thyroid surgery, very few individuals die in thyroid storm or crisis. When that does occur, neither the treating physician nor the examining pathologist may entertain the possibility. The usual clinical laboratory tests for hyperthyroidism can be successfully carried out with blood obtained after death. The analysis of blood for the level of thyroid-stimulating hormone is most useful to determine the state of thyroid activity. Insofar as these determinations are concerned, the blood is stable for many hours after death. The histologic examination can go hand in hand to point to thyroid storm as a cause of death.

The hemoglobinopathy situation. Perhaps as many as 12 percent of blacks have a hemoglobinopathy, some life-threatening, others not. The S-S hemoglobinopathy causes death in sickle cell crisis. The S-A hemoglobinopathy is usually considered not to be life-threatening. However, forensic pathologists occasionally encounter cases in which S-A hemoglobinopathy is present, with massive sickling of red blood cells. In some instances, a minor infection or other anoxia-producing episode appears to have precipitated the sickling and death. The usefulness and reliability of hemoglobin electrophoresis performed on blood specimens obtained after death is undeniable. Blood specimens retained so long after death as to be hemolyzed (and sometimes even decomposing samples) have been successfully used to demonstrate hemoglobinopathies. Infarcts of the S-A node of the heart, with resulting sudden and unexpected death, have been found to result from hemoglobinopathy.

The digitalis overdose. With the advent of radioimmunoassay, analyses for digitalis are commonly performed in the clinical laboratory. The variation in levels of digitalis in the bloodstream of those being treated with the drug is well known. Toxic levels may appear in some subjects even though the dosage may be within the usual therapeutic range. Digitalis assays may be carried out, using blood specimens collected after death, provided hemolysis is not great. In the event of hemolysis, analysis of the vitreous humor for digitalis (digoxin and/or digitoxin) can be used. Instances of digitalis overdose, both intentional and accidental, may be proved by such analyses. The author has seen suicidal overdose of digitalis in individuals who have not been treated with the drug, but who have access to it through a family member or acquaintance.

The apparent drowning victim. There have been many techniques designed to prove that a body found floating in water died by drowning. Gettler sought to prove this by comparing the concentration of chloride in the serum collected from right and left sides of the heart. He argued that the chloride concentration in the blood returning to the heart from the lungs would be lower than that found in the blood coming to the heart from the peripheral areas of the body. This, he held, was true in drowning in fresh water; in seawater drowning, because of the high chloride content of the water itself, the left heart's blood would have a greater concentration than the blood collected from the opposite side of the heart.

Despite this reasonable hypothesis and a not inconsiderable quantity of analytical supporting evidence, this ''test'' or ''proof'' of drowning is far from infallible. False negatives and false positives are encountered because:

1. When the drowning is of the ''dry'' type, where because of glottic spasm, little or no water entered the lungs, changes in the chloride concentration would not be expected.

2. Drownings do occur in brackish water. This may prevent the expected electrolyte change because an unpredictable amount of salt is present in the water. Layering of fresh and salt water may also be encountered.

3. External cardiac massage and extensive resuscitative efforts may cause postmortem mixing of blood from the two sides of the heart and confuse the results.

4. If the drowning was not witnessed, then perhaps the subject did not drown! In such an instance, a negative determination might be viewed as a false negative when the test is really pointing to the true cause of death!

5. In many instances, the blood is badly hemolyzed. Because of this, the serum chloride levels are very high and may obscure smaller, more meaningful differences. (Hemolysis occurs as a part of the decomposition process. Many floating bodies are recovered so long after death that decomposition has long since prevented any reasonable examination of the blood chloride levels.)

Because of the foregoing, interest in the Gettler test for drowning has decreased, and substitutes have appeared. One such is the determination of the specific gravity of the serum, comparing Sp. Gr. rather than chloride. However, only the substance measured has changed, not the hypothesis for its analysis, and, as with chloride concentrations, false negatives and false positives are expected and found—for much the same reasons. Osmolality is one more approach to the same problem, with the same drawbacks as the others.

Obviously, these analytical methods do not constitute proof of drowning. Such determinations are productive of misleading data that can be misinterpreted and misapplied. There is no drowning test in which real confidence can be placed. It is far better to be aware of this and not attempt to perform spurious tests.

The foregoing short description of the usefulness of clinical laboratory (and histology laboratory) analyses, techniques, and instruments in the resolution of problems of forensic importance should merely open the door to a fascinating employment of laboratory skills. One final observation: Remember that if the analysis is to be of maximum use to law enforcement personnel, attorneys, and the courts, the results must be expressed in easy-to-understand language, both on the report and later, if necessary, in the courtroom. Your expertise as a laboratorian should not be compromised by impossible-to-understand technical jargon.

If fear of the forensic is eliminated, then you—either pathologist or technologist—can help resolve issues at law.

1. Oppitz, E. A new color method for proof of sperm in moral crimes. *Arkiv für Krimin* 144 (1969): 145-148

2. Petty, C.S., and Stone, I.C. Medical and forensic investigation of sexual assault. American Society of Clinical Pathologists, Forensic Pathology Workshop, Chicago, Ill., March 1977

3. Adams, E.G., and Wraxall, B.G. Phosphatases in body fluids: The differentiation of seminal and vaginal secretions. *Forensic Sci* 3 (1974): 57-62

4. Rolfe, H.C., Curle, D., and Simmons, D. A histological technique for forensic ballistics. *J Forensic Med* 18 (1971): 47-52

20

When You're Called as an Expert Witness

Lawrence A. Reynolds Jr.

Whatever position you hold in the laboratory, you may be subpoenaed to testify in court as an expert witness. How will you feel when you take the oath for the first time? Probably a bit apprehensive. And totally unprepared. That's how I felt the first time I testified in court.

I've given evidence in more than 100 trials since then. Most of these were criminal cases, in which I testified as the prosecution's expert forensic chemist. Over the years I have developed some guidelines that help me during court appearances. Perhaps you will find them useful when—as may happen sometime—you have your day in court.

Just what *is* an expert witness? It is someone whose education, training, and knowledge are impressive enough for the court to rely upon. As an expert witness, you are usually required to testify as to exactly what kind of test you performed. You may also be asked to interpret the results of the test.

In other instances—usually in criminal trials—the expert witness may be asked to testify as a link in a legal chain of evidence. For example, you may testify that you took custody of a sample of blood in a drunk-driving case. When you testify in this capacity, you give evidence only to your direct knowledge of the facts, as they pertain to the evidence being presented.

If you are called to testify in a case, you will first hear about it when you are subpoenaed. The subpoena will be requested by the lawyer who wants your testimony. The authority to issue subpoenas ultimately comes from the court. Most subpoenas are sent by first-class mail. You should honor a subpoena sent in this manner, even though the law requires a subpoena to be hand-delivered. In other instances, the subpoena may be sent by registered mail. Most states consider a subpoena that is sent by registered mail to be hand-delivered. My rule: Honor *all* subpoenas.

The subpoena names the attorney who is requesting your appearance in court. Contact him immediately. Ask him exactly what he wants. What information will he require? What pieces of evidence will he need? When is the case scheduled for trial? And, equally important, discuss your witness fee.

You may legitimately charge a fee as an expert witness. This fee is compensation for your time—*not* for your testimony. How do you set your fee? You will have to review analyses, confer with attorneys, and spend some time in court. Do some figuring. If extensive travel or other pretrial expenses are involved, it is proper to ask for some—or all—of your fee in advance. Work out these money matters well before the trial. The courtroom is never the place to negotiate a fee.

Stay in close touch with the attorney who has subpoenaed you. Changes in pleas may occur. The trial date may be changed. It is your responsibility to keep informed of all of these changes. When the trial date has been confirmed, make an appointment with the attorney for a pretrial conference. These conferences are very important to the expert witness. The lawyer is usually not familiar with your area of expertise, so be prepared to give him as much information as possible. This allows the attorney to ask the right kind of questions when he puts you on the witness stand.

This pretrial conference will also familiarize you with all aspects of the case. When you get on the stand, you can stick to information that is relevant and pass over matters that aren't. You may wish to draw up a list of questions to help the attorney present your testimony to the court.

On the first day of the trial, you and the other witnesses will be sworn in and then sequestered until each of you is summoned to testify. The judge will instruct you not to discuss the case with any other witnesses before you leave the courtroom. From my own observations, however, these instructions are heeded only about half of the time. Don't you disregard them. You may find yourself facing a contempt-of-court charge if you do.

A bailiff will lead you into the courtroom and direct you to the witness chair after you are summoned to give evidence. You will then be sworn in by the bailiff, if you were not present at the initial taking of the oath.

You will then be qualified as an expert witness. It is the custom in some courts to simply ask the expert witness to state his qualifications. In other jurisdictions, this task is conducted by the attorney who has subpoenaed the expert. In either case, you should be prepared to provide information that will include: your education—undergraduate and graduate, including major, thesis subject, degrees, and dates of graduation; place and date of hospital and laboratory training; specialty training; certification and licenses; work experience; publications; membership in professional organizations; and experience with this type of case.

I have found that the jury tends to be more impressed if I recite my qualifications without having to resort to a printed résumé. However, it is legally acceptable to have this information readily available in print, if you need to read from it while giving your qualifications.

You will usually be accepted as an expert witness after reciting your qualifications. Most often, the opposing attorney will stipulate that you are an expert. The judge will be the one who makes the final ruling if the opposing attorney chooses to challenge your qualifications as an expert witness.

Now that you have been qualified, the attorney whose subpoena summoned you to court will begin his direct examination. Here are some tips to keep in mind as you give evidence. By following them, you will help your lawyer present his case. You will also enhance the jurors' estimate of your credibility as a witness.

1. Have your facts ready, in orderly sequence. Bring all of your notes with you, and be prepared to refer to them.

2. Your expert opinion means just that. You may offer an opinion, if you are asked for one, on matters for which you are fully qualified. But you do not have to evaluate, interpret, or offer an opinion on anything that falls outside the area of your professional expertise.

3. Look cool. How you look has a bearing on what you say. The court may find it difficult to believe that the casually or sloppily attired witness is the professional he claims to be.

4. Be cool. You should always remain calm and controlled when on the witness stand. Never argue with an attorney. Never show your temper. Emotional behavior will only be used against you, and it will undermine your testimony.

5. Direct your testimony to the jury, and not to the attorney or the judge. The jurors need to hear your testimony; they are the ones who must reach a verdict. Remember, too, that the jury is composed of laymen. Structure your testimony so that each juror will get a clear understanding of what you are saying.

The opposing attorney will begin questioning you after your direct examination has been completed. This is one aspect of your court appearance that can never be completely mastered. Lawyers use a wide variety of legal tricks on cross-examination. These ploys are designed to intimidate a witness and discredit his testimony. Here are some of the tactics I've encountered.

Excessive questioning. This is an attempt to wear you down and tire you on the witness stand. The questions usually have little or no significance. One lawyer spent an hour asking me where I kept my test tubes, how large they were, and what kind of soap I used to clean them. This lawyer was trying to force me to give a careless reply. He was hoping that he could then cast doubt on the rest of my testimony.

No questioning. Your testimony may have such a damaging effect that the opposing attorney would prefer that the jury doesn't hear it a second time. The less said by you, he reasons, the less impressed the jury will be by the evidence you have given.

Personality change. This tactic is often used on persons who are testifying for the first time. The opposing attorney will approach you before the trial begins. He will converse with you in a friendly manner. He may even continue in this vein during the first few minutes of cross-examination. Then he suddenly turns on you. He becomes nasty and abrasive. This can be a most unsettling experience for the newcomer on the witness stand.

Homework. Sometimes an opposing attorney can surprise you by displaying unexpected knowledge of your own field of expertise. But no matter how much homework he has done, the opposing attorney possesses only limited knowledge on the subject. He'll eventually run out of questions. You can easily turn this tactic to your advantage by demonstrating that you know more about the subject than he does. I was recently asked why I had not performed a Beame test on a sample of marijuana. I politely replied that the Beame test hadn't been used in the lab since the 1940s.

Publications. You may be asked if you have read a certain author's publication. Do you agree with it? If your answer is Yes, the attorney will then quote some statement by the author that supports his client's case. You can avoid this embarrassment by knowing exactly what the author has written *before* you answer any questions. Attorneys sometimes quote out of context, so consider asking the judge for permission to read the entire article before replying to the question.

Possibility of error. The attorney will attack such points as the chain of evidence, collection procedures, or the possibility that a specimen was contaminated. The lawyer will try to convince the jury that the testimony that you presented on direct examination may be false, misleading, or in error. This is why it is absolutely essential that you get as much information as possible at the time you collect a patient's specimen.

The specimen container must be marked so that you can identify it on the witness stand—years later, if need be. If you pass on any evidence, record when the incident occurred, what the evidence was, and who received the specimen. I have seen more cases thrown out of court for "poor chain of evidence" reasons than for any other single cause.

Another expert. The opposition may bring in another expert to refute your testimony. When this happens, the jury is most likely to favor the expert who presents the most understandable and believable testimony. I once testified for the prosecution in a case involving some tests for LSD that I had conducted. The defense brought in an expert who said my test results were wrong. I told the district attorney to ask the defense expert how many LSD tests he had conducted during his professional career. His answer, "None."

Witness fee. This tactic may be used to suggest to the jury that since you are being paid, the testimony you present may not be free of bias or prejudice. You can counter this suggestion by explaining to the jury that you are being paid for your time and that your time is *all* you're being paid for.

One of the toughest parts of an opposing attorney's job is trying to discredit the testimony of an expert witness. The attorney is at a distinct disadvantage as long as the expert conducts himself as a professional on the witness stand. And in the minds of the jurors, your testimony will provide one of the most powerful pieces of evidence that they will use in deciding the outcome of a court case involving laboratory data.

21

I Was a Link in a Chain of Evidence

Vicki Salmon, MT(ASCP)

Most laboratorians don't know a darn thing about the law. Why should we? We are thoroughly familiar with the language of the lab, of course. But throw us a phrase like *res ipsa loquitur,* and then watch our minds go blank. Until my home telephone rang one night several years ago, all I knew about the law was what I'd learned watching Perry Mason on television. That phone call changed my life. It threw me into a criminal case, in which I became a link in a chain of evidence.

The call was from the night nursing supervisor. There are 15 techs in our hospital, and it was my turn to take evening calls. "There's been a bad traffic accident," she said. "Two cars. The driver of one car is seriously injured, and we need a crossmatch."

The patient was in the emergency room when I arrived minutes later. She was a teenager. They already had her in a hospital gown. A physician and a nurse worked desperately to save her life. A policeman stood nearby, taking statements in a whisper. I performed a venipuncture and hurried to the lab.

The telephone rang before the patient's blood sample had clotted. It was the nurse up in the emergency room. "The police have brought in the driver of the other car," she told me. "A blood alcohol has to be drawn." I rushed back.

The suspected drunk driver was an attractive woman in her late 20s. She didn't appear injured, and I really didn't pay much attention to her. I was the only tech in the hospital, and my mind was on that crossmatch. A policeman pointed at the suspect. "Get a sample of her blood for evidence," he said.

I had the procedure for drawing blood alcohols down pat. There are specific instructions on this subject posted in the lab. These instructions

FIGURE 21-1

Directions for Drawing Blood for Alcohol Content

Mary Lanning Hospital, Hastings, Neb.

1. Blood for alcohol content may be drawn by nursing personnel, medical technologists, or physicians upon the orders of the police department, sheriff, or the state highway patrol.

2. When a blood alcohol is requested during the hours when technologists are in the laboratory, the medical technologists will collect the specimen. However, between the hours of 8 p.m. and 6 a.m., the nursing supervisor may collect the specimen.

3. Supplies for the collection of blood alcohols are kept in the north cupboard in the outpatient drawing area. Directions for collection are posted on the inside of the door.

4. **Procedure:**

   A. Clean the arm with benzalkonium chloride (aqueous 1.750 dil.). *Do not use alcohol on the skin.*

   B. Either a Vacutainer with needle or disposable syringe can be used for collection.

   C. Place 5 cc of blood in a gray-stoppered vacuum-collection tube and mix by inverting five or six times.

vary from state to state, depending upon how the laws and the rules of evidence are written. Consult with a lawyer if you contemplate posting them in your lab. You can see our requirements for blood alcohols in Figure 21-1.

I told the woman that I was going to perform a venipuncture. She said O.K. and gave me her arm. I carefully swabbed the area with benzalkonium chloride, rather than alcohol, so that the test results would not be

D. A label must be placed on the tube stating the name of the patient, the time and date the specimen was collected, and by whom the specimen was collected. Place the label at the top edge of the tube and stopper to form a seal.

E. The tube is then given to the police officer, sheriff, or highway patrolman, and he will obtain the analysis. If the test is to be performed here, place the tube in the metal box, lock the box, and place it in the under-the-counter refrigerator in the outpatient drawing area. Urine is handled in the same manner.

F. A charge of $2.50 is made for this service. This is charged through the laboratory on a laboratory charge slip. The charge is not made to the individual patient, but is made to either the city police department or the state highway patrol. An information slip is to be filled out. These will be found in the box with the collection supplies. The laboratory will then make the charge.

G. The attached requisition is to be filled out by the nurse or medical technologist collecting the specimen. Place this requisition in the box with the specimen.

5. On the advice of our attorney, it has been ascertained that the patient's authorization is not necessary if the officer requests it and the patient voluntarily submits. The law presently permits this procedure by official law enforcement people, and, if the individual in question refuses the examination, his driver's license can be automatically suspended.

contaminated. I handed the container to the policeman when I was finished. He sealed it, and we both initialed and dated it. From past experience, I knew that the police chemist would subsequently test this blood sample.

I returned to the lab, where it took me about 45 minutes to do the crossmatch. I gave the test results to the night nursing supervisor. "I don't think that injured girl is going to make it," she told me. The nurse was right. When I returned to work the next day, I learned that the girl had died. It seemed such a tragedy: another young life lost in a pointless accident. A double tragedy, I thought, because the older woman would probably be charged with manslaughter.

It was almost a year after the girl had died when my doorbell rang one evening. I opened the door, and a big deputy sheriff handed me a subpoena. I was thoroughly intimidated. I studied the subpoena after he left. I was being summoned as a witness for the prosecution. I was ordered to testify about the events that took place on the night I drew blood from the female drunk-driving suspect presumed responsible for the accident. I took it for granted that it was a manslaughter case. I didn't even bother to contact the prosecutor for advice. That's how naive I was.

I told the chief tech that I'd been subpoenaed, and he arranged for me to have the afternoon off on the day of the trial. I didn't even bother to review the old hospital records. After all, I told myself, I had played such a small part in the case.

I arrived at the courthouse in my work clothes on the day of the trial. My mind went totally blank as I sat on a bench in the corridor outside the courtroom. Was I scared? I was so nervous I actually broke out in blotches!

A bailiff called me into the courtroom. There was no jury; the trial was being conducted before a judge. I took the stand, and the prosecutor started questioning me. First, he asked about my professional qualifications. I told him that I had spent three years in college, followed by a one-year internship. I started to relax—a little. The prosecutor next asked me about the events on the night I drew the suspect's blood. As the defendant stared at me, I described exactly what happened. The prosecutor thanked me and sat down.

I took a deep breath. I had seen enough television to know that my cross-examination was coming next. The lawyer representing the defendant started in on me. His patronizing tone and his line of questioning made me feel ignorant and embarrassed. He did such a tough job questioning me that the only thing I remember about him is his red hair.

He asked me all kinds of questions. He made much of the fact that I had been out of training for only two years. How many times had I drawn blood? Several hundred times, I replied. What kind of container had I put the defendant's blood sample in? A 5 cc stoppered tube containing an anticoagulant, I replied. What are the chemicals in this anticoagulant? Potassium oxalate and sodium fluoride, I replied. What do these chemicals do? It went on and on and on.

After a while, he stopped and looked at his notes. There was a slight smile on his lips when he turned to face me. I had the feeling that I was turning into a solid, giant blotch as he asked: "Did you feel that the woman now in this courtroom was drunk on the night that you took a sample of her blood?"

I shook my head. "I'm really not qualified to answer that question," I replied. It must have been the right answer. The lawyer sighed and waved his hand in dismissal. Then he said that he had no more questions. I couldn't get out of that courtroom fast enough!

I didn't see anything about the outcome of the trial in the newspaper, as I had expected to. It wasn't until I decided to write about my day in court that I learned what happened after I left the witness stand. Here's what I discovered.

I had been subpoenaed to court as a link in the prosecutor's chain of evidence. The prosecutor put several witnesses on the stand, starting with the policeman who had arrived at the scene of the accident. This officer was the first link. The policeman who took statements in the emergency room was the second link. I was the third link. The police chemist who tested the defendant's blood was the fourth link. It was the prosecutor's job to link all of this testimony together to prove his case. The defense attorney tried to break these links.

I next discovered that I hadn't been giving evidence in a manslaughter case, as I had assumed. The defendant had been tried on a simple drunk-driving charge. The prosecutor had developed evidence before the trial, proving that the accident had been caused by the girl who was killed. This meant that the prosecutor could only try the defendant as a drunk driver. And the judge had dismissed *that* charge after hearing all of the evidence. No wonder I couldn't find anything about the case in the newspaper.

I also learned that I had acted properly on the witness stand. Why? Because I stuck to the truth. Because I followed lab procedures, right down to the letter. And because I wouldn't respond to questions that I could not answer. No wonder the defense attorney dismissed me when I said I wasn't qualified to say whether the defendant was drunk. He hadn't been able to trip me up.

My single day in court convinced me that I'll never be a legal expert. It also convinced me that I never want to see a subpoena again.

22

The Case of the Elusive Contaminant

Joyce Yeast, Ph.D.

The results of a series of tests I once ran were challenged in a lawsuit. Though I wasn't named in the suit myself, I was called in to testify as an expert witness—and certainly I had a stake in the outcome of the case, since my professional work was in question. Though the circumstances were rather unique, don't bet that something similar couldn't happen to you someday.

I was owner and laboratory director of a medical diagnostic laboratory at the time my story begins. Our facilities were located in the farm belt, and we conducted tests in commercial bacteriology, mycology, and biochemistry. Some of our work involved testing samples of farm animal feeds, such as haylage and silage, for protein, vitamin A, nitrates, urea, and additives. While this particular part of my job was routine, I always treated each of these tests as though a human life were involved.

One morning, a veterinarian brought a sample of pellets to my lab. The veterinarian was in charge of research at a large feed manufacturing company. I looked at the pellets he handed me. I couldn't identify them. They looked something like dog food.

"I want you to run a salmonella isolation test on this sample," he said. "When can I get test results?"

I studied the pellets. "I don't have anyone trained to handle the job," I replied, "so I'll do it myself. I should have the results in a few days." I didn't ask the veterinarian any questions. Laboratory protocol dictates that tests of this nature should be conducted blind.

I tested the pellet sample, using a technique similar to that for testing stool specimens for salmonella. This test involves introducing the sample into tetrathionate and selenite broth. After incubation, the sample is transferred to brilliant green sulfa and other identifying media. Serological typing is done on suspect colonies.

My tests were negative for the presence of salmonella in all of its more than 2,100 varieties. I filled out the appropriate test forms and then telephoned the veterinarian.

These tests for salmonella continued for more than a month. I received a sample of similar pellets almost weekly. All test results remained negative. Was I curious about the material I was testing? Of course, but speculation is idle when specific test results are required.

Several months passed, and then I received a letter from an attorney in another town. The letter asked me to contact him immediately. I dialed his number and introduced myself. "I represent an insurance company," he told me. "We are the insurer for a feed manufacturing company in your town. We are also the insurer for a small firm that sells this feed. Both of these companies are accused of supplying contaminated cattle feed to a dairy farm where sal . . . salmo . . ."

"Salmonellosis," I said, immediately aware that the lawyer was on unfamiliar ground.

"Right, salmonellosis," he replied. "At any rate, salmonellosis broke out at this dairy. A number of cows died. Some of the hired hands came down with the disease. I understand you tested this feed for salmonella, and didn't find it."

"I tested some pelleted samples for salmonella," I said. "I was never told where the samples came from. I didn't even know the samples were cattle feed."

The lawyer sighed. "The trial is about to start. I'll be sending you a subpoena. I want you to testify as one of our expert witnesses. The subpoena will tell you when to come to my office. Bring all of your records with you."

I went to the lawyer's office at the required time, accompanied by the veterinarian. My first impression of this lawyer was unfavorable. He wasn't a farm boy and knew nothing about the cattle and feed business.

He hadn't done his homework on lab procedures, either. I decided to ask some questions.

"When did salmonellosis break out at the farm?"

The lawyer looked at his notes. "It happened before you were asked to conduct your tests," he said. "The county health department came in and conducted tests at the farm. These tests were positive for salmonella. You were asked to test the same feed used at the farm after the feed manufacturer and the feed company were sued."

I nodded, thinking here was a case of too little and too late. "Well, there was no salmonella in the samples I tested," I said.

"Then what could have happened?" the lawyer said.

"It may very well be that the farm workers gave the salmonella to the cattle," I replied. "The epidemic might have been caused by humans, and not the feed."

"How can that happen?" he asked.

As diplomatically as possible, the veterinarian and I did our best to enlighten the attorney. I showed him all of my test reports. I explained my test procedures. I described varieties of salmonella and their symptoms. We didn't seem to be making much of an impression.

"I don't know," the lawyer said at one point. "Maybe we should settle out of court. Throw in the towel."

"Look," I said, "you have been hired to put up the best defense possible. We'll give you all the help we can."

I testified several days later. The insurance company lawyer put me on the stand. I outlined my qualifications as a laboratorian. Then I explained how I performed my tests, what salmonella is, and how it is transmitted.

The lawyer representing the farm owner asked very few questions. Did I find salmonella in the samples I tested? What's the difference between a microbiologist and a bacteriologist? Then he dismissed me. I had been on the witness stand less than 20 minutes.

I returned to my lab. The veterinarian telephoned me the next day. "We lost the case," he said. "The jury brought in a judgment for $39,000. They believed our feed caused the salmonellosis."

What had gone wrong? Even though I wouldn't have to pay any part of the award, my professional curiosity was aroused. The feed manufacturing company accepted the jury's decision and proceeded to determine the source of the harmful organism. The company asked me to do further tests on raw materials they had used to manufacture the pellets. Here is what I discovered.

The feed manufacturer bought its raw material from a number of sources. This raw material is called tankage, and it contains things like waste meat, offal, bone meal, and fish meal. The feed manufacturer heats the tankage to kill any harmful organisms that may be present. After additional processing, the tankage is turned into meal and then shipped from the plant as feed pellets.

The veterinarian and I backtracked to the sources supplying the raw tankage. I began running salmonella isolation tests on this raw material and—just as you may have guessed—I found salmonella in nearly 75 percent of the samples.

There were still unanswered questions. If the raw tankage contained salmonella, why wasn't it killed when it was heated in the manufacturing plant? Our tests showed it was. Then what went wrong? We did some more detective work. Additional tests showed that the contaminated tankage was handled in the same carriers after it was heat-treated. You can see what happened. The pellet samples I had been testing were free of any salmonella; it was being re-introduced during packaging.

Things have changed for the better since then. Worried legislators wrote stiff laws that mandate Federal checks at various points between feed and food suppliers, manufacturers, and the finished product. The history of all too many industries shows that meaningful quality-control checks often have to be forced on manufacturers. For the manufacturer that I worked for, the impetus to more thorough quality control came at a high price.

23

Rape Cases: Fail-Safe Test Handling

James A. Terzian, M.D., and
Bettina G. Martin, M.S., HT (ASCP)

Your hospital laboratory *must* be able to provide expert clinical evidence and testimony in cases involving an alleged rape. Here's why. Federal crime statistics show that 67,131 rape cases were reported in the United States in 1978. The charges against many of the defendants in these cases were dismissed prior to trial. Less than 34 percent of the rape cases that did go to trial resulted in convictions. What's going wrong? Many clearly guilty rapists may go free because laboratorians improperly collect or handle evidence that could lead to convictions.

There has been an effort in hospitals all across the country to organize health teams that are expertly trained to collect clinical evidence from rape victims. All of us have a key part to play in this effort. We must be especially concerned with the chain of evidence that we collect. This chain is composed of a number of links, with each link representing a systematic procedure performed by a physician or a laboratorian. The first link in this chain is forged when the victim seeks medical attention. The chain becomes complete after all lab reports have been verified, signed, and turned over to the hospital administrator.

We updated our protocol for maintaining the integrity of the chain of evidence in rape cases. Much of the initial work on this protocol was done by Ellie Bechtold, M.D. First we decided that we needed a locked box in which reports and specimens taken from the victim could be stored when the clinical pathology attending physician or resident could not immediately examine them. We also needed special containers holding all of the forms and specimen collection equipment that must be readily available when a rape victim is physically examined. Our answer to both needs is what we call the medicolegal lockbox. The contents of the box are shown in Table 23-1.

TABLE 23-1

Contents of the Medicolegal Lockbox

Forms

- Consent for pelvic examination
- Physician's record
- Release of information
- Clinical and anatomical lab requisitions to microbiology, immunology, chemistry, and cytology
- Confidential records envelope, preaddressed to the hospital administrator
- A ballpoint pen to complete forms.

Specimen collection equipment

- Sterile medicine dropper for collection of infant cytology smears and secretions for acid phosphatase
- Plain microslides for cytology and gonococcal smears
- Diamond-tipped pencil for labeling microslides
- Paper clips to separate microslides in fixative
- Cytology fixative (95% alcohol)
- Cardboard slide holder for gonococcal smears
- Culture tubes for microbiology
- Plain blood tubes for chemistry (acid phosphatase)

Specimen record book

The following are to be completed:

- Date and hour of examination
- Patient's name
- Physician's *printed* name
- Itemized list of all specimens, including the source of each specimen
- Signatures of physician and witness

Here's how our medicolegal lockbox system works. The attending physician uses the forms inside the box to take the patient's history, obtain signed releases, and order tests. A witness is always present throughout the examination. This witness should be a woman, preferably a nurse or a seasoned laboratorian. We follow these guidelines for obtaining specimens:

A primary laboratory objective in proving rape is verification that spermatozoa are present in cytological specimens taken from the patient. (Caution: All cytological specimens *must* be taken by aspiration, to protect spermatozoa from crushing and air-drying.) The presence of acid phosphatase in fluid specimens collected in the examination may be equally acceptable as legal evidence of rape.[1] In most cases, we also collect medically important smears and cultures for gonococci, and blood for VDRL and alcohol measurements.

The victim's undergarments and outer clothing may also contain important forensic evidence. Retain those portions of the patient's clothing that you believe contain male ejaculate. Label this evidence. Some police departments prefer to test this evidence in their own laboratories. In other areas, the investigating officer or the prosecutor may ask you to perform these tests. Check with your laboratory director if you are unsure of local requirements. Here's a tip: Do *not* fold or crumple these suspect garments. Seminal fluid becomes fragile after it dries and must be handled with care to insure verification of the presence of spermatozoa.

We forge another link in our chain of evidence by labeling each specimen with the victim's full name, the source of each specimen, the determination to be performed, and the date each specimen was taken. The clinical pathology resident distributes these specimens to the appropriate section of the laboratory. The technologist receiving the specimens signs for them in the specimen record book. A written report of these test results, verified and signed by an attending pathologist, is then delivered to the medical records department. Cytology reports are hand-carried to the hospital administrator's office.

The examining physician forges the final link in our chain of evidence. Each medicolegal box contains an envelope that is preaddressed to the hospital administrator. The physician places in this envelope the victim's records, the consent form, and the release form. The envelope is sealed and then hand-carried to the hospital administrator's office, where it becomes part of the patient's confidential record.

Suppose the victim is examined at night, when the hospital is virtually deserted? All important medicolegal specimens and paperwork are locked inside the medicolegal box at the conclusion of the examination. We then place the medicolegal box in a secure area, insuring that the custody will remain unbroken until the hospital administrator and the laboratory crew arrive. The keys for these boxes, by the way, are kept in the locked narcotics cupboard in the emergency room, in a secured area of the clinical pathology director's office, and in the hospital administrator's office.

We have several of these medicolegal boxes available so that one of them can be brought back to the laboratory and replenished while others remain available for immediate use. The contents of each box are periodically checked and replenished by technologists or emergency-room personnel.

At our hospital, the clinical laboratory director and his supervisors are responsible for educating the staff as to the standard operating procedure for the proper handling of evidence in rape cases. A written protocol means nothing unless everyone on the staff fully understands the importance of safeguarding the chain of evidence. We periodically review this written protocol with the day, evening, and night staffs. Policy changes are similarly reviewed, with copies of these changes sent for posting in the hospital administration office and in the emergency room.

Our inexpensive medicolegal lockbox system is a legally sound approach for preserving a chain of evidence that may be used in court against an accused rapist. Knowing exactly how the system operates, our laboratorians are confident that they won't somehow interfere with the due process of law.

1. Schumann, G.B., Badawy, S., Peglow, A., and Henry, J.B. Prostatic acid phosphatase: Current assessment in vaginal fluid of alleged rape victims. *Am J Clin Path* 66 (1976): 944-952

V
LABORATORY SAFETY

24

Hidden Laboratory Hazards

Patricia A. Flury, MT

Safety in the laboratory is a hot item. Hardly a journal goes to press without some mention of the subject, but little is really being done to provide laboratory employees with a safer place to work.

One reason is lack of interest, but in many labs, there is also a lack of understanding about what constitutes a safe laboratory. Furthermore, providing a safe laboratory costs money, and many hospitals are not prepared to spend the necessary dollars.

Another reason for foot-dragging on safety is that, to date, not many laboratories have been inspected by the Occupational Safety and Health Administration, and sad though it may be, it has only been since the Occupational Safety and Health Act was passed in 1970 that anybody has really concerned himself with lessening the dangers in the laboratory and providing a safe and healthy work place for laboratory employees.

However, reluctance and ignorance are no longer an excuse for neglecting lab safety. Federal regulatory agencies are scrutinizing clinical laboratories more closely than before, and it's high time for all of us to put some good, commonsense safety rules into effect in our labs.

Examples of lab accidents. Perhaps by looking at some of the laboratory accidents cited in the 1975 edition of "Case Histories of

Accidents in the Chemical Industry,'' published by the Manufacturing Chemists Association, we can all pick up a few pointers. A number of hazards involving laboratory chemical explosions are examined.

In one case, a bottle of chromous chloride solution exploded on a storeroom shelf, scattering debris into the adjoining laboratory. The top of the bottle was found with the plastic seal intact. Also found were remains of the label—dated 1968! Normal heating and cooling over a period of time probably created moisture in sufficient quantity to react with the solution and build up excessive pressure.

Personnel were at fault in permitting this outdated reagent to remain in stock. This points to the need to have hazardous chemicals clearly and properly labeled with name, date received, expiration date, and particular hazard, if any, indicated. All supply labels should be checked at least twice a year and outdated material disposed of.

Several case histories relate to chemical explosions while a laboratory worker was mixing certain reagents. In one instance, while disposing of waste solvents used for chromatography, a tech added chloroform to a residue bottle containing other solvents, including acetone. The bottle exploded and injured two persons. Technologists should be made aware of those chemicals that are dangerous when mixed together—even in a drainpipe during disposal.

If you've ever wondered why safety experts make such a point about properly securing gas cylinders, the following accident description will give you the answer:

A worker was moving a compressed gas cylinder by scooting it across the floor with one end propped on his shoulder. Suddenly, the valve came off the cylinder, and the worker found himself wrestling with a 215-pound steel monster gone wild. He was unable to hold it, and the cylinder spun and careened around the room, leaving a path of destruction in its wake. A painter was knocked from his scaffold, another gas cylinder was knocked over and its valve bent, concrete blocks were broken loose from a wall, and an electrician made the run of his life with the cylinder in hot pursuit.

Fortunately, there were no fatalities, and you can't help but chuckle a little at the picture of the cylinder on the loose. However, 2,200 pounds per square inch of compressed gas is no laughing matter. The damage could have been far worse, considering the explosive potential of compressed gas. Needless to say, compressed gas cylinders must be properly secured and capped when not in use.

TABLE 24-1

How Safe Is Your Laboratory?

If you're curious about whether you're following good safety practices in your laboratory, take this little test. It's far from all inclusive, but it's a good start. If you can honestly answer Yes to all these questions, you're on the right track.

1. Do you have an adequate supply of personal protection equipment (face masks, shields, goggles, gloves, aprons) readily available and in good condition?
2. Do you have ample safety showers, eyewashes, fire extinguishers, fire blankets, etc.—and is this equipment checked regularly?
3. Are there prominent signs that identify the above items?
4. Is eating and smoking prohibited in your laboratory?
5. Is your laboratory clean, neat, and well housekept?
6. Do you have a safety manual for all employees?
7. Are all flammables stored in containers approved by Underwriters Laboratories or Factory Mutual?
8. Are all electrical outlets grounded? Don't answer this one until you look. There is scarcely a laboratory with all three-prong plugs.
9. Do you have explosion-proof refrigerators in your laboratory?
10. Is your working supply of acids and flammable and combustible materials kept to a minimum (one or two days' supply)?
11. Are all compressed gas tanks properly secured and capped when not being utilized?
12. Do your employees know exactly what to do in case of a fire or accident?
13. Do you have ventilation hoods in those sections of your laboratory where they're needed, such as bacteriology and chemistry?
14. Do your employees in the radioimmunoassay section wear radiation exposure badges, and is there proper disposal of waste materials from this area?
15. Do you have a designated safety officer in your laboratory?

Lacerations. One common accident involves lacerations sustained by laboratory workers and cleaning personnel when removing plastic liners from trash cans. People who drop broken glass or needles into ordinary trash containers are worse than thoughtless. Each laboratory should have marked disposal containers for broken glass and dirty needles, and the contents should not be transferred to another trash container. The entire container should be disposed of daily. (In our laboratory, we use wide-mouth, plastic gallon jugs.)

In our state, a neighboring county has a law that reads: ''It shall be unlawful for any person to discard any hypodermic syringe or needle, designed principally for subcutaneous injection, without first rendering such hypodermic syringe or needle useless by *destruction or mutilation of the syringe barrel and needle.''* (Violation of the law resulting in conviction is punishable by a fine of up to $500.)

In response to this law, many hospitals and labs require techs to break needles before discarding them. Most punctured fingers occur when techs are attempting ''destruction or mutilation'' of needles. Techs should stop this practice immediately and discard needles whole into special containers, as described above. It is management's responsibility to insure destruction of needles thereafter. In our hospital, all discarded needle containers are removed daily by housekeeping to a large, *locked* dumpster in the trash area.

Eye safety. A special safety note from the American Society for the Prevention of Blindness is directed at those who wear corrective lenses. The society urges workers *not* to wear contact lenses if they work in a chemistry laboratory or with caustics or combustibles in any laboratory. There have been cases of fumes or flash explosions that have caused contact lenses to adhere so tightly to the eyeball that large areas of dried cornea were removed from the eye when the lenses were taken out.

Sodium azide. Perhaps the lack of concern for safety in the clinical laboratory is best exemplified by the problems of sodium azide. The potential dangers of sodium azide have been known since 1973, yet little was done to avoid the hazard until newspapers played up an alert issued by the National Institute for Occupational Safety and Health (NIOSH). The NIOSH report noted: ''These explosions have the propensity to propel metallic objects over a wide area and the potential for causing serious injury to exposed workers and others in the vicinity.''

NIOSH also reported a violent azide explosion that occurred during the repair of a constant-temperature bath in which sodium azide had been used as a preservative. Obviously, sodium azide is dangerous. It should be used with extreme caution only by those thoroughly aware of the problem and able to take necessary precautions.

During visits to several laboratories this year, I noted numerous safety violations. A few of the most common were: safety-shower handles placed out of reach; fire extinguishers outdated or inaccessible; food and coffee everywhere; laboratories so cluttered and overcrowded that the hallway served as the storeroom; personnel wearing open-toed shoes, sandals, or sneakers; laboratories with only one exit; poor lighting; poor ventilation; too few eyewash showers, fire blankets, etc., and no signs indicating where they were located; no posted fire evacuation plan; improper storage; outdated reagents; no water fountain; and inadequate bathroom facilities.

Because many employers are so negligent about safety in the work place, enormous power has been placed in the hands of the Occupational Safety and Health Administration. OSHA has enforcement as well as regulatory powers. To date, the agency hasn't flexed its muscles much in the clinical laboratory, but beware.

OSHA inspectors would have a field day in most clinical laboratories. OSHA requires employers to provide employees with a work place *free* of hazards or environmental factors that may cause sickness or impair the health and well-being of employees. The health factors that we should be concerned about are chemicals (use and storage), fumes, acids, biological hazards, housekeeping, personal cleanliness, potable water supply, proper laboratory design, adequate lighting and ventilation, radiation safety, waste disposal, and even temperature extremes.

25

Radiation: How to Keep It Tamed

Christine Woodrum, RT, CNMT

"CAUTION! RADIOACTIVE MATERIALS." This warning sign, which hangs outside the door of our nuclear medicine laboratory, never fails to catch the eye of every medical technologist who walks through the door—the first time.

But after working in the lab for a few months, the tech walks right past the sign without even noticing it. The bright yellow and magenta colors gradually fade into the background and become invisible.

That describes the situation supervisors face in insuring radiation safety in the lab. Of course, we post warnings, give detailed instructions about safe laboratory procedures, and provide the necessary safety equipment. These are stipulated by law. In our lab, we even go beyond what's required. But when people work daily with radionuclides, they tend to stop worrying about the dangers and sometimes start to take unnecessary chances.

The problem is magnified by the fact that radioactive lab materials usually come in a beguilingly ordinary liquid form that masquerades as a harmless solution. To technologists who work with solutions all day, radioactive solutions begin to look like just more of the same. This situation is particularly insidious in the regular clinical lab, where radionuclides are used for blood work studies and other routine procedures, but where there is less emphasis on radiation safety than in the nuclear medicine lab.

In some labs, another factor tends to lull people into a false sense of security. When radionuclides are used only for diagnostic studies—as is the case in our lab—and not for therapy, the amounts handled are extremely minute. Radiation levels are very low, and techs are tempted to think that a little extra exposure can't do much harm.

No one can afford to take this attitude, least of all a supervisor. We already know that radiation—even minute amounts of it—can cause serious disease, including hepatoma, carcinoma, leukemia, and congenital malformations. Though we don't yet know all the long-range effects of radiation, there's no doubt of its gravely harmful potential.

Certainly, we owe it to laboratorians to guarantee that they aren't subjected to any radiation on the job beyond what is absolutely necessary. In fact, we are charged with this task. Your hospital could be held responsible for an employee's health problem 30 years from now—even if the employee quits his job tomorrow—if it can be shown that you failed to enforce accepted safety standards while the employee was working for you.

What can you do? In our lab, we approached the problem from two directions. First, we attempted to eliminate the possibility of any unnecessary radiation by tightening our existing rules and procedures. Then, because there was still room for human error, we stepped up our efforts to develop a safety-consciousness among our technologists. This included updating our safety manual and talking up safety louder and more often at our regular biweekly department meetings.

Regulations. Some of our rules and procedures are mandatory. The Nuclear Regulatory Commission requires them of every hospital laboratory licensed to use radioactive materials. In addition to displaying the warning sign outside our door, we must prominently post the Commission's "Standards of Radiation Protection." We're also required to post a list informing employees where to find our radiation safety manual and our manual of standard operating procedure.

The NRC also instructs us about how to keep an accurate record of every employee's exposure to radiation, limit an employee's radiation total to the required minimum, deal with accidental exposure and disposal of contaminated materials, monitor personnel and equipment to measure radiation, and install and use safety equipment.

In addition, the Commonwealth of Pennsylvania requires us to post its own "Standards for Protection Against Radiation."

These regulatory agencies have valid reasons for their posting requirements. They are responsible for protecting the public against the misuse of radioactive materials. Certainly, laboratorians are a part of that public. The regulations themselves aren't the problem. The problem is to insure that they are carried out to the letter.

Limiting exposure. There are three basic elements to consider in dealing with radiation safety: time, distance, and shielding. During any procedure involving radioactive materials, a laboratorian should be exposed for the shortest possible time at the greatest possible distance using a maximum amount of shielding.

Laboratorians are strictly limited as to the amount of radiation they may receive. For example, during any one calendar quarter, hands, forearms, feet, and ankles may not be exposed to more than a total of 18¾ rems. In our lab, techs wear film badges which record the radiation absorbed on the job. We log totals daily, including time spent moonlighting on other jobs. Every month, we send the film badges back to the manufacturer, who returns a printout for each employee, listing radiation exposure for the month, quarter, year, and total lifetime.

In looking for ways to limit exposure to the shortest time, you naturally try to pare down every laboratory procedure to its essentials so that there are no extra steps to add to exposure time. But what do you do when a laboratorian stops to talk for a minute in the middle of a procedure? These things do happen, and you can't afford to ignore them. In our lab, when a supervisor notices an incident like this, she jots it down and brings it up at the next safety session.

Often, you have similar problems in dealing with the distance factor. In our lab, we work with technetium a great deal—for brain scans, as well as for cardiac, liver, kidney, bone, placental, and lung studies. The laboratorian injects it into the patient's vein in liquid form. When she works with technetium in a vial, she wears gloves and holds the tube with tongs, in order to put as much space as possible between herself and the radioactivity.

Sometimes, a tech decides to save time by holding the vial with her gloved hand, figuring nothing much can happen by ignoring the distance factor for a moment. To prove just what *does* happen, I designed the accompanying illustrations (Figure 25-1), which show the difference in

FIGURE 25-1

Effect of Distance on Exposure to Radiation

The intensity of radiation (I) for a dosage of radioactive material that radiates energy per unit of time (E) is inversely proportional to the square of the distance (d^2) from the source; or $E = I \div d^2$. Suppose a dosage of technetium 99^m radiates 20 milliroentgens per hour at a distance of one foot in air:

Situation I

Then, at a distance of 2 feet in air, radiation would be:

$E = \frac{20}{2^2} = 5$ milliroentgens per hour*

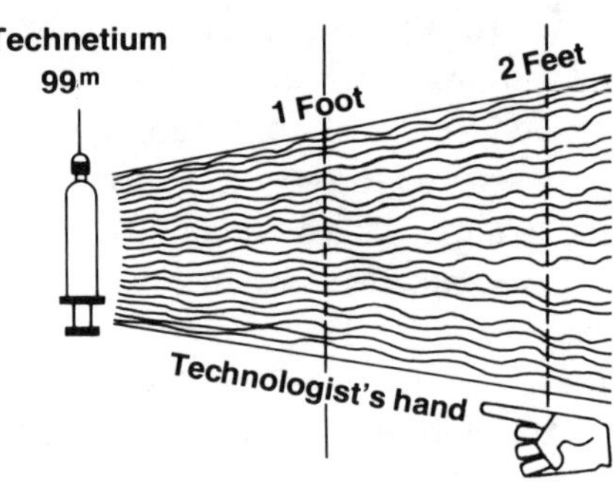

Situation II

And at a distance of ½ foot in air, radiation would be:

$E = \frac{20}{(1/2)^2} = 80$ milliroentgens per hour*

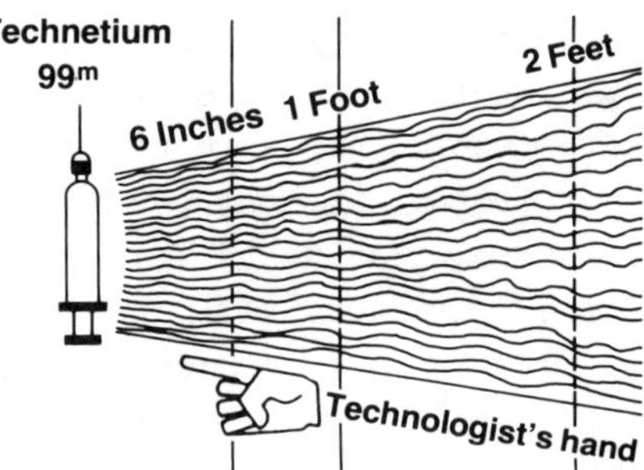

Situation III

At a distance of ⅛ inch in air, radiation would be:

$E = \frac{20}{(1/96)^2} = 184{,}320$ milliroentgens per hour*

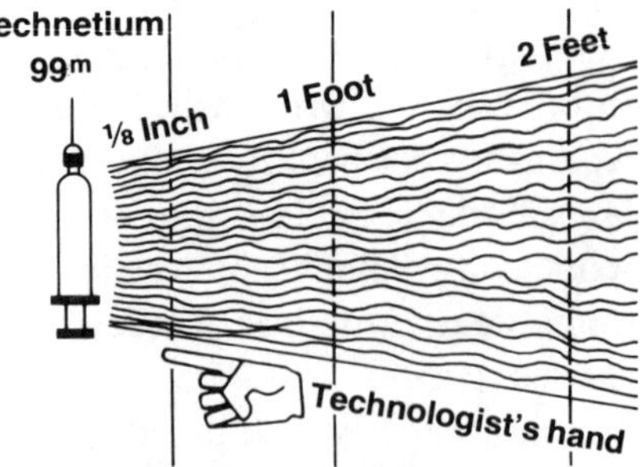

*These equations are for the purpose of dramatizing the danger of working with radioactive materials and do not set forth the specific conditions under which these materials can be used with absolute safety.

exposure that distance makes when a technician is working with technetium-99m.

Suppose a dosage of technetium-99m radiates 20 milliroentgens per hour at a distance of one foot. The tech who uses the tongs to put 6 inches between her fingers and the test tube is exposed to about 80 milliroentgens per hour of radiation, a relatively minor amount. But all radiation is subject to the inverse square law. In other words, the intensity of radiation at a given distance from a source is inversely proportional to the square of that distance. The tech who ignores the tongs receives a dose of approximately 184,320 milliroentgens per hour. When laboratorians can see dramatic evidence of the difference in exposure, they are much more likely to follow standard procedure the next time.

We solved some of our shielding problems by building protection into the system. For example, on one counter we set up a permanent barrier of lead shielding bricks that separates the laboratorian from the vials she is working with. She can reach around the barrier to work with the vials, but the bricks prevent any unnecessary radiation from reaching her. We have made these bricks ourselves—shaping lead into forms about 2 × 2 × 8 inches—and you can, too, if you have an ample supply of lead.

We also do everything we can to shield the laboratorian when she's working with patients. When she injects a patient with a radioactive material, she must use a lead syringe shield—that's standard procedure. But here again, there's room for error. If the shield is the type that wraps around the syringe, it can become worn and crack after repeated use. This happened to a shield we received from a medical supply company during a promotional campaign. Now we use only the screw-on type. But even the best shields are worthless if technologists forget to use them—as sometimes happens. Here again, we rely on graphic evidence during our regular safety sessions to drive home the point that standard procedures are for the laboratorians' own benefit.

As a check on all of our safety procedures, we use a Geiger-Müller counter to monitor every area where we've used radioactive materials. The Federal government suggests that this be done weekly. We think it's important to monitor daily, once in the morning and once in the evening. Just recently, we had to decontaminate the room of a patient, in for a brain scan, who was injected with 20 millicuries of technetium and then went into a seizure, urinating on the floor. We grabbed our emergency equipment from the drum we keep outside the lab door, donned disposable boots, gloves, and coats, and went to work scrubbing the area with decontaminating foam. After scrubbing thoroughly, we still detected contamination.

The problem was the cracks in the tile floor. Finally, we got the radioactivity reading down under the required background level of 0.06 milliroentgens per hour. Of course, this emergency wasn't detected through monitoring. But a daily monitoring would have revealed a few drops of urine on the floor that otherwise might not be noticed.

In some cases, eliminating hazards involves doing away with time-honored traditions—and this may be the toughest task any supervisor has to face. Nobody wants to be the one to forbid life's small pleasures, such as snacking, coffee drinking, and smoking. Although these activities were never allowed in our lab, we didn't succeed in stopping them until we took a firm stand and outlawed them altogether. We just couldn't take the chance of having contaminated material on gloves transferred to the mouth by a cigarette or cup.

Tightening rules. To make the policy stick, we wrote it into our procedure manual and made it clear that any infraction would result in a written warning to the offender. To ease the transition, we installed a refrigerator away from the laboratory area.

After tightening rules and weeding out hazards, we tackled our safety manual. Our lab was now a safer place to work, and we wanted our manual to reflect that fact. Getting everything down in black and white would be evidence to all that our renewed interest in safety was not transitory—that we intended to follow through. Also, it would assure that everyone would be held to the same high standards.

How did the techs react to the new radiation safety rules? We were pleasantly surprised. Instead of feeling resentful, they gave us their full cooperation. It made a big difference that they realized we meant business. But also, I think, they were impressed by the fact that these rules reflected our very real concern for their safety. That was probably the most important factor of all.

26

Setting Up a Lab Safety Program

Gretchen Evenson, MT(ASCP),
and Pamela Krueger, MT(ASCP)

Assumptions can be just as fatal as laboratory accidents. We assumed that most hospital labs in our area had a safety program. We were dead wrong. We discovered that developing safety programs seemed to be at the bottom of their list of priorities, based on a survey requesting details of such programs. And only a handful of replies trickled in.

What does it take to convince our colleagues that a comprehensive safety program saves lives, money, as well as time? Perhaps a few horror stories will help. Later, for those of you who still have not instituted a laboratory safety program, we'll provide you with the details for setting one up.

A lab in our state used a titrator to determine Stat chloride levels. To save time, the nitric-acetic diluent was made in one-liter volumes and stored in a glass container under the counter where the titrator was located. The hood under which they made the diluent was in a room across the hall. This meant that somebody had to carry a large, heavy container across a busy hall and into an equally busy lab. One day, the tech carrying the diluent dropped it. The acidic mixture spread rapidly over the stone floor, making it extremely slippery. The tech slipped and fell as she attempted to pick up broken shards of glass. She was eight months pregnant.

TABLE 26-1

Suggested Topics for a Safety Manual

OBJECTIVES

Each employee, as he is trained in any laboratory department, should be in-serviced in the safety policies as well as the technical procedures. The objectives should state what every employee must know to function safely in the laboratory. All objectives must be completely defined in the body of the manual.

PERSONAL SAFETY POLICIES

Clothing:
Laboratorians work in an environment exposing them to infections, caustic materials, and instrument hazards. Proper attire is mandated. Lab coats will be worn at all times, plus hard shoes covering the entire foot. Jewelry will be minimal. Long hair will be tied at the back of the neck.

Eyes:
Safety glasses or goggles will be worn in designated lab areas. If an eye accident occurs, be sure that effective eyewashes are immediately available.

Personal habits:
Eating, smoking, and drinking will be confined to designated places outside the work area. Frequent hand washing is essential for the safety of patients and laboratorians.

Pipetting:
There will be no pipetting by mouth. Mechanical pipettes and bulbs are available to reduce the risk of infection and ingestion of toxic substances.

TECHNICAL SAFETY POLICIES

Fire:
The lab must have fire extinguishers, fire blankets, and safety sprinklers to handle all types of fires. Each laboratorian must know the location of these devices and how to use them. All fire escape routes will be clearly marked.

Chemical and electrical hazards:
This section of your manual will include what to do for spills, how to properly dispose of chemicals, and how to handle electric safety problems.

Radiation:
Policies governing storage and disposal of radioactive material will be strictly enforced. Laboratorians will be regularly monitored for radiation exposure.

Infection control/Isolation procedures:
Patient isolation instructions must be visible as soon as a technologist enters the room. Instructions for the proper disposal of contaminated cultures and specimens, plus procedures for handling high-risk organisms, must also be clearly posted.

Ventilation:
The lab must have an adequate ventilation system to safely route toxic materials and combustion end products out of the laboratory. Laboratorians will prepare all reagents under a properly ventilated hood.

Compressed gases and air lines:
All compressed gas tanks must be stored in a cool place, away from the main work area. Tanks must be chained to the wall or securely mounted on the floor. All regulator connections will be checked for leaks. Air lines will be monitored for pressure and oxygen content.

Labeling:
All dangerous substances must be properly identified.

FIRST AID

Kits:
First-aid kits will be located in every lab department. These kits will be periodically checked to verify their contents. Laboratorians must know whom to contact when an accident requires medical attention.

Accident reports:
Laboratorians sustaining injuries will fill out forms describing the accident. These forms will ask the victim how the accident could have been prevented. The safety team will use these completed forms as a guide in investigating each accident and determining how similar accidents can be prevented.

HOUSEKEEPING

This section of the safety manual will tell housekeeping employees who work in the lab area how they can avoid accidents. These employees should receive the same in-service training given to laboratorians. Remember: Housekeeping employees see more back corners than anyone else. With training, they can discover problems that could lead to injuries.

This accident never would have occurred if the diluent had been stored in an unbreakable container. And the tech should have realized the danger of slipping and falling on an acid-drenched floor. A comprehensive safety program, with an emphasis on what to do when spills occur, could have prevented this accident.

Another potentially lethal accident recently occurred in our own hospital. We have a unique blood gas lab; it is centrally located and provides services for our surgical and intensive-care patients. A flame photometer for determining potassium levels is in this lab. One day the photometer developed ignition problems. The whole burner assembly suddenly exploded. The force of the blast raised the instrument right off the counter! We later discovered that the explosion was caused by an oxygen leak into the central air line feeding into the photometer. Fortunately, there were no injuries.

This explosion made us examine our safety program. We now take care to continually monitor the central air line throughout the hospital for oxygen content. We went off the central air line in the blood gas lab and now use our own compressors. Several factors may have caused the oxygen leak. We *do* know that this kind of accident will never happen again.

A final horror story. A microbiology tech in a Midwest hospital gave a trainee an unknown organism to identify. Neither the tech nor the trainee knew what the organism was. It was Coccidioides. The trainee was hospitalized with lesions on his lungs. Many of his colleagues who were exposed to this pathogen lost valuable time from work. This tragedy could have been avoided with a safety program that taught laboratorians to treat *all* organisms as potential pathogens.

The need for a safety program in all labs should now be clearly evident. How can you develop one for your lab? The most important step is to organize a lab safety team. This team can eventually work with the hospital's safety committee. To get the widest possible representation, your team should include:

- the administrative technologist,
- one technologist from every major lab department,
- one tech from the evening and overnight shifts,
- a housekeeping employee,
- a security employee, and
- a plant operations employee.

Get information on state and Federal safety standards after your team has been selected. Such organizations as the National Fire Protection Agency and OSHA have helpful publications, as do some lab services/ suppliers.

Your safety committee must then meet on a regular schedule while formulating its program. We suggest meeting once a week for an in-depth evaluation of your laboratory's potential hazards and for the development of a prevention program.

When you have determined the specifics of your safety program, you must present them in an organized and candid fashion. A safety manual is the best way to do this. It can act as a quick reference for handling emergencies but, more important, it can provide all staff members with the policies they must incorporate into their daily routine. Table 26-1 shows suggested topics to be included in your safety manual.

We have found that the best safety program in the world is meaningless unless the safety team makes spot checks to see how laboratorians respond to emergency situations. For example, we have a fire-alarm program. We suddenly drop a sign reading, "I am a fire" near techs in a work area. Then we monitor how long it takes these techs to trigger the fire alarms. You don't have to limit this technique to fire drills. You can use a variety of "I am a ___" signs, since the objectives in your safety manual will spell out exactly what to do in *all* emergency situations.

Even after in-service training, it may be difficult to get your laboratorians to immediately accept a comprehensive safety program. Expect to hear, "I've been doing it this way for years. Why should I wear safety glasses now?" To combat this attitude, send safety team members out on patrols to remind offenders.

What should they say to someone who is violating a safety procedure? Remind the offender that medical technologists are professionals who believe that the patient always comes first. How can a tech truly help that patient if he is sick or disabled as a result of an accident that could have been prevented?

27

How OSHA Operates

Christopher J. Bale

He shocked the laboratory personnel of Good Samaritan Hospital in Dayton, Ohio, when he showed up unannounced.

"You always live with the fear that an OSHA inspector will arrive on your doorstep," said Shirley Pohl, the lab's managing director. "But still it took us by surprise."

The visitor from the Occupational Safety and Health Administration was responding to a complaint about air quality in the histology department. It had been filed by an employee whose name the agency held in confidence.

The inspector's presence touched off mild tremors of panic under waves of disbelief. "Four years earlier, when we built the new lab, we designed everything to meet OSHA requirements," Pohl recalled. "In most respects, we overcompensated. For instance, we put an eyewash and shower station in the blood bank. And here we were being inspected."

Good Samaritan eventually received a clean bill of OSHA health. But its experience underscores the vagaries of life in the era of work-place regulation that began with the Occupational Safety and Health Act of 1970.

Unless a lab has had specific experience with OSHA, it probably lives under a cloud of uncertainties about OSHA enforcement methods. Here is a rundown of what the agency looks for in a complaint, when and how it makes inspections, how it responds, and the postinspection possibilities a lab can expect:

Complaints. Most OSHA inspections are triggered by formal or informal complaints by workers or their representatives. OSHA also

TABLE 27-1

Occupational Safety and Health Administration Regional Offices

Region 1—Connecticut, Maine, Massachusetts, New Hampshire, Rhode Island, Vermont:

JFK Federal Building, Room 1804
Government Center
Boston, Mass. 02203
Phone: (617) 223-6712

Region 2—New York, New Jersey, Puerto Rico, Virgin Islands:

1515 Broadway, Room 3445
New York, N.Y. 10036
Phone: (212) 944-3426

Region 3—Delaware, District of Columbia, Maryland, Pennsylvania, Virginia, West Virginia:

Gateway Building, Suite 2100
3535 Market St.
Philadelphia, Pa. 19104
Phone: (215) 596-1201

Region 4—Alabama, Florida, Georgia, Kentucky, Mississippi, North Carolina, South Carolina, Tennessee:

1375 Peachtree St. NE, Suite 587
Atlanta, Ga. 30309
Phone: (404) 881-3573

Region 5—Illinois, Indiana, Michigan, Minnesota, Ohio, Wisconsin:

230 S. Dearborn St., Room 3263
Chicago, Ill. 60604
Phone (312) 353-2220

conducts "programmed" inspections of high-risk industries, but hospitals and labs are far down this list.

By law, OSHA must follow up any formal complaint with an on-site inspection. Also, its policy has been to conduct an on-site inspection whenever it receives a "serious" informal complaint.

The agency has 10 regional offices (see Table 27-1) and 84 area centers around the country. They are listed under the U.S. Department of

Region 6—Arkansas, Louisiana, New Mexico, Oklahoma, Texas:

555 Griffin Square Building, Room 602
Dallas, Tex. 75202
Phone: (214) 767-4731

Region 7—Iowa, Kansas, Missouri, Nebraska:

911 Walnut St., Room 3000
Kansas City, Mo. 64106
Phone: (816) 374-5861

Region 8—Colorado, Montana, North Dakota, South Dakota, Utah, Wyoming:
1961 Stout St., Room 15042
Denver, Colo. 80294
Phone: (303) 837-3883

Region 9—Arizona, California, Hawaii, Nevada, American Samoa, Guam, Trust Territory of the Pacific Islands:

450 Golden Gate Ave., Room 9470
Box 36017
San Francisco, Calif. 94102
Phone: (415) 556-0584

Region 10—Alaska, Idaho, Oregon, Washington:

Federal Office Building, Room 6048
909 First Ave.
Seattle, Wash. 98174
Phone: (206) 442-5930

Labor in the phone book and generally serve as the initial screening center for employee complaints or questions. Inspectors are based at the area centers.

"The most important thing for anyone registering a complaint is specificity," said Nathan Richmond, assistant administrator for the Philadelphia regional OSHA office. "If there's a problem with fumes, the employee should try to find out the type of fumes, where they're coming from, and other details."

Second, employees should remember that the agency can deal only with health and safety problems. "We get calls on workers' compensation and many personnel issues that are out of our jurisdiction," Richmond said.

Moreover, the hard-pressed agency (complaint inspections are increasing 30 percent a year) asks complainants to use common sense. "Before an employee files with us, we suggest that all possible internal channels be exhausted to resolve the matter."

Inspections. Once a formal complaint or serious informal complaint is registered, OSHA schedules an inspector for an on-site investigation. The law forbids advance notice of the visit to an employer, except in rare circumstances such as imminent danger.

Once on site, the inspector should explain the nature of the complaint and how he plans to proceed with his inspection. After he conducts the necessary investigation, the inspector can either: 1) call the area director and issue the lab a citation on the spot, or 2) discuss the findings and possible citation with the employer and refer the case to the area office for a decision.

"In our case, the inspector was very professional and extremely objective," Shirley Pohl recalled. "He carefully explained everything he intended to do. He told us what tests he wanted to conduct and that he'd want to check the employee health records for any hint of illness related to the possible problem.

"He sampled extensively in the morgue and histology department for xylene, ethanol, and formalin. Before he left, he explained that if we violated any standards, we'd be given a time period in which to rectify the situation, and that we had the right to appeal for an extension. Only if we missed that deadline would a fine be levied. He also noted we had the right to contest the findings, the time period for making the corrections, and the amount of the fine."

Good Samaritan was told it would hear one way or another in three to four weeks. It was closer to nine weeks, and the news was delivered both by phone and by certified mail to the hospital administrator. In this case, at least, the news was worth waiting for.

"There was only one caveat," Pohl explained. "We were warned to be on the lookout for the formalin standard being developed by OSHA. Once that is published, we'll have to be sure we're in compliance, as we were with the other two."

Compliance consultation. "The suddenness of the inspection was somewhat traumatic," Pohl admitted. "But now that it's over—successfully—it's a great relief to know, for certain, that we meet the standards."

Pohl said the hospital never considered voluntarily inviting OSHA in for an evaluation before its unexpected arrival because "that would be like asking the IRS to audit your tax return."

In fact, the law forbids OSHA from "evaluating" a lab for compliance. "We're an enforcement agency, and if we go into a work place, it must be for an inspection," Richmond explained.

Nevertheless, Congress and OSHA recognized the need for impartial assistance for doubt-plagued employers. Currently, OSHA contracts with the labor departments in 24 states (and private firms in the rest) to offer free consultation to employers with specific questions. However, "they don't do a total assessment of compliance," Richmond noted. "A call to an OSHA regional office can get an employer in touch with the proper office. The call is in confidence and won't trigger an inspection."

Standards. OSHA, of course, is responsible for promulgating legally enforceable standards, and employers are responsible for familiarizing themselves with them. OSHA doesn't develop standards aimed at labs or hospitals exclusively, but instead establishes cross-industry categories such as toxic and hazardous substances, personal protective equipment, and so on. Standards are formulated through a series of OSHA advisory committees, then proposed for public comment, reassessed, and issued in final form.

Procedure changes. A General Accounting Office report determined that the agency has been increasingly saddled with demands stemming from the growing number of complaints. To reduce unnecessary inspections, it advised OSHA to adopt better screening methods for informal complaints and also urged Congress to repeal that portion of the law requiring on-site inspections for every formal complaint.

At the same time, GAO criticized OSHA complaint inspection procedures, saying they should not be limited to the problem identified by an employee, but in fact should be a comprehensive survey of all possible hazards.

That means laboratory employees will have to judge more carefully those gray-area safety and health concerns they might want to report. For lab managers, it means the chances of an inspection will be reduced, but the inspections that take place are likely to be more comprehensive.

28

Lab Safety Programs: Voluntary vs. Imposed

Michael Guarnieri, Ph.D., M.P.H.,
and S.R. Guarnieri, M.D., M.P.H.

How safe is safe enough? That question may have no answer. It's hard enough to determine the risk in any activity, much less assign a value to it. But the question holds important implications for clinical laboratories. Supervisors and directors must provide an acceptably safe work environment, and they must be prepared to deal with others' attempts to define what precautions must be taken and what risks may be allowed.

Safety has been a major issue in laboratory medicine for several years, and it seems likely that the subject will receive increased attention in the near future. Until now, the approach to laboratory safety has been haphazard if not irrational. Government regulations have been lacking in some areas, overdone in others, and actually counterproductive in a few cases. Unless laboratorians take the initiative in defining and dealing with the problem of safety, they can look forward to even more stringent legislation and more costly and inefficient requirements.

Several problems unique to the clinical laboratory complicate the already difficult task of risk analysis and reduction. For one thing, laboratories are particularly vulnerable to the efforts of government regulators and private-sector safety lobbyists. Laboratories are highly visible, and their records are open. It's easier for the government to enforce laws covering gram amounts of toxic chemicals in laboratories than those applying to tons of hazardous wastes discharged by industries.

Since laboratories are subject to government regulation in other areas, such as quality control and personnel standards, overregulation in the area of safety may become a matter of course. And although the number of toxic chemicals in the average lab is probably only a fraction of what can be found in the household-products section of a supermarket, laboratories *seem* to be dangerous places.

The early notions of occupational safety involved vague ideas about preventing property damage and personal injury, ambiguous statements about human error, and widespread disagreement about what actually caused accidents. And in the past, government actually resisted involvement in safety matters. Often it took a major disaster to stimulate truly necessary legislation. Much of the resulting law is a hodgepodge of building, plumbing, fire, and electrical codes.

Growth of regulation. Government's involvement in safety regulation grew as government itself expanded. Various agencies began regulating in their own areas of responsibility, and the results have often been confusing, the regulations themselves conflicting. The Joint Commission on Accreditation of Hospitals requires that infectious wastes be burned, but the Environmental Protection Agency's clean-air standards have made most hospital incinerators obsolete.

Growth of a "safety industry" has also spurred the trend toward increased regulation. Manufacturers push hard for laws promoting their products, and the results are often less than rational. In some states, for example, labs must store solvents in metal cabinets. They are large and expensive, and recent studies have shown that wooden cabinets are not only cheaper but safer. The metal cabinets act like ovens, transferring heat to the solvents faster than a burning wooden enclosure would. The cabinets also represent bomb-like threats to firemen.

Perhaps the greatest incentive for a more reasoned approach to safety has come from applying an economic yardstick to human injuries. Although putting a price tag on injury seems to be grim and inhumane, it has helped provide justification for expenditures on safety precautions.

One method, the "human capital" approach, derives a monetary value for accidents by determining the value of future earnings that would be lost as a result of the disability. How much would it cost if an employee developed hepatitis from an accidental exposure? How much would it cost to reduce hepatitis risk by 50 or 75 percent?

TABLE 28-1

A Three-by-Three Safety Analysis for Phlebotomy

TASK: Venipuncture

TYPES OF HAZARDS: Needles, glassware, alcohol, centrifuge, frightened or hostile patients, slips, falls, startled reactions, fainting.

	Before	During	After
Person	Technician properly instructed. Patient calm, not likely to move when blood is drawn. Anticipate subalert reactions.	Patient stable and secure. No distraction from patient's spouse or children.	Patient is all right before leaving. Bleeding stopped. Appropriate first aid for patient distress.
Place	Drawing station free of obstacles, no chance for visitor to slip or bump sharp objects. Drawing chair secure. All supplies on hand and in working order. Building, fire, and other codes met.	Instructions posted in case of emergency. Centrifuge, refrigerator, and sample-storage areas satisfactory.	All work areas clean. Needles clipped and correctly disposed. Infectious material processed.
Task	Samples correspond to request; patient correctly identified.	Correct technique.	Specimens properly stored. Necessary instructions to patient for subsequent specimen collections. Janitorial service informed about disposal practices.

Which would be cheaper: to compensate an employee with job-related liver damage (renal dialysis costs $15,000 to $25,000 a year) or to protect employees against renal toxins? Looking at the problem in this way makes it possible to quantitate or assign dollar values to safety.

Systematic approaches to accidents. Safety experts have taken this approach even further. Using computer models, they analyze the probability of accidents, project what the effects would be should the mishaps occur, and estimate the costs of different protection systems. Theoretically, one can buy various grades of safety.

Theories about the nature of accidents have also changed in recent years. Safety experts have downgraded the role of "human error" and begun looking at uncontrolled energy as the underlying cause of accidents. Burns are caused by uncontrolled thermal energy, for example. Mechanical energy produces cuts and abrasions. Biochemical energy causes disease. Unlike human conduct, most forms of energy can be readily controlled. Failure to control the energy is a failure of the system, not of the person who is a part of the system.

A technologist transferring an infectious agent may be distracted and spill some of the material—a common occurrence in laboratories. Whether or not the incident results in damage or injury depends on the controls built into the system. Were the techniques and equipment correct? Was the technologist wearing protective clothing? If the system is adequate, there are no penalties for the mistake.

Ironically, the new systematic approaches to risk analysis and prevention have opened the door to more governmental regulation. They have given regulators objective standards on which to base their claims of the need for legislation. Unfortunately, although the basis may be objective, the process of developing the regulations is as subjective as any other government activity and as vulnerable to political influences.

Laboratories should take advantage of the new systematic approaches to safety by instituting their own programs. That may also help them avoid having the government impose its often irrational, inefficient regulations.

Perhaps the simplest approach is for the lab to implement industrial hygiene principles:

- Shield people from hazards by using protective clothing, glasses, and the like.

- Shield hazards from people by using hoods, solvent storage rooms, controlled-access refrigerators, and other safety devices.
- Establish and adhere to waste collection and disposal procedures to cut down on the accumulation of hazardous materials.
- Try to eliminate dangerous processes or materials by substituting less dangerous ones whenever it's possible.

Of course, it's not possible to afford total protection through these general measures. A laboratory cannot completely shield employees from exposure to toxic reagents, for example. But a more specific analysis of individual situations within a lab can help you apply the principles and help keep uncontrolled energy to a minimum.

The best person to analyze a work situation is the individual who performs the task. As the one most familiar with the activity, he is best able to assess its risks. And the analysis itself makes the employee more aware of potential problems. The technologist is more likely to remember safety precautions that he helped develop than those that are imposed upon him.

Safety analysis. In our laboratory, we have asked technicians and technologists to analyze the safety aspects and potential hazards of each procedure they perform. In order to do this, they look at three elements—the people, the place, and the task—at each of three points in time—before, during, and after the procedure is performed. Table 28-1 shows an analysis of venipuncture using this method. The method allows almost any potential hazard to be uncovered, from the beginning of the safety analysis to the end.

Such studies also focus on areas that are easy to overlook. In the phlebotomy study, for example, we discovered that alcohol and needles at one drawing station were stored in floor-level cabinets, within easy reach of children who were often in the area.

And by analyzing events through to their conclusions, we have minimized even secondary hazards. We can plan to deal not only with the immediate effects, but also with any others that might develop.

In the case of a hazardous spill, for example, the three-by-three study would make cleanup a part of the protocol—which might be forgotten if someone were seriously injured and being tended to. With someone specifically assigned to clean up the spill, no one else would be injured while the first casualty was being treated.

Lab safety programs like ours, instituted voluntarily on a lab-by-lab basis, are far preferable to regulations imposed by governments. An individual program addresses a laboratory's real needs.

Government regulations, on the other hand, can bring waste and inefficiency, which actually add to the dangers in a lab. The money spent to meet unnecessary requirements cuts into the funds for needed safety equipment, education, and salaries for competent personnel. And voluntary programs such as ours may be the only way to stave off increased interference by the regulatory agencies.

VI
INSPECTION

29

Getting Ready for Inspection

Peggy Leverton, MT

If your lab has never been visited by inspectors, you might as well put out the welcome mat because they're on their way.

Even if the second Clinical Laboratory Improvement Act is never enacted, the Department of Health and Human Services (HHS) will accomplish its objectives through regulation. And one of those objectives is on-site inspections. Almost all laboratories in the country will be subject to the same kind of close scrutiny independent laboratories now undergo.

As of now, some laboratories host several inspecting agencies while others see none. Depending on how large your lab is, where it does business, and the kinds of testing you do, you can be visited by inspectors from HHS, JCAH, OSHA, CDC, CAP, Medicare, and city or state agencies. Or none of the above.

Although some labs will see more inspectors in the future, fortunately others will see fewer. There's currently a trend toward agencies granting each other equivalency. That is, in the interest of efficiency, one agency may delegate its regulatory functions to another when it considers the other agency's standards equivalent to or higher than its own. When an independent lab is both interstate-licensed and Medicare-certified, for example, examiners often conduct a single inspection for both programs. Then instead of having five or six inspectors descend on your lab during the year, you'll have only one or two.

Fortunately, too, most agencies have the same goal—to keep clinical laboratory testing standards high. Although some, like the CDC, are more thorough than others, and some, like OSHA, limit inspections to specific areas, most look for the same kinds of things when they visit. They want to see evidence that your laboratory is handling its testing in an acceptable manner. If you're in shape to pass one inspection, you can probably pass the others.

In any case, it's impossible to prepare for visits from inspectors because what they're looking for can't be whipped into shape in a matter of days or even weeks. They want to see your personnel policy manual, your procedure manuals, and your testing and quality-control records. If you've been informed of an inspection in advance, you'll probably have a week or so to make sure these things are up to date, but you can hardly start from scratch.

Besides, agencies like CDC and OSHA sometimes drop in unannounced and stay for as long as three days. It's pretty hard to prepare for visits like that. The only way you can be sure your lab is ready to pass any inspection any time is to make sure your standards remain acceptable all year round.

I do think it's useful, however, to know what to expect when the inspectors arrive—what they usually ask to see, whom they want to talk to, and what happens if you don't pass. When I worked in a doctor's office that was licensed by the State of California and also by Medicare, I found out what goes on because I personally guided inspectors through three inspections—two state and one Federal.

The state inspections were for California and Medicare licensure during two different years. The Federal inspection was, in effect, an inspection of the state inspection. In developing national standards, the Federal government picked 126 labs at random to evaluate, and ours was one of them. They were checking to make sure we met all the criteria and that the state inspectors had been strict enough.

Before the first inspection, I didn't know what to expect. I read all the laws I could find and checked back through records of previous inspections, but there were a lot of things I couldn't determine myself.

But now that I've been through three inspections and found out what they're like, I thought a checklist might help other supervisors who face their first inspections. So here it is.

Not all items apply to every lab, of course, because thoroughness varies according to the program being checked, but the checklist can be used as a general guide to what to expect from a comprehensive laboratory inspection.

Personnel policy manual. Although personnel requirements differ from state to state and program to program, all inspectors want to see the personnel policy manual. They want to find out whether everyone in your lab is qualified for his job under the program being checked—and in California, of course, this means that everyone must have a valid license.

Make sure your manual includes information about hours worked, overtime, vacations, holidays, and special benefits, as well as evidence of adequate health supervision. In California, the minimum requirement is a chest X-ray and an annual blood test. We also include copies of our laboratory personnel qualification appraisal forms.

In addition to having a licensed laboratory director, Medicare requires that there must also be at least a part-time technical supervisor—a pathologist, Ph.D., or physician qualifying under a grandfather clause.

Procedure manual. This is carefully examined. It must include instructions for blood drawing, finger sticks, urine collection, and culture collection, as well as test procedures.

For our state inspection, we must include the following information: name of test, specific up-to-date instructions, standards and controls used, instructions for specimen collection and handling to insure test reliability, references for technical data, initials and date to indicate annual review by the lab director. If any changes have been written in, these must also be dated and initialed by the director.

Internal quality-control records. The key word in all inspections is documentation, but this is especially true in the area of internal quality control. It's not enough to practice quality control. Your records must show that you do.

To make sure we meet this requirement, we keep records showing standards and control values for every test we do. We record these daily or whenever we run the test, and we include both normal and abnormal controls. We keep a record of the percent transmittance or optical density reading of any test that doesn't involve a digital readout. We check each colorimetric test for linearity when a new lot, reagent, or kit is used. Then we do parallel testing and record the results.

But we can't stop there. We must calculate a monthly mean and two standard deviations for each test, as well as a daily indication of shifts and trends. Inspectors consider manufacturers' insert values for their controls to be only an indicator and won't accept them. However, some manufacturers of control sera offer a computer service that does these computations for you if you mail them a record of your daily control values. They'll even provide you with printed graph forms that indicate the two standard deviation ranges on which you can show the daily shifts and trends.

We must also have a written out-of-control procedure, including a definition of out-of-control, a way of identifying shifts and trends, a method of noting and recording out-of-control results, and a remedial action plan. And we keep a fully documented out-of-control log that explains what went wrong and what we did to correct it.

We need even more records for some tests, such as syphilis serologies. If we do rapid plasma reagins, for example, inspectors check to see if we run a weakly reactive and negative as well as a reactive control. We must be able to show that we check the needle calibration and the revolutions per minute of the rotator on the day of the run.

Our records must show the antigen source, the antigen lot number, and the results of the three controls. The ambient temperature of the lab must also be indicated. And we must have reference materials on hand, as well.

Proficiency-testing results. If your laboratory is required to participate in a proficiency-testing program, the inspectors will want to see these results, so keep them on hand for at least a year. In my experience, these records are examined carefully to make sure that certain commonly performed procedures are within standards and to see if there are any problem areas.

If any test has been outside the two standard deviation ranges twice in a row, expect to be called on it. You must be able to show inspectors that you've been making an effort to correct any problems and haven't been turning out questionable results.

On-site proficiency testing. One of the best ways to check testing in the lab is to see firsthand how it's done. Some inspectors arrive with a test sample and watch while technologists analyze it. Others introduce a sample into the stream of that day's routine specimens. Then the inspectors review the testing method used and check the result to make sure it's accurate.

Instrument maintenance. This is another high-priority item on inspectors' checklists. They want to see a written plan for regular instrument maintenance and a record of when and how this maintenance was carried out.

Inspectors in California ask to see evidence that we inspect all our instruments and equipment semiannually for proper operation and calibration. But they also want to see that we attend to details. When we check line voltages, cords, and plugs, for example, we don't assume the inspectors take it for granted. We put it down in black and white on our records.

These records must also have some indication that we validate all instruments every day or with each use if we don't use them daily. For example, we're required to check our spectrophotometers with a didymium filter and our colorimeters with a solution of known optical density. And our daily quality-control records must show volume checks on automatic dilutors and heat checks on all heat blocks, refrigerators, or instruments with built-in heating elements.

Specimen accession and laboratory report cards. The inspectors want to make sure there is some way of following the results of a patient's test from the original order to the chart. So they check daily records that must show the tests that were ordered and collected, the patient's name, the date, and the doctor who ordered the tests.

We must also keep a permanent lab record and chart copy with the patient's name, the date when the test was ordered, the results of any procedures carried out, and the normal values. If any tests are sent out, we include the name and address of the referral lab with the results. If we run cultures, our lab copy must include a flow sheet of techniques and results used to identify the organisms.

We're also asked to provide an approximation of the number of tests we've done during the year, broken down by each laboratory specialty.

Our billing is checked, too. Whenever we send a test out to a reference lab, the bill must include the name and address of the reference lab with a notation of their charge to us as well as our charge to the patient.

Storage and labeling of reagents. When the inspectors have finished poring over your records, don't be surprised if they take a look into your refrigerators and cabinets. They aren't just checking to see whether you have food in them—although they do that, too. They want to check that all reagents and kits show the dates they were received, opened, and prepared, plus their expiration dates.

Microbiology is another area that requires extensive documentation. During our inspections, we have to show that we check reagents like indole and oxidase for reactivity and deterioration on the day of use with a known positive and negative organism. We must also show that we check all media for sterility and performance when we receive it, even if it's been tested by the manufacturer. And indicator tape isn't considered adequate for autoclaving. We must show that we use live-spore ampules or spore strips.

Safety. This is another area that's examined closely. OSHA sets the standards for all clinical laboratories except those in Federal, state, and municipal hospitals, and it has its own inspectors. But in a comprehensive inspection, any inspector will check your compliance with OSHA standards if they apply to your laboratory.

The inspection includes fire and safety equipment, ventilation, proper storage of dangerous and flammable materials, and acceptable sanitary conditions. Inspectors also look to see whether you have written and posted emergency procedures. They want to make sure you have a running log of illnesses and accidents, including a detailed report of every job-related accident plus an annual survey of these injuries and illnesses.

The inspectors also check for biohazards, using standards developed by the National Institutes of Health. They want to make sure you have fire extinguishers, safety showers, and other required safety equipment in the work areas—and that all employees know how to use them. To find this out, they talk to the employees themselves.

They also check to make sure that food isn't taken into areas where biohazardous materials are handled—and that smoking isn't allowed. They want to see how you handle toxic substances and whether you have negative-air-flow ventilation where it's required. And where bioassay studies are done, they'll look at your method of decontamination.

But this list is far from complete. If you have questions about your ability to comply with OSHA standards for clinical labs, you should get in touch with OSHA directly (see Table 27-1). For a copy of NIH biohazard standards, write to the Superintendent of Documents, U.S. Government Printing Office, Washington, D.C. 20242.

Facilities. Before they leave, the inspectors check the lab's physical arrangements. They note whether lighting, ventilation, and humidity are adequate, as well as work space and overall cleanliness and order.

As soon as the inspection is over, the inspectors give you an oral or written report outlining the areas in which your laboratory is weak or doesn't comply with the law. At the same time, they're helpful about offering suggestions about what measures you can institute to bring the lab into compliance.

The follow-up differs from program to program, but shortly after our state inspections, we receive a written document in the mail. It lists any inadequacies point by point and requests that we file a proposed plan of action along with a timetable for correcting these inadequacies. About a month later, there's a brief reinspection to make sure we've made the corrections.

A final note: If you need help or have any questions about regulations that apply to your lab, call your state health department. It's an invaluable source of information. Or you may want to invest in another excellent source—the current edition of the Laboratory Regulation Manual, published by Aspen Systems Corp., 20010 Century Blvd., Germantown, Md. 20767.

If your lab has never been inspected, you probably have a lot to do to get it ready. Now is the time to start. Then whether the inspectors give your laboratory four hours' notice or arrive unannounced, you can greet them with confidence.

30

We Volunteered for Federal Inspection

Ted Street, M.B.A.

Many hospital laboratories look upon the Medicare regulations and their mandated inspections with misgivings if not outright trepidation. In our hospital laboratory, we know we're ready for them. We've been passing HEW licensure inspections for several years now on a voluntary basis.

While we're not the only hospital laboratory under HEW (now called Health and Human Services) licensure, our situation is rare. We first became involved with the inspections in 1968, a year after the original Clinical Laboratory Improvement Act mandated them for laboratories engaged in interstate testing. Since our work consisted almost exclusively of serving a 750-bed medical center, we were not covered by CLIA '67. But when a nearby independent lab asked us to handle some of their reference work in blood banking and microbiology, we needed HEW licensure in those areas in order to accept.

We received the license for those divisions and maintained it by passing the annual HEW inspection. In 1974, we decided to seek voluntary licensure for the rest of the laboratory. We obtained it gradually, one division at a time, and finished the process in 1978 when our hematology section passed muster.

Why did we volunteer for the additional licensure? For one thing, we saw it as another way of assuring ourselves we were maintaining a high performance level. For another, we expected the CLIA requirements to be extended eventually to hospital laboratories. We were right. We feel our voluntary compliance with the CLIA standards has prepared us for the mandated Medicare regulations that went into effect in November 1978. The two sets of criteria are practically identical. In fact, our HEW (HHS) inspection can count as our Medicare inspection as well.

We did not need a crystal ball to predict what the Medicare regulations would be. They were first published in the Federal Register in September 1974. The Medicare guidelines apply to any laboratory that receives reimbursement under that program. They were equivalent to those set by the Joint Commission on Accreditation of Hospitals, but much less stringent than the CLIA '67 standards. Although the new Medicare standards were published in 1974, they were not to go into effect until November 1978. We decided not to wait.

From the start, we've fared very well with the HEW inspections. In every area, we found we satisfied most of the procedures requirements simply because they represented good laboratory practices. Also, we were already in compliance with the personnel qualifications. Our only major deficiency was in the paperwork needed to prove we were living up to the standards.

Coming up with the required documentation was no simple matter, though. Before seeking licensure in each lab division, we had to completely rewrite the procedure manual. That meant checking and updating references and putting the manual into the mandated format.

We had to establish maintenance logs for our instruments. And we had to revise our method for handling out-of-control results. Instead of merely throwing out the results as we had been doing, we had to keep records showing that they had, in fact, been discarded. We had to create forms to show that we checked temperatures on refrigerators and incubators as often as we did. The supervisor in each division was responsible for developing these and all other necessary records.

Each year when the inspector arrived to check our licensed sections, we asked him to go through one or two additional divisions. In that way, we gradually added routine chemistry, urinalysis, clinical immunology, and hematology to the originally licensed blood banking and microbiology divisions. When we set up our new radioimmunoassay division, we made sure it would pass inspection too.

The inspections, carried out for HEW by the Center for Disease Control, have not been traumatic. The inspector reviews our manuals, maintenance and quality-control logs, and worksheets. He goes through personnel files to assure that competency requirements have been met, and he checks on safety and other environmental factors.

HEW (HHS) does not revoke a license immediately if an inspector uncovers a deficiency. Instead, it issues a warning. The lab must respond within 10 days, stating that the problem has been corrected or detailing plans to correct it. There's also an appeal process if the lab feels an adverse finding is unwarranted. The agency will listen to reason: It changed a ruling against us after we appealed and successfully argued our position.

This incident concerned our quality-control testing of a commercial reagent. The inspector found us deficient for not following the manufacturer's procedure in checking the product. We didn't use the company's technique because we thought it was faulty and that our own way was better. A few letters and phone calls to the CDC convinced them we were right. Shortly afterward, they changed the wording of the regulation in question to allow labs to use their own testing procedure for checking reagents if the procedure is either equivalent or superior to the manufacturer's.

Few well-run hospital laboratories will have difficulty meeting the Medicare regulations for practices and instrumentation. As we found with the HEW standards, most labs should already be up to par—except perhaps for the documentation. On the other hand, the medical personnel regulations may cause a hardship for many laboratories, particularly smaller ones.

The CDC regulations set education and experience standards for most laboratory jobs—from director to aide. Their requirement that supervisors have at least six years' professional experience is likely to be troublesome. Since our lab is large and turnover is low, we have plenty of experienced techs from whom to draw our supervisors. Smaller labs with higher turnover won't be as fortunate. The problem may spill over into labs that do have veteran technologists—when the have-nots try luring them away.

The Medicare inspections should not be too formidable. There may be variations in procedure from place to place, though, because the job is being delegated to state agencies. Our inspections are now being handled by the Kansas Department of Health and Environment, for example. CDC makes spot checks to insure that the inspecting agency in each state is maintaining the Federal standards.

One other aspect of our HEW licensure has been the proficiency testing we've undergone several times each year. CDC sends us unknown specimens, and we analyze them. Significant discrepancies in results on two consecutive tests could mean suspension or revocation of our license. The proficiency tests have not been a problem for us, nor would they be for any laboratory that obtains accurate results as a matter of course.

Complying with the HEW standards has required an expenditure of time and money, although not as much of either as we had expected at the start. Providing the required documentation was the most difficult part for us. But once each department had its record-keeping system in order, maintaining it has not been time-consuming.

In order to meet certain guidelines, we also may have purchased a few special supplies that we would not otherwise have needed. But on the whole, we've looked on our outlay for voluntary licensure as a necessary cost of maintaining excellent patient care.

31

Learning Through Inspections: An Inspector's View

Jackie Blakeney, MT(ASCP)

"The CAP inspector just telephoned. He would like to schedule our inspection for a week from Tuesday. You better give everything a last-minute check."

There was a time when that news would have put me in a tailspin. I would have worried frantically until the day of the inspection that I'd forgotten or misinterpreted something from the checklist. Those days are gone. Now I can greet an inspection from any agency without the least apprehension. Inspectors are no longer a source of mysterious foreboding for me. The reason: I've been an inspector myself.

My title was not actually inspector, but for the past two years I've assisted a pathologist in carrying out CAP inspections. That means I've visited numerous hospital and independent laboratories to evaluate their operations point-by-point. In the process, I've picked up valuable ideas to apply in my own laboratory and learned a lot about the inspection process itself.

The most important thing I have learned is that inspections should not be viewed as formal fault-finding sessions, but rather as opportunities for continuing education. Chances are, if your lab is CAP-accredited, the person handling the inspection will be someone like me. And I know that my main purpose during a visit is to be helpful.

My first experience on the other side of the checklist came two years ago. Four of the six pathologists in my laboratory are certified CAP inspectors, and they handle most of the inspections in southern Mississippi and an occasional one in neighboring states. When one of the younger pathologists was preparing for his first inspection, he invited my chief technologist and me to join him.

I was flattered but somewhat apprehensive about my ability to handle the job. Although pathologists must fulfill certain requirements to become a CAP inspector, as described in the accompanying box, there are no set requirements for inspector assistants. Each pathologist-inspector may choose his own team.

So, equipped with my 10 years of laboratory experience and armed with a well-sharpened pencil and the checklist, I faced that first inspection with a great deal of trepidation—almost as much as I used to feel when I was the one being inspected. Somehow, I made it through that day without any serious problems. My main difficulty was nervousness and, because of that, the tendency to hold too firmly to the point-by-point checklist. Since that time, I've learned to relax and make the most of each experience.

What's an inspection like from the inspector's point of view? Our team consists of the pathologist and two to four technologist assistants, depending on the size of the facility being inspected. Six of our laboratory's experienced technologists participate, taking turns going on the trips. All of us have studied the CAP's detailed inspection manual, and about two weeks to a month before we make a visit, we get information about the lab we are going to inspect.

This material from the CAP describes the lab's previous inspection, including notations about any deficiencies that were found. We also see the lab director's responses to a preinspection questionnaire. All this material gives us a good idea of what to expect and lets us prepare for special situations. If the lab uses an instrument we've never seen before, we have a chance to find out in advance how it works and what we should look for.

The inspections last most of a full working day. While the pathologist meets with the lab director and, in most cases, the facility's administrator, we technologists work with our counterparts. We inspect almost exclusively within our areas of expertise—the microbiologist from our team works in microbiology, the chemist in chemistry, and so on.

We follow the checklists, of course, which run from about five pages for urinalysis to more than 30 in microbiology. (See Figures 31-1 to 31-5.) The questions, which CAP updates periodically, can be answered as Yes, No, or Not Applicable. A negative answer represents a deficiency, and if we mark one, we usually pencil in an explanatory comment. We technologists do not have the authority to award deficiencies on our own. Instead we bring them up to the pathologist, who makes the final decision.

The laboratory being inspected receives copies of the checklist in advance, so its personnel know just what questions to expect. But as I've learned since that first time out, strict reliance on the format is not the most useful approach. I prefer to have an open dialogue that goes beyond the Yes or No answers required on the questionnaire. Laboratory operations are rarely so clear-cut that they can be described in a word.

If I notice something that doesn't seem correct, I feel I should be able to offer some advice on how to improve it. And I'm always open to explanations about why something is set up the way it is. It seems that I always come away from an inspection with an idea for improving my own operation—a helpful record form, an easy way of calibrating pipettes, and the like.

At the end of the day, the inspection team meets briefly to discuss our findings. Then we meet with the director and others from the lab who have participated in the inspection. Each of the inspecting technologists presents the results from his section, pointing out the good as well as the not so good.

We technologists have to be ready to defend our criticism with good sound reasons. We also try to make our comments as constructive as

The Making of an Inspector

What does it take for a pathologist to become an inspector in CAP's Inspection and Accreditation Program? Mostly the desire. According to CAP, any fellow of the college whose own laboratory is accredited under the program is eligible. He may become an inspector either by attending one of the Clinical Laboratory Improvement Seminars, which CAP presents occasionally in various locations around the country, or by receiving on-the-job training from an experienced inspector. In a few special cases, a CAP regional commissioner may appoint a pathologist without prior training to inspect a lab.

possible, offering suggestions for improvements when applicable. These summation meetings must be handled with tact because by the end of the day, we're all pretty tired and nerves can be a bit frayed.

How can laboratories make the most of these inspections? For one thing, they should use them as opportunities for continuing education. That means involving as many technologists as possible in preparing for inspections.

When the advance questionnaires arrive, the lab director should distribute them to the various departments. The supervisor or technologist who will handle the inspection for a given area should not be the only one to see or study the checklists. Individuals who work at the

FIGURE 31-1

CAP Inspection Checklist
Specimen Collection

	Phase	Circle one
Are syringes and needles stored (and disposed of) in such a manner to be reasonably inaccessible to unauthorized persons?	I	YES NO N/A
SPECIMEN COLLECTION PROCEDURES:		
Is there a procedure manual for the proper collection and handling of specimens?	II	YES NO N/A
The manner in which this standard is met may vary with hospital and independent laboratories. The intent is to provide instructions for personnel who are collecting and handling specimens before the specimens reach the laboratory.		
DOES IT INCLUDE PERTINENT INFORMATION WHEN NECESSARY REGARDING:		
Preparation of the patient?	I	YES NO N/A
Type of specimen to be collected?	I	YES NO N/A
Need for special timing for collection of specimens?	I	YES NO N/A
Need for preservative or anticoagulant?	I	YES NO N/A

benches and with the instruments—those who are responsible for implementing the laboratory's basic policies and procedures—should also go over the questions. It's a good idea to schedule a dry-run inspection, too, with the supervisor or senior tech playing the role of inspector.

This advance work does not mean that the laboratory should engage in a mad rush to achieve compliance. It's not possible to change basic procedures in a matter of weeks, and attempts to do so will prove only to be counterproductive. But the preparations let the laboratory clear up minor points and help those who will handle the inspection know what to expect.

	Phase	Circle one
Need for special handling between time of collection and time received by the laboratory (i.e, refrigeration, immediate delivery)?	I	YES NO N/A
Instructions for proper labeling?	I	YES NO N/A
Need for clinical data (age, sex, type of test, diagnosis)?	I	YES NO N/A
DISTRIBUTION OF SPECIMEN COLLECTION MANUAL:		
Hospital laboratories: Is the specimen collection manual distributed to all nursing stations (floors, OR, OPD) and other locations where specimens are collected?	II	YES NO N/A
Nonhospital Laboratories: Are instructions for proper preparation of patients and collection of specimens supplied to all specimen collection areas and physician clients?	II	YES NO N/A

This checklist and those in Figures 31-2 to 31-5 are only a fraction of the entire CAP inspection list. Phase II questions are considered more crucial than Phase I items.

FIGURE 31-2

CAP Inspection Checklist
Hematology

	Phase	Circle one		
Is the anticoagulant used one which will not adversely effect cellular characteristics?	II	YES	NO	N/A
Are capillary samples adequately identified? .	II	YES	NO	N/A
Are specimens checked for clots (visual or applicator stick) prior to testing?	I	YES	NO	N/A
REAGENTS:				
Are all reagents properly labeled and dated?	II	YES	NO	N/A
Are all reagents being used within their expiration date?	II	YES	NO	N/A
PROCEDURE MANUAL:				
Is the procedure manual written?	II	YES	NO	N/A
Is it complete (i.e., includes all tests offered by the section)?	II	YES	NO	N/A
Is it reviewed annually?	II	YES	NO	N/A
Is it available at the bench or in the work area?	II	YES	NO	N/A

Note:
Card files are acceptable for quick reference at the workbench, provided that a complete manual is available for reference and the cards correspond to the complete manual.

DOES THIS MANUAL INCLUDE:				
Patient preparation (fasting, time of collections, or other conditions if necessary)?	I	YES	NO	N/A
Proper collection of specimen (type, amount, timing)?	I	YES	NO	N/A
Proper handling of specimen (preservative, anticoagulant, need for immediate delivery to the laboratory)?	I	YES	NO	N/A

FIGURE 31-3

CAP Inspection Checklist
Clinical Chemistry

	Phase	Circle one		
Does the person in charge of clinical chemistry have education and experience equivalent to an MT(ASCP) and at least 4 years experience under a qualified director?*	II	YES	NO	N/A
Are the results of tests run by the night and weekend personnel reviewed by the clinical chemist, the pathologist, supervisor, or chief technologist?	II	YES	NO	N/A
PHYSICAL FACILITIES: CLINICAL CHEMISTRY				
Space: Is sufficient space provided for:				
The overall workload of the department?	I	YES	NO	N/A
Administrative functions?	I	YES	NO	N/A
Clerical work?	I	YES	NO	N/A
Technical work (open bench space)?	I	YES	NO	N/A
Instruments?	I	YES	NO	N/A
Shelf storage (materials, reagents, and supplies)?	I	YES	NO	N/A
Refrigerated storage?	I	YES	NO	N/A
Is space used efficiently?	I	YES	NO	N/A
Are work areas shaded from direct sunlight?	I	YES	NO	N/A
HOUSEKEEPING:				
Are floors and benches free of clutter?	I	YES	NO	N/A
Are floors, benches, and sinks clean and well maintained?	II	YES	NO	N/A
UTILITIES:				
Provisions should be adequate for the types of procedures done and for the workload of the department in regard to:				
Water taps, sinks, and drains?	I	YES	NO	N/A

*Required for both CLIA '67 and Medicare.

FIGURE 31-4

CAP Inspection Checklist
Blood Bank

	Phase	Circle one
Timer checked at least monthly?	I	YES NO N/A
Speed checked at least monthly by tachometer (mechanical, strobe, or light cell type)?	II	YES NO N/A
Are unsatisfactory instruments (speed or time off, bearings worn, shaft bent, etc.) taken out of service?	I	YES NO N/A

REAGENT CONTROL: EXAMINE THE REAGENTS IN CURRENT USE. ARE THE FOLLOWING IN DATE:

	Phase	Circle one
Anti-A serum	II	YES NO N/A
Anti-B serum	II	YES NO N/A
Anti-A, B (O) serum	II	YES NO N/A
Anti-Rh_0 (D)	II	YES NO N/A
Anti-rh′ (C)	II	YES NO N/A
Anti-Rh_0rh′(CD)	II	YES NO N/A
Anti-hr′ (Little C)	II	YES NO N/A
Anti-rh″ (E)	II	YES NO N/A
Anti-rh″ (E)	II	YES NO N/A
Antiglobulin (Coombs) serum	II	YES NO N/A
A-Cells	II	YES NO N/A
B-Cells	II	YES NO N/A
Antibody screen cells	II	YES NO N/A
Antibody panel cells	II	YES NO N/A
Sensitized cells (Coombs control)	II	YES NO N/A

Current use of outdated reagents is a phase II deficiency except for rare types which may not be commercially available. These must be used with appropriate controls.

FIGURE 31-5

CAP Inspection Checklist
Serology

Does the procedure manual include:	Phase	Circle one
Patient preparation (timed specimens, paired sera)?	I	YES NO N/A
Proper collection of specimen (type, amount, preservative if necessary)?	I	YES NO N/A
Preparation of reagents, standards, and controls (source of supply, storage, shelf life)?	I	YES NO N/A
Methodology?	I	YES NO N/A
Derivation of results (calculation, definitions of 1+, 2+ reactions, interpretation of agglutinations)?	I	YES NO N/A
Controls and criteria for unacceptable control results?	I	YES NO N/A
Notes?	I	YES NO N/A
References?	I	YES NO N/A
Are all changes dated and initialed by the pathologist or supervisor?	II	YES NO N/A
PROCESS CONTROL:		
Are controls run daily with each batch of tests?	II	YES NO N/A
ANTISTREPTOLYSIN TITER:		
Positive controls?	II	YES NO N/A
Negative controls?	II	YES NO N/A
C-REACTIVE PROTEIN:		
Positive controls?	II	YES NO N/A
Negative controls?	II	YES NO N/A
RHEUMATOID FACTOR:		
Positive controls?	II	YES NO N/A
Negative controls?	II	YES NO N/A
LATEX AGGLUTINATION:		
Positive controls?	II	YES NO N/A

Having the bench technologists study the questionnaires and get involved with the preparations is a valuable continuing-education activity for a couple of reasons. For one thing, it provides a review of procedures. But perhaps more important, it demonstrates the rationale behind many of the things they're asked to do in their jobs.

It seems to me that the medical-technologist education programs don't do as well as they should in preparing technologists for the record keeping and documentation that are required for a laboratory's certification or accreditation. Many technologists have little idea of what an inspection entails, and this makes some of the work they do to meet the requirements seem unnecessary or perhaps even silly. Studying the checklists help dispel such misconceptions.

More than 1,600 laboratories participate in the CAP's Inspection and Accreditation Program. Each is inspected every other year, with about 600 pathologist inspectors carrying out the 800 annual evaluations.

The inspectors usually choose their teams from among their own laboratory's technologists. But technologists who know of an inspector from another lab in their area should tell him if they are interested in assisting. Not every supervisor or senior technologist will have a chance to go on inspections, but I'd certainly advise those who do get the opportunity to take advantage of it. On the other hand, any pathologist who wishes can become an inspector. And I'd recommend that they take advantage of that opportunity, too—if only for the benefits it can provide their technologists who get a chance to go along.

My bosses are happy to have me and our other team members involved. They gladly arrange for our release from regular duties and schedule the inspections to fit as conveniently as possible into our lab's routine. CAP pays all our expenses for attending the inspections. We technologists receive notations of our participation for our personnel files. The pathologists also receive continuing-education credits for taking part.

Our greatest compensation comes when it's time for our laboratory to be inspected. We're prepared to meet the requirements, but we're not expected to be perfect. Even the best of the labs we inspect have a few deficiencies. And we know that the person on the other side of the checklist is not our opponent. We've been there many times ourselves.

32

Students as Laboratory "Inspectors"

William O. Umiker, M.D., and
Joseph Meier, MT(ASCP)

In 1975, 1977, and 1979, the years between CAP inspections, our laboratory underwent remarkably thorough self-inspections. The in-house inspections were remarkable in another respect as well: The inspectors were our medical technology students.

We have always encouraged our students to play an active role in the lab. At our 300-bed hospital, we have no separate "practice" or "student" lab, for example, where students perform simulated tests on hand-me-down equipment. Our students train on our best instruments. And once they master the basics, they help with the daily workload: running tests, phoning Stat reports, and taking calls from hospital floor nurses. These added responsibilities motivate the students and help them realize the importance of their work.

In 1975, after the CAP notified us that we were due for a self-inspection, we discussed how our students could best learn from the exercise. We decided that, instead of being observers, the students would act as section supervisors and inspectors and conduct the inspection themselves.

While we agreed that the students could certainly benefit from the experience, we had some reservations about the idea. Would a student inspection live up to the CAP standards for in-house inspections? Could our students understand all the questions on the CAP inspector's list? Finally, would the supervisors go for the idea? Or would they resent having students inspect their sections and point out their deficiencies?

When we talked it over with the supervisors, they agreed to a student inspection, provided that the technologists would take over and repeat the inspection if the students couldn't handle the job. Understandably, they were concerned about the quality of the inspection. After we got their approval, we decided to give the idea a try.

We began by dividing our nine students into two groups. Four served as inspectors, another as chief inspector. The remaining four were named section supervisors, one each for blood banking, hematology, microbiology, and chemistry. To insure that they would know what they were doing, we assigned students only to those areas of the lab where they'd completed their benchwork training and received an acceptable grade. The only area not under student inspection was tissue pathology, which is done by the pathologist.

Next came the preparation. We handed out copies of the CAP checklists to the student supervisors. Our real section supervisors, the quality-control coordinator, and the safety coordinator all helped the student supervisors prepare the forms before the inspection-time deadline.

Meanwhile, the four student inspectors met with their student chief inspector to review the CAP inspector's manual and checklists. During this preinspection briefing, the chief inspector referred students with any questions to the appropriate lab personnel, including the lab director. Since several members of our staff have served on CAP inspection teams for many years, students found no shortage of expert advice.

The inspection came off without a hitch. It took longer than usual, and the students required some help from the staff to complete the inspection. But overall, it was a success—the supervisors agreed that a follow-up inspection wasn't necessary. We were so pleased with the results that we held a student inspection again in 1977 and 1979.

At the summation meeting, students discussed their findings with the supervisors and lab director, just as real inspectors would do after an official CAP inspection.

The students were enthusiastic about their participation. For many, it wasn't only an achievement, but an educational experience as well. Here are some of their comments:

"It made me realize how much more is involved in a laboratory than merely performing routine analyses."

''The quality control and safety measures are much more complicated than I thought.''

''I never realized how much I didn't know about laboratory operations and guidelines.''

''There are many aspects of the laboratory that cannot possibly be learned in one year. This inspection brought to light some of these hidden activities.''

The section supervisors, while not as enthusiastic as the students, agreed that it was an adequate inspection of the lab. The technologists who were most critical of the students' inspection were the same ones who criticize the students' benchwork performance most severely—and for that matter are most critical of the official CAP pathologist inspectors. For the technologist who is used to being regarded as infallible by his students, it probably wasn't very palatable having them point out his deficiencies.

Looking back on our student inspections, we've noticed some encouraging results. Student inspections have uncovered more deficiencies in our lab than the outside CAP inspectors did during their inspections. Students detected some things that outside observers could not. For instance, while performing their benchwork assignments, students noted a technologist who skipped logging a daily equipment temperature reading and recorded two days' readings with one day's finding. (In our lab, we call this practice ''QC sink testing.'') The students also claimed that they saw some mouth pipetting, although the supervisors maintained this is never allowed.

In its guidelines, the CAP emphasizes that laboratory personnel should learn from an inspection—they should learn the causes of deficiencies and how to correct them. It's obvious, of course, that students don't have the expertise to provide this sort of instruction, and we certainly aren't suggesting that students should ever replace outside inspectors.

But for self-inspections, we feel that students can be competent inspectors. Since we're always checking for problems developing in our lab, self-inspections don't usually reveal any striking surprises—whether they're conducted by students or staff. Our real learning experiences result from outside inspections. Indeed, the chief benefit of an official CAP inspection has always been the fresh outlook and expert advice from inspectors who can offer many suggestions for correcting deficiencies.

Since our last student inspection, we've come up with some ideas for improvements. Our biggest problem has been getting the students adequately prepared. For our next self-inspection, we will give the students more time to prepare and also hold formal meetings with the lab director so he can brief the students on everything he expects to be accomplished. We're also going to stress the importance of tact and courtesy to the students. Some of the technologists have felt that a few students took advantage of their temporary authority and became too demanding.

We're also thinking of pairing each student with an experienced technologist who would serve as the student's advisor. We're even considering a student inspection for CAP inspection years, as a dry run before the official one.

A final piece of advice: If your students or supervisors don't go for the idea of a student inspection, don't push it. Although it worked in our lab, that's no guarantee it will work in yours. But if you do decide to use students as inspectors someday, you might well find that will be the day your students mature into responsible laboratorians.

VII
LABORATORY FRAUD

33

A Lab That Went Wrong

Jane C. Monaghan

Laboratory fraud makes headlines, and sometimes more than headlines: It has also been the subject of television exposés, Congressional hearings, and countless legislative efforts on both state and national levels.

Some laboratorians feel that all this adverse publicity is unwarranted and that the vast majority of laboratories do good, honest work from which they reap honest profits. They complain bitterly that the few dishonest people in clinical laboratories are making the whole profession look bad.

One New Jersey laboratory inspector forcefully takes issue with that point of view: "I'm sick and tired of the tut-tut attitude I hear from people and read in most journals—that there are a few bad eggs, and we're all getting blasted because of them. Well, in my experience, it isn't just a few bad eggs. And as far as financial skulduggery goes, it's pretty widespread."

The controversy points up one important fact: Laboratory fraud is a subject that must be carefully examined by laboratorians themselves as well as by outside inspectors and investigators.

This is the story of one laboratory that made unpleasant headlines. If we can learn what set of circumstances combined to permit abuse, perhaps we can also learn what might be done to prevent it.

On Sunday, March 14, 1976, the headline, "Lab Accused of Faking," was bannered across page one of *The Record,* a major suburban newspaper in affluent Bergen County, N.J. The laboratory in question: Englewood Clinical Laboratories, an independent lab in Englewood, N.J., a populous suburb of New York City. The story: In sworn statements, two technicians who had worked in the lab said they had been told to write in normal results for certain tests without performing them, and another tech was instructed to write up phony quality-control charts before a state inspection. And there was more. Much more. The two-part report was the result of months of careful investigation and exhaustive research. It was some story.

The reporter who wrote it had been alerted to the possibility of finding laboratory abuse—and a dramatic story—when the New Jersey State Commission of Investigation held hearings on Medicaid fraud in June 1975. During those hearings, the commission learned that "potentially dangerous conditions and techniques" existed in 20 of the 500 labs in the state. The newsman found one of them in his own backyard.

Englewood Clinical Laboratories was essentially a one-man show. Its owner, Harry Pieratos, was a hardworking, ambitious man who had worked his way up in the laboratory world. He had started his career in hospital laboratories, but for the past 18 years, he had owned and operated his own labs. From his first one-room lab with $200 worth of basic equipment, he'd progressed to an eight-room facility equipped with multichannel analyzers and cell counters. He was chief tech, supervisor, and for all practical purposes, "management" since the physician-director spent no more than about 14 hours a week in the lab.

According to Pieratos, the laboratory had 20 full-time and part-time employees. State inspectors evaluating the lab for Medicare certification listed 12 qualified technologists and technicians. This staff ran tests daily on upwards of 500 or 600 specimens, picked up by lab delivery men from about 130 doctors in the area. Precise daily workload figures were difficult to determine, state inspectors said, because there was no accession book, as such. Separate books or parts of books were kept for each physician, medical group, or nursing home. But whatever the actual workload was, it was too much for the staff. In the words of the state inspectors: "The laboratory does not employ sufficient personnel to handle the workload demand."

The laboratory offered its physician-users a full range of services in chemistry, hematology, serology, bacteriology, and antibody screening (in some cases, regardless of its qualifications to do so). The specimens were picked up on one day, and results were sent back on the next. Fast service and low prices were apparently what sold doctors on the lab.

Fast service and low prices were also what got the lab in trouble. New Jersey's Assistant Commissioner of Health, Division of Laboratories and Epidemiology, Dr. Martin Goldfield, sees it this way: "When a laboratory and all its people know that it's a money mill, it's hard to convince them that it's the results that are important. It's easy to develop attitudes that justify the idea that if something breaks down, they can write in a fictitious result because of the time and money pressures."

Whatever the reasons for doing it, there's ample evidence that fictitious results were commonly written in at the laboratory. Not only did lab employees give sworn statements to that effect, but state inspectors on their Medicare certification visit found numerous instances of employees entering in patient records results different from what were shown on instrument printouts. "When we had the opportunity to compare patient results copied onto worksheets with the corresponding results on those printouts . . . we found very many serious discrepancies."

This is only one of 47 deficiencies that the inspectors found. Many others, detailed in 19 single-spaced, typewritten pages, are equally disturbing. Here's a brief sampling:

"Suitable records of real test results are not maintained since all instrument printouts are destroyed almost immediately."

"Laboratory still performs all bacteriology [including Medicare and Medicaid specimens] on the premises although certification in this specialty was deleted on Feb. 17, 1975."

"Culture methods used are totally unacceptable."

"The laboratory manual is completely unacceptable. It consists of a mixture of old procedures no longer in use and new methods that are in use. . . . Some methods do not appear at all, and none indicate review by director or supervisor."

"The laboratory accepts specimens that are obviously unfit for analysis. For example, we observed: a prothrombin time specimen that had been collected, and stored unseparated, two days earlier . . . we observed a specimen accepted for blood culturing that consisted of a drop of clotted blood at the bottom of a nonsterile Vacutainer tube."

"Records documenting the routine precision of each method are of dubious value since control records sometimes show results for days on which the laboratory is closed. . . ."

"Control limits for standards and reference samples are not recorded and displayed. . . . Nothing like an out-of-control result ever appeared on any of the control worksheets, although . . . we observed, on printouts that had not yet been destroyed, control results that were out by as much as 100 percent. More important, there was no documentation of action taken to check the obviously spurious patient results (most were, like control, 100 percent higher than median normal value), although these results had been copied onto worksheets as normal values."

The Medicare survey of Englewood Clinical Lab was conducted on Dec. 4 and Dec. 9, 1975, and the laboratory's proposed plan of correction was returned to the state Department of Laboratories on Feb. 5, 1976. Pieratos said that corrections would be made by Feb. 15, and the state inspectors made their postcertification revisit on Feb. 27. Their findings: Thirty-three of the 47 deficiencies were uncorrected. The very first item on the revisit report is indicative of the whole: "It is evident from the uncorrected deficiencies documented below that the laboratory director still does not spend an adequate amount of time directing and supervising the laboratory."

This second report documented again such deficiencies as inadequate personnel, poor specimen labeling and handling, inaccurate reporting of results, accepting unfit specimens, and "completely unacceptable" quality-control and laboratory manuals.

On March 16, the principal medical technologist conducting the surveys recommended that Medicare certification be denied the laboratory. That recommendation was approved and forwarded to the regional Bureau of Health Insurance office in New York City, and that certification was officially terminated on May 1. The laboratory, however, had already shut down operations in April.

You're no doubt wondering how such conditions could exist in a laboratory. How could it continue to operate like that? Why was nothing done earlier to close the lab? What about all the rules and regulations that *you* routinely follow? Why not this laboratory?

Let's try to answer some of those questions. Until very recently, clinical laboratory regulation on the state level in New Jersey (and many other states) was not adequate "to safeguard the public's interest and insure that the performance of laboratory services meets high standards of public health care," as the state Commission of Investigation described it. That observation was part of a lengthy statement prepared by the Commission, in April 1975, to urge passage of the New Jersey

Clinical Laboratory Improvement Act. In July 1975, that act did indeed become law, but because of bureaucratic red tape and a lack of adequate funding to get the program off the ground, it had not been completely implemented a year later.

All right, then, what about Federal controls? If states don't regulate laboratories strictly enough, what about Medicare regulations and CDC regulations under CLIA 1967? Englewood Clinical Lab had been certified to do Medicare and Medicaid testing, and the lab had passed certification inspections with only minor deficiencies in 1973. In 1974, more serious deficiencies were noted, and the lab was requested to withdraw from bacteriology testing for Medicare. The state inspectors, however, have only the power to inspect and report such deficiencies. Enforcement of the Medicare law and disciplinary actions are a matter for the Federal government. In this case, as the inspectors reported in their last visit, the laboratory was still performing bacteriology tests—and presumably getting paid for them—even though their certification had already been rescinded in that specialty.

The tougher and more strictly adhered-to standards of the Federal CLIA 1967 didn't apply to Englewood Clinical since it was not engaged in interstate commerce. Interestingly enough, the lab had sought a CDC license and been denied it.

So there you have it, a pattern of regulations and standards that this laboratory was able to skirt or avoid altogether: state regulations that weren't stringent enough, then passage of a state law without the means to implement it; Medicare regulations that the Federal government finds difficult, if not impossible, to enforce; and CDC standards that apply to all too few laboratories.

Stricter and more strictly enforced regulations aren't the only answer to lab fraud, and many conscientious laboratorians find them a pain in the neck, but a pathologist in a CDC-licensed laboratory had this to say on the subject of regulations:

"For many years, I complained about the detail involved in the Federal regulations, but I've found that as we grew larger, they really only forced us to do what we'd have had to do anyhow. You can only depend on the goodwill of the technical staff to a certain point, and then you need records and documentation."

Ignored and unenforced regulations aren't the whole Englewood Clinical story, either. To explain it more completely, we must take a closer look at the cast of characters playing out that story.

The laboratory director. Mark Mankoff, M.D., is a board-certified pathologist and, under the old law, the only person in the lab who must be licensed by the state. That license is issued by the state Board of Medical Examiners, and until 1973, any physician could automatically qualify as the director of a laboratory. Dr. Mankoff was also the part-time director of a laboratory in Bronx, N.Y., and he had a private practice of psychiatry (yes, psychiatry) in New York City. "What you have here," says Assistant Commissioner Goldfield, "is an example of a very common practice—someone directing a lab on paper. He didn't really direct it and claims total ignorance of what went on."

Adds Joseph O'Brien, M.D., of Metpath, a major independent lab in New Jersey, "I have very little sympathy for the position he finds himself in. For a fee, he allowed his name to be used, and I can't be sympathetic with that. If you're responsible for the output of a lab, you're responsible. And that means totally responsible. There's no way of shirking it. Generally speaking, part-time directorships aren't very useful arrangements, and I think they're much to be discouraged."

Another New Jersey pathologist had been approached by the lab owner some years ago and asked to take the post of part-time director of Englewood Clinical. "I turned it down. It was just too much money for too little on my part. The in-house duties would have been negligible, and as I recall, the salary that he mentioned was $40,000."

As for disciplinary action, that power lies with the Board of Medical Examiners. It could revoke or suspend the director's license and fine him up to $500 for each instance of unprofessional conduct.

The lab owner. Characterized as energetic and hardworking, Harry Pieratos was a self-made man who literally carved his own success in a competitive, highly specialized, and fast-changing business—running an independent clinical laboratory. And the place was run like a discount outlet—the main criteria being to move the merchandise and make money. Proof that the lab was profitable came from Pieratos himself in an interview. Explaining away the technicians' statements that they had been instructed to fake tests, he suggested it was because they were jealous of him. "Those boys, they see me with the big cars, the big house (reportedly worth $160,000 in 1976); they resent it."

One physician-observer of the case described the basic problem thus: "It's poor perception of what it takes to run a quality lab." His statement is amply documented in the Medicare certification reports: hit-or-miss scheduling and poor personnel records, complete lack of attention to quality control, disastrous record keeping, and faulty reporting of results.

Oversight? Carelessness? Deliberate fraud? The authorities would have to determine that.

The technicians. What would you do if you worked in a laboratory that you suspected was turning out false reports? Or doing poor work? Would you quit? Would you report the conditions you saw? To whom? What kind of documentation would you need? Falsifying patient records is a serious accusation. Could your motives be suspect if you reported it? Could you be blackballed from other labs if you made such accusations? Or maybe, if you were young, inexperienced, and just working part time to earn some extra expense money, you might think it was "just the way they do things here," as some of the techs at Englewood Clinical admitted in the newspaper report.

Medical technologists and technicians are in a spot when they see irregularities in a lab. They fear—and with some reason—that their employer or others in the laboratory field might take it out on them somehow if they describe to the authorities practices that don't conform to accepted standards. That's why the ASMT urged inclusion of an employee-protection provision in the pending Clinical Laboratory Improvement Act. This provision would keep an employer from discriminating in any way against an employee who testified or helped in an investigation of his laboratory.

Dr. Paul A. Brown, chairman of the board of Metpath and an ardent advocate of the stricter quality-assurance program embodied in CLIA, sees the technicians as the real heroes in the Englewood case. "They're the only reason the lab was caught," he told me. "They put their moral convictions ahead of their economic position, so to speak, and that's an important point to make: Lab techs are professionals. If they want the respect that's due them as professionals and if they're being paid as professionals, they should function as such. I give those people who brought it out in the open at Englewood Clinical a lot of credit.

"One irate technologist is one thing," he continued, "but when you have a group of techs who are concerned professionally, then you've got something to work with. As a competitor with that lab, I can't say anything about it. Nobody would believe it—one laboratory complaining about another. Even when I testify at Congressional hearings, I'm sticking my neck out because people accuse me of having my own ax to grind. But a technologist has no such competitive interest.''

Dr. Goldfield of the New Jersey Division of Laboratories believes that the techs could have gone still further: ''Those technicians would have done well to call our people immediately and describe what was going on. We would have honored their confidentiality, investigated their allegations, and uncovered the problems there long before we did—we had suspected problems there for some time.''

In principle, then, there's little disagreement that technologists should contact the authorities and disclose any irregularities they know about. In practice, that's much more easily said than done. It takes nerve, a knowledge of whom to contact—and a lot of professionalism.

The physicians using the lab. If doctors suspect that the lab they're using doesn't do quality work, they have an effective way of showing their disapproval: They can take their business elsewhere.

But in the case of Englewood Clinical, the lab seemed to have a loyal following of physicians, and the lab's markedly lower prices were a recurring theme with people who commented on the case. Would a physician let price alone determine the lab he uses? This story Dr. Brown tells suggests the answer: ''I was talking to some well-trained physicians here in New Jersey and told them the lab they were using was poor. One of them said to me, 'Look, I know it's poor; last week I sent them a sample of colored water and got back a complete blood count. But they're charging me 50 cents for a blood count, and you're charging me \$3.' '' Rhetorically, Dr. Brown asks, ''What do you say to that?''

What many observers might think about it is that the doctor would probably charge his patients the same \$4 or \$5 for a blood count, regardless of where the work was done. The difference being, of course, that he'd pocket \$2.50 more if he sent it to the lab with lower prices.

Both Dr. Brown and his associate, Dr. O'Brien, feel that private practitioners should know more about the labs they use. ''They're placing a large portion of their clinical judgment in the hands of an outsider,'' O'Brien points out, ''and they should take the time to visit the laboratory they're using and get some insight into its operation.''

''A doctor would never think of sending a patient to a hospital he knows nothing about,'' adds Dr. Brown, ''but they seldom bother to evaluate laboratories. Some 10 percent of the national health-care dollar is being spent on lab work, and the average doctor may spend some

$3,000 to $5,000 a year on lab testing—he should take an interest in where that money is being spent.''

Still another economic element must be considered in this case—and in the case of any lab profiting from poor work—and that's the reimbursement system third parties developed to pay for lab work. ''If we tried to, we couldn't have set up a system that begged for more misuse,'' says Assistant Commissioner Goldfield.

''First of all, it's based on the concept of payment per test, so that cost-effectiveness, such as automating and charging by the panel, is actually discouraged. A laboratory can realize greater profit if it charges by the test—even though testing may be done on multichannel automated equipment—and this kind of abuse is common. Another common trick is charging for a more expensive test—such as the old rabbit test for pregnancy—and actually performing another cheaper one, in this case the two-minute slide test.

''Moreover, third-party payers have taken no interest in stopping such practices. They are more interested in competing for Federal dollars. If they can show the Government how cost-efficient *they* are, by having the lowest administrative costs in relation to total disbursements, they strengthen their position as the Government's fiscal intermediaries. The more they pay out, the better they look.

''What we have, then, is a reimbursement system creating inordinate profits in the laboratory; they, in turn, lead to great self-interest in increasing the workload and all the abuses that can precipitate, including everything from sink testing to kickbacks and other illegal payments. The end result of all this is a corruption of the entire independent laboratory process, and we have found this condition to be widespread.''

Now that New Jersey has its Clinical Laboratory Improvement Act, it should be more difficult to do anything illegal. But there are problems in administering the law.

''The main problem is money,'' says Dr. Goldfield. ''I understand that the newspaper spent about as much in six months investigating that one laboratory as we have in our budget for a year. Estimates show that you need about $1,000 per lab to get a program like ours off the ground, and the budget [for the first year] is $90,000—or about $180 for each of the 500 labs in our program. I couldn't at first even offer a prospective director of the program a competitive salary.''

Dr. Goldfield's department was hampered by the red tape involved in establishing a licensure procedure and licensure fees, to say nothing of the actual process of licensing the state's laboratories. As he points out, it was difficult to use the powers in the law to suspend or revoke a lab's license when the lab hadn't yet been granted one!

But Englewood Clinical was closed and had to meet certain requirements before it could reopen. Among them, said Dr. Goldfield, "The laboratory must demonstrate its ability to perform adequately and in the public interest before we grant it approval. Further, we're not permitting any lab to open even with a licensed director until that director provides us with a signed, fully documented statement describing how much time he'll spend in the laboratory and assuring us that he's aware of the responsibilities he's undertaking."

From this, it looks as if the right steps have been taken to tighten up on the directors and managers of laboratories in the state—and they, after all, are legally responsible for the lab. All laboratorians, though, should remember that they share the responsibility for what goes out of the lab and, if necessary, in their duty to report practices that aren't in the best interests of patients whose work is being done.

By way of a wrap-up, let's look at what happened to the characters in the story. Dr. Mankoff, the lab director, resigned his post, claiming he didn't have the necessary time to correct the deficiencies since his position with the lab was part time.

The owner, Harry Pieratos, after denying test faking and claiming he was the victim of a smear campaign, put the lab up for sale and took a vacation.

The laboratory was ordered to pay $23,000 in fines—$100 for each of 230 instances of failing to report a positive VDRL. As a spokesman at the state health department wryly commented, "That just shows you the level of regulatory authority we've had—if the only thing we can nail them on is a failure to report at $100 a clip."

And even though it was surrounded by scandal, the lab drew prospective buyers. Now, under new ownership and directorship—and a new name—it has received provisional state approval to reopen for limited testing only.

While some of the circumstances—like the reimbursement system—that gave rise to abuses in this lab remain unchanged, others have improved. Let's hope that the improvements will prevail. Let's hope, too, that the telling of this story will persuade other laboratorians to speak up like the professionals they are whenever and wherever they see abuses.

34

Theft of Services: The Lab That Never Was

MLO staff

On June 25, 1976, two New York pathologists pleaded guilty to criminal charges stemming from a laboratory theft-of-services case. Since the case did not go to trial, some of the details may never be known. But what is known adds up to another flagrant example of laboratory abuse.

The story begins in 1972, in Mount Kisco, N.Y. This small town is located in upper Westchester County, less than an hour by car from New York City. It is a town that abounds in physicians, and a private clinical laboratory had just been formed: Consulting Pathologists Laboratory, Inc. The principal officers of this corporation were Martin Lefkowitz, M.D., and Naomi Kaplan, M.D.

CPL, as the laboratory came to be known, did not occupy the two principals on a full-time basis. Dr. Lefkowitz was also head of the division of pathology at the Westchester Medical Center, in nearby Grasslands. Dr. Kaplan also had other employment. She was director of laboratories at the Peekskill Community Hospital and the Julia Butterfield Hospital, both private hospitals.

CPL was utilized mainly by general practitioners. A CPL messenger regularly picked up specimens at the offices of physicians. Test results were said to have been highly accurate. Delays were unheard of. Prices were most reasonable.

CPL performed a variety of clinical tests, but its specialty appears to have been histology. The generalist who referred tests to the laboratory knew that he had immediate rapport with highly qualified pathologists. Whether the case involved a sebaceous cyst or a wart, Dr. Lefkowitz or Dr. Kaplan was readily available when an informed opinion was required.

CPL and its two principals enjoyed an excellent reputation for more than two years. But in December 1974, ugly rumors came to the attention of the authorities. The Westchester County Parkway Police heard the first of these rumors. It was alleged that a substantial portion of CPL's histology work was being done by county technologists, on county time, at the Westchester Medical Center in Grasslands. It was said that Dr. Lefkowitz was paying some of his county employees "a little something extra" to perform CPL's tests.

The county police are not equipped for a full investigation into such a rarefied area as questionable laboratory practices. However, they took the case as far as they could. At the same time, an internal auditing procedure was being undertaken at Grasslands by Dr. Joseph A. Cimino, the county health commissioner.

The investigation. In early 1975, the evidence developed by the police and Dr. Cimino was forwarded to Carl A. Vergari, the county district attorney. Vergari assigned the case to Arthur L. Del Negro Jr., chief of the frauds bureau. Del Negro passed the case along to Martin E. Smith, his deputy bureau chief.

Smith reviewed the evidence and determined that he had grounds to request two search warrants. The places where Smith wanted to conduct searches were: Consulting Pathologists Laboratory, Inc., in Mount Kisco, and the county laboratory facility under the control of Dr. Lefkowitz, at Grasslands.

The search warrants were simultaneously executed at 1 p.m. on Jan. 31, 1975. An assistant district attorney named Jonathan Z. Friedman was one of the officers who entered CPL's offices. Friedman brought an informed presence to the proceedings; he had once worked as a lab assistant at the Brooklyn State Hospital.

"It was while I was in college, and later in law school," Friedman recalls. "I worked summers in chemistry, hematology, and histology. I also did a bit of cytology. When we had autopsies, I worked in the autopsy room."

CPL was located on the third floor of a red brick medical building. Here's how Friedman remembers it:

"They occupied one large room, with a dividing partition and a small front office. One technologist was on duty. The lab was outfitted to perform cytological tests. Cytology work was, in fact, being done on the premises. But as far as histology work was concerned, the technologist employed by CPL was not fully qualified to perform histological tests. We believe that there was no activity at CPL other than cytology."

Friedman and his colleagues identified themselves to the startled tech, displayed their search warrant, and then started bundling up all of the items cited in the warrant. The county police drove off with half a vanful of slides, documents, and books.

Del Negro, Smith, and a detachment of investigators entered the county lab facility at Grasslands, while Friedman and his squad of police conducted their search at CPL. Here's how Del Negro recalls the scene:

"We were looking for histological specimens embedded in paraffin blocks. Bottles, vials—all preceded with the letter 'X.' We had information that work being done for CPL at Grasslands was shown in the county accession books preceded with the letter 'X.'"

The district attorney's men returned to the courthouse at the county seat in White Plains. They spent the next six weeks cataloging their evidence, guided by experts in the laboratory field. By March 1975, they felt that their case was strong enough to present to the grand jury.

The indictment. The grand jury heard the secret testimony of 41 witnesses as it considered the prosecution's case. Dr. Lefkowitz and Dr. Kaplan waived immunity and testified at length before the grand jury. It was also during this period, in April 1975, that Dr. Lefkowitz was removed from his $49,000-a-year position at Grasslands.

On May 12, 1975, the grand jury voted a 39-count indictment against Dr. Lefkowitz, Dr. Kaplan, and CPL. The two physician-defendants were accused of:

- Twenty-five counts of rewarding official misconduct in the second degree;
- Seven counts of falsifying business records in the first degree;
- Three counts of tampering with public records in the first degree;
- One count each of grand larceny in the second degree, grand larceny in the third degree, theft of services, as well as official misconduct.

Vergari outlined the case against the two physicians and CPL on the day of the indictment. He said that from May 12, 1972, until January 1975, "All histological specimens received by the defendants were sent to either Grasslands or Peekskill Community Hospital for testing. The patients were then billed by the defendants through Consulting Pathologists Laboratory, Inc., for work that was actually performed by county employees, or by Peekskill Hospital employees, with the resources and facilities of these two institutions.

"During this period," Vergari continued, "the defendants processed 2,362 histology tests at Grasslands, and received $15,296.70. In addition, the defendants are charged with having more than 400 blood specimens tested at Grasslands, from June 1972, through January 1975, for which they received $1,300 from private patients."

Vergari said that the two defendants had also received $1,000 from the Westchester County Department of Social Services, during a three-year period, for work that was actually performed by county employees, using county supplies, at Grasslands.

The defendants were further accused of paying fees of from $60 to more than $1,000 to six employees of the division of pathology at Grasslands, ostensibly for performing CPL's tests.

Vergari added that an additional 1,776 of CPL's tests had actually been performed at Peekskill Hospital, for a total value of $16,127.

"The grand jury filed no charges against the defendants in connection with the Peekskill Hospital billings," Vergari noted. "Testimony from the [Peekskill] hospital administrator indicated that the practice was known to him, and condoned. The counts charging tampering with public records in the first degree relate to charges that the defendants caused the falsification of laboratory records in Grasslands Hospital, to attempt to cover up their activities."

Vergari concluded: "The defendants, whose operations through Consulting Pathologists Laboratory, Inc., over the three-year period in question were in excess of $124,000, faced possible prison terms of up to seven years. The corporate defendant (CPL) faced more than $380,000 in fines, upon conviction."

Dr. Lefkowitz and Dr. Kaplan surrendered themselves on the day of the indictment. After they had been photographed and fingerprinted, county detectives brought the two physicians to the county courthouse, where they were arraigned. They pleaded not guilty to all charges and were released on their own recognizance.

The defendants retained attorneys, and, following extensive motions and discovery procedures, a series of plea-bargaining meetings between the defense and the prosecution began.

The sentencing. On May 5, 1976, Dr. Lefkowitz and Dr. Kaplan stood before Judge Isaac Rubin. The defendants pleaded guilty to parts of the indictment. Dr. Lefkowitz pleaded guilty to the felony of rewarding official misconduct in the second degree. Dr. Kaplan pleaded guilty to the misdemeanor of aiding and abetting official misconduct.

Between the time of this hearing and sentencing, on June 25, Judge Rubin received presentence reports on the two defendants. These reports are usually prepared by the county probation department, and judges tend to rely heavily on them. These reports are confidential, though Rubin was to hint at their contents when he pronounced sentence on the two doctors.

Dr. Lefkowitz was sentenced first. Rubin mentioned a number of letters that had been received from physicians, praising the defendant. "There was never a hint of unsound medical practice in CPL's activities," Rubin noted. The judge described Dr. Lefkowitz as "one of the outstanding pathologists in this area . . . conscientious and meticulous . . . one of the experts in the country. . . ."

"It always grieves the court," Rubin continued, "to have a man of your standing come before it. You have dishonored yourself . . . you have suffered great disgrace and great anguish. You have received a great deal of adverse publicity. In all probability, you will be brought before the Westchester County Medical Society. In my opinion, you have suffered enough. The people would gain nothing by imprisoning you. You are not a threat to the community."

Then the judge swiftly passed sentence: a fine of $2,000, and five years' probation. "I will consider an earlier release if the probation department so recommends," Rubin added.

Dr. Kaplan was next. One of her lawyers spoke for her as she stood before the judge, hands clasped at her waist. "This is an unusual case, and this is an unusual person with an unblemished record," the lawyer told the judge. "She is a director of two laboratories, where she is vitally needed."

The lawyer cited Dr. Kaplan's work in numerous voluntary charities. He noted her distinguished service as an inspector with the American Association of Blood Banks.

"She has a husband and four young children," the lawyer continued. He described her involvement with CPL as "a worthy and unselfish purpose, to provide low-cost medical service to the citizens of Westchester County. A singular and unfortunate set of circumstances brought her into conflict with the law. She has already undergone great personal anguish and suffering . . ."

The judge looked at a sheaf of probation reports. When the lawyer finished, Rubin then told Dr. Kaplan:

"I am very aggrieved to have a person of your high professional standing before me today. You really were a victim of circumstances in your lack of knowledge of business practices. Your involvement was minor, compared with Dr. Lefkowitz's."

Rubin noted that the probation report included many favorable letters, plus praise of Dr. Kaplan from the hospital administrator at Peekskill, where many of CPL's tests had actually been performed.

"I hope that you will not be affected in any way by the sentence pronounced here today," Rubin said. "It is really unfortunate . . . a technical violation of the law . . . I will show as much leniency as I can."

Then the judge pronounced sentence: a fine of $1,000 and a conditional discharge, the condition being that she perform *pro bono publico* work during a one-year period. Rubin added that he would grant a probation department request to release Dr. Kaplan earlier, if such a request was made.

Sentence was then passed upon CPL. This corporate entity, which is considered a separate and living thing under the law, pleaded guilty to 34 counts of larceny in the third degree; rewarding official misconduct in the second degree; falsifying business records in the first degree; and theft of services. Rubin fined CPL $5,000, and the attorney representing Dr. Lefkowitz immediately handed the bailiff a certified check in this amount.

Judge Rubin had alluded to the possibility of professional sanctions against the two convicted physicians. The New York State Department of Health in Albany refused to comment on that possibility. What punitive actions might they take in a case like this? Anything from censure to the revocation of a license to practice medicine.

A source close to Dr. Kaplan said that her share of CPL's profits amounted to something less than $3,000 over a three-year period.

"I think the problem arose when it turned out that these doctors, because of their other obligations, found it difficult to conduct all of the tests at CPL's headquarters,'' Dr. Kaplan's spokesman continued. ''And they both had responsibilities at their own hospitals. They developed a habit of bringing certain tests to the hospitals.''

How did District Attorney Vergari and his staff feel about the case? Vergari readily conceded that the people's case against Dr. Lefkowitz and Dr. Kaplan—and CPL—had been an unusual one.

''It's the first in my experience of 29 years of law enforcement,'' Vergari said. ''I don't think that it was a foolproof scheme. Once we became aware of it, it was pretty easy to prove. But it's unique. I've never run across anything quite like it before.''

35

Rooting Out Medicare-Medicaid Cheats

Christopher J. Bale

Acting on the premise that the first step in cutting the Government health bill is to reduce cheating in existing programs, Congress enacted the Medicare-Medicaid Anti-Fraud and Abuse Amendments.

It should come as no surprise to laboratory directors, who have repeatedly felt the sting of adverse publicity, that many of the law's provisions affect them directly.

The amendments do not radically revise the Government-sponsored programs, but they dramatically raise the penalties for wrongdoers and create means of detecting the claim-hungry termites in the Medicare-Medicaid woodwork.

The ownership disclosure provisions in the law are perhaps the most significant for lab operators. Essentially, they required that HEW—now called Health and Human Services (HHS)—draw up regulations to apply to any "entity" that "furnishes or arranges to furnish" reimbursable services.

The law spells out that "entity" includes independent clinical laboratories, as well as renal care facilities and health maintenance organizations. Excluded are individual and group practitioners.

As a condition of certification for participation in the Medicare-Medicaid programs, these "entities" have to file regularly the names of anyone with "an ownership or control interest" in the company. These are people with a 5 percent or more interest in the company, or a "5 percent or greater interest in any mortgage, note, deed of trust secured (in whole or part) by the providing entity."

In corporations, the names of officers and board members are required. The provision applies to owners in partnerships as well.

But that's not all. The Government is also empowered to request "full and complete" ownership information on subcontractors with whom a provider has had more than $25,000 in total business transactions in the previous 12 months.

Moreover, according to the law, HHS can order a full record of any "significant business transactions" that have taken place between a provider and a wholly owned supplier or subcontractor over the past five years.

Easier access to ownership and financial data is just one detection strategy in an array the amendments contain. Strengthening the investigative capability of states and Professional Standards Review Organizations is another.

Beyond the institutional review responsibilities that PSROs already possess, the amendments direct PSROs to begin monitoring noninstitutional ambulatory care within two years after they are operational. This covers physician lab work. Instances of possible abuse or fraud they spot are to be turned over to the state anti-fraud units. (The law authorizes and encourages the states to form these units by offering up to $500,000 in Federal subsidies.)

Further, HHS must grant any PSRO requests for responsibility to review services furnished by shared health facilities.

A "shared health facility" is the statute's term for "Medicaid mill." It is defined basically as two or more doctors sharing a common location and staff or equipment. At the location, there must be a person who "manages, controls, or supervises substantial aspects" of the operation, makes staff support available to the doctors, and is compensated on a percentage of gross.

In addition, at least one of the practitioners must receive more than $5,000 in any one month from the Government for services rendered, or the practitioners in aggregate must receive more than $40,000 over 12 months.

Until a PSRO decides to step in, however, states have and will continue to have policing authority over shared health facilities. And in a sense, states are asked to monitor PSROs because the amendments make clear that if a state provides reasonable documentation that a PSRO is not operating effectively—for example, if it is approving inappropriate care which results in increased benefits—then HHS can withdraw the PSRO's authority until corrections are made.

Among the other important provisions:

Prohibition against assignment. Assignment of claims is allowed now only as a condition of a doctor's employment with a hospital or clinic, as an agreement with a Government agency, or at a court's order. An arrangement between an agency and a physician is permitted if the compensation paid to the agent is unrelated "directly or indirectly to the amount of such payments or billings . . . and is not dependent upon the actual collection of any such payment."

Uniform reporting. HEW was to develop a uniform reporting system whereby it could compare efficiency and utilization among all facilities including HMOs, hospitals, skilled nursing care facilities, intermediate-care facilities, "and other types of health organizations."

Nomination of intermediaries. HEW was to develop guidelines and criteria for measuring what constitutes effective and efficient program administration or designate regional or national intermediaries for a class of providers if increased efficiency and utilization are likely to result.

Abuses now become felonies. Prior to the amendments, it was only a misdemeanor to defraud, take kickbacks, or otherwise cheat the Government health programs. No longer. Such transgressions are now felonies, with violators punishable with up to five years in prison and/or a $25,000 fine. Convicted practitioners, moreover, are to be suspended from participation in Medicare and Medicaid for "an amount of time" deemed appropriate by the Federal government.

Aside from the subsidies to encourage state anti-fraud units, the law has no specific enforcement provisions. House-Senate conferees knocked out a provision that HEW be given the authority to initiate suits against alleged defrauders.

One reason this provision failed was the promise by the attorney general that the Justice Department would give Medicare-Medicaid law enforcement its highest priority. In fact, just before the House voted on the bill's final version, the attorney general announced that 350 FBI agents were receiving special training in Medicare-Medicaid auditing. Additionally, 1,100 agents were being trained for general health-related investigations.

And don't forget HEW itself. Joseph Califano, then Secretary of HEW, denied reports that his department was about to abandon its so-called "Project Integrity" to root out abuses in Medicaid, which he estimated was costing $1 billion annually in ineligible claims.

On the contrary, he said, HEW had screened 250 million claims and turned up 47,000 involving doctors and pharmacies "which appear to us improper or questionable."

Of these cases, 2,500 were being investigated on a state-by-state basis for criminal prosecution or civil action. As these were processed, he added, more cases were to be submitted for action.

VIII UNIONIZATION

36

Union Activity in U.S. Hospitals

Jane C. Monaghan

Since the early 1970s, collective bargaining activity among hospital workers in the U.S. has increased substantially, mainly because the National Labor Relations Act was amended in August 1974 to bring all nonprofit hospitals under the act. Before that, hospitals could recognize unions voluntarily, but were not forced to do so by law. In 1971, according to the American Hospital Association, about 1,100 hospitals had union contracts; by 1976, more than 1,500 had them.

Another indication of growing union activity among hospitals comes from statistics compiled by the National Labor Relations Board. In fiscal 1975, 542 representation elections were held among health-care workers. In these elections, employees vote on whether or not they want to be represented by a particular union. Unions won 330 (61 percent) of those elections. That figure is all the more remarkable when you realize that for the same period unions won less than 48 percent of the representation elections in *all* industries.

Nor do officials of the AHA see a slackening of union activity among hospital employees. "The health-care industry is going through the same experience that other industrial and commercial firms did when they became covered by the act. First, there's a tremendous amount of organizing and acceptance of the unions. Then after a while, the novelty wears off, and organizing activity slows down—as it has in other sectors of the economy.''

The net result of stepped-up union activity is that hospital employees are beginning to get higher pay and better fringe benefits—whether or not they're union members. Here's how one union organizer on the West Coast puts it: ''We're finding hospitals are beginning to give much more substantial pay increases and much more liberal fringe benefit packages than they ever did before. Just the potential of a union coming into the hospital is upgrading the entire system—more in line with non-health-care workers.''

Laboratorians are also joining unions—though not to the extent that some other groups of hospital employees are. The reason, largely, is that many medical technologists have trouble reconciling the idea of professionalism with unionization.

One collective-bargaining advocate described the feeling this way: ''Medical technologists can't equate being professional with being concerned about their own socioeconomic matters. Many of them haven't yet opened their eyes to the fact that other professionals are organizing successfully—from physicians to teachers to university professors—to say nothing of the American Nurses' Association, which now considers collective bargaining to be just another part of its professional activities.''

Recognizing—and attempting to combat—the prejudice that laboratorians may have against unionization, some professional groups have taken a slightly different tack toward organizing. The ASMT, for example, set up its own collective bargaining arm, the National Economic Council. Though the NEC has since been dissolved, it left behind some strong local chapters in the Pacific Northwest, representing some 1,300 hospital employees, some of whom have already become affiliated with an international union.

The California Association of Medical Laboratory Technologists also joined forces with a collective-bargaining group, the Engineers and Scientists of California. In addition to its West Coast activity, CAMLT/ESC's national organization, the National Economic Council of Scientists, has been organizing drives and conducting collective-bargaining activities across the country—from Florida to Ohio to Arizona. According to its figures, CAMLT/ESC represents about 2,500 medical technologists in California, and the NECS, several hundred in other parts of the country. These groups, like the NEC before them, place strong emphasis on professionalism as well as on the economic advantages of collective bargaining.

Also recognizing how strong the idea of professionalism can be among health-care employees, at least one union—the Retail Clerks International Association—has established a separate professional division in an attempt to make membership more attractive.

Most other unions representing hospital workers put laboratory technologists and technicians into bargaining units that represent other technical employees as well as professionals. Such units may include dental assistants, autopsy techs, blood gas techs, ophthalmology techs, and respiratory therapists. Or in some cases, the units may be limited to professional employees, such as medical technologists, physical therapists, psychotherapists, and registered dietitians.

Now let's take a look at the national and international unions that are most active in organizing health-care employees.

Service Employees International Union represents the largest number of hospital and health-care workers in the country. Its total membership is 550,000, and about one-third of those are health-care workers. About 15,000 members in some 25 locals are LPNs and other technical and professional employees, including laboratorians. The largest number of technical employees represented by SEIU are located in the states of California, Colorado, Massachusetts, Michigan, and New York, and also in Washington, D.C.

National Union of Hospital and Health Care Workers. Formerly Local 1199 of the Retail, Wholesale, and Department Store Workers Union, this is now Division 1199 of that union, and an independent union in its own right. Of its 100,000 members, all of whom are in the health-care field, some 60,000 are in the New York City area. The union's greatest strength lies in the Northeast, including these other cities: Boston, Philadelphia, Baltimore, Rochester, N.Y., and Springfield, Mass. The union is also active in the states of Connecticut, Rhode Island, Virginia, West Virginia, and Kentucky, and it has scattered locals throughout several Midwestern states.

American Federation of State, County, and Municipal Employees. As its name suggests, the vast majority of this union's members are public employees. Of them, about 150,000, or 20 percent of total union membership, are health-care workers. Membership is concentrated mostly in the East and Midwest, with especially large representation in New York, Pennsylvania, and Michigan.

Retail Clerks International Association, with its separate professional division, has been particularly strong in organizing pharmacists, among other health-care workers. Out of a total 650,000 members (it's one of the largest unions in the U.S.), some 30,000 are health-care workers and pharmacists. These health-care workers are represented by 60 to 70 locals across the country, with the greatest concentration being in the Midwest, the Far West, and on the East Coast.

Other large unions, such as the Teamsters International and the Communications Workers, have begun to organize health-care workers, but so far their efforts and health-care membership haven't matched the other unions mentioned here.

What about strike activity? According to American Hospital Association data, 20 strikes occurred in hospitals from August 1974 (when the law was amended) through July 1975, though hospital services were completely stopped in only three cases.

But more strikes are likely. In these days of government and public outcry against soaring hospital costs (and payroll consumes well over half of hospital expenses), upcoming union contract negotiations will run into heavy going from hospital administrations saying they simply haven't got the money. And such negotiating impasses often mean just one thing: strike.

37

Avoiding Union Organization

Howard C. Hay, J.D.

It's sad but true that most hospitals and laboratories that get unions bring them on themselves. Management frequently has ignored legitimate grievances to the point where the employees turn to unionization as a last resort. Matters reach this pass, not because the employer has evil intent to abuse and exploit his employees, but because he neglects employee-relations problems. Errors of omission are more to blame than errors of commission.

It's particularly important for lab management to examine its employee-relations practices now, because since the National Labor Relations Act was amended in 1974 to include nonprofit institutions, efforts to unionize labs have increased dramatically. To tap this lucrative new source of members, unions are sending in their most experienced organizers. All too often, these lucky organizers encounter laboratory managers, supervisors, and employees who have little, if any, familiarity with the very real practical and legal problems that can arise when a union enters the picture—and even less knowledge of how to avoid union organization.

The keys to avoiding union organization in the lab are to avoid problem areas that make employees feel the need for representation and to know your legal rights in fighting a union. In this effort, it's important to distinguish between two separate periods: First, the "pre-union" period, before any union activity; second, the "pre-election" period, which extends from the time union organizers appear on the scene right up to the representation election. Although both periods are important, management's actions are legally more limited after organization begins.

Thus the pre-union period is vital. This is the time when management can build good relations with its employees, making unionization unnecessary. To do so, management must establish the following four policies:

First, make one person directly and personally responsible for employee relations. My experience has been that the vast majority of medical laboratories that encounter union activity do not have one person explicitly charged with the responsibility for employee relations as a *priority* part of his job. While this is more frequently a problem with medium-size to smaller laboratories, the problem also arises with large laboratories where responsibility for employee relations is shared by so many people that individual accountability is lost.

Why one person responsible? So that person can and will develop rapport with all lab personnel; take the necessary time to talk with employees concerning their complaints and problems as they arise; provide—or see that others provide—relief where relief is possible and, equally important, an explanation where no relief is possible; train and evaluate supervisors in fair handling of their employees; make sure that the hospital is spending its benefit dollars in areas of greatest concern to its employees; and keep abreast of wages and benefits paid by competitors and other medical employers in the area.

The laboratory must assist this person by sending him or her to conferences on employee relations and by educating him or her in other ways on performing personnel functions more skillfully.

When one person discharges these responsibilities as a priority part of his or her job, balancing the legitimate needs of the employees against the legitimate needs of the employer, the single greatest cause of union organization will be eliminated.

Second, have a definite system for periodic wage reviews. Set regular specified times, known to each employee, when he or she will be reviewed for an increase. There are numerous examples of an employer's failure to make periodic reviews leading to such a sense of frustration and lack of progress among the employees that they were driven into a union.

Every employee needs the definite assurance that he will be reviewed regularly for an increase, and management needs this check against errors of omission. The system is a built-in safeguard against inadvertently failing to periodically review each employee's performance and grant wage increases when appropriate.

Of course, the system you choose depends on your particular circumstances, your starting rates, and what your competitors are doing. My experience convinces me that employees making less than $12,000 per year should be reviewed more than once a year. Moreover, there are varying schools of thought on the extent to which such periodic reviews should generate automatic versus merit increases. Sometimes, hospitals are forced to rely on automatic increases because of their great size or the difficulty of making careful merit judgments concerning employee work performance.

Yet lab techs normally react more favorably to merit reviews when they are properly done, and lab supervisors find that they get better effort, motivation, and skills when merit increases are fairly given. Thus, the proper mix of merit and automatic increases depends on your particular laboratory and your own philosophy. The key is to have a well-publicized system that provides a sense of progress for employees and a check against your own errors of omission.

These first two steps—one person responsible for employee relations and a system for periodic wage reviews known to employees—are critical. Once they have been taken, management must make certain that employee problems and complaints are given a hearing.

Set up a simple grievance procedure for individual complaints. The procedure could provide, for example, that the employee can raise his problem orally with his supervisor, who must provide an answer to the employee. If the employee doesn't get a reasonably prompt answer or if he isn't satisfied with the answer he gets, he may take his problem to the person who is handling employee relations, and finally, directly to the person responsible for the entire laboratory.

This way, employees will be confident that they can raise individual complaints with management and get straight answers. Equally important, the laboratory will find out what its employees are concerned about, and its front-line supervisors should become more responsive to legitimate employee beefs.

The success of any such program depends on the laboratory's genuine commitment to make it work. Make sure employees know they can use the procedure without recrimination. Don't put this procedure in unless you mean it and are willing to put in the time and energy to solve legitimate complaints and answer those complaints that have no easy solution.

The fourth policy is similar to the third—only the scale is changed—and requires the same sense of genuine commitment if it is to work.

Hold periodic meetings between managers and small groups of employees, at which time the employees are encouraged to bring up any problems they are having in the laboratory (other than clearly individual grievances that should go through the grievance procedure that was described above).

Normally, such meetings are scheduled every two to three months. Employees participate on a first-come, first-served basis. If more than 20 employees sign up for the meeting, preference is given to those who have not previously participated. At the meeting, employees may raise virtually any problem they have, and day-to-day operational headaches generally consume the majority of time. However, employees do ask questions such as, "What is the hospital doing about providing a cost-of-living increase?" and, "Has the hospital considered adding a dental plan to the benefit package?"

The person responsible for employee relations answers those questions he can immediately and promises a later reply to the problems that require study, fuller consideration, or specific action. Within three weeks after the meeting, a written summary of all the questions and answers is posted on the employee bulletin board. Whenever specific action has resulted or will result from an employee's question, that action is noted.

As a result of these meetings, productive changes have been made at many labs—changes that posed no real problem for management, yet had become a source of genuine irritation to some employees. Moreover, my experience has been that employees accept an honest No to a request when management explains its answer, demonstrating that the majority of employees don't expect a utopia nearly so much as thoughtful consideration of and response to their concerns.

One note of caution: There are some legal restrictions involved in the use of such group meetings. The National Labor Relations Act makes it an unfair labor practice for an employer to dominate or interfere with the formation or administration of any labor organization. Obviously, that prohibition makes sense in most instances, except that "labor organization" is defined so broadly by the act that the group of randomly selected employees attending a meeting might be considered a "labor organization." Thus, the meetings could be viewed as a potential unfair labor practice.

Such an interpretation is obviously an extremely unfortunate one and benefits no one but organized labor. There is simply no reason why employees and their employers should not have the opportunity to sit down and work out their problems between themselves—no reason, that is, except organized labor's recognition that such a procedure is extremely effective in eliminating the lab's need for a union. The legal restrictions do, however, point up the need for careful legal guidance concerning the manner in which these group meetings can be conducted and maintained.

These, then, are the four steps that should be taken during the preunion period. But what if it's too late and union activity has already begun? Legal rules change at this point, and the employer has very little freedom to modify his past practices concerning wages, benefits, and working conditions.

For example, management can normally grant wage increases, additional holidays, and better insurance coverage to its employees whenever it sees fit without any obligation to justify or explain its actions. However, from the time the employer becomes aware that union organizing has begun, he can't do any of these things unless he can prove that the motivation for doing it was unrelated to the union. This is frequently very hard to do, and the consequences can be serious.

If the employer can't prove his case, he may be charged with committing an unfair labor practice. In some instances, the entire election may be set aside by the National Labor Relations Board. In one case, an employer gave across-the-board increases to employees after organizing activity had begun. The union lost the election and filed a protest. Because the employer couldn't prove that the increases were unrelated to union activity, the NLRB ruled that the union was elected as the employees' collective bargaining agent as redress for the employer's unfair labor practice.

Because violations of the National Labor Relations Act can be treated so severely, many administrations simply freeze when a union appears on the scene. They figure it's safer to do nothing than to take a chance of committing an unfair labor practice.

However, there are a number of things management *can* do to fight a union during the pre-election period. These actions are specifically covered in Section 8(c) of the NLRA as follows: "The expressing of any views, argument, or opinion, or the dissemination thereof, whether in writing, printed, graphic, or visual form, shall not constitute or be evidence of an unfair labor practice under any provisions of this act, if such expression contains no threat of reprisal, or force, or promise of benefit."

The key to union opposition during the pre-election period thus becomes communication—**reminding employees of what they already have, showing them how the union could adversely affect that situation,** and demonstrating that management is more capable than the union of bringing about improvements in the future.

Of course, there are several traditional methods of communication that form the backbone of any good pre-election campaign. These include one-on-one candid discussions between supervisors and employees; group meetings, and particularly the question-and-answer exchanges that should follow; succinct bulletins summarizing the disadvantages of a union; and occasional letters to the employee's home.

In addition, there are several somewhat newer communication techniques that can be extremely effective in illustrating the disadvantages of a union. For example, I have developed a booklet to **demonstrate to employees the unreliability of the union's pre-election promises and claims.** This booklet contains several pages, each with a separate "union guarantee." A typical statement reads: "I GUARANTEE: that if my union wins the election, my union will get you a ___ cent per hour wage increase in the very first union contract." There is then a line for the official union representative to sign his name and the date, so that the employee will have the union's guarantee in writing.

Distributing such a booklet invariably makes an important point to the employees: Because union organizers have no way at all of guaranteeing any improvements if the union wins, the organizer cannot sign. He thus is forced to confirm what management has been saying all along—that the union can't deliver on its promises.

The booklet also provides strong ammunition for the pro-management employee who wants to fight the union, yet frequently has insufficient material or information to do so. The refusal of the union organizer to sign the employee's booklet provides quite a talking point for him.

Another effective communication technique is a contest, with cash prizes, in which employees attempt to guess the union profit if the union wins the election and gets a three-year contract. Employees are given such information as union dues, initiation fees, number of employees, annual turnover, and so on. They're then asked to figure out how much money the union stands to gain if it wins the election. Employees are generally astounded at how much money is at stake. In one such contest held recently at a 60-person lab, the correct answer was $35,000. This technique points up the fact that unions aren't in the organizing business out of altruism—they're in it to make money. It puts the union on the defensive in a way that a written bulletin or a speech could never do.

Written material can also be extremely effective, particularly if it's published by a disinterested third party, such as a newspaper or magazine. Such items have more credibility than the typical bulletin or letter prepared by management. For example, there was a recent article in the *Los Angeles Times* noting that unemployment in California was at an all-time high "because of union strikes." The story also mentioned that strikers are not entitled to unemployment insurance. These were the very points laboratory management had been emphasizing to its personnel, with little effect, until the employees read the independent newspaper article.

Similarly, several recent court decisions have held that Seventh-Day Adventists could be required to join a union and pay dues despite their genuine religious conviction to the contrary.

One such decision, and the newspaper reports about it, proved very helpful in a recent campaign in persuading several Jehovah's Witnesses to vote—and to vote against the union—because of the inevitable infringement of their religious freedom. Giving them a copy of the decision itself provided the turning point in our efforts to convince them. It also demonstrated to other thinking employees the loss of individual freedom that a union entails.

In other circumstances, we have provided Supreme Court decisions or NLRB decisions explaining that the payment of merit wage increases must stop immediately if the union wins the election, or that strikers can be replaced permanently by new employees.

These are some techniques that have proved effective during the pre-election period. Of course, such communication efforts are at best only short-term solutions, designed to secure for employer and employee a second chance to work together without the interference and disadvantages of a union. The long-term solution is to practice the four pre-union recommendations discussed earlier. Employers who do so will find that their personnel are far more satisfied with their working environment, and far less susceptible to a union's seductive sales pitch to acquire more membership dues.

38

We Were Forced to Join a Union

Pam Troyer, MT(ASCP)SBB, and
Barbara E. Goerger, MT(ASCP)

Unionization was an area foreign to most of us working in the lab at a nonprofit volunteer blood center in a Midwestern state. We had always assumed that we could not be forced to join a union. We were wrong. We were once a happy and cohesive group of techs, and we could take our grievances directly to management. No more. Now we confront management only at the bargaining table. Here's the unhappy story of how we became unionized because of our ignorance of the labor laws.

The possibility of a union was nothing new to our large blood bank. Clerical, maintenance, and blood custodial employees had petitioned to be considered a bargaining group associated with a union as far back as 1970. Naturally, the administration opposed this move, arguing that the National Labor Relations Act exempted nonprofit hospitals from unionization. Both sides retained lawyers, and the matter passed through a number of hearings before state and Federal agencies.

We paid little attention to these hearings. The 25 lab employees felt sympathy toward these nonprofessional employees who wanted to join a union. We felt their complaints were legitimate. But we knew that their situation differed greatly from ours. We were professionals, and we took our problems to management. They were semiskilled workers and unable to develop one-to-one relations with the administration.

This initial petition to hold a union election was eventually turned down by the National Labor Relations Board (NLRB), which ruled that a union could not be formed because our blood center was exempt from union activities as a "nonprofit charity organization."

The years passed, and the law was changed. The National Labor Relations Act was amended in August 1974, bringing all nonprofit hospitals under the act. Before that, of course, hospitals could recognize unions voluntarily, but were not forced to do so by law. This single piece of legislation would change our professional lives, though we didn't know it at the time. Indeed, I can't recall anyone in the lab even mentioning it.

The nonprofessional employees remained dissatisfied with their lot, and they found another union willing to represent them. A new petition was filed with management, which rejected it on the same grounds given in 1970. Then the matter went to the NLRB. We paid little attention to these arguments. We somehow assumed that, even if the petition were granted, it would apply only to a union limited in membership to nonprofessional employees.

We received our first surprise six months later, when the NLRB ruled that the employees at our facility had the right to hold a union election. All at once, the light began to dawn upon us. We started asking questions. Was there even a remote chance that we could be required to join a union? Would we then be compelled to pay dues for salaries and benefits that we felt were quite adequate?

We arranged a meeting with the lawyer who had represented the blood center during both attempts to organize the nontechnical employees. It was then that we learned that during the final stages of the NLRB hearings, the blood center had agreed to have as many employees as possible included in the union election. This meant that we were being lumped in with blood custodians, maintenance men, and typists! Why?

"We wanted a bargaining unit as large as possible, with common interests," the lawyer told us as we sat in stunned silence. "Under the circumstances, we felt that the skills in your group were not sufficiently definable to separate you for labor relations purposes. The NLRB agreed with us, simply on the basis that the duties you perform in the laboratory are not clearly defined as a skill."

The next shock came when he told us that the union had made a quiet attempt to include the nurses in the organizing petition. This request had subsequently been withdrawn. Why?

''Well, the nurses could have been in the group if the union asked them,'' the lawyer continued. ''But we weren't going to agree to put them in because their bylaws show nursing to be a definable profession, so the union backed off.

''Traditionally, the labor law says that professionals can elect to be in a larger bargaining unit composed of persons with fewer skills than they have,'' the lawyer explained. ''They also have the option of electing to stay out. That's the classic position for the defined professions. Unfortunately, the law does not give techs the same option. You don't have a definable skill in the legal sense. Nothing personal or judgmental,'' he reassured us. ''We think you're good, but that's what the law is at this point.''

One of us pointed out that management and the union seemed to have reached an accord not to press the nurses for inclusion in a single union. Why hadn't we been included in this accord? ''We're professionals, too,'' someone said.

The lawyer shrugged. ''At some point in the future, either your group or other groups like you will have to educate the NLRB to agree with you. Right now, the NLRB doesn't view you as professionals. The only way the law is changed is by legislation or by a series of cases that litigate the matter. We made a judgment that we did not feel that starting litigation in this area was the best use of our money. We looked at the law very carefully, and we made a judgment that we could not consider the lab as a separate group for bargaining purposes. The NLRB agreed with us, and so did the union.''

We were hurt and angry when the lawyer left the room. Some of us felt that we had been used as pawns in a chess game between management and the nonprofessional employees. Others said that the administration had deliberately included us in the union bargaining unit in the hope that our total laboratory votes would defeat an attempt to create a union shop.

Morale plummeted in the days that followed. We contacted the district representative of the AFL-CIO, and he confirmed everything that the blood center's lawyer had told us about the NLRB ruling. The only way we could defeat an attempt to become unionized, he told us, was by voting against it in a union representation election. Assuming, he added with a smile, that we had the votes to do it.

We were bombarded with leaflets from union and management as the election drew near. One letter from the union really upset many of us. ''Just a few words to the people working in the lab,'' it read. ''In all frankness, we have to admit that those of you on the higher rungs of the ladder of staff positions (medical technologists, etc.) will probably stand to gain somewhat less than those of you with more limited professional training (lab aides, etc.). Nevertheless, we are firmly convinced that union representation is, in the long run, in the best interest of all blood center employees, professional as well as nonprofessional.''

So even the union conceded that we were professionals! Not that this bid for our votes would make any difference in how we voted.

In desperation, we sought last-minute legal advice. All of us in the lab chipped in $5 apiece, and we hired our own lawyer. Was there any way we could be considered a separate entity as techs and then form what would amount to a professional union? The lawyer said he would study this possibility.

But we were too late. Our lawyer told us that he felt we had a very good case for being considered as a separate bargaining unit. ``But you waited too long,'' he told us. ``Matters have proceeded too far. You should have come to me much earlier. Your union election will be held next week, and there is no time left to file the proper petition to the NLRB.''

Election day arrived. Almost all of us in the lab voted against joining the union. Then we waited for the votes to be tallied. There were a lot of long faces when the results were announced: We had been defeated by six votes! Now we were part of a union shop.

Many questions remain in our minds. Why didn't management tell us earlier of its decision not to dispute our inclusion in the bargaining unit? Why does the NLRB consider nurses to be professionals, while even degreed techs are apparently regarded as having a lower order of skills? And how, in a democracy, can an individual be forced to join a union against his own will?

To a large extent, we can only blame ourselves. We should have been more enlightened. We should have sought advice from our professional societies. We should have hired a lawyer much earlier. We should have known the law. There were alternatives open to us, if we had only realized it in time.

39

Creating a Strike Contingency Plan

Frank Greaves, MT(ASCP)

Imagine for a moment that you are the chief technologist, and you are alone in the laboratory of a 550-bed hospital. Your employees are all out on strike. Your routine workload is waiting to be drawn, and 15 physicians are all calling for Stat requests. What are you going to do?

It's too late to start planning for a strike when your employees are out pounding the picket line. And don't think that *your* laboratory will somehow remain immune to union activity, either. Hospital strikes became a nationwide reality with the passage of the 1974 amendment to the Taft-Hartley Act, removing hospitals' exemption from union activity—including strikes. Now is the time to ask yourself what you would do in the event of a strike.

There are many ways to plan for a strike, and I will discuss all of them, including a specific strike plan that we have developed. *Your* first priority should be attempting to keep your employees from joining a union. The only effective way to resist unionization is to satisfy the physical and psychological needs of your employees. This responsibility doesn't belong to the hospital administration alone; it also falls on the shoulders of every first-line supervisor.

If the majority of your employees are dissatisfied, it's probably only a matter of time until a union attempts to organize them. You should know all the rules and regulations concerning these activities in advance, and you must abide by them. These Federal regulations prohibit any action threatening reprisals for joining a union, asking employees questions about union activities or their feelings about a union, and assigning work on the basis of union affiliation.

You could be forced into a National Labor Relations Board election if you break just *one* of these rules. You might also discover that you have been unionized without benefit of an NLRB election. Hold seminars or inservice training sessions on these rules and their ramifications now, and make sure that all supervisory personnel attend.

"Plan for the worst and hope for the best" still holds true. Even if your hospital is not unionized, you should still prepare for a strike. Consider these factors in tailoring your strike contingency plan:

- How many beds do you serve?
- How extensive might the strike be? Will it involve all departments? What percentage of the employees will go on strike?
- How many supervisory employees will you be able to count on?
- Will nonstriking employees cross the picket line?
- Can striking employees be replaced during the strike?
- What are the ordering patterns of the physicians you serve?
- What instruments do you have? How do you use them?
- How can you streamline your testing procedures without cutting back on patient service?
- How many weeks before your supplies are exhausted?
- Can more supplies be obtained after your stocks are exhausted? Will your vendors cross the picket line?
- How long can the institution stand the strike?

We recently considered all of these questions. Then we developed a highly specific strike plan for our 550-bed hospital. This plan assumes that all of our nonsupervisory personnel would be out on strike. Following, in a somewhat abbreviated form, is the text of our contingency plan:

Laboratory Procedures in Case of a Strike

There are five basic considerations in formulating operating procedures during a strike. They are: establishing test priorities, utilization of supervisory personnel, instruments, supplies, and engineering.

Test priorities. It is estimated that up to half of our laboratory tests could be eliminated without adversely affecting patient care. The medical staff will be asked to understand our situation and eliminate all unnecessary tests. Physicians will also be asked to furnish patients with written requests for all necessary laboratory tests. These tests can be drawn on admission. Fasting requirements can be met outside the hospital.

Only tests shown on the Stat list will be run. Specimens for testing will be drawn by all available personnel between the hours of 6 a.m. and 8 a.m. During the day, one supervisor from hematology, clinical chemistry, and microbiology will be designated to draw blood.

Full service will be provided on all other tests within two days, except for profiles. No profile testing will be conducted during the strike. We will limit tests to those the physician feels are pertinent to each patient's situation. These test priorities will be reviewed daily to determine if it is possible to add some services or curtail others. We will also consider using local and out-of-state reference laboratories for some of our tests.

Utilization of supervisory personnel. The chemistry section will be operated seven days a week by the assistant lab manager, the section head of chemistry, and the research and development technologist. These personnel will also work a 16-hour shift every third day, to include evening hours.

The microbiology section will be operated seven days a week by the section heads of microbiology and mycology, and the assistant chief technologist. They will also work a 16-hour shift every third day, to include evening hours.

The section heads of urinalysis, hematology, serology, and the blood bank are to operate their respective departments seven days a week during the first shift. They will also work a 16-hour shift every third day, to include evening hours.

The educational coordinator will work in hematology seven days a week, plus a 16-hour shift every third day, to include evening hours.

The section head of the evening shift will work evenings seven days a week, in addition to a 16-hour shift every third day, to include the hours of the first shift.

The histology section will be covered six days a week by the section head of histology. Extra hours beyond the regulation eight hours daily will be worked as needed, to make up for the lack of staff.

If the third shift cannot be staffed, it is to be rotated among the lab manager, the assistant lab manager, the section head of chemistry, the research and development technologist, and the chief technologist.

The laboratory manager will function as the lab's liaison with the nursing services. He will also direct laboratory operations from the lab's communication data area. He will constantly monitor the situation and make appropriate recommendations to administration concerning laboratory functions.

Utilization of instruments. All tests on the Stat list will be run. Instruments, including the automated analyzers, will be operated 16 hours a day. Tests not on the Stat list will be shipped to an outside lab.

Supplies. The lab currently has supplies to operate for one month. This inventory could be increased over a 10-day period, so that the lab could then operate for six months.

Engineering. Supervisory personnel have a very good background in instrument maintenance. Most minor problems can be handled by existing expertise and spare parts. All lab procedures have suitable backup equipment. This equipment may be used in the event of a serious instrument malfunction that cannot be repaired by lab personnel.

Conclusions. This strike contingency plan could be maintained for at least four weeks if the supervisors are motivated to rally to the situation. Supervisors are expected to suffer psychologically after one month. Production will drop. We would then probably have to curtail our services and rely heavily on reference laboratories.

40

Working Nonunion in a Union Lab

Marlene A. Brownson, CLA(ASCP)

Not everything about work in a laboratory is taught in school—as I learned on the first day of my first job after graduation. In fact, as a fresh-out-of-school certified laboratory assistant, I had no idea that hospitals even experienced the problem that was to cause me so much distress. The problem was a union.

My lessons began that first day when the chief technologist and the union chairman, who was also a tech, argued about whether my job should be covered by the union. The hospital's local consists mostly of service workers—secretaries, custodians, and kitchen personnel. In the laboratory, it also includes phlebotomists and techs who have not passed their ASCP certification exams. Our laboratory has several techs who were trained in the military or on the job and are not ASCP-certified. They are in the union. The ASCP techs, even though they do about the same jobs as the others, are exempt from the union. And of course, the supervisors are nonunion. Since I was the first CLA to be hired by the hospital, mine was a special case.

The personnel department listed me as nonunion, claiming that my ASCP certification made me ineligible for membership. The chief tech also said my job was too important to be covered by the union. The union chairman disagreed and filed a grievance. He argued that a pharmacy worker with the word "certified" in his job title was in the union. Since my title also had the word "certified," I should be covered, too.

Nothing ever came of the grievance. I'm still listed as nonunion, but as far as I know, the question was never officially settled. I worried about it for a long time. Being a pawn in a power struggle between management and union gave me an uncomfortable feeling.

I also felt caught in the middle of controversy between my union and nonunion co-workers. Both groups approached me, one to extol the union's virtues, the other to warn me of its faults. I was never given a choice, but if I had been, I know I would have decided against the union.

My initial feeling was that, as a professional, I did not belong in a service workers' union. Other drawbacks of the union became apparent after I'd been on the job awhile. Although the local probably has won better wages and benefits for most of the hospital's employees, it seemed to concern itself with many petty issues. These often involved the kinds of tasks certain workers could or could not perform, and the resulting restrictions made life in the laboratory more difficult than necessary.

For example, I have seen a phlebotomist with spare time after pickups watch a secretary do the work of two when another clerical person was out sick. The union phlebotomist was prohibited from helping because secretarial work was not in her job description. Similarly, nonunion supervisors are not allowed to do benchwork, so they can't help out when we're in a bind.

Management was not entirely blameless in the situation. The chief tech made no effort to hide his dislike for the union and often ignored contract provisions. He also scheduled staff meetings for nonunion techs only. These closed meetings set us apart from the others and widened the gulf between the two groups. The chief tech recently quit, primarily because of his constant problems with the union.

The situation in the laboratory reached a climax in the spring of my third year when the union voted to strike. Their action left only seven of us in the laboratory, doing the work normally performed by 20 in serving our 226-bed hospital. It was rough at first, but we managed very well. Everyone pitched in. Supervisors worked at the bench. Techs typed, filed, and charted their own work. The personnel director mopped and waxed floors. The work was hard, but we felt proud of the fact that our small group of professionals was getting the job done in a crisis.

While the situation inside the hospital was well under control, outside was a different story. After the first week of the strike, the mood turned ugly. Tires were slashed on the cars of nonunion personnel. Off-duty workers were followed and threatened. At one point, a few strikers blocked the driveway to the emergency entrance, jeopardizing the lives of patients.

The hospital offered room and board to anyone who wanted to avoid harassment from the strikers. This allowed techs on call to stay overnight, as I did on several occasions. It was hard enough crossing the picket line in the morning. Coming in for Stat work in the middle of the night was something that few of us wanted to try.

The strike ended after five and a half weeks, but the disruption it caused in the laboratory may never be healed. It was impossible to welcome back all the strikers as if nothing had happened. Those of us who had stayed on the job felt that some of the strikers' actions were unforgivable—and a few of us told them so. The most aggressive strikers seemed changed, as if their personalities had been altered by their activities on the picket line. More than one friendship was destroyed.

Before the strike, the laboratory staff had had a lot of fun together off the job. We would go on canoe trips, play volleyball on Saturday afternoons, and have frequent parties. Those days are gone.

The atmosphere in the laboratory has become less tense with the passage of time. But even today, a year after the strike, there are still conflicts between union and nonunion workers. Some of the wounds may never heal.

41

I Scabbed a Strike

Josephine Soublet, MT(ASCP)

"If union members vote to strike, will you go out with us?"

A very vocal, pro-union technologist asked me that question. Our contract, which covered all the technologists at the 17 Kaiser facilities in northern California, had expired on March 1, 1978, and the possibility of a strike was a major topic of discussion in our lab. We had taken a straw vote, and most of the techs had been against a strike. But management was sticking to its original offer, union negotiators were determined to win us a big settlement, and we were caught in the middle.

I didn't want to strike. First of all, I consider myself a professional, a cut above a retail clerk or a bus driver. I feel I can earn a just wage without resorting to a blackmail tactic like a strike. In addition, I don't think my parents took on extra jobs to put me through college so I could walk a picket line like a longshoreman. And finally, I really don't think strikes are effective.

I had to answer, "No, I will not support a strike."

A day after that conversation, I started getting pressure from other people. A technologist I trained with 10 years ago accused me of making a deal with management. He said he had heard I was going to work 18-hour shifts during the strike and make hundreds of dollars in overtime pay. Of course, I denied his accusations, but my protest fell on deaf ears.

Another technologist told me that if I worked during the strike, I could be transferred to an unfamiliar department and be expected to produce satisfactory results regardless of my lack of proficiency. And if I refused to work in another department, I could be dismissed, and the union wouldn't lift a finger to help me. I knew this was just a threat, and it only made me more determined to work if there was a strike.

The excitement and controversy among technologists over a strike was partly due to the novelty of union representation at Kaiser. We originally belonged to the California Association of Medical Laboratory Technologists (CAMLT), a professional organization that mainly dealt with continuing education and only incidentally negotiated our contract. Some of the CAMLT members later suggested we loosely affiliate ourselves with a union for lobbying power in Washington and more clout at the bargaining table.

In September 1974, we affiliated with the Engineers and Scientists of California, a union that also represents welding engineers and electric company linemen. About a year after that, several organizational meetings were held, and we found that we no longer belonged to CAMLT, but were full-fledged members of the union. The union negotiated our contract in 1976 and now was busy bargaining for us once again.

On Saturday before the Monday strike deadline, management and union leaders held a final bargaining session. I called the Kaiser hot line, a phone number that gives current reports of hospital activities, to find out what had happened at the noontime negotiations. To my dismay, I learned that the union had stuck to its original demands, management had refused to budge, and the Federal negotiator had recessed the meeting less than an hour after it started.

My first reaction was disbelief: I thought it was just company propaganda. But when I checked with our laboratory representative, she assured me it was accurate. Barring an 11th-hour settlement, it looked as if a strike was inevitable.

I was furious! The union's demands—which included such requests as a fixed dollar amount per tech per year for educational benefits *plus* paid education time—far exceeded the salary and benefits that most of the techs said they'd settle for. It was painfully obvious that the union *wanted* a strike.

Monday morning came without word of a settlement. While the news media rushed to cover "the first technologist strike ever at Kaiser," I stayed home and worried. Because I work the 1 to 9 p.m. shift, I still had time before going to the laboratory. And I was not looking forward to it. When I finally got into my car to drive to work, I prayed for a flat tire or a minor accident—anything to delay my arrival.

I had expected to be greeted by pickets, but the hospital entrance looked strangely deserted when I arrived. Inside, I found another surprise: The lab was literally crawling with people. In addition to exempt employees like the education coordinator and the laboratory director, there were assorted staff physicians, three pathologists, four cytotechnologists, four other scab technologists, eight students, two lab aides, and a hospital administrator. The noise level was high, but confusion seemed to be minimal.

The doctors helping out in chemistry had been assigned to only one or two instruments each, and they all were busy with their individual tests. Surprisingly, most of the routine work had been done. I checked results, filled in slips, performed a few tests, and cleaned counters.

At about 4 p.m., our crew began to dwindle. Most of the lab was quiet, except for the blood bank. In a cold, calculating move, management had refused to cancel two aneurysm operations scheduled for that day. Many of the striking technologists were bitter, and on that point I agreed with them. A real tragedy could have occurred if rookies under pressure had been required to set up all the blood for the two patients. Fortunately, a regular blood bank technologist had decided to scab the strike. On that day, he personally set up more than 10 units of blood, and he refused to leave until both patients had stabilized.

The strikers were furious when they heard that news. If a regular blood bank technologist had not been in the lab, they said, management would have been forced to agree to the union's demands. Perhaps that's true, but at what price? Can professionals in good conscience weigh the lives of two patients against educational leave and tuition reimbursement? I think not.

By the third day of the strike, we had established a routine that centered around the coffee pot. Management supported our work efforts, and in addition to sending a memo praising us and asking for staff cooperation, they provided pastry for our daily coffee break and microwave dinners for the evening crew.

One unusual benefit of working during the strike was being able to talk to the staff physicians who were helping out in the lab. We had some lively discussions about lab procedures, hospital policies, and staffing problems.

On one occasion, for example, I remarked to a urologist that microscopic examinations of clear, yellow urine with normal specific gravities and dipsticks were a waste of time because 99 out of 100 are normal. He reminded me that the lab is not a casino and we're not here to play percentages. "It's that abnormal 1 percent we're looking for. *That's* the patient we want to find," he said. He did agree with me that techs should be able to report microscopically normal urines as normal rather than wasting time listing 0-1 WBCs, few squamous, and the like.

Another popular topic among the physicians was Stats. A gynecologist was upset by the excessive number of Stat pregnancy tests we do to rule out ectopic pregnancies. He maintained that a gynecologist who can't diagnose an ectopic pregnancy without a pregnancy test ought to be a podiatrist.

On the other hand, a dermatologist told me that Stat VDRLs would be helpful to his department. He said that having to wait 24 to 48 hours to confirm syphilis before prescribing penicillin caused many unsuspecting persons to be exposed to the disease. I suggested his patients might read a book or watch TV for a few nights.

One charge the striking technologists leveled at our temporary staff was that unqualified individuals were turning out questionable results. In fact, while the turnaround time for Stats was definitely longer during the strike, the quality of results was well within acceptable limits. Most of the physicians grumbled about standardizing instruments and running controls, but they still did them. And after a little bit of practice, a few of them were more proficient than some of our regular technologists.

Of course, we also had our problems. Some physicians were cranky, a few found the work boring, most were messy, and *all* had bad handwriting. But even with the problems, the majority of physicians made few complaints—and showed a great deal of respect for the expertise of the techs who worked during the walkout. Whenever a doctor was unsure of a technique or result, he consulted one of us. In fact, some days it seemed as if I spent the entire eight hours giving instructions on quality control, preventive maintenance, and other lab procedures.

Unfortunately, the strike took an ugly turn that made management even more determined to stand by its original offer. On Thursday of the first week of the strike, I got a threatening phone call. An unfamiliar male voice told me there was a contract out on me. Another tech was similarly threatened. We both reported the incident to the police and the administration.

The following day, someone pasted a poison label on a container I had left in the lab refrigerator. Names, addresses, and phone numbers of all scabs were distributed at a rally held by striking techs in a nearby park. Management offered to get us unlisted phone numbers, but I don't think there were any takers.

About a week later, I discovered that someone had put sugar in my gas tank. Although the job was botched and damage was minimal (a more experienced thug could have done two to three thousand dollars' damage), the message was clear: The strike had become more important than human dignity, honesty, and morality. I changed my parking spot and bought a locking gas cap, but I refused to strike.

Our workload at the lab fluctuated. On some days we actually had time to sit around and chat, but by the end of the second week, our workload was almost equal to its prestrike level. We continued to juggle schedules, send out selected tests to commercial labs, and encourage doctors to delay routine orders.

Ten days after the strike began, management agreed to a second bargaining session, which proved futile. Then on Wednesday of the third week of the strike, we heard our first bit of encouraging news: Management had made an offer that seemed acceptable to the union negotiators, and a general meeting was called for Thursday night. At the meeting, members voted to ratify the contract, and the union announced the strike would end at 7 a.m. the following Monday. After three weeks and hundreds of cups of coffee, Kaiser's first laboratory technologist strike was over.

The irony of the walkout was that the union leaders wound up accepting almost exactly what had been offered to them before the strike. They had strongly opposed a three-year contract, for example, but finally agreed to a two-and-a-half-year settlement, and most of the other demands lost out, too. The union probably could have gained the same concessions with some straight, serious bargaining. And it would have been done without a strike.

The technologists who struck learned a lesson, too. Most of them honestly believed the hospital could not survive without them. They figured the strike would last two or three days and management would beg them to come back. Only the union leaders knew it would last as long as it did, and they didn't care about the rank-and-file technologists. As long as they got us a raise, they knew they could ask us for higher union dues, which is exactly what happened.

Needless to say, there was mistrust and anger among the technologists after the strike. Most of the strikers refused to speak to the scabs for about a week. They were particularly upset with the student technologists who had worked 10- and 12-hour shifts to keep the lab running smoothly. Gradually, however, things shifted back to normal. Almost. Nothing will ever erase the fact of the strike.

But now its effects are much less apparent. And it was a learning experience for everybody. Strikers were suddenly faced with empty pay envelopes and the reality of management's and the union leadership's indifference to their wants and needs. Many physicians saw the other side of a Stat for the first time.

And I learned how lonely a solitary stand on principles can be.

42

The Case for Unionization

David N. Buhr, MT(ASCP)

So much misinformation and so many false statements have been broadcast about unions in the health-care field that I think it's time to set the record straight. I've been a member of a national union for several years now, and there's a lot of positive information I'd like to share.

First, let me clear up some common misapprehensions: Contrary to popular belief, the average union member is not a wild-eyed, tire-slashing radical who would cut corners on patient care for a $10 pay raise. I've been a union steward in my laboratory for more than two years and a rank-and-file member for several years before that. I've yet to see any violence in connection with my union's activities. I haven't even witnessed a strike. Our members are ordinary, law-abiding citizens who have one thing in common: We believe that in negotiating with management, we have more clout as a group than as individuals.

Unions aren't always necessary. Some laboratories already have a fair system for assigning work, giving out raises, and handling promotions. They don't fire employees without warning, and they have a mechanism for dealing with their employees' grievances. When this is the case, there's no need for a union to represent employees.

But when a laboratory deals with employees on a paternalistic or authoritarian level, I think employees should band together to protect their own interests. They should form a union that will prod management to set up a system for dealing with their needs and problems.

Occasionally, this leads to a strike. When management ignores employees' grievances, employees should have the right to strike. This doesn't necessarily mean a strike will occur. But the right to strike gives employees their greatest bargaining leverage.

I'm opposed to striking when it interferes with patient care. In our 360-bed VA hospital, union members, as Federal employees, are expressly forbidden by law to strike—and we honor that law. But we retain the right to bargain collectively with the administration over every issue except salaries. This is handled at the national level.

Our union has established a smooth working relationship with our hospital's management. When we meet over the bargaining table, we protect our members' interests, and the administration protects the hospital's. Twenty-five years ago this would not have been possible. But collective bargaining has come a long way in the past few years. Where there are unions, most hospital administrations have accepted them as a fact of life—and find they can work with them constructively.

Unions have become a big part of the hospital scene. Among those active in organizing hospital workers are: Service Employees International Union; National Union of Hospital and Health Care Workers; American Federation of State, County, and Municipal Employees; and Retail Clerks International Association. My own union, the American Federation of Government Employees, is only one of several that organize Federal employees.

But the union movement in the health-care industry is still in its infancy. Whereas organized labor has lost some of its clout in other industries in recent years, it is gaining influence in the health-care field.

Wherever working conditions and salaries are poor, unions will attempt to organize. Women, who have resisted joining in the past because they often worked part time, are joining now as full-time members of the labor force.

I don't see that this growth is any cause for alarm among administrators. We all have the same goal in the long run—quality care for our patients. The union wants this as much as the administration does. In fact, over the years, the rights and benefits that hospital unions have won for their members have helped upgrade the entire health-care profession.

It's well known that just the potential of a union coming into a hospital often has the effect of pushing management to upgrade employees' salaries and fringe benefits. And any gains, of course, must benefit union and nonunion employees alike.

Unions have improved life for hospital employees in a number of other ways, too. Here are the most common situations that our local chapter deals with:

Employee grievances. As a union steward, I listen to grievances brought to me by union members, counsel them on what to do, and sometimes intercede on their behalf.

Say a technologist is up for a merit increase, but doesn't get it—and doesn't know why he didn't get it. According to the union's agreement with the administration, the supervisor is supposed to warn an employee that his work is unacceptable early enough so he can do something about it. If he gives the employee an unsatisfactory rating on his permanent record without notifying the employee, the employee has a legitimate grievance. When this happens—and it has happened more than once—I speak to the supervisor and ask him to clear the record.

I also make sure union members aren't passed over when it comes to promotions. If an employee who has put in for a promotion is ignored during the selection process—and he's qualified for the job in question—that's a legitimate grievance. This seldom happens in our hospital because a union representative sits in on every meeting of the hospital's promotion panel, which decides what candidates are eligible to be considered for job promotions.

Under this system, every employee, nonunion as well as union, has an equal chance for promotion based on a point system—so many points for education, so many for experience, and so on. At meetings, the panelists look over the qualifications of employees whose names have been submitted for consideration. They then select a pool of five or six candidates for each job made up of the top scorers.

It's a fair system. And every hospital employee benefits from having a union representative on the panel, because all the other panelists represent management.

Discipline. Unions have been instrumental in formulating the formal disciplinary procedure that has become the standard throughout business and industry.

Before this system came into use, an employee could be fired without warning on the basis of flimsy evidence. Now in most laboratories, a supervisor must go through a three-step procedure that includes written documentation of inadequacy. This procedure benefits the employees in two ways: It gives them a chance to present their side of the story when there might be mitigating circumstances; and, when the criticism is justified, it gives them a chance to improve before any further disciplinary action is taken.

Supervisors complain that unions keep them from getting rid of inefficient employees quickly. But I doubt that many of them really want to go back to the old ways. The formal system is fair. Most supervisors wouldn't want to work under a system themselves in which they could be fired capriciously. By now almost every laboratory, union or nonunion, has adopted some version of the formal system.

As a steward, I counsel union members who are in trouble with their supervisors and help when I can. Suppose a technologist has been coming in late for weeks and his supervisor writes up a formal complaint. I talk to the employee to hear his side of the story. If I find this employee hasn't been late in five years until recently and then was late only because of difficult family problems, I'll speak to the supervisor to suggest this be taken into consideration before making the next disciplinary move.

But I'm not out to bury a union member's mistakes. If someone has been coming in late for no good reason, I'll try to persuade him to change his ways. But if he doesn't, I'm not going to defend him in a disciplinary proceeding. Despite what many people seem to think, unions don't want to be in the position of defending uncooperative or lazy employees. We only want to make certain that employees who are in trouble with their supervisors for any reason will be given a fair shake.

As a matter of fact, I never simply take a union member's version as gospel. Whenever I get a complaint, I spend a lot of time checking out the facts. I talk to everyone involved and try to piece together an accurate picture of what happened.

If a technologist complained that his supervisor had unjustly accused him of falsifying test results, for example, and we didn't check out the facts before starting grievance proceedings, evidence of altered or missing test records would be very embarrassing. Even worse, we would lose credibility with the administration, which would make future negotiations more difficult.

Gripes. A gripe is a minor complaint that doesn't necessarily demand action. But as a steward, I try to iron out these minor problems if they warrant attention. Acting as the third party in a dispute, I find I can often defuse a potentially explosive situation.

Suppose a technologist is assigned to work for a particular weekend and has made personal plans for the following weekend. If his supervisor spoils these plans by asking him at the last minute to switch weekends and he complains to me, I'll speak to the supervisor to see whether something can be done.

In such cases, I'm not interested in gaining favored treatment for the union member. I just want to make sure the change was fair and necessary. In fact, this kind of intervention can sometimes benefit a whole department. For example, if I find the last-minute switch was caused by poor planning, I'll recommend improvements that may lead to more efficient scheduling in the future. Of course, if I find the last-minute switch was unavoidable, I readily accede to the supervisor.

In general, our union members get their money's worth. On the national level, the union works to influence legislation that might affect them adversely.

At the local level, besides handling specific complaints and problems, union officials deal with problems of general concern to all members. We negotiate contracts with the administration, put on training seminars dealing with such topics as equal employment opportunity, hold monthly training sessions for stewards, hold meetings of the union's executive board, and meet once a month with personnel officers to discuss problems that have come up. Recently, at one of these meetings, we discussed the scarcity of parking space and how more could be allocated to employees.

I'm surprised more technologists don't join unions. Evidently, many are under the impression that they have to choose between union membership and membership in a professional organization. They don't. They can let professional organizations represent them in such matters as licensure and continuing education—and the union in things like wages, hours, and working conditions. That's what I do, and I've benefited.

43

The Union Threat: What Supervisors Need to Know

Carl W. Mantey, M.H.A.

Laboratory supervisors think of themselves in a variety of terms. Few, however, would be likely to define themselves as: "(An) individual having authority, in the interest of the employer, to hire, transfer, suspend, lay off, recall, promote, discharge, assign, reward, or discipline other employees, or responsibility to direct them, or to adjust their grievances, or to effectively recommend such action."

That definition of a supervisor is one of the most important, though. It's the one contained in the National Labor Relations Act, which guarantees the right of workers to organize.

The words became important for most laboratories in 1974, when nonprofit hospitals were brought under the NLRA. Since then, union activity in hospitals has been intense. In 1975, for example, 542 representation elections were held among health-care workers. Unions won bargaining rights in 330 of those contests. As the labor-management conflict has grown, supervisors have been caught in the middle—between top administration and the organizing employees.

It's an important position. In many cases, supervisors are the key elements in determining whether or not a unionizing effort is successful—both in their general management activities, which can create a climate favorable or unfavorable for a union, and in direct campaigning

FIGURE 43-1

Some Things Supervisors Can Do Regarding Union Activity

1. Tell employees that if a majority of them select the union, the administration will have to deal with it on all their daily problems involving wages, hours, and other conditions of employment. Advise them that the hospital would prefer to continue working with them directly on such matters.
2. Emphasize that you and other members of management are always willing to discuss any subject of interest to them. Point out how earlier problems have been resolved through such discussions.
3. Remind employees of the benefits they currently enjoy, all of which have been obtained without union representation. Avoid promises or threats, either direct or veiled.
4. Point out how wages, benefits, and working conditions compare favorably with other hospitals in the area, whether unionized or not. Information should be factual.
5. Advise employees of the disadvantages of belonging to a union, such as the expense of initiation fees, monthly dues, fines, strike assessments, and membership rules restricting their personal freedom. Quote from the union's constitution and bylaws granting it authority to impose punishment and discipline against its members and giving the international organization power over the local.
6. Tell employees there is a possibility that a union will call a strike or work stoppage even though many workers may not want one and even though the administration is willing to negotiate or has already been bargaining.
7. Point out that any strike can cost employees money in lost wages.
8. Explain that in negotiating with the union, the administration does not have to agree to all of its terms, and certainly not to any that are not in the economic interest of the hospital.
9. Relate any experience you may have had with unions, especially the one seeking to represent the employees. Be factual.
10. Inform employees of anything you know about the union or its officers. One way would be to distribute reprints of articles about them. In some cases, the union will have been the subject of a Congressional or other investigation. News stories about the inquiries can be revealing. Be sure the material is factual and applies only to the union seeking representation. Identify the source of your information.

11. Tell employees your opinion about union policies and union leaders, even though in uncomplimentary terms. Be factually correct.
12. Point out any untrue or misleading statements made by an organizer, in a handbill, or through any other medium of union propaganda. You may always give employees the facts.
13. Tell employees that they are free to join or not to join any organization without prejudice to their status with the company.
14. Advise the workers that merely signing a union authorization card or application for membership does not mean they must vote for the union. They should know, though, that in some cases, the union may use the signed authorization cards to obtain bargaining rights *without* an NLRB election.
15. Inform employees of the NLRB election procedures and the importance of voting, and emphasize the secrecy of the ballot.
16. Tell employees about their legal rights. The hospital should not, however, encourage or finance employee suits or other legal actions.
17. Make and consistently enforce rules limiting solicitation of membership or discussion of union affairs to outside working time so that it will not interfere with an employee's own work or impede the work of others. Remember, however, an employee can solicit members and discuss unionism on his own time, even on hospital premises, when it does not interrupt work.
18. Restrict the distribution of all union literature to the nonworking areas of the hospital. Union material may be prohibited from bulletin boards, but only if their use is limited to official hospital correspondence.
19. Restrict the wearing of union buttons to areas where there is no patient contact. A general prohibition of buttons would probably be considered an unfair labor practice. However, the National Labor Relations Board would accept the patient-area restriction because of the potentially damaging psychological effects of the displays.
20. Enforce all other hospital rules impartially in accordance with established procedures. You may discipline or discharge for cause if the action is taken without regard to the employee's union status. Avoid taking such action before a representation election; be sure you can document your assertions.

(These guidelines were adapted from a list prepared by the Texas Association of Business.)

against any union threats. In many cases, workers vote in union elections either for or against their immediate supervisors, rather than the institution as a whole.

Although the responsibility is great, a supervisor's position in regard to the union is not always clear. The language of the act is open to interpretation by the National Labor Relations Board and the courts, and it can be difficult to keep up with the many decisions. In fact, a recent study found that two-thirds of hospital administrators had *no* working knowledge of the act.

The law is clear about at least one point: Supervisors are considered

FIGURE 43-2

Some Things Supervisors Can't Do Regarding Union Activity

1. Promise employees a pay increase, promotion, benefit, or special favor if they stay out of the union or vote against it.
2. Threaten loss of job, reduction of income, or discontinuance of privileges or benefits presently enjoyed.
3. Discharge, discipline, or lay off an employee because of his activities in behalf of the union or threaten to do so.
4. Threaten any of the above acts through a third party.
5. Spy on union meetings. Parking across the street from a union hall would be a suspect activity.
6. Conduct yourself in a way that would indicate you are watching employees to determine whether or not they are participating in union activities.
7. Discriminate against workers actively supporting the union by intentionally assigning undesirable work.
8. Transfer employees prejudicially because of union affiliation.
9. Show partiality to nonunion employees over those active in behalf of the union.
10. Discipline or penalize employees supporting a union for an action permitted to nonunion workers.
11. Separate pro-union workers from the other workers through assignments or transfers.

part of management and are required to support its position in any union conflict. Failure to do so can be grounds for dismissal.

It is top management's responsibility, though, to help supervisors meet a union threat. Administrators should keep themselves informed about the law and its interpretations, and then pass along the information to middle management. Labor-relations workshops, perhaps presented by expert consultants, should be given before an organizing effort is even apparent. Then if a unionization attempt does come about, supervisors should be apprised of the situation as it develops and of the steps they should take to counter it.

12. Ask employees how they intend to vote in a union election.
13. Question workers about whether or not they belong to a union or have signed an application or authorization card. This point also applies to job applicants.
14. Inquire about the internal affairs of the union. Some employees may volunteer such information. It is not an unfair labor practice to listen, but you may not ask questions to obtain additional information.
15. Ask employees about the union sentiments of their co-workers.
16. Say that the administration will not deal with the union.
17. Urge employees to persuade others to oppose the union or stay out of it.
18. Give financial support or assistance to a union, its representative, or employees. This restriction is to avoid administration's favoring one union over another.
19. Make speeches to assemblies of employees on hospital time within the 24-hour period before a representative election.
20. Call employees to your office or visit their homes to discuss the union. The location is the important point here. Although you can give your opinion about the union, to do so in some settings could be construed as an implied threat. The best place for such conversations is an open area with several people present.

(These guidelines were adapted from a list prepared by the Texas Association of Business.)

Supervisors also have the responsibility to keep the administration informed about the situation in their departments. This point is particularly important prior to the appearance of any unionizing effort. In many cases, employees become involved with unions because of dissatisfaction with working conditions and management, rather than wages and benefits. If supervisors give administrators the impression that all is well when it really is not, small problems can fester into major ones.

When an organizing attempt cannot be avoided, supervisors become a hospital's first line of defense. Although their conduct during this period is limited by law, supervisors should remember two points. First, they may continue to carry out all of their management responsibilities: They may hire, fire, discipline, and make work assignments *as long as these actions are not related to the union effort*. Second, they can actively campaign against the union.

Since the NLRA restrictions are often ambiguous, there are pitfalls in both areas. And the penalty for mistakes can be severe. If a manager is found by the National Labor Relations Board to have committed an unfair labor practice, if he threatened firing someone for his pro-union activities, for example, a union can be granted bargaining rights regardless of the outcome of a representation election.

The accompanying list of dos and don'ts should help supervisors avoid mistakes. These guidelines should also assist them in carrying out the most effective defense against a union threat.

IX
PERSONNEL PRACTICES

44

What's Legal in Employment Practices

Walter L. Scott, Ph.D.

Staffing is an ongoing chore for clinical laboratory managers and supervisors. Many laboratory administrators have lightened that burden by relinquishing some staffing tasks to the personnel department; however, clinical lab personnel must fit such unique requirements that effective staffing demands significant lab input. It follows that the laboratory supervisor must keep abreast of the legal considerations of the hiring process—and promotion, firing, and a wide variety of other employer-employee relationships.

This involves an awareness of a fast-growing body of law. On all levels, government is showing an increasing determination to intervene in the employment processes of all industries, including health care. Over the past dozen-or-so years, regulatory lawmaking has intensified. The laboratory manager must know the law in order to avert costly litigation, unfavorable publicity, and the possible erosion of employee morale. Legal fees, court costs, fines, and an overburdened laboratory staff in the absence of workers called to testify are some of the debits accruing to an institution involved in such litigation. Violators risk huge penalties. Among corporate employers, for example, A.T.&T. paid a settlement of $38 million in penalties and increased pay in one year alone, with additional payments in subsequent years.

To avoid legal difficulties, you should be aware of the laws that affect laboratories as employers. Following is a rundown of the pertinent laws now on the books and, after that, some pointers about how to comply with them.

The foundation for much of the law affecting employers is the **14th Amendment** to the Constitution, adopted more than 100 years ago. Its "equal protection" clause directed that no state "deprive any person of life, liberty, or property without due process of law; nor deny to any person within its jurisdiction the equal protection of the law."

From the same era came the **Civil Rights Acts of 1866, 1870, and 1871.** These acts granted to all persons the equal protection of the law previously enjoyed only by white citizens. The acts also provided that those who deprive others of their rights should be liable to the injured party.

Workers who felt they had been discriminated against were still relying on these pioneering civil rights acts until fairly recently. For example, in the case of Brown v. Gaston County Dyeing Machine Co., the Fourth Circuit Court of Appeals ruled, under the Civil Rights Act of 1866, that a black denied a job because of his race was entitled to back pay for the period in which he suffered discrimination—from the time he applied for a job in 1960 until he was employed in 1961.

Now supplementing these early civil rights laws is the comprehensive **Civil Rights Act of 1964.** It forbids employment practices discriminatory for reasons of race, color, religion, sex, or national origin. It is important to note that this law covers a wide variety of the many aspects of employment, including recruiting, interviewing, advertising, application forms, employment tests, pay, training programs, and work and shift assignments.

This broad-gauged act applies to state and local governments, educational institutions, establishments employing 15 or more persons, and organizations participating in Federally funded programs, such as Medicare. Under the act, the employer is implicitly obliged to make restitution to all persons who have been denied equal employment opportunity. This may require instituting pay raises, granting back pay, or other corrective measures.

Amendments passed in 1972 added greater impact to the Civil Rights Act of 1964 by creating the **Equal Employment Opportunity Commission,** which functions to enforce the law and investigate claims of discrimination.

Judicial decisions based on the Civil Rights Act of 1964 have more clearly defined and enlarged the scope of the legislation. One line of decisions in particular applies to the lab. It started in 1971 with a U.S. Supreme Court ruling in the case of Griggs v. Duke Power Co.

In that case, several blacks charged discrimination when they were denied maintenance and repair jobs because they did not have high school diplomas. While the employer required this of all applicants, the high court ruled against the power company. The Court held that it is the burden of the employer to show that "any given requirement must have a manifest relationship to the employment in question." In this example, the company failed to show why a high school diploma was needed to perform maintenance work. In the Court's opinion, what is required ". . . is the removal of artificial, arbitrary, and unnecessary barriers to employment when the barriers operate invidiously to discriminate."

This reasoning was applied to a laboratory situation in a New York case, Townsend v. Nassau County Medical Center (see Washington Report, *MLO,* March 1976). In this case, the U.S. District Court, Eastern District of New York, ruled under the Civil Rights Act of 1964 that Nassau County violated the rights of Margaret Townsend, RMT, by demoting her from Medical Technologist I (blood bank supervisor) to the lower-paying classification of Laboratory Technician II because she had no college degree.

The court said: "There is no evidence that persons who possess a degree perform better in blood banking in terms of identifiable criteria than those that do not." Also, "evidence fails to support the proposition that acceptable college programs relate to the practical demands of the blood bank."

Nassau County appealed, and the decision was eventually reversed by the Second Circuit Court of Appeals.

Laboratorians should realize, however, that a similar challenge might someday be upheld, with serious ramifications impinging on the whole spectrum of laboratory job qualifications, educational requirements, professional certification, and licensure.

Though the civil rights laws may be the major kind of legislation that laboratory managers must comply with, they are by no means the only ones. Other laws that affect the employer-employee relationship are:

The Fair Labor Standards Act of 1938 (Wage and Hour Law) is administered and enforced by the Wage and Hour Division of the

Department of Labor. It requires payment of at least the minimum wage and time and a half for overtime. It sets a minimum age of 16 for employment. Professional, administrative, executive, and sales personnel are excluded from the minimum wage and overtime requirements. It is interesting to note that medical laboratory technologists and technicians are not excluded as professionals from the Wage and Hour Law provisions. This law affects laboratory recruitment by influencing decisions on scheduling overtime, hiring additional employees, and automating more fully.

The Labor-Management Relations Act of 1947 (Taft-Hartley Act) makes it illegal to refuse to hire an otherwise qualified applicant because he is or is not a member of some particular union. Furthermore, the law forbids any recruiting activities that tend to encourage or discourage membership in any particular labor organization.

The Equal Pay Act of 1963 was passed as an amendment to the Fair Labor Standards Act, and is often summarized in the phrase, "Equal pay for equal work." It deals primarily with wage discrimination on the basis of sex. I can recall, in the recent past, situations in the lab in which male supervisors or section chiefs were paid substantially more than females in positions of equal skill, effort, responsibility, and similar working conditions—definitely an illegal situation.

Under this law, employers must keep records on wages, hours, and other items listed below. Most of this information on laboratory employees would be kept for ordinary business reasons, as well as to comply with other laws and regulations. Records of the following are required:

Name, home address, and if under age 19, birthdate; sex and occupation; hour and day of workweek and shift; regular hourly pay rate; hours worked each workday and total hours worked each workweek; total daily or weekly straight-time earnings; total overtime pay for the workweek; deductions or additions to wages; total wages paid each pay period; date of payment and pay period covered.

Executive Orders 11246 and 11375, signed by President Lyndon B. Johnson, forbid discrimination by race, color, religion, national origin, or sex in establishments operating under Federal contracts. The Office of Federal Contract Compliance (OFCC) was established to see that Federal contractors adhere to the requirements of the orders. An employer who is found to be noncompliant can be penalized and may lose his Government contract (or license). In meeting Government requirements, an employer may have to adopt an "Affirmative Action" program. This may require the institution to draw up a plan of action showing discrimination prevention as well as a plan to correct past employment inequities.

Age Discrimination in Employment Act of 1967 deals with discrimination against persons between 40 and 65 years of age in employment and employment advertising. It applies to establishments employing 25 or more persons. In addition, Executive Order 11141 prohibits age discrimination by Federal contractors.

Those are the laws that affect the relationship between employers and employees. What can you do to avoid time-consuming and possibly expensive litigation over your employment practices? Here are some suggestions:

1. Know the law. Ignorance is no defense when the law is broken. When in doubt, call the nearest office of the EEOC (listed in the white pages of the telephone directory under United States Government).

2. Have a knowledgeable advisor for personnel administrative matters or have a legal counselor. A relatively small investment can avert very expensive penalties, court costs, and attorney fees.

3. Have a job description prepared before interviewing applicants. Be as specific as you require for the job; however, be able to show how each requirement is "job-related."

4. Have each applicant complete an application form.

5. Have a list of precise qualifications. Remember that rejection of an applicant is acceptable only when based on qualifications. If an applicant is obviously unsuitable, have a list of "knockout" questions available so the applicant can disqualify himself. For example: "Are you willing to stand continuously for periods of up to three to five hours?" "Do you accept the risk of possible contraction of hepatitis or other diseases related to this position?" "Will you be able to work rotating shifts?" "Can you work weekends?"

6. Be able to prove that the person hired was better qualified.

The best safeguard is to know your vulnerability regarding your employment practices.

45

Affirmative Action: What It Really Means

Neal M. Hoffman, M.P.A., and
Bettina G. Martin, M.S., HT(ASCP)

Mention affirmative action at your next coffee break or administrative meeting and you're likely to stir a spirited discussion. In fact, the merits of the concept have been argued throughout the country during the '70s, and the Supreme Court has several times wrestled with the question of what its limits should be.

The results of this national debate will be important for society as a whole, but they should be of particular interest to laboratorians: Many hospitals, and almost all of the larger ones, are required by law to have affirmative-action programs.

For all the high emotions that affirmative action evokes and the wide-ranging effects it can have, surprisingly few of us actually know what its goals are, how they are set, or what actions are being taken to accomplish them. All too often, the heated discussions that take place about the issue are based on unfounded opinion, not often enough on the facts.

While there are legitimate grounds for differences—the Supreme Court's decisions on the matter have been neither definitive nor unanimous—the arguments should be based on accurate information. Let's look at what affirmative action means and, at the same time, clear up some common misconceptions about it.

Much of the confusion about affirmative action derives from the fact that the term is used to cover a lot of territory. In general, affirmative action is a plan for positive steps that an organization will take to insure equal opportunities for everyone, regardless of race, creed, color, national origin, sex, marital status, age, or disability. A variety of state and Federal laws and executive orders define these programs and spell out who must adopt them. The different rules and regulations require different actions and apply in different cases.

The affirmative-action requirements that most often apply to hospitals are those administered by the Office of Federal Contract Compliance. Any employer holding Federal contracts or subcontracts totaling more than $10,000 a year must have an affirmative-action program for women and minorities, including blacks, Hispanics, Asians, American Indians, and Vietnam War veterans. If the contracts total more than $50,000, the program must be written.

In addition, an employer with more than $2,500 in Federal contracts must also have an affirmative-action program for the handicapped. (These programs are discussed in Chapter 49.)

Since many Federal research grants are considered to be contracts, almost all university-affiliated hospitals are covered by these contract-compliance requirements. In addition, many states have similar regulations that apply to government institutions or contractors. In New York, for example, all state facilities must have affirmative-action programs.

Employers who have been found by the courts to have discriminated in the past may also be required to have affirmative-action programs. Some companies—including A.T.&T.—have agreed to legally binding programs when faced with discrimination suits. And finally, many employers have adopted purely voluntary programs.

Individual programs vary widely. For one reason, many different laws and orders govern them. For another, the regulations usually state broad guidelines for the programs and leave the means for implementing them up to the institution or company. Most programs, though, are similar to the ones for Federal contractors.

Generally speaking, there are three basic elements in an affirmative-action program: a utilization analysis of current employment to show how many women and minority members are employed in comparison with their availability, a statement of hiring and promotion goals and a timetable for correcting any deficiencies uncovered by the study, and a plan for attaining the goals.

Along with defining what affirmative action is, it may be helpful to talk about what it isn't. We've found there are three major misconceptions on the subject: that affirmative action means "hiring by the numbers" or setting quotas for hiring women or minority members; that it calls for "reverse discrimination" against white males; and that it leads to a lowering of standards.

We would like to debunk these myths. In doing so, we think it will be easier to understand what affirmative action is and how it can be applied to your laboratory situation.

Myth No. 1: Hiring by the numbers. Some see affirmative action as a quota system that precludes hiring white males until a certain number of women or minority members have been hired.

The truth is that the guidelines for Federal contractors specifically prohibit quotas. "Goals may not be rigid and inflexible quotas . . . but must be targets reasonably attainable by means of applying every good faith effort to make . . . the program work," the regulations state. This position is close to the one taken by the Supreme Court in its 1979 Bakke decision. In that case, the Court ruled that race could be used as a factor in the admission process, but it outlawed numerical quotas.

If hiring and promotion goals may not be quotas, then what are they? Simply put, they are statements by the employer about the number of women or minority members it will try to place in each job. The aim is to let them reach a level of employment that would be achieved by drawing without bias from the available labor pool. Obviously, defining the available labor pool is an important—and difficult—part of the process. That's where the utilization and availability studies come in.

The Federal guidelines require an employer to do a study and set a goal for women and each of the identifiable minorities in each of its job classifications. In doing so, it must take into account a variety of factors. Among other things, it must consider the minority population of the surrounding area, the degree of minority unemployment, and the availability of minorities with the necessary skills for the job. The demographic information for these studies comes from the census, Department of Labor studies, professional organizations, and any other sources that are available to the employer.

Clearly, the utilization studies and goal setting can involve a complex statistical analysis, which is usually done by an affirmative-action office. Let's look at one example of how the process might work:

Suppose women make up 38 percent of the work force in your recruitment area, the nationwide figure based on the 1970 census. In that case, they should make up about the same overall proportion of your employees, and that proportion should also hold for each job classification.

When you consider the availability of those with particular skills, the process may be a bit different. As a hypothetical example, if only 10 percent of the technologists in your recruitment area are black, you can be expected to have only that proportion of blacks among your technologists, regardless of their proportion in the overall work force.

Much of the criticism of affirmative action as "hiring by the numbers" derives from the statistical nature of these utilization studies. But some employers further this misconception by approaching the studies as abstract numerical exercises. In their attempts to prepare a plan that complies with the letter of the law, they often spend more time and effort devising goals than trying to achieve them. They forget the purpose of the goals and lose sight of the fact that they should be achievable objectives.

Ample evidence of the need for goals can be found by looking at the situation now and in the recent past. Here are some of the facts: Unemployment for blacks continues to be about twice that for whites. In 1974, blacks made up a larger proportion of the poor than they did in 1959. Similar statistics hold for women and other minorities. Between 1960 and 1975, the unemployment rate for women increased faster than it did for men. In 1977, women employed full time had a median annual income of $8,814 compared with $15,070 for men. It's not only reasonable but clearly necessary to set goals to rectify these inequities.

Myth No. 2: Affirmative action calls for reverse discrimination. Some people see any preferential treatment of minorities or women as discrimination against the majority of white males in the work force.

The truth is that the Federal guidelines require employers to take positive steps to recruit, hire, train, and promote minorities and women. The OFCC regulations state that the employer must: "Base decisions on employment so as to further the principle of equal employment opportunity," and "insure that promotion decisions are in accord with" those same principles.

In other words, if it should come to the hypothetically abundant but actually infrequent pair of equally qualified candidates, the employer must give preference to the one who will further affirmative action.

The affirmative-action program agreed to by A.T.&T., in fact, went beyond that. In order to meet its goals, the company agreed to fill jobs by hiring or promoting "basically qualified" workers over the "best qualified" or most senior. When they did, it was called an "override," and there have been more than 40,000 of them since 1973.

A group of "overridden" employees took the company to court, claiming reverse discrimination—that their rights had been violated because of preferential treatment given to others on the basis of race or sex. A Federal district court disagreed, saying that the color and sex consciousness of the program was justified in order to remedy past discrimination. That decision was affirmed in circuit court on appeal, and the Supreme Court declined to hear the case.

Such direct conflicts between the interests of individual employees are perhaps the most dramatic aspect of affirmative-action programs. But as equal-employment goals are reached, the number of these conflicts will necessarily decrease. Meanwhile, there are other steps employers can take toward their goals to diminish the likelihood of these clashes.

The recruitment process offers one obvious area for effective action. As the proportion of minority and women candidates increases, their proportion among those hired will rise naturally. The supervisor or director with hiring responsibility should work closely with the search committee or personnel office, explaining the needs of the position and suggesting areas where qualified minority candidates are likely to be recruited.

They should also be on the alert for and encourage promotable minority and women employees already on staff. In one medical center, for example, a qualified woman employee felt she had been denied a promotion opportunity. She went to the affirmative-action officer with her story, and he brought it to the attention of the hospital administration. The woman got the position, and the word of the affirmative-action officer was a big help. A supervisor can play the same kind of role.

Myth No. 3: Affirmative action leads to lower standards. Believers of this myth claim that in order to find enough qualified women or minority employees, qualifications must be relaxed.

The truth is that in many cases, this means that employers must simply do away with practices that clearly have discriminated against certain groups in the past—such as a requirement that all hospital maintenance workers should be men.

Few would argue with the removal of clearly arbitrary policies, but in fact, such restrictions played a large part in creating the disparities that affirmative action seeks to correct. Very often the restrictions were more tradition than policy and were defended by saying, "We've always done it this way."

In recent years, the courts have ruled that an employment policy that has a disproportionately negative effect on any group is unlawful unless there is a compelling business necessity for it. And courts have defined compelling business necessity very narrowly.

A requirement that all employees in a job be at least 5 feet 7 inches, for example, would effectively screen out most women and a disproportionate number of Hispanic and Asian men. If the job involved having to reach seven feet into the air, the employer might claim a business necessity. But if it were possible to change the nature of the job or provide platforms for the employees, the claim would be disallowed.

Other qualification requirements may be more subtly restrictive. A rule that a technologist must have at least four years of continuous service in order to qualify for a supervisory position would discriminate against a woman whose employment was interrupted for maternity leave. It's unfortunate—and intolerable—that removing such unfair and unnecessary standards is seen by some as lowering standards.

There are, of course, occasional abuses in which employers' misguided attempts to meet goals have resulted in placing individuals in jobs for which they are obviously unqualified. This does great harm to the institution and the employees and adds to the myth of lowering standards. Fortunately, such cases are very rare.

Employers find, in fact, that affirmative-action programs actually improve rather than lower the quality of work. By opening opportunities to a wider spectrum of employees, employers find they have a larger, more diverse pool of talent to draw from. Morale is likely to go up and turnover down as a large segment of employees who once felt they were in dead-end jobs are able to see new opportunities in areas from which they were once barred.

The success of affirmative action depends in large measure on the supervisors and directors who do the actual hiring, firing, and promoting. A fair and open-minded attitude on the part of these decision makers is more important than any formal program. Discrimination is a deeply ingrained habit that, if unchecked, will perpetuate deprivation, unemployment, and other ills of society. As with any habit, the first step toward a cure is an awareness of the problem. The next step is a commitment to solve it.

The greatest obstacle to equal employment is a lack of understanding. If a hospital does have an affirmative-action officer, laboratorians should work closely with that officer to uncover and remove any discriminatory situations. The program should be explained in newsletters or other in-house publications. Seminars for airing grievances about the program or explaining controversial issues should be encouraged.

The discussion of affirmative action that begins on a coffee break or at an administrative meeting should lead to a thorough study of what each person can do to further the cause of equal opportunity for all.

46

Promoting Without Discrimination

Robert M. Dews

You have known for several days now that your chief tech will be leaving at the end of the month. While you're pleased that he can move to a more responsible position, there is one question you dread facing. It's not, "Who will take his place?" but, "What do I tell the losers?"

Of the four eligible candidates, you have a gut feeling that Linda Goodhart is the most logical replacement for the chief tech position—that she'll fit right in with the administration. But you must admit that your "I-had-a-gut-feeling-that-she-was-the-best-person-for-the-job" reasoning might sound a little weak to the other three candidates—the losers. When you further explain that she would fit in with the administration, they probably still would not concede your superior administrative judgment. To answer their questions, you need a good, factual, easily documented explanation for your decision. Finding this explanation is a problem you feel had best be tackled right away.

You search the four personnel folders and hope that somehow they'll shed some light on the logic of your choice. But even a cursory glance tells you your logic isn't there. For a brief escapist moment, you fondle the idea that maybe the other three candidates won't ask. But quicker than you can say equal employment opportunity, the thought of Maxwell Harrington snaps you back to reality.

Maxwell Harrington is not only one of the most competitive techs in the lab, he is black. He will ask. He is probably the only one who would really press the issue, though. The other two would probably just walk back to the bench after hearing you incant, "Gee, with so many highly qualified techs to choose from, it really was a difficult decision, but I chose the one I thought would do the lab the most good."

This has always worked in the past. Especially with Miss Grogan. Those platitudes would bring tears to Miss Grogan's eyes. Of the final four, she has the most seniority, which certainly deserves some consideration. As for Bill Bottomly, your newest senior tech, he probably doesn't expect the job anyway. He has been a senior tech for only two years now, and the others have at least five years more seniority. Besides being low man on the totem pole, Bill is white, Anglo-Saxon, and male, so there's no way he can accuse you of discrimination.

It looks as if your only problem will be with Maxwell, and then his major complaint will probably be that you didn't promote him because he's black. He may also remind you of the existence of a document called the affirmative-action plan and the department's EEO policy that says something about preferentially promoting minority employees. This is not to mention your own boss, who said just the other day that it would look good, affirmative-actionwise, if we had some minority members in higher positions. Well, maybe Linda Goodhart isn't the most "logical" choice after all. But if you promote Maxwell, Linda will no doubt point out that the affirmative-action plan applies to sex discrimination, too, and that you're nothing but a chauvinist.

Obviously, more than casual research is needed to solve this dilemma. For one thing, you'll have to go back and actually read the departmental affirmative-action plan and EEO policy statement to find out exactly where you stand. Do you have to promote minorities in *preference* to nonminorities? Are you legally required to have a given percentage of women in "positions of responsibility"?

No matter how carefully you study the statement, you can't find a definite yes-or-no answer to those questions. You don't even find a "yes, but." What you *do* find is a discussion of how unfortunate it is that minorities and women have been denied equal opportunity for advancement, with which you wholeheartedly agree. Unfortunately, this doesn't help you choose your next chief tech. It doesn't tell you whom you can and can't promote. What it does is give you a mandate to insure equal opportunity for all employees in your promotion practices. Terrific!

The EEO policy statement further points out that in hiring or promoting employees, you must evaluate them on an *equal basis* and on *job-related* activities or qualifications. What does this mean? Well, in this particular situation, it means that all your employees should have an equal opportunity to be promoted to chief tech and that your choice must be based only on job-related activities or qualifications.

What else does the EEO policy statement say about minorities and promotions? It says that if disproportionately few members of a minority group are represented in your work force, then this fact alone is evidence that an "adverse effect" against that minority group exists. This doesn't mean that you necessarily discriminated against that minority group. It simply means they are not represented as well as they should be and that you *might* have discriminated against them.

The EEO policy also says that if an adverse effect is shown, it is up to you, the supervisor, to show that your promotional practices were not based on discriminatory practices. This means that if Maxwell files a complaint with the Equal Employment Opportunity Commission charging that you have disproportionately few blacks in the lab and alleging that he was denied the promotion because he is black, then he has established grounds for an investigation. He has shown that an "adverse effect" against blacks exists. Then, the burden is on you to prove that you denied Maxwell the promotion, not because he is black, but because the individual you promoted is better qualified. If you can prove this, you can promote anyone you want to chief tech, as long as he's the best qualified individual, and you can prove it.

This brings you right back to the original problem: How do you prove your decision is the right one and not a frivolous product of your prejudices and personal preferences? Since performance appraisals are about the only documentation you have of your employees' work, their importance has increased phenomenally!

Having done your homework, you once again pull out the performance appraisals of the final four. This time, you review them with two important guidelines in mind: job relatedness and equality in evaluation. You get no further than the first area of appraisal when you realize you're in trouble. Is "attitude" a measure of performance or personality? If it is a measure of performance, is it job-related? The senior tech job description shows you that a good attitude is not a requirement for the job. That takes care of that—if it's not job-related, it's not a fair measure of performance.

Looking at the other headings on the performance appraisal, you come to "skills—accuracy, neatness, quantity and quality of work produced." Now *that's* job-related! The question becomes, how do you measure the skills of the final four? What concrete, observable actions of theirs made you appraise them the way you did? Why did you rate Maxwell a grade 2 "good" and Miss Grogan a grade 3 "good"? What differentiates the two? For that matter, what differentiates "acceptable" from "outstanding" skills?

To answer these questions, you decide to make new special promotional performance appraisals, as free of your personal prejudices as possible. You will evaluate each candidate's observable actions that are directly related to the job. The good feeling you have comes not only from knowing you'll give all four fair and equal treatment, but from an intellectual curiosity about how valid your original decision was. Is Linda Goodhart really the best qualified person for the job, or was your original decision influenced by her charming personality?

As a starting point, you go back to the original job description of the senior tech, specifying the skills and duties necessary for the position. Under skills, for example, it calls for, "thorough knowledge of the principles and laboratory applications of clinical chemistry, current laboratory methods, equipment, and materials."

Next, you establish definitions for poor, good, and outstanding performance of this skill. The definitions look something like this:

Poor performance of this skill is exemplified by such actions as failure to apply correct formulas for calculating results, attempting to use improper reagents, inappropriate use of instruments, or failing to maintain instruments in optimal conditions. Documentation should be specific, such as, "Incorrectly calibrated DK-2 for phosphate analysis," or, "Used wrong stain on prepared slides," or, "Failed to report results in correct units."

Good performance of this skill is exemplified by such actions as correctly calibrating instruments and maintaining them in optimal condition, using appropriate reagents in analyses, reporting results in acceptable ways, and using proper stains on prepared slides.

Outstanding performance is exemplified by such actions as establishing and setting up operating conditions and calibrations for new procedures; developing more accurate, faster, or more efficient ways of performing analyses; improving reporting methods, either by lowering costs, providing faster reporting procedures, or improving readability of reports; developing new reagents or stains to help in performing analyses; or improving methods of using old reagents.

After doing this for all major skills and duties, you have the basis for a job-related performance appraisal—one specifically job-related to the position of senior tech in your laboratory. And looking over your revised performance appraisal, you feel the effort was worth it. You've not only avoided the effects of any prejudices, but you've given your employees, and yourself, a clearer understanding of how you judge performance.

Now you're ready to prepare the four special performance appraisals with your new definitions of poor, good, and outstanding. This time, you have specific job-related actions in mind. The fact that Linda Goodhart walks around the laboratory beaming and smiling and telling everyone how lucky she is to work here shows she has a good attitude, but is it job-related? Is it as job-related as the fact that Bill Bottomly spends 15 to 30 minutes after work every day planning the next day's work? Both have good attitudes, but how are they related to doing the job? Linda's attitude makes her pleasant to be with, but Bill's attitude makes his section more efficient. This efficiency is easily documented by the greater number of analyses his section gets out, as well as better organization of the workflow.

What about Maxwell and Miss Grogan? Maxwell is an aggressive, hardworking employee—at least he always seems busier than anyone else. However, a closer examination reveals that many of his actions don't really improve his job performance. Sure, he has a neat work area, and he's always busy rearranging his reagents and equipment. But in terms of the number of analyses done in his section, his record is not significantly better than the other candidates'. When you consider Miss Grogan's performance record, you note that her analyses are always neat, accurate, and on time, but as far as original contributions to the laboratory, you see nothing in her record that's above average for her position.

In reviewing the performance of the four, you realize that many things that made the biggest impression on you aren't job-related at all. For example, are Miss Grogan's 30 years of experience job-related? Yes, to a degree, but her experience doesn't seem to help her do her job better than the others. Another thing: You had always rated Linda high in job knowledge. She knows a lot about biochemistry, for sure. If any of the techs has a question about biochemistry, they go right to her for the answer. But does this extra knowledge help Linda do her job? Well, not really. Beyond a basic understanding of the fundamentals of the tests performed, additional knowledge about esoteric biochemical mechanisms doesn't really help. In terms of job-related knowledge, it's more important to know how to keep the analyzer working than to know the reaction mechanism for converting sugar to protein.

Finally, after reviewing the new appraisals of knowledge, skills, and work habits and how they relate to the official job description, you find your next chief tech. He is Bill Bottomly.

You have also found the answer to the question that was bugging you most. When the losers ask, "Why did you promote him instead of me?" you'll know what to say. To Linda, you'll respond: "Linda, your pleasant personality certainly makes the laboratory a nicer place to work, and your superior knowledge of biochemistry is unquestioned, but I promoted Bill because of the way he organizes the work in his section. By optimizing the use of instrumentation, he increased his section's productivity 35 percent during the year."

To Maxwell, you'll say: "Maxwell, I really appreciate the way you keep your work area organized. Your efforts at keeping the laboratory clean and orderly make a definite contribution, but I promoted Bill because he organized the workflow and instrument use in his section to increase the weekly number of tests run from 350 to 475."

To Miss Grogan, your answer will be: "Miss Grogan, the fact that I can always count on your section to get out its share of the work makes it easier for me to plan the laboratory workload, and I appreciate your 30 years of service. I promoted Bill, however, because he not only gets out his share of the work, he also is constantly searching for and finding ways to get more done. His efforts along these lines have reduced the cost per test in his section from $2.75 to $1.25 over the past two years. This compares with no reduction at all in your section and a less than 75 cents per test reduction in the others."

And while you realize that, sure, Linda Goodhart would have fit in with the administration, when it comes down to documented, job-related performance, the facts point to Bill Bottomly. And documented, job-related performance is the only criterion that will stand up under the cross-examination of the other candidates and the Equal Employment Opportunity Commission.

47

Firing According to the Rules

Bettina G. Martin, M.S., HT(ASCP),
and Vincent Scicchitano

"You're fired!"

These are among the most powerful words a laboratory supervisor or director ever has to say to an employee. They are the last resort, used only after all other possible solutions to the problem have failed. The words represent a point of no return, a complete break. Maybe.

The fact is that terminations are not automatically final. With the increasing unionization of the health-care field and the multitude of government agencies watching over employee rights, almost any laboratorian who is fired has some avenue of appeal. And unless the termination is not only justified but handled according to strict procedures, the challenge will probably be successful. The hospital may even be ordered to reinstate the employee, and he's not likely to return a better or happier worker for the experience.

The employee-rights field is governed by a complex set of laws and regulations that are constantly evolving. To get an idea of their complexity, consider all of the groups and agencies that operate in the field:

- State and Federal civil rights agencies and the Federal Equal Employment Opportunity Commission have jurisdiction in cases of alleged discrimination.

- The National Labor Relations Board and state labor boards rule on complaints that terminations were related to union activities, and if your lab is already unionized, any firing will probably be subject to arbitration.
- Labs that work on Federal contracts are answerable for employment practices to the Office of Federal Contract Compliance.
- Finally, any employee who has been discharged can always take his case to court for a ruling under the Fair Labor Standards Act and still other labor laws.

The field is so complex and changeable that personnel officers spend much of their time trying to keep up with developments. A laboratory supervisor or director certainly wouldn't be expected to know all the finer points of labor law. But there are a few general rules you should be aware of before you consider that ultimate solution to an employee problem. If you follow these rules, the words "You're fired!" should indeed be final.

The first rule is that any termination must be made according to an established policy that applies equally to all employees. The second is that any disciplinary action—and the reasons for it—must be well documented. As an independent arbitrator wrote in a recent decision involving our hospital, "In labor relations, it is well recognized that the discharge of an employee is comparable to capital punishment under the penal code. Guilt must be proved beyond a reasonable doubt."

Disciplinary policy. It is generally accepted in the employee-relations field that a three-stage disciplinary policy, providing for progressively severe action at each step, is the most effective. After all, the object is to get rid of the problem, not the person, and to help the worker improve, not to punish him.

Except for instances of gross misconduct, such as falsification of test results, a termination will not be upheld unless you can demonstrate that you've tried to correct the offense through less drastic action. And you'll never be able to prove incompetence as a reason for firing unless you've pointed out to the worker what his shortcomings are and made every effort to show him how to perform his duties correctly.

The policy's first stage should be a meeting with the employee to tell him that his performance is unacceptable. You should be as specific as possible in pointing out the offense, and you should be as helpful as possible in discussing ways to improve the situation. After you've talked with the employee, make a record of the meeting for your files, including a summary of what was said.

Ideally, the meeting will correct the problem, but if it doesn't, the next step in the disciplinary procedure is a written warning. Make two copies—one to give the employee and the other to put in his personnel file. The document should refer to the earlier discussion of the problem, spell out your complaints, and state that disciplinary action will be taken if the offense continues.

At no time—either orally or in writing—should you mention the possibility of dismissal, even if you consider it a friendly warning rather than a threat. It may seem natural to say, "Listen, Jack, if you keep coming in an hour late every day, you're going to get fired." But arbitrators have consistently ruled that from the time such a statement is made, management is working toward the employee's discharge, not trying to avoid it.

The third stage of the progressive policy is actual disciplinary action. This stage should also allow for progressively severe measures, perhaps starting with a reprimand and continuing to demotion, and, finally, termination. If your lab is unionized, the contract may have provisions for suspension, loss of vacation time, and fines as disciplinary measures.

If the process does reach the ultimate step, it's best that the worker's supervisor not handle the termination interview. The lab director or personnel administrator, through training and experience, is better qualified to deal with that situation. And if the firing should be overturned, it would almost certainly be easier for the supervisor and employee to reestablish a relationship if they haven't gone through a dismissal confrontation together.

Your three-stage policy should be written out from start to finish, and any disciplinary action you take should be based on that document. This will not only help you act consistently in disciplinary matters, but it will also bolster your argument if you do have to prove you acted fairly. In addition, it will provide a guide to your employees, showing what you expect from them and what they can expect from you.

The personnel department should help develop your disciplinary policy, and you should consult with someone from that office before taking any action under it. Of course, any disciplinary measures you take should be endorsed by the administration. The successful policy gives an errant employee every opportunity to mend his ways. If he cannot, the policy insures that any firing done with just cause won't be overturned because it was mishandled.

Employee conduct. Defining just cause can also be a bit difficult. There are only two basic reasons for dismissal: incompetence or misconduct. And the ways an employer can limit or dictate employee conduct are subject to continual reinterpretation. Dress codes and hair-length regulations are a good example of how standards can change.

Regulations governing employee appearance were challenged frequently, and often successfully, in the '70s. But the pendulum began to swing the other way at the end of that decade. Instead of ruling in favor of employees, the courts have been giving management more latitude in setting dress and appearance standards.

You still cannot arbitrarily dictate the type of clothes your workers wear. But in the laboratory, there are many good reasons for having some regulations. Techs performing certain procedures might be required to wear safety equipment, for example. Phlebotomists and others who go out to the wards can logically be required to wear clothes that distinguish them clearly from patients and visitors. And you may and should demand that personal hygiene be maintained.

Whatever your lab's dress code or other personnel regulations may be, they must be clearly spelled out as established policy. You may not charge a worker with misconduct unless he knows that the behavior is unacceptable. And you must enforce the regulations fairly and consistently. You may not discipline one worker for an activity that another does with impunity.

Some cases of misconduct are obvious grounds for immediate dismissal. In the lab, these include falsifying test results, breaching the confidentiality of patient records, theft, drinking on the job, and drug abuse. Other serious offenses, such as rudeness to a patient, might be tolerated only once or twice before dismissal.

The most troublesome cases are those in which the transgressions are minor but the cumulative effect is intolerable: an employee who is continually late, for example. In these situations, you must be able to show a pattern of misconduct and to demonstrate that the progressive disciplinary policy was unable to correct the problem.

Incompetence. Of all the grounds for dismissal, incompetence may be the most difficult to sustain. Again, you must be able to document a clear pattern, and it should be one that was evident from a fairly early point in the worker's employment. It would be difficult to prove that someone who has handled a job successfully for several years had suddenly become incompetent.

Suppose, for example, that one of your late-shift technologists has a year to go until retirement. He has been a marginal worker on the night crew for four years and you've stuck with him mainly because of the trouble you've had filling the late slots. But now you're planning to change your schedule so that all the techs work rotating shifts. You're positive that the marginal worker won't be able to handle the faster pace of daytime duty. Can you fire him because of incompetence? Not a chance.

For one thing, you haven't given this tech the opportunity to prove himself. For another, in the absence of any evidence of incompetence, he'll be able to make a plausible case that you're trying to oust him because of his age. You simply have to make the best of the situation and put up with this tech's shortcomings until he does, in fact, retire.

No termination policy or performance manual can cover every eventuality. Even the most detailed ones are useless if the supervisor does not supply that indispensable ingredient: good judgment. The requirements set out in your personnel regulations provide the yardsticks for measuring performance, and your disciplinary policy provides the means for handling infractions. But it's up to the supervisor to use them wisely.

It helps to keep the policies in perspective. Discipline, even firing, is not meant to hurt or punish the individual. Its purpose is to help you achieve your ultimate objective: the efficient functioning of your laboratory to provide optimum patient care.

48

Documentation for Employee Management

Larry A. Stanifer, M.P.H.

When bench technologists move up into the supervisory ranks, they suddenly find themselves confronted with management chores that leave them uncomfortable at best. They have no experience at job interviewing, employee counseling, or hiring and firing. For some reason, these highly trained individuals almost always forget one of the tools that made them technically competent—and hence promotable—in the first place: good documentation.

If you suggest that managers need to document their work, most new supervisors will offer a variety of excuses: "I don't have the time." "I don't know what to document." "A good manager should keep all that information in his head." "What good does it do, anyway?"

In fact, documentation can do a lot of good, for the new supervisor or for the old hand. By using the appropriate forms, managers can systematize promotions, raises, work assignments, discipline, and counseling for all their employees.

Consistency is not only more efficient, it's more fair. Employees understand and accept management decisions more readily when they can see—on paper—that they are being evaluated by the same standards as their colleagues. The right documentation can help managers avoid misunderstandings and even legal problems.

Pre-employment. One of the first things managers need to document is the pre-employment interview with a job applicant. The following story illustrates the complications you can avoid by using a form like that shown in Figure 48-1.

A Virginia manufacturer advertised for a secretary and interviewed four applicants, including Jane Doe, a married woman in her late 20s. She was not hired and three months later hit the company with a sex-discrimination complaint. She charged that she had been treated rudely and had been asked, among other things, if she was pregnant. The company denied any rudeness or discrimination, but offered to apologize anyway.

That wasn't enough. More than 21 months after the interview, the Equal Employment Opportunity Commission formally subpoenaed documents, memoranda, notes, applications, and statements detailing why Jane Doe was not hired. The agency turned the incident into a full-blown investigation, demanding exhaustive information on the company's employment by sex and by race.

The lesson for managers: Protect yourself and your institution with documentation when interviewing, counseling, or disciplining. Develop a checklist so that you cover the same information with every employee or job applicant. Consistency goes with documentation. If you cannot demonstrate that you have given the same information and asked the same questions in each person's interview, you become vulnerable to charges of discrimination.

Orientation. After you have hired someone, you should continue to use documentation, beginning with the first-day orientation program. The checklist in Figure 48-2 constitutes a record of your discussion. The employee can't complain later on that you never told him about the dress code, for instance, or about attendance rules. And if he does complain, you need only show him his own signature on the orientation checklist.

More important, the checklist saves you time by laying out in order all the important questions to ask. You don't have to worry that you've forgotten some important point.

Finally, the checklist can help prevent misunderstandings and pave the way to employee satisfaction. For example, asking a new employee not just his full name but how he would like to be known (the first point on the checklist) can help considerably in making him feel comfortable in your laboratory.

FIGURE 48-1

This form insures fair, consistent interviewing and encourages the applicant to open up. Keep written comments brief; talk means more here.

Pre-employment Evaluation Interview

Applicant: Donna Hendricks

Interviewer: Larry A. Stanifer

Vacant job title: Section head-chemistry

Date: June 7, 1981

1. What do you feel were your major responsibilities in your last job?

   Supervised special chemistry section.

2. What are some things you feel you have done particularly well or in which you have achieved the greatest success, and why do you feel this way?

   I improved department work flow and quality control.

3. What do you feel has been your greatest frustration or disappointment on your job, and why do you feel this way?

   No authority in personnel management: hiring, firing, etc. No input in decision making policies.

4. How many hours do you feel a person should devote to his job?

   At least 8 hours a day.

5. What do you feel is a satisfactory attendance record?

   Fewer than 5 days missing per year.

6. What kind of people do you like working with? What kind of people do you find most difficult to work with? How have you successfully worked with this type of person?

   Like: flexible, open minded people. Dislike: aggressive people. Have not worked well with aggressive people.

7. What are some things in a job that are important to you and why?

   Professional and peer recognition, benefits and salary.

8. What are some things you would like to avoid in a job and why?

   Dictitorial management policies.

9. What is your overall career objective? What have you done outside your job to achieve this objective?

   Lab management. Nothing

10. What position would you expect to progress to in five years? Ten years?

    5 years: chief tech
    10 years: higher management

11. What are your current salary expectations? How have you arrived at this figure? What would you consider satisfactory salary progression from this point?

    15 per cent increase to change jobs, and because of added duties, 10 per cent per year increase.

FIGURE 48-2

A thorough orientation gets a new employee off on the right foot. This form helps the supervisor remember all the essential items and lets the employee know exactly what's expected of him.

Laboratory Orientation Checklist

Employee's name KRISTA HERBERT Supervisor L. Stanifer

Employment date May 14, 1981

☑ 1. Ask the employee his full name and the name he prefers to be called.

☑ 2. Provide a job description for the employee, and explain his responsibilities and duties.

☑ 3. Explain proper dress, and have the employee sign that he has read and understood the dress code.

☑ 4. Explain the departmental organization.

☑ 5. Inform the employee of starting and quitting time, lunch period, breaks, personal relief, and other details that apply specifically to his job.

☑ 6. Describe departmental method for handling tardiness and absenteeism.

☑ 7. Explain how the employee will be paid, when, where, rate of pay, and method of increases.

☑ 8. Inform the employee of location of procedure and policy manuals and other sources of information.

☑ 9. Inform the employee of location of bulletin boards and the necessity of reading them daily.

☑ 10. Inform the employee of location of locker room, lounge, restrooms, hospital entrances, exits, and parking lots.

☑ 11. Familiarize the employee with working area and any other department with which he will have contact.

☑ 12. Indicate your willingness to help the employee with any work problems, and invite questions and free communication in the future.

☑ 13. Have the employee complete the following items before allowing him to enter his work area.

a. Read hospital and departmental safety rules. . . . . Yes ✓ date 5/14/81
b. Read hospital disaster plan. . . . . Yes ✓ date 5/14/81
c. Read hospital fire plan. . . . . Yes ✓ date 5/14/81
d. Passed pseudo isochromatic color perception test . . . . . Yes ✓ date 5/14/81

Krista Herbert
Employee's signature

Larry A. Stanifer
Supervisor's signature

During the orientation, you should stress the importance of open communication. You might get things off on the right foot by giving the new employee a copy of the checklist and going over it with him. Encourage him to come to you with any questions.

Set up a meeting after a few weeks to talk about any problems that may have developed. You might ask the employee to jot down questions that come up so you can go over them during your first follow-up meeting. Keep a record of your discussion, using the counseling form shown in Figure 48-3. This same form should be used anytime you counsel employees.

Discipline and counseling. These are tough skills for anyone to acquire—and particularly for technologists who move up from a bench job to section supervisor. Though expert in their own areas, these employees are not often expert managers. One difficult adjustment they must make is assuming a position of authority with their former co-workers. This can be especially uncomfortable when it comes time to discipline someone who is consistently tardy, for example, or a sloppy record keeper.

Documentation helps take the anxiety out of these difficult tasks. It is important to remember first that counseling does not have to be negative. After all, good management is mostly a matter of common courtesy and communication. You will find that if you make time for the orientation session and the follow-up meetings, you will end up with a more valuable employee. The forms help you make that good beginning. You will have less need to police your staff because everyone will have a better understanding of laboratory policy.

When disciplinary action becomes necessary, you should take a number of private measures before beginning the formal, documented process of correction:

1. You, the supervisor, should consider your own possible responsibility for the situation, including any personal bias.

2. You should try to look at the problem through the eyes of the employee, other employees, and your own immediate supervisor.

3. Finally, you should consider such complicating factors as the employee's past record, the morale of other employees in the same section, the type and seriousness of the infraction, and such extenuating circumstances as an unusually heavy workload—a big influx of Stats or emergency room cases, say—at the time of the incident in question.

Throughout the course of the disciplinary action, the supervisor should regard himself as a counselor rather than a judge and try to solve the problem both to protect the laboratory's position and to allow the employee to save face. This requires consistency in making and enforcing rules.

FIGURE 48-3

When informal methods fail, the documented disciplinary process can still help resolve problems amicably. It can also prevent legal and unemployment compensation disputes.

Documentation of Employee Counseling

Harrison Alsup
Person involved

Larry A. Stanifer-office manager — April 9, 1981
Person preparing report and his title — Date

A. Brief description of events necessitating this counseling session:
On april 7, 1981, Harrison Alsup was to report to work at 6:30 A.M. It was noticed at about 8:30 A.M. that he had not arrived. He was called at home and arrived to begin his run at 9:20 A.M. When Harrison arrived at the hospital he tried to call me, but could not reach me, Julie Guthrie was then called.

B. Employee's statement:
Forgot to set my alarm clock

C. Action taken on counseling given: Harrison was informed of the following: many people, both patients and hospital employees depend on his being on time. Doctors both here and at the hospitals where he picks up specimens are waiting for him. Reports must be held up getting to patients' charts when he is late. It is noted that this is the first time this has happened and Harrison said he just did not set his alarm clock.

Harrison Alsup
Signature of person involved

Larry A. Stanifer — Lynn F. Blake, M.D.
Signature of person preparing report — Reviewed by: Signature and title

It is difficult for the employee to save face if you jump on him for being five minutes late, then look the other way when the chemistry supervisor walks in 10 minutes later without explanation. Likewise, you cannot let rules slide for six months and then have sudden disciplinary purges.

Report of Corrective Interview

Date January 21, 1981

Employee Mary B. Payne

Department Laboratory - Chemistry

Please describe briefly the infraction with which the employee is charged:

In 1980, Mary was tardy for a total of 8 hrs, 47 min. On this date Mary was tardy again for 25 min. and has no excuse. Mary is habitually five to ten min. late.

What actions will be taken to improve this infraction?

If Mary is tardy again during the next 90 day probation period (1/21/81 to 4/21/81) she will be sent home and suspended for three days without pay.

Mary B. Payne
Employee's signature
(This does not indicate agreement, only review of above.)

This form documents: verbal reprimand ______
written reprimand ✓
termination ______

Larry McNeilly
Personnel director

Lynn F. Blake, M.D.
Department head

When it becomes apparent that your counseling is not achieving the desired results, you should start to document a systematic process of discipline. Actual discipline should be kept impersonal. People are disciplined for what they have done and not because of who they are. The use of forms helps maintain this needed distinction.

Begin the disciplinary process by speaking to the employee about his failure to measure up. Tell him that if the problem continues, formal discipline will result. But don't suggest dismissal, even as a friendly warning. (For further details, see Chapter 47.)

If it becomes necessary to follow up this oral notice, use the form shown in Figure 48-3. When you meet to discuss the problem, give the employee time to read your "charge" on this corrective interview form. Let him add any pertinent comments he may have and sign the document. He keeps a copy, and the other copy goes in his personnel file.

Schedule a follow-up meeting with the employee in about two weeks. Making use of the corrective interview form again, state whether or not the employee has corrected the problem. If he has not, stress the importance of the needed change and set up another meeting in three to five working days.

This process may seem drawn out, but it is intended both to solve problems amicably and to protect yourself from the charge of discrimination should dismissal become necessary. To demonstrate your fairness, you may later have to show that you counseled the employee a number of times over several weeks.

The documents become your proof. If the employee never corrects the infraction, he will at least not be able to claim he was kept in the dark about the need for improvements. Be sure that in the counseling session and on the interview form you tell the employee what *specific* changes you want.

Avoid abstractions. You should say exactly how the employee should be handling the problem and how he has failed to do so. If you don't tell him what he is doing wrong, how can he correct it?

Remember: Counseling can iron out many personnel problems as long as you are consistent and fair. If a supervisor is fair, employees will seldom complain even when they are written up.

Repeated disregard for laboratory rules may eventually lead to suspending the employee without pay. And if the problem persists even after the suspension, dismissal may be the only solution. By then, you should have a detailed documentary record of the case, describing all pertinent instances of failure and demonstrating that you followed a progressive system of discipline.

Your documentation will have kept the employee informed of his status at every step in the disciplinary process. He will not have been subjected, as too often happens, to a sudden release of pent-up managerial objections. Documentation can also prevent unjustified unemployment insurance claims, preventing increases in the hospital's insurance payments.

You may want to develop additional forms to use in your own laboratory. You may also find it helpful to keep a sample of each form, filled out and encased in plastic, in a ring binder. This way, supervisors will not have to go to the chief technologist or the laboratory director every time they have to write up a disciplinary problem. The samples will answer any questions. Each supervisor should, of course, have an adequate supply of forms in his possession.

Documentation won't cure all your managerial problems. But properly used, it can help correct them with a minimum of anxiety and misunderstanding for you and your staff.

49

Helping Handicapped Employees

V. Beverly Rogers, MT(ASCP)SBB

It's hard enough to move ahead with a physical disability without coming up against someone who is standing in the way.

One of the greatest problems for the handicapped is having others set limits for them. Like everyone else, they need to feel that there's always more to learn, that there's room to move ahead. They need to stretch their abilities to the limit. Perhaps, in order to compensate for their physical limitations, they need this even more than those who don't have handicaps.

How do I know? Because I'm handicapped myself. During a rewarding career in the laboratory, I've found that the supervisors who helped me most were the ones who encouraged me to use all my abilities and then stepped aside to let me do it. They didn't try to set limits for me, nor did they try to do too much for me. They knew I couldn't do things exactly the way everyone else did them. But they were wise enough to let me figure out how to accommodate my work to my disability, and they let me make my own mistakes.

My first supervisor had the right idea. I had just graduated from a two-year program in medical technology geared to the handicapped at Alfred University in Alfred, N.Y. In an interview, I had somehow convinced a skeptical pathologist that I could do venipunctures—though

I wasn't so sure myself—and I reported to the blood bank for my first day of work.

The technologist who supervised the department took me out on the floor and, after showing me the venipuncture technique on two or three patients, left me in a patient's room with instructions to finish drawing the patient's blood while she went to "get something from the lab."

I was stunned. The patient had several visitors, and everyone looked at me expectantly. This is it, I thought, as I picked up the syringe. I'm going to muff it. I could feel beads of sweat form on my brow. Then, almost as if by magic, blood began to appear in the tube. Somehow I had inserted the needle into the patient's arm and miraculously found a vein.

When the tube was full, I released the tourniquet, withdrew the needle, and followed the procedure through to completion. My supervisor suddenly appeared in the doorway, a bright smile on her face. "I knew you could do it," she said.

This is a great moment for any new phlebotomist. But for me it was a major triumph because I was performing the task with one arm. The other had been paralyzed since I had a bout with polio at the age of two.

Since that first patient in 1956, I've logged several thousand phlebotomies from both patients and donors. I've worked in every department of the laboratory on all shifts, including those no one wants. I've gone back to school for my B.A. in medical technology and earned my ASCP certification. And today, after qualifying for specialty certification in blood banking, I supervise the blood transfusion service of a 240-bed hospital. I think I've proved that the handicapped can make it if they're given a chance.

It hasn't always been easy. Even as a small child, I had to struggle to be allowed to live a normal life. Today, educators recognize that handicapped children learn better when they attend school with normal children, and more handicapped children are being "mainstreamed" into regular classes. But when I was a child, a handicapped child's right to be educated wasn't even recognized, and my parents had to fight to get me into public school.

My parents understood my ambitions and urged me to go after whatever interested me. They never stood in my way. But not everyone offered the same encouragement. After high school, as a handicapped person, I came under the sponsorship of New York State's rehabilitation program. My ambition was to become a teacher, but my job counselors discouraged me. Instead, they suggested laboratory technology. It's ironic that at a time when so much progress was being made in other fields, so little was known about dealing with individual handicaps. My counselors actually thought that medical technology would be easier for me than teaching.

Employment Laws That Affect the Handicapped

Since the Rehabilitation Act of 1973 became law, Federal contractors and subcontractors have been required to take affirmative action in hiring qualified handicapped individuals. But the handicapped weren't granted full civil rights until June 1977 when Congress enacted section 504 of the Rehabilitation Act.

This legislation makes it illegal for any organization that receives Federal funds to deny jobs to the handicapped based on their handicaps. The handicap itself is no longer considered a valid reason to deny a job to a qualified person.

In addition, an employer must do what he can to help a handicapped individual who is otherwise qualified for the work. This can mean providing support services, such as career counseling, as well as removing physical barriers. It can also mean restructuring jobs or providing modified work schedules for handicapped employees.

In the past, responsibility for succeeding in a job was placed on the shoulders of the handicapped employee himself. Now employers are being asked to carry part of the burden. Employers who receive Federal funds must make a reasonable effort to provide the handicapped with equal access to all their programs and activities.

In order to insure them equal opportunity, special treatment may be necessary. Obviously, it doesn't do much good to offer a job on the third floor of a walk-up building to an applicant in a wheelchair unless you provide an elevator that will take him there.

Every handicap must be treated on an individual basis, so regulations regarding physical access are purposely vague. But there are some requirements. For example, all public buildings constructed after 1975 must be built so that they're accessible by wheelchair. That means they must be equipped with ramps, handrails, elevators, and wide doors. Older buildings must be altered only to the extent that programs conducted in them are accessible to the handicapped, unless this puts undue hardship on the employer. But any major alterations must include plans to accommodate the handicapped.

For more details, write for "Affirmative Action for Disabled People." This booklet is available free from the President's Committee on the Employment of the Handicapped, 1111 20th St., Washington, D.C. 20036.

In retrospect, the advice was good but for the wrong reasons. I'm sure the counselors didn't realize how much physical involvement is required of lab techs. Any student who has mastered the fine art of quantitative analysis or worked in a chemistry or biology lab knows how valuable a second hand can be. Many times during my classes at Alfred University, I was challenged to figure out a way to substitute for that second hand.

As I mentioned earlier, our classes were geared to the handicapped—though we had nonhandicapped students as well—and our teachers tried to challenge our ingenuity. They'd say, "Here's a task. See if you can find a way to do it." I always came up with something. In bacteriology, for example, I used a series of clamps lined up on a stand to hold test tubes for culturing.

I've used the same approach on the job. There are many ways to set up a laboratory procedure, and I'd find one that worked for me. Usually a simple device did the trick. Often I'd discover that a particular procedure didn't really require two hands.

Of course, sometimes I did need help. Although my handicap has never stopped me from trying things I want to do, I've always been aware of my own limitations, and I've had to accept the fact that I can't do everything for myself.

During the time when I was a chemistry supervisor, for example, I was never able to fasten those tiny tubes onto those tiny plastic couplers of an automated analyzer. They invariably leaked all over me. I've learned that when I'm up against something I can't do, I should simply ask for help.

Everyone is always willing to give me that extra hand I need. Sometimes too willing. One of the most exasperating things about being handicapped is having people rush over to help you do something you can do perfectly well for yourself. That used to happen all the time, especially before my colleagues in a particular lab got to know me. I was always happy when I settled into a job and my fellow techs saw that I could do the work as well as anyone else in the laboratory—using my own system.

Looking back on my career, I'm proud of the contribution I've been able to make. Unfortunately, not many of my handicapped colleagues have been as lucky. They've been largely ignored in the job market, and as a result, they make up a large percentage of the country's unemployed. This is a serious problem when you consider there are 28 million adults in this country who are classified as handicapped. As some of our activists have put it, blacks used to sit in the back of the bus, but the handicapped weren't even on the bus.

Things are looking up, though. We've worked hard at sensitizing the public to our needs, and we're beginning to see results. Special parking spaces are being set aside for us. Buses are being equipped with "kneeling" steps that make it easier to get on and off. Cuts are being made in curbs at street corners, and guide dogs are being allowed in places they've never been before. The handicapped are beginning to get around because the obstacles that have been in our way are being removed.

But even more important, our civil rights are finally being recognized (see accompanying box). It's now illegal for Federal agencies and any firms or institutions that receive Federal funds to discriminate against handicapped individuals. Federal agencies and contractors must take affirmative action to hire the handicapped. The Federal government must provide every handicapped individual with an education, job counseling, and job placement help.

This means that the handicapped will soon be entering the job market in large numbers. When this happens, I hope some will consider the field of medical technology as a career. And I hope laboratories will welcome them with open arms.

There's no reason in the world a paraplegic in a wheelchair, for example, can't become a blood bank specialist. A work counter can easily be adjusted to fit above a wheelchair. If someone who is handicapped is qualified to do the work, his supervisor should be willing to make accommodations to his disability.

Supervising the handicapped doesn't require any special gifts. In some respects, it's easier than supervising others. To most handicapped persons, a job is precious. We don't take it for granted. We don't have to be motivated because we're already highly motivated, especially if we see we'll be given the same chance to advance as others.

But a certain amount of flexibility is called for. Supervisors must be willing to adjust schedules, reshape jobs, or make whatever adjustments are necessary to allow the handicapped to do their jobs. Often these adjustments are minor. For example, someone who tires after several hours on his feet can be assigned some sit-down tasks. Or someone with limited vision can be given jobs that don't require reading fine print.

Working with the handicapped can be a rewarding experience for everyone. One reason the handicapped have been excluded in the past is that others focused on their differences—and they feared what they didn't understand. When they work alongside the handicapped on a daily basis, they have a chance to see that in most respects we're pretty much like anybody else. That's healthy for everyone.

50

What Supervisors Owe Their Employees

Ted Street, M.B.A.

No supervisor gets very far through the use of authority alone. Power and obligation go hand in hand. To inspire an employee's best efforts, you must offer something in return. In exactly the same way that he has obligations to you, you have obligations to him.

This simple fact of organizational life has been known for years, yet many managers and supervisors seem oblivious to it. They focus so intently on their employees' obligations to them that they forget how important their own obligations are.

I suppose this is only natural. After all, an obligation is something we are bound to do—whether we want to or not. It may be a debt our conscience prods us to pay or something to get out of the way so we can move ahead. And it's easy to resent duties that we have no choice about.

But there's no need to look at obligations in a negative light. They can be viewed positively. When you fulfill obligations to your employees, you are earning a higher level of performance from them.

What exactly does a laboratory manager or supervisor owe his employees? I think he has three basic obligations:

Loyalty. Loyalty is a two-way street. You can't expect employees to be loyal to you unless you are loyal to them. If, for example, a technologist gets into a scrape with the nursing staff as a result of trying to do a better job, you should support him.

Even if he steps on some toes, he deserves your public support. Then, in private, you can try to find out how he got himself into trouble so he can avoid it in the future. Nothing sours an employee faster than to find out that his supervisor is going to stand by and watch him go down for the third time without offering a hand.

When one of your staff makes a mistake, it pays to give him the benefit of the doubt. Reacting with anger or righteous indignation can do more damage than the mistake itself. Obviously, you won't carry this policy so far that you condone repeated errors. But I find it pays dividends to deal with minor problems patiently.

Fairness and consistency. Employees want to know where they stand. In enforcing and interpreting your administration's policies, it doesn't matter so much whether you're hard as a rock or the world's biggest pushover. Employees have an amazing ability to adjust to a variety of management styles.

What drives them up the wall is a supervisor who flip-flops. One day he can't do enough for them, and the next day he's ready to throw the book at them for every minor infraction. Whatever management style you choose, you owe it to your staff to use it consistently.

Your staff members also deserve to be treated fairly. Whether you are disciplining, giving out work assignments, or doing favors, you should be prepared to take the same stance toward one employee that you've taken toward another in a similar situation. Employees hate to see supervisors play favorites, even when they aren't personally victimized. They want to know that the same rules apply to everyone so that they have a fair chance to become winners themselves.

Opportunity. No one wants to feel locked into a particular job with no chance to move up. As supervisor, you hold the key.

There are many ways you can help your staff develop their capabilities. You can encourage them to get the training they need to take the next step up the career ladder. You can give time off for attending conferences for professional growth. You can provide your own continuing education sessions.

I'm also a strong believer in delegation. Not only does this give your people a chance to expand their horizons and stretch their capabilities, but by training others to handle some of your responsibilities, you're paving the way for moving up yourself.

When an employee does an especially good job, it's important to give him recognition. This should be done judiciously, of course. If you give out praise too lavishly, employees will soon see it as automatic—and meaningless. But any job that's done particularly well deserves praise. And any employee who knows he deserves praise wants to hear it.

If someone on your staff deserves a promotion, let the administration and your superiors know about it. Don't worry about losing a good worker. If he's sharp and ready to move on, you're going to lose him eventually anyway. It's better to keep him in the organization than lose him altogether.

Everyone, no matter what level he's at, should feel that he can move up. You've got to make this possible by providing a career ladder from bottom to top. Not everyone will use it, but everyone needs to know the ladder is there and the climb is possible.

51

Upgrading the Status of Part-Time Techs

Lyle L. Bulgrin, MT(ASCP)

Part-time technologists perform an important, perhaps indispensable, role in the clinical laboratory. Unfortunately, employers often treat them more as second-class citizens than as the valuable employees they are. As a chief technologist, I'm in favor of making the best use of part-time employees and giving them the respect, recognition, and rewards they deserve. The two parts of that statement are, I believe, closely related.

Some of the widely held attitudes toward part-timers are simply unfounded generalizations. A few that I've encountered frequently: Part-timers are only working to keep themselves busy, to earn money for vacations, or to put children through school; they'll quit when they lose interest in the job or make enough money. They have jobs, not careers, so they don't care about advancement or continuing education.

Those statements may be true of some part-time employees. But they are also true of some full-timers. In my experience, part-timers as a group are just as dedicated, knowledgeable, and professional as anyone else. They simply work fewer hours.

The most extreme of the unenlightened attitudes I've seen toward part-timers was held by the large hospital where I worked some years ago. They refused to hire part-timers at all, thus denying themselves a large pool of talent and an extremely helpful scheduling tool.

More frequent is the laboratory that takes advantage of part-timers — literally. It views them as cut-rate labor, a source of saving on salaries and benefits. That approach, taken by most of the hospitals I'm familiar with, leads to obvious inequities and is ultimately counterproductive.

My own hospital is probably typical. Our personnel policy handbook states that employee benefits apply only to full-time employees, those who work at least 40 hours a week. That means part-timers receive no sick days. If they're ill when scheduled to work, they lose pay. The same is true if they miss work for jury duty. Nor does the hospital reimburse part-timers for attending educational programs held off the premises. All of these benefits are given to full-timers.

Salary policies are even more unfair. Starting salaries for full- and part-time employees who do the same job are equal. But when the hospital awards raises or cost-of-living adjustments, the part-timer receives only half the percentage increase of a full-time employee. And if a full-time person changes to part time, his salary reverts back to the base level.

The differences in benefits and salaries are wrong in the first place because they are unfair. Part- and full-time technologists work side-by-side. Part-timers must be just as qualified. They must work just as hard and produce at the same rate. They must assume the same responsibility for the quality of their work. Why should they earn less?

The policies are also wrong because they are misguided. The obvious inequities only lead to management problems that end up costing the hospital money.

A staffing problem I encountered recently shows the false economy of one of our policies on part-timers. We had a downturn in workload, and I found myself slightly overstaffed. One of my technologists was willing to work fewer hours, and that would have been the perfect solution. The hospital would have been paying only for the number of technologist hours it needed. The technologist would have been satisfied working less time. And I would have been happy to retain her services.

She was not willing to take the cut in hourly pay the policy stipulated, though. And I can't blame her. She would have been doing the same work, just for fewer hours each week.

She was an excellent technologist. I couldn't replace her with a comparable part-timer because I could not have found one. Nor could I do without her completely. My only choice—and hers—was to continue as we were, overstaffed. The hospital's policy, which was supposed to save on salaries, forced me to pay more for personnel than was necessary.

Other staffing inefficiencies that result from the policies toward part-timers are not as easily measured. Who knows how many good technologists have turned down the chance to work in our laboratory because of the poor treatment of part-timers? Or how many workshops or continuing education programs my technologists have passed up because they would not be reimbursed? How have these policies hurt the quality of our service? How many times has a part-timer worked when ill rather than lose a day's pay? How have the inequalities between technologists affected morale? Though the cost of these problems cannot be tallied to the penny, I believe it's more than the hospital can afford.

The situation is improving. A few years ago, our part-timers were finally given prorated vacations. And now a new personnel director is reviewing all of our policies toward them. I hope more inequities are removed.

Equal Rights for Part-Timers?

Where is it written that part-time employees are entitled to the same salary and benefits as full-timers? Apparently, nowhere. State labor laws vary, of course, but generally have little to say about part-timers. The Federal laws do touch on the subject, but very lightly.

The Employee Retirement Income Security Act, which regulates pension plans, extends its protection to any employee who works at least 1,000 hours a year, or about half time. The Fair Labor Standards Act, which sets hourly wage practices, does mandate equal pay for equal work. But the provision applies to employees of the opposite sex who perform the same job, not to full- and part-time employees who do.

The law allows different wage rates for different hours worked at a given job, provided the policy is applied equally to men and women. But if all part-time workers in a position were one sex and the difference in hours between full- and part-time was slight, the employees would have a persuasive argument that they were being discriminated against on the basis of sex.

Employers have much latitude in the way they can treat part-time workers. The salaries and benefits given them, therefore, are a direct function of their perceived value. It's up to laboratory managers and directors to let administrators know just how much part-time technologists mean to the lab.

The happiness of my part-time employees is important to me because I couldn't operate the laboratory without them. The lab serves a 245-bed general hospital. We provide services 24 hours a day, seven days a week, with a staff of 17 full-time and 11 part-time technologists. The full-timers work 40 hours per week. The part-timers work an average of 24 hours a week, but their schedules can vary widely. That variation is what helps me make the best use of their time. Let's see why:

Staffing efficiency. A laboratory with a workload that requires an exact number of full-time employees is rare, and the situation is probably temporary as well. Workload in most laboratories fluctuates so that an exact number of full-time technologists is almost always too many or too few. Part-time employees are the most economical way to adjust staff size to fit changing needs.

Again my lab provides a good example. For the moment, our workload is up, and we're temporarily understaffed. To get the job done, I have to ask some technologists to work extra hours. My choice? Part-timers, of course. It would cost me half as much again to use a full-timer. According to the Federal wage-and-hour laws, an hourly employee who works more than 40 hours per week is entitled to overtime pay—one and a half times the normal rate. As it is, the part-timers simply work an extra day at the regular rate. It seems shortsighted indeed to discriminate against the people who make such savings possible.

Scheduling flexibility. Most chief technologists find scheduling to be a real headache. It is not easy to assign weekend and holiday coverage or to compensate for vacations and sick days. Part-timers can help, either by filling in on special occasions or by providing a flexible element in the regular rotations.

A few years ago, I had a part-time technologist who worked only weekends—every weekend. That's the way she wanted it. Her preference made scheduling easier for me because it lightened the weekend load for all the other technologists.

Now we operate with about half our staff on Saturdays and slightly less on Sundays. Full- and part-time technologists share the weekend duty about equally. Everyone works every other Saturday and every fourth or fifth Sunday. That gives both full- and part-timers a free weekend every other week. And by scheduling part-timers for Fridays and Mondays, I'm able to give full-timers a three-day weekend every other week. We're in direct competition for technologists with three larger hospitals within a 25-mile radius, and these long weekends are an important selling point.

The part-time technologists also help me meet emergency scheduling needs. Since we have a regular contingent of part-timers, I never have to worry about coming up with replacements for others who are out sick or on some other emergency leave. A quick phone call or two to my part-timers is all it takes to solve the problem.

Source of talent. Part-timers would prove helpful to any laboratory, I'm sure. But for our hospital, they are an absolute necessity. I simply could not find enough qualified technologists to operate the laboratory without them.

At one time, our hematology department was staffed entirely by part-time technologists. And for more than two years, we wouldn't have been able to maintain a microbiology department if it hadn't been for a talented, experienced part-timer who carried it along.

Why do some technologists choose to work short weeks? I've found two basic reasons: Some older technologists want to increase their leisure time yet remain productive and keep up to date professionally. Some younger women prefer to have more time to spend at home during child-rearing years. But they also want to continue their professional development. Neither reason makes the part-timer an employment risk. If anything, both indicate excellent motivation.

Whatever reasons part-timers have for being part-timers, we managers should be thankful that they have them. They may not work full time, but they are full-fledged members of the laboratory team.

X

CERTIFICATION AND LICENSURE

52

Issues in Licensing

Christopher J. Bale

What's wrong with the licensure system of the nation's health professions? And how is it to be rectified?

The questions are getting old enough to creak. They've been asked repeatedly since 1971. That's when the Department of Health, Education, and Welfare (now called the Department of Health and Human Services) published its now-famous "Report on Licensure and Related Health Personnel Credentialing." That document described numerous administrative and procedural wrenches lodged in the state licensure machinery, problems reemphasized two years later in a subsequent HEW paper titled, "Developments in Health Manpower Licensing."

Yet another HEW report, "Credentialing Health Manpower," appeared in July 1977. Its purpose: to crystallize current thought on how best to cope with the certification-licensure conundrum. And in January 1978, representatives of scores of health professions met in Arlington, Va., to discuss this 1977 report's recommendations.

The conference didn't result in official pronouncements or policy developments. No one, including the sponsoring National Health Council, expected it to.

Clearly, licensure problems identified by HEW in 1971 and 1973 hadn't disappeared or been purged. Conference representatives from the clinical laboratory field and other health professions bemoaned the varying requirements, responsibilities, and controls that characterize the present system and impede career and geographic mobility.

Further, they questioned the ability and willingness of licensure boards to implement adequate continuing competence mechanisms and to take disciplinary action when needed. Many wondered whether licensure was the most appropriate credentialing route for the majority—or even any—of the health professions.

The 1977 HEW report served as the centerpiece for the discussions. Among its recommendations was one—on criteria for further state licensure decisions—that suggested that states should consider the licensing of additional categories of health personnel "with caution and deliberation."

A "criteria" workshop generated a complaint that was reiterated in all the workshops on licensure, standards, competency measurement, and continued competency. Put simply, it was: Enforcement is an absolutely essential element of licensure.

"The assumption that licensure is equated with an assurance of competence is unfounded," said Charles Bagley, M.D., secretary for the Maryland Board of Medical Examiners.

The statement seemed to strike at the heart of the licensure issues. "Why license at all? Licensure is supposed to insure competence, but too often it proves not to," he added.

Bob Bergeron, an official of the Connecticut Hospital Association, agreed. "Some boards in our state can't do a proper job because they are two-person operations," he noted. "They're moving paper and licensing professionals, but they can't police their professions effectively. They can't do much more than mail out pieces of paper."

Indeed, legislative commitment to funding and molding a licensure board that has clout emerged as a unanimous recommendation from the criteria workshop. And it wasn't the only workshop to voice this sentiment.

The criteria workshop also recommended that states consider the cost, especially the hidden cost, of creating new licensure boards. Legislatures should recognize that all regulation, including licensing a health profession, increases management time and cost for employers.

Also debated were the merits of licensure versus other forms of credentialing. A dietitian pointed out that "everyone here seems to favor licensing. Certification has worked very well for us."

Susan Hillbrath, an official of the American Occupational Therapy Association, responded that certification has not proved an ideal method for her group's members.

"The problem is that certification is voluntary," she said. "In our field, we have well-intentioned, noncertified people who give patients arts and crafts, but no therapy. Others are just incompetent. The AOTA, which certifies occupational therapists, can't do anything about the people who call themselves 'occupational therapists' and get hired by institutions that are not concerned about credentials.

"When an incompetent, noncertified practitioner is exposed in the newspapers, all of us in the profession, including the certified members, get a bad name," she continued. "If there's a better way, we'd certainly like to try it.

"Maybe licensure isn't such a hot approach right now," she added. "It has its problems. But I think we can deal with the trouble and should start by cleaning up the laws to make them fairer, tougher, and more realistic."

Toward that end, the criteria workshop also recommended the use of "sunset" legislation to periodically review the need for existing licensure boards. It also suggested more moves toward reciprocity arrangements between states, and a clearinghouse of all state licensing laws affecting the health professions, and studies of those laws. Additionally, the panel endorsed experiments to improve licensing laws, such as those achieved in Minnesota and Wisconsin.

A second criteria workshop, held concurrently with the first, concluded that regulation of the health professions is necessary and desirable. But licensure, the group decided, is the least desirable form of regulation and should be considered a "last resort." A certification system is preferable, it concluded.

The findings from an "improved licensure procedures" workshop paralleled those of the criteria workshops. For instance, that panel advocated centralizing all boards in a state in order to increase cost-effectiveness, accountability, and continuity.

This workshop further called for greater use of national examinations and their recognition by states as one valid device for measuring competency.

What of all these calls for action? Undoubtedly, they were heard by Harris S. Cohen, Ph.D., who was the principal author of the 1977 HEW report.

"That report was meant to stimulate public, state, and private association moves to improve what everyone concedes needs improvement," he explains. "I think the conference showed that there's momentum for change, but that there's a long way to go."

The National Health Council, many of whose members are the associations affected by credentialing methods, intends to direct the recommendations emerging from the conference to "the appropriate groups," be they state licensing boards, the Federal government, associations, or the NHC itself.

Although no new conference has been scheduled by NHC or anyone else, "we won't let the issue drop," an NHC spokesman said. "The subject of credentialing is too controversial and too important. No one wants the Federal government to step in and dictate credentialing for the health professions. And the threat of that happening is too real right now for anyone to forget these issues just because one conference is complete."

53

Certifying the Certifiers: The NCHCA

Christopher J. Bale

It took seven years of remarkable cooperation and determined effort, but it finally happened. The formation in December 1977 of the voluntary, non-Federal National Commission for Health Certifying Agencies opened up a new chapter in credentialing history.

Professionals representing some 65 health organizations met in Miami and hammered out bylaws and preliminary criteria that would enable the new commission to, in effect, certify the certifiers of the country's health professionals.

While the NCHCA is not all the Department of Health, Education, and Welfare might have liked it to be—at least not yet—it is being hailed by government and private agencies alike as a landmark achievement—and the first step toward wiping out the present system's disarray.

Since 1928, when the ASCP's board of registry awarded its first medical technology certificate, the number of organizations setting standards for laboratory personnel has grown steadily. Today, dozens of national and state organizations certify and register individuals in various clinical laboratory disciplines (see Table 53-1). Instead of providing a set of reliable standards for laboratory performance, they form an alphabet soup of certification activities that often overlap, duplicate, and even contradict each other.

The reason for the certification explosion is simple enough. As technology developed, laboratory specialists proliferated, and so did the organizations formed to serve their interests. No group wants its members under the thumb of another organization, particularly if that organization has the power to restrain or limit the members' scope of practice.

TABLE 53-1

Laboratory Certifiers and the Professionals They Certify

American Board of Bioanalysis
Bioanalyst laboratory director
Clinical laboratory director
Bioanalyst clinical laboratory director

American Board of Clinical Chemistry
Clinical chemist (Ph.D.)

American Board of Medical Microbiology
Director in microbiology (Ph.D.)

American Medical Technologists
Medical laboratory technician MLT(AMT)
Medical technologist MT(AMT)

American Registry of Radiologic Technologists
Registered nuclear medicine technologist RT(ARRT)

American Society of Clinical Pathologists
Certified laboratory assistant CLA (ASCP)
Chemistry technologist C(ASCP)
Specialist in chemistry SC(ASCP)
Cytotechnologist CT(ASCP)
Hematology technologist H(ASCP)
Specialist in hematology SH(ASCP)
Histologic technician HT(ASCP)
Medical laboratory technician MLT(ASCP)
Medical technologist MT(ASCP)
Microbiology technologist M(ASCP)
Specialist in microbiology SM(ASCP)
Nuclear medicine technologist NM(ASCP)
Specialist in blood bank technology SBB(ASCP)
(certified jointly with the American Association of Blood Banks)

That was the situation in 1977 when the ASMT finally decided to end its representation on the ASCP board of registry. ASMT officials said one important reason for the split was their inability to convince the ASCP that the board of registry should be reorganized into an autonomous certifying body, independent of the pathologists' group.

HEW Proficiency Examination
Clinical laboratory technologist
Cytotechnologist

International Academy of Cytology
Cytotechnologist (CMIAC)

International Society for Clinical Laboratory Technology
Registered laboratory technician RLT(ISCLT)
Registered medical technologist RMT(ISCLT)

National Certification Agency for Medical Laboratory Personnel
Clinical laboratory technician CLT(NCAMLP)
Clinical laboratory scientist CLS(NCAMLP)
Proposed future category:
Clinical laboratory practitioner CLP(NCAMLP)

National Registry in Clinical Chemistry
Clinical chemist
Clinical chemist technologist

National Registry of Microbiologists
Technologist in microbiology
Supervisor in microbiology

Nuclear Medicine Technology Board
Certified nuclear medicine technologist

The following laboratory groups do not certify members, but they are contributing organizations to the NCHCA:

American Association of Blood Banks

American Society for Medical Technology

American Society for Microbiology

National Society for Histotechnology

The ASMT's concern grew from the Federal Trade Commission's announced intention to investigate competitive problems in health-care delivery. Specifically, the FTC was expected to look into professional organizations' certification activities and determine whether or not they constituted conflicts of interest.

After years of talking about the need for an independent certifying body for medical technologists that would not report ultimately to any single professional organization, the ASMT decided to take action. It threw its energies into helping form a new certifying body, the National Certification Agency for Medical Laboratory Personnel, and the NCHCA to certify the certifiers.

What will the new commission mean for certifying agencies and those who are certified in the clinical lab field? There are several ramifications:

Greater credibility. The overwhelming opinion is that certification will be a more meaningful term. Glenda Price of the ASMT was elected vice-speaker for the NCHCA general assembly. She pointed out, "In the past, no one has ever known what various certifications mean. Now all the groups that belong to NCHCA can say, 'Here are the . . . standards met by the groups that certify personnel in our profession.' "

In agreement is David J. La Fond, M.D., who since 1974 has acted as the ASCP's liaison with the steering committee, piecing together the commission concept. "Patients and the Government will be the real beneficiaries," he said. "They can be assured that a certificate on the wall of any professional certified by an NCHCA agency is meaningful, and not the product of a certification mill."

No consolidation of certification agencies. The commission was created to codify high standards for certifying bodies and to make sure they are met. How many certifying bodies exist to serve a profession is irrelevant as far as the NCHCA is concerned.

"There's no intention whatsoever to compare certifying groups within a profession," said William Samuels, executive director of the American Society of Allied Health Professions and the NCHCA steering committee's director. "The only judgment NCHCA makes is whether certifiers meet the standards."

Compatible certifying systems. Dr. La Fond expressed the hope that the commission will lead to a uniformity of definitions among certifying agencies within the same professions. "It would be nice, for instance, for 'technologist' to have the same meaning in all lab-related organizations," he pointed out.

"Toward that end, occupationally related NCHCA agencies would have to work among themselves to be sure their certification standards are the same or complementary," said Harris S. Cohen, Ph.D., who for several years has chaired HEW's (now the Department of Health and Human Services) Committee on Health Manpower Credentialing.

For the immediate and foreseeable future, the commission sees its major role as assuring that agencies in the certification business are doing a good job. Here's its strategy, as outlined in the bylaws.

An executive council will confer, revoke, or reclassify an agency's membership in NCHCA based on the recommendations of a membership committee. Member agencies will be assigned to one of two categories. Category A will include private nongovernmental bodies that conduct a national certification program for a health profession or occupation.

Category B will consist of any other national organization, governmental or private, that has an interest in certifying—but does not actually certify—health-care practitioners.

Certifying agencies become conditional members simply by submitting an application. Then the membership committee and the executive council have up to 12 months to decide whether the organization meets NCHCA criteria (see Table 53-2) for membership.

The executive council may extend the conditional acceptance an extra 12 months if it feels the applicant hasn't met the criteria but can do so, given that additional time. The bid is rejected if the council judges that the deficiencies cannot be corrected within a year's time.

Steering committee director Samuels noted that "there is no grandfathering. All organizations, even those founding agencies that worked on this for two and three years, must go through the acceptance process. Everyone starts at square one."

To encourage participation, NCHCA organizers agreed to keep annual per-member dues as low as possible: $500 for the right to vote on creation of the commission, its bylaws, and officers; $500 for first-year dues; $1,000 for the second year; and $2,000 for the third year.

From the start, the private-sector agencies pioneering the commission recognized the advantages of working closely with Government agencies like the watchdog FTC.

"The steering committee regularly checked with FTC officials for their view of how we were proceeding," Samuels explained. "If they saw trouble with a path we were taking, we'd ask them to point us in a safe direction. Our philosophy with the FTC, as with all other governmental bodies, was to show them where we were going at each step so they could help us steer clear of pitfalls."

For that reason, the steering committee also kept close contact with Harris Cohen at HEW's Office of Health Policy, Research, and Statistics. Cohen, in fact, attended the December 1977 Miami meeting and was headlined at the press conference announcing NCHCA's birth.

Actually, the steering committee's work over the previous three years ran parallel to HEW's broad initiatives to formulate a cohesive policy on health manpower credentialing. HEW's deep involvement began in the late 1960s when Congress, bewildered by the proliferation of health-care professions, was suddenly overwhelmed by requests for manpower-training funds. Complaints about charlatans and poorly trained health practitioners were proliferating as well.

Congress asked HEW's help on two fronts—certification and licensure. Since 1971, HEW has been sponsoring papers, conferences, and studies on how best to revamp the credentialing system. HEW's strategy was, and has been, not to issue Federal fiats but to stimulate public and state action.

TABLE 53-2

Criteria That Every Member Agency of NCHCA Must Meet

Purpose:

To evaluate individuals who want to enter, continue, or advance in their health profession—and to certify and credential those who meet the required standards.

Structure:

The organization must be nongovernmental, national, and independent. No parent organization may influence or finance the agency's certification activities, and by 1982, the certifying component of a nonprofit association must be administratively independent.

The agency's governing body must include individuals from the discipline being certified who are selected by their professional peers and barred from choosing their own successors. In decision making, the agency will consider input from its consumers, its professionals, and the employers of individuals being certified. The certifying body of a professional organization must be separate from its accrediting body.

Resources:
The organization must prove that it can afford to carry out certification adequately and that its staff is well qualified to do so.

Evaluation mechanism:
It must be objective, fair, and based on the knowledge and skills needed. The organization must periodically review its evaluation mechanism to insure continued relevance; protect the security of its examinations; and prove that its passing requirements and evaluation methods are fair, reliable, and valid.

Public information:
The association must publicize its certification responsibilities, furnish material about its testing procedures, and publish a summary of each test and of its certification activities. It must also publicize its activities that are unrelated to certification.

Responsibilities to applicants:
It may not discriminate as to age, sex, religion, or national origin. It must provide all applicants with information about its certification programs and the educational or employment background required for certification. It must provide a means for evaluating and certifying individuals who are skilled but lack a formal education, give proctored tests at accessible sites throughout the country at least once a year, provide test results promptly, including information about areas of deficiency, and keep results confidential. A formal appeals procedure must be outlined in its examination announcements.

Responsibilities to the public and employers of certified personnel:
The organization must insure that it adequately measures the knowledge and skills needed in the profession and awards certification only to qualified individuals. It must publish a list of certified individuals.

Recertification:
It must have or be developing a plan for recertification to measure continued competence or to increase competence.

Responsibilities to the NCHCA:
It must regularly provide the commission with copies of all publications related to its certifying process, notify the commission of all major changes in its testing administration or procedures, and undergo re-evaluation by the commission at five-year intervals.

In July 1977, HEW summarized six years of thought and talk in a 26-page report, ''Credentialing Health Manpower.'' More frequently referred to as the Cohen report, it spelled out six recommendations. The first called for a national, non-Federal certification commission. The second, for national standards in certification and licensure. The third and fourth covered criteria for state licensure decisions and improved licensure procedures. Recommendations five and six called for all credentialing bodies to promote the use of mechanisms for measuring competence and continued competence, respectively.

Six months later, Recommendation One became a reality upon the NCHCA's formation in Miami. As the steering committee director William Samuels said, ''The private sector viewed Recommendation One as an endorsement of what we were trying to accomplish.''

Also, Recommendation Six seemed partially satisfied. Among the commission's criteria for approval is one saying that an agency must itself have a recertification mechanism for proving a professional's continued competence.

Many in the private sector believe NCHCA also conforms with Recommendation Two—calling for national certification standards—since it lists standards that all member agencies must meet.

But Harris Cohen didn't see it that way. ''I'd say NCHCA is the fulfillment of Recommendation One, but not Two,'' he said. ''NCHCA establishes standards for certifying agencies. Recommendation Two addresses standards for personnel within a profession, advising that related professions work together to make certification requirements sensible from one level to the next.''

Where more than one agency certifies a single level within a profession, Cohen said that differences should come to an end. ''I don't believe we should eliminate competition among certifying bodies,'' he continued, ''only that the competition should not revolve around standards. Certification agencies must eventually agree on the basic skills, knowledge, and competency needed at a given level to assure public safety, and set those as their standards. Anytime a certification agency requires less or more than those basic elements, it runs a risk.''

Why can't an agency require skills or knowledge beyond what is essential to public safety? ''Because if a Federal regulator like the FTC, or any lawyer, demonstrates that they are extraneous, that is, not absolutely necessary to performing at a given level, the additional requirements could be construed as barriers to entry and mobility.''

Lagging behind right now is the effort to renovate state licensing structures. "In terms of the national strategy, the commission's formation is a tremendous thing," said ASMT's Glenda Price. "But that represents just one aspect of the Cohen report. Licensing is the other function that has to be strengthened and coordinated.

"In our field, for example, California's licensing procedures are unique, and that state accepts nothing else," she continued. "I can't believe their needs are so unique that some reciprocal agreement can't be arranged."

Nor could HEW. That's why the Cohen report urged states to adopt relevant national examinations and standards. It also said that states should:

- assign high priority to disciplinary procedures and responsibilities;
- expand membership on licensure boards to include effective representation of consumers and other functionally related health professions; and
- establish linkages with other licensing boards and government agencies responsible for planning, developing, and monitoring health manpower and service.

The Cohen report also cautioned the states to deliberate carefully before launching new licensure boards. HEW had grave reservations about the anticipated proliferation of licensed health occupations, and the report suggested that states should consider the following points before acting:

How will unregulated practice clearly endanger the public health? Can the public be effectively protected by means other than licensure? How will the public benefit by a license's assurance of initial and continuing competence? Why is licensure the most effective form of regulation? What impact will the newly licensed category have on the authority and scope of practice of previously licensed categories?

What's lacking in the movement to improve licensure is a focal point to bring state licensure boards and professional associations together. Cohen said, "We intend to do everything we can to encourage meetings, discussions, studies, and eventually, real progress toward a more ordered licensing system. That's one reason behind the July 1977 report—to serve as a catalyst. But our job hasn't ended with the report."

54

California's Model Licensure Law

David J. Kull

California is known in laboratory circles for its strict licensure law. How strict is it? A list of requirements for various categories of laboratorians is given below, so you can judge for yourself.

Another measure of the state's rigorous standards, though, can be found in the law's provisions for reciprocity. The State Department of Health is permitted to waive its qualifying test for any person who has passed the examination of an accrediting board whose requirements are deemed equal to or greater than California's. So far, not one has met the department's standards, but some boards are being considered.

Under the law, which was adopted in 1938 and has been revised several times since, the state issues full licenses to laboratorians in eight categories. They range from "bioanalyst," who is authorized to direct multiservice labs, to "limited technologist," who may perform tests only within his special area of expertise. Most of the state's 20,000 licensed laboratorians are technologists. The state also issues temporary licenses to persons working on the training requirements for permanent licensing.

Although the health department does not license phlebotomists, aides, or technicians, it does spell out qualifications for persons holding those jobs and specifies the duties they can perform.

A phlebotomist, for example, must receive 10 hours of training from a licensed physician or bioanalyst before he is permitted to perform venipuncture. A laboratory aide may engage in such activities as labeling, centrifuging, preparing media, and transcribing results. But only licensed personnel are allowed to make quantitative measurements, perform mathematical calculations relative to test results, and standardize or calibrate instruments.

The California law, which also provides for licensing and regulating laboratories, is administered and enforced by Laboratory Field Services, a division of the state health department. The division is meagerly staffed. Twenty examiners are responsible for overseeing the state's 2,000 hospital and independent laboratories. They make periodic visits to the laboratories to assure that only licensed personnel perform the specified duties, that there is sufficient supervision, and that the other regulations are being followed.

The categories of California licensure are as follows:

CLINICAL LABORATORY BIOANALYST

Minimum Requirements

A master's degree in one of the biological sciences, including 45 credits in 10 prescribed subject areas, plus four years' experience as a licensed technologist performing work "embracing the various fields of laboratory activity."

Examination

Written, oral, and practical.

Permitted activities

Direction of a multiservice laboratory. Other than these licensed bioanalysts, the only individuals permitted to direct a multiservice laboratory are appropriately licensed physicians.

CLINICAL CHEMIST OR CLINICAL MICROBIOLOGIST

Minimum requirements

A master's degree in the specialty in which licensing is sought, including 30 credits in that area, plus one year of directed study and three years' experience, or four years' experience. Two years' experience must be at the supervisory level.

Examination

Written and oral.

Permitted activities

Direction of a laboratory that provides services only within the area of specialization.

CLINICAL LABORATORY TECHNOLOGIST

Minimum requirements
Baccalaureate degree in clinical laboratory science, including one year's study consisting primarily of training; or baccalaureate degree, plus one year as a licensed technologist trainee; or 90 credits, plus two years as a technologist trainee; or 120 credits, plus one year as a licensed trainee. If the nonlaboratory science degree or credits are used for eligibility, a certain number of courses must be in specified areas. A higher proportion of laboratory courses is prescribed if an applicant earned the degree or credits after July 1973.
Examination
Written.
Permitted activities
Performance and supervision of laboratory procedures.

CLINICAL LABORATORY TECHNOLOGIST—LIMITED

Licenses are granted in chemistry, microbiology, immunohematology, and toxicology.
Minimum requirements
Baccalaureate degree in the specialty for which license is sought, plus one year of postgraduate training or experience in the specialized field.
Examination
Written.
Permitted activities
Performance or supervision of procedures only in the science covered by the license.

All examinations are prepared by the ASMT and edited and approved by the California Laboratory Field Services. They are offered twice a year at several locations. The application fee for bioanalysts, chemists, and microbiologists is $25, and their annual renewal fee is $20. The application fee for technologists and limited technologists is $15. Their renewal fee is $6 per year.

55

How to Classify HEW Techs

John Davidson

Ever since the HEW proficiency examination was first administered in 1975, laboratory managers have been faced with a difficult question: How should technologists who pass the exam be classified? Should an HEW tech be considered a full-fledged technologist and be paid the same as an ASCP-certified technologist? Or should the ASCP-certified technologist be paid more based on his educational background?

Many labs have refused to admit that a problem exists. Others have been in a holding pattern—the easiest solution being to do nothing at all. Still others are confused by the HEW requirements. Perhaps we ought to take a closer look at the original purpose of the proficiency exam.

The proficiency exams are part of the procedure by which HEW (now the Department of Health and Human Services) qualifies laboratories to be eligible for Medicare-Medicaid reimbursement. According to current regulations, laboratories must have "a sufficient number of properly qualified technical personnel for the volume and diversity of tests performed," among other requirements.

The personnel qualifications include education, training, and experience, but do not require certification by any professional group. A laboratorian who does not automatically qualify as a technologist by holding a bachelor's degree in medical technology may take the proficiency exam. If he passes, he will be considered a qualified Clinical Laboratory Technologist (CLT).

And that's where the conflict arises: In one laboratory, a CLT may be paid the same rate as an ASCP-certified technologist, while in another laboratory he may be paid on an entirely different scale.

FIGURE 55-1

Position Description for MT-HEW

WENTWORTH-DOUGLASS HOSPITAL
DOVER, NEW HAMPSHIRE

TITLE: Medical Technologist-HEW GRADE________ CODE________

REPORTS TO: Section Chief DEPT: Laboratory

Main Function:

Performs a wide variety of tests and procedures to provide information for the diagnosis and treatment of the patient's condition. Draws specimens according to the tests ordered.

Duties and Responsibilities:

Under general supervision and following department and hospital policies and practices, performs routine tests and procedures in all laboratory disciplines.

Maintains laboratory areas and equipment in a safe and sanitary condition. As assigned, may be responsible for a subsection of the laboratory. May draw blood for transfusion and perform a physical exam of the donor, as required.

Records and reports test results following departmental procedures. Maintains the quality control program, forwards specimens to reference laboratories as requested. Reports abnormal results immediately. Prepares bacteriological media and chemical reagents, as needed.

Individuals in this classification are expected to utilize a high degree of initiative and judgment in the performance of tests and examination of specimens. Individuals must have four years' experience, pass the HEW proficiency exam, and demonstrate equal capabilities of a graduate medical technologist with at least one year's experience in this hospital laboratory; or have a degree in a related field plus HEW proficiency and six months' experience in this hospital laboratory.

May be required to work on-call shifts, weekends, or rotating shifts.

Performs other duties as requested or as needed.

This double standard is not new: Military-trained technologists have faced the same problem for years. As long as they stay in Government laboratories, they do the same work as ASCP-certified technologists—and may even supervise them. Yet once military-trained technologists apply for a job in a civilian lab, they are often told they cannot be paid the same as ASCP-certified technologists, even though they have the same amount of training and experience.

Probably the most controversial issue created by the double standard is the question of equal pay for equal work. If HEW (HHS) techs are legally qualified to perform the same duties as ASCP-certified technologists—and are in fact performing the same duties—they are entitled to the same pay. Whether certified and noncertified personnel should do the same work is still being debated and is something the new Clinical Laboratory Improvement Act should clear up—if and when it is passed.

Are technologists who pass HEW's proficiency exam indeed equal to those certified by the ASCP? And do most laboratories recognize them as such? To find out, I sent questionnaires to 500 laboratories, ranging in size from 100 to 400 beds, and asked the following questions:

1. Do you pay CLTs the same as ASCP-certified technologists?

2. Do you have a separate pay category for CLTs?

3. Do you consider an individual who has a degree in a related field and passed the HEW proficiency exam equal to an ASCP-certified technologist?

4. Do you classify CLTs with MLTs, giving consideration to years of experience and increasing their pay accordingly?

I received 190 responses, and the answers show how many different ways laboratories classify CLTs. Here are some of the results:

Forty-two said they pay CLTs the same as certified technologists; 65 said they did not; and 16 said they pay CLTs the same as certified technologists only if they are doing the same work. The remainder said they either did not have any CLTs or have not had to face the problem. Two labs pay a bonus to techs who pass the HEW proficiency exam—one bonus is $75 a month, the other $14 a week.

Of those respondents who do not pay CLTs the same as certified technologists, only 28 said they have a separate pay category for CLTs, but 43 said that if a tech has a degree in a related field and passes the proficiency exam, he is considered equal to a certified technologist. A mere 16 respondents classify CLTs with MLTs and increase their pay based on the number of years' experience.

In addition to answering the survey's questions, many of the respondents supplied additional comments. One said that he originally gave CLTs the same salary and benefits as certified technologists, but now worries about what he calls a flood of technologists in the field who may not be as well versed in theory as they should be. Another said he was told by a JCAH inspector that both ASCP-certified technologists and CLTs are considered qualified technologists. Others interpret various Federal personnel standards as giving the two groups equal status and are afraid to pay CLTs less than certified technologists on legal grounds.

What's the best way to classify HEW (HHS) techs? There's no easy answer, but we've solved the problem at our 200-bed hospital laboratory by creating a separate job category for techs who pass the proficiency exam. Here's how it works:

We've been classifying laboratory personnel in four job categories: MT(ASCP), MT-HEW, MLT(ASCP), and CLA(ASCP). A different job description exists for each job category. Thus an HEW tech will be performing some—but not all—of the same job functions as an ASCP-certified technologist. Our job description for an HEW tech is shown in Figure 55-1.

The starting salary range for HEW (HHS) techs is 8 percent below that for MTs. In order for a tech to move up to the MT-HEW job category, he must have four years' experience and pass the HEW proficiency exam. One year's experience must be in our hospital laboratory. A laboratorian can also be classified in the MT-HEW category if he has a degree in a related field, passes the proficiency exam, and has six months' experience in our lab. We set the experience requirements to insure that techs who pass the proficiency exam are as capable as graduate medical technologists.

We think it's a fair system because it upgrades those who have passed the HEW test, but still distinguishes certified technologists. Since we instituted this system, we've had no complaints from either ASCP-certified or HEW-proficient technologists.

If and when a new version of CLIA comes out of Congress, the problem of proficiency and certification may finally be cleared up, eliminating the dilemma that many laboratories now face. Meanwhile, creating a separate job category for HEW (HHS) techs is a fair and practical compromise that worked in our lab. It can work in yours, too.

56

State Licensure Laws for Laboratorians

David J. Kull

It's not only what you are. Where you are located in the country often determines whether you qualify as a laboratory director, supervisor, technologist, or technician.

Personnel standards vary widely among the states. In Arizona, only a physician or osteopath may serve as laboratory director, while in California, a physician or bioanalyst may direct a multiservice lab. A supervisor in Connecticut needs at least a bachelor's degree, but in Oregon you're eligible if you have three years of college along with laboratory experience. Technologists in most states may show a combination of some college and some experience (or certification or successful completion of an examination) in place of a bachelor's degree; in Georgia, you must also pass an exam. New Hampshire lists a bachelor's degree as one way to rank as a technician, although most states call for only a certain number of college credits or hours, or a high school diploma combined with lab training or experience.

While Federal regulations establish nationwide standards for different classifications of laboratories, state rules frequently impose additional personnel requirements. These requirements also apply, of course, to labs not covered by the Federal programs, those that neither receive Medicare reimbursements nor engage in interstate commerce.

Even HEW (now the Department of Health and Human Services)-proposed personnel standards would not eliminate the state-by-state variations. The pending Federal standards may, in fact, make state provisions loom larger by contrast. The HEW plan would ease qualification requirements for laboratory directors, a level of responsibility that states generally accord the greatest attention in their codes.

TABLE 56-1

The States with Personnel Standards for Clinical Laboratories

	Director	Supervisor	Technologist	Technician
ALABAMA	O ●	●	●	●
ALASKA				
ARIZONA	X			
ARKANSAS	O			
CALIFORNIA	X		X	
COLORADO				
CONNECTICUT	X	X		
DELAWARE	X			
DISTRICT OF COLUMBIA	X	X	X	X
FLORIDA	X	X	X	X
GEORGIA	X	X	X	X
HAWAII	X	X	X	X
IDAHO				
ILLINOIS	O ●	X	X	X
INDIANA				
IOWA				
KANSAS	O			
KENTUCKY	●	●	●	●
LOUISIANA				
MAINE	●			
MARYLAND	X	X		
MASSACHUSETTS*	O ●			
MICHIGAN	X	X		
MINNESOTA	O			
MISSISSIPPI	O			
MISSOURI				
MONTANA				

The scope of state licensure varies as much as the conditions for eligibility. Some states regulate only independent laboratories, others only hospital labs, and still others apply separate standards to the two categories. Some states don't license at all, but regulate hospital labs through hospital laws. And in a few states, strict rules are on the books but not enforced.

	Director	Supervisor	Technologist	Technician
NEBRASKA				
NEVADA	X	X	X	X
NEW HAMPSHIRE*	X	X	X	X
NEW JERSEY	X	X	X	X
NEW MEXICO				
NEW YORK	X	X	X	
NORTH CAROLINA	O			
NORTH DAKOTA				
OHIO				
OKLAHOMA				
OREGON	X	X		
PENNSYLVANIA	X	X	X	
RHODE ISLAND	●			
SOUTH CAROLINA*	X	X	X	X
SOUTH DAKOTA				
TENNESSEE	X	X	X	X
TEXAS	X			
UTAH**	X	X	X	
VERMONT				
VIRGINIA				
WASHINGTON				
WEST VIRGINIA				
WISCONSIN	X			
WYOMING				

X Same rules, all labs
O Hospital labs
● Independent labs

* Not enforced
** Voluntary program

Here, then, is a rundown of laboratory licensure:

ALABAMA

Hospital laboratories must be directed by a physician or a committee of the medical staff. The following regulations apply to independent laboratories.

Director

Physician with two years' laboratory experience; or
Doctorate in chemistry, biology, or physical sciences; or
Microbiologist certified by the American Board of Medical Microbiology or clinical chemist certified by the American Board of Clinical Chemistry; or
Other specialist certified by national board with standards acceptable to the state health department; or
Individual with four years' experience and general lab training under licensed lab director.

Supervisor

Physician with two years' experience; or
Doctorate in chemical, physical, or biological sciences; or
Master's degree in those areas with four years' experience; or
Completion of 90 semester hours or more of study in those areas, with six years' experience.

Technologist

Bachelor's degree in medical technology; or
Three years or 90 semester hours in approved courses in approved school of medical technology; or
At least three years of study in chemical, physical, or biological science with one year's experience or training covering the specialties in which tests are to be performed.

Technician

Must meet the requirements for CLA or MLT, or have had training in a military lab.

ALASKA

No requirements.

ARIZONA

Director

In all labs, must be a licensed physician or osteopath, or hold advanced degree in chemical or biological science. Requirements do not apply to those licensed before 1964.

ARKANSAS

Under hospital licensure law, hospital labs must be directed by a member of the medical staff. Independent labs are not regulated.

CALIFORNIA

All clinical labs.

Director

Any multiservice lab must be directed by a licensed physician or bioanalyst. Minimum requirements for bioanalyst are a master's degree in a biological science, including 45 credits in 10 prescribed areas; plus four years' experience as a licensed technologist; plus successful completion of written, oral, and practical examinations.

Laboratorians providing service only in chemistry or microbiology may be directed by licensed clinical chemists or clinical microbiologists. Requirements are a master's degree in appropriate specialty, including 30 credit hours in that area; plus one year of directed study and three years' experience, or four years' experience (in either case, two years must be at the supervisory level); and successful completion of written and oral examinations.

Technologist

Bachelor's degree in clinical laboratory science, including one year's study consisting primarily of training; or

Bachelor's degree, plus one year as a licensed technologist trainee; or

Ninety credits, plus two years as a licensed trainee; or

One hundred and twenty credits, plus one year as a licensed trainee.

If a nonlaboratory degree or credits are used for eligibility, a certain number of the courses must be in specified areas.

Limited technologist licenses are granted for chemistry, microbiology, immunohematology, and toxicology. Applicants must have a bachelor's degree in the specialty, plus one year of training or experience in the specialized field. All technologist applicants must pass a written exam.

COLORADO

No requirements.

CONNECTICUT

All clinical labs.

Director

Pathologist licensed in Connecticut, and certified by the American Board of Pathology, or equivalent qualifications; or

Physician, veterinarian, or dentist, licensed in Connecticut, whose qualifications to perform tests are acceptable to the Commissioner of Health; or

Doctorate or comparable degree with a major in chemical, physical, or biological science (applicant must also satisfy the proficiency requirements for registration); or

A person with proven ability in a lab specialty, which qualifies him in the eyes of the Commissioner of Health.

Supervisor
Physician; or
Doctorate in a science, plus two years' specialty experience; or
Master's degree in a science, plus four years' experience, with two years spent in a specialty; or
Bachelor's degree, plus six years' experience, with two years spent in a specialty.

DELAWARE
All clinical labs.

Director
Physician board-certified or -eligible in pathology or one of laboratory specialties; or
Doctorate in chemical, physical, or biological science, if certified in one of the laboratory specialties; or
Laboratorian with four years' general experience in a clinical lab.

DISTRICT OF COLUMBIA
All laboratorians in the district are considered to be engaged in interstate commerce and come under Federal standards.

FLORIDA
All clinical labs.

Director
Physician; or
Doctorate in chemical, physical, or biological science certified by the American Board of Clinical Chemistry, the American Board of Medical Microbiology, or another national accrediting board, plus four years' experience, two of them in acquiring proficiency in a specialty.

Supervisor
Physician; or
Doctorate in chemical, physical, or biological science, plus two year's experience in a special field; or
Master's degree in one of those sciences and four years' experience, two of which must be in a special field; or
Bachelor's degree in one of those sciences plus six years' experience, two of which must be in a special field; or
Three years' academic study, with a minimum of 70 semester hours, plus seven years' experience; or
Two years' academic study, with a minimum of 60 semester hours, plus 10 years' experience.

Technologist
Bachelor's degree in medical technology; or

Three years' academic study, with a minimum of 90 semester hours, meeting requirements for entrance into a 12-month school of medical technology; or
Bachelor's degree in a chemical, physical, or biological science, and one year's experience in a special field; or
Three years' academic study, with a minimum of 90 semester hours, plus one year's experience in an accredited lab; or
Two years' academic study, with a minimum of 60 semester hours, plus four years' experience in an accredited lab.

Technician
Two years' academic study, with a minimum of 60 semester hours in a chemical, physical, or biological science; or
High school education and completion of a minimum of 12 months in an accredited school, plus one year's experience; or
High school education and two years' experience as a technician trained in an accredited lab; or
High school education, plus one year's experience as a technician trainee in a program approved by the Council on Medical Education of the American Medical Association; or
High school education and two years' experience in an accredited lab.

GEORGIA
All clinical labs.

Director
Licensed physician, certified by the American Board of Pathology, the American Osteopathic Board of Pathology, the American Board of Medical Microbiology, or the American Board of Clinical Chemistry; or
Doctorate in a chemical or biological science, and certified by ABMM or ABCC.

Supervisor
Licensed physician; or
Doctorate in a chemical, physical, or biological science, and two years' pertinent lab experience, or
Master's degree in a chemical, physical, or biological science and/or a medical technology discipline, with three years' pertinent experience, or
Qualified clinical lab technologist, with four years' pertinent lab experience.

Technologist
Bachelor's degree in medical technology; or
Three years of college with a minimum of 135 quarter-credit hours and completion of at least 12 months' training in an approved school of medical technology;
Bachelor's degree in a chemical, physical, or biological science, and one year's pertinent lab experience; or
Three years of college, plus two years' experience; or
Four years' experience as a technician.
All applicants must pass an exam.

Technician

Two years of college; or

High school diploma, with completion of a 12-month technician training course or with two years' experience as a clinical lab technician trainee.

All applicants must pass an exam.

HAWAII

All clinical labs.

Director

Physician; or

Doctor of veterinary medicine, plus one year's lab or teaching experience; or

Doctorate in a basic medical science; or

Master's degree in a medical science, plus three years' lab or teaching experience; or

Five years' lab or teaching experience in a basic medical science.

Supervisor

Doctorate, plus one year's experience and successful completion of an exam; or

Master's degree, plus two years' experience and exam; or

Bachelor's degree, plus three years' experience and exam.

Technologist

Bachelor of science or equivalent degree, with instruction in biological or chemical sciences or medical technology; or

ASCP certification or eligibility for certification.

Technician

Associate degree with 60 credit hours, plus six months' training or experience; or

High school diploma, plus one year of lab training and experience; or

High school diploma, plus training as a lab assistant, plus three years' experience, plus a letter of recommendation from person under whom applicant trained.

IDAHO

No requirements.

ILLINOIS

Hospital and independent laboratories are regulated under different laws. Except for the requirements for directors, however, personnel standards for both types of labs are essentially the same.

Director

In hospital labs, the director must be a physician with qualifications acceptable to the Department of Public Health. Independent lab standards for director are:

Physician, with one year's training in lab procedures; or

Physician who is board-certified or -eligible; or

Doctorate in chemical or biological science, plus one year's training and two years' lab experience; or
Master's degree in basic science, plus one year's training and two years' experience in any discipline covered by the lab that is not included in the degree.

Supervisor
Doctorate, with two years' experience; or
Master's degree and four years' experience; or
Bachelor's degree and six years' experience, or
Qualified medical technologist and six years' experience.

Technologist
Bachelor's degree in medical technology; or
Bachelor's degree, plus one year's experience; or
At least 90 hours' college work, plus 12 months' training in a school of medical technology.

INDIANA
No requirements.

IOWA
No requirements.

KANSAS
No personnel standards for independent labs. Under the state's hospital licensure law, hospital labs must be directed by a pathologist or a staff physician.

KENTUCKY
No standards for hospital labs. Requirements for independent labs are:

Director
Pathologist board-certified or-eligible; or
Physician certified in one of the laboratory specialties by an approved national accrediting board; or
Physician with at least two years' general laboratory training; or
Doctorate in a chemical, physical, or biological science; plus certification by an approved national accrediting board; or
Doctorate in one of the three sciences, plus two years' experience in a specialty.
Individual may qualify under grandfather clause if he directed a clinical lab for a year between January 1968 and May 1977 and meets one of these requirements:
Master's degree in one of the three sciences, plus four years' experience; or
Bachelor's degree in one of three sciences, plus six years' experience; or
Successful completion of approved exam.

Supervisor
Physician; or
Doctorate in one of the three sciences, plus two years' experience in a laboratory

specialty; or
Master's degree in one of the three sciences, plus three years' experience, two in a specialty; or
Qualified technologist with four years' experience, two in a specialty.
In cytotechnology, supervisor may qualify with four years' experience during preceding 10 years.
If individual supervised in a clinical lab prior to 1968, he may qualify as supervisor with a combination of 15 years of experience and education. If individual supervised in a clinical lab in Kentucky for at least one year prior to May 1977, he may continue in that capacity, although a proficiency exam may be required.

Technologist
Bachelor's degree in medical technology; or
Bachelor's degree in one of the basic sciences, plus one year's training or experience in a laboratory specialty; or
At least 90 credits of college study plus a year's training in approved medical technology school or equivalent training and experience; or
Successful completion of approved examination.
Grandfather provisions apply to those who worked as technologists prior to 1968.

Cytotechnologist
At least two years' college study, including specified science courses, plus 12 months in approved cytotechnology training program or six months' training and two years' experience; or
High school diploma with six months' training and two years' experience prior to May 1977; or
Successful completion of HEW examination.

Technician
At least 60 credit hours, including study in chemistry, biology, and medical laboratory techniques; or
High school diploma, plus one year's training in approved program or two years' experience or completion of military medical laboratory procedures course of at least 50 weeks' duration.
An individual may qualify as a technician if he performed the duties of a technician for at least five years prior to 1968, or for only one year if the experience was within the state.

LOUISIANA
No requirements.

MAINE
The state sets no personnel standards for hospital labs. Independent lab requirements are:

Director
Licensed physician, certified by the American Board of Pathology, the American Osteopathic Board of Pathology, or equivalent; or
Licensed physician with special qualifications acceptable to the Health Department and the Commission.

MARYLAND
All clinical labs.

Director
Physician; or
Doctorate with a chemistry or biology major, plus two years' experience.

Supervisor
Bachelor's or associate degree, with a chemistry or biology major, or an MT (ASCP) with one year's experience.

MASSACHUSETTS
Under hospital licensure law, hospital labs must be under supervision of a pathologist. The following personnel standards for independent laboratories are included in a law that has not been implemented.

Director
Physician board-certified in anatomical or clinical pathology by the American Board of Pathology or by at least one laboratory specialty—the American Board of Medical Microbiology, the American Board of Clinical Chemistry, or other board acceptable to the state health department; or
Doctorate in chemical, physical, or biological science, plus certification by ABMM, ABCC, or other acceptable board.
An individual who has directed a clinical lab for 12 consecutive months during 1971-1975 may qualify as a director with:
Master's degree in chemical, physical, or biological sciences, plus four years' experience; or
Bachelor's degree in chemical, physical, or biological sciences, with six years' experience; or
Successful completion of HEW director's exam.

MICHIGAN
All clinical labs.

Director
Physician certified by the American Board of Pathology in a specific field of study; or
Certification in specific lab departments, plus a doctorate or master's degree in the specific area of study, plus required years of experience.

Supervisor
Must meet educational requirements for director in supervising specialty, plus one year's experience; or
A combination of seven years of appropriate education, training, and experience, plus achieving a satisfactory grade in an exam conducted under department sponsorship.

MINNESOTA
Under hospital licensure law, hospital laboratories must be directed by physicians. The state sets no personnel standards for independent labs.

MISSISSIPPI
Under hospital licensure law, hospital labs must be directed by physicians or laboratory specialists holding doctorates. The state sets no personnel standards for independent labs.

MISSOURI
No requirements.

MONTANA
No requirements.

NEBRASKA
No requirements.

NEVADA
All clinical labs.

Director
Pathologist, or
Physician with approved certification and four years' lab training and experience; or
Physician with approved experience who passes an exam; or
Doctorate in chemical, physical, or biological science, with four years' lab training and experience.

Technologist
Bachelor's degree in medical technology; or
Three years' study of medical technology, plus one year's training; or
Bachelor of science, with three years' experience or one year's training; or
A year's training in medical technology and six years' experience.

Technician
High school diploma, with one year's training; or
Two years' experience as a technician trainee.

NEW HAMPSHIRE

The State Department of Health and Welfare adopted the following regulations for all clinical laboratories in September 1979. According to observers in the state, the regulations are not yet being enforced.

Director

Doctorate in chemistry, biology, microbiology, public health, medicine, osteopathy, pharmacy, dentistry, or veterinary medicine, plus two years' laboratory experience; or

State-approved certification by American Board of Pathology, American Osteopathic Board of Pathology, American Board of Medical Microbiology, American Board of Bioanalysis, American Board of Clinical Chemistry, or other acceptable national accrediting agencies.

The above regulations do not apply to those operating clinical laboratories prior to July 1979.

Supervisor

Doctorate in a clinical laboratory field, plus two years' experience; or

Master's degree in medical technology or the biological, physical, chemical, or public health laboratory sciences, plus four years' experience; or

Bachelor's degree in one of the basic sciences, plus six years' experience.

Applicants may also be required to pass an examination. These requirements do not apply to those acting as supervisors prior to September 1979.

Technologist

Bachelor's degree in a basic science and one year of training as a medical technologist; or

At least 90 semester hours, including 24 hours in the basic sciences, plus two years' training or experience; or

Successful completion of HEW proficiency examination.

These regulations do not apply to those working as technologists prior to September 1979.

Cytotechnologist

At least two years of college, including 12 semester hours in biology, and 12 months' training in cytotechnology or six months' training and six months' experience; or

For those trained prior to 1969, high school diploma, plus six months' training and two years' experience in cytotechnology.

Applicants may be required to pass an examination. These regulations do not apply to those working as cytotechnologists prior to September 1979.

Technician

Bachelor's degree in basic sciences; or

Associate degree from medical technology program; or

At least 60 semester hours of college work, including minimum hours in specified subjects; or
High school diploma, plus one year's approved training and three years of experience.
An exam may be required. The regulations do not apply to those working as technicians prior to September 1979.

NEW JERSEY
All clinical labs.

Director
Pathologist board-certified or -eligible; or
Physician certified in one of the lab specialties by an approved national accrediting board; or
Physician with at least four years' general laboratory training, two of which were spent acquiring proficiency in a specialty; or
Doctorate in a chemical, physical, or biological science, plus certification by an approved national accrediting board; or
Doctorate in one of the three sciences, plus four years' experience, two in a specialty.
Other than board-certified pathologists, applicants for a director's license must pass an examination covering all laboratory disciplines.
The requirements do not apply to those acting as directors prior to July 1971.

Supervisor
Physician or doctorate in one of the three basic sciences, plus two years' experience in a laboratory specialty; or
Master's degree in one of the three sciences, plus four years' experience, two in a specialty; or
Qualified technologist with six years' experience, two in a specialty.
In cytotechnology, supervisor may qualify with four years' experience during preceding 10 years.
For supervisors first qualifying prior to July 1971, at least 15 years' experience and education prior to January 1968 would meet the requirements.

Technologist
Bachelor's degree in medical technology; or
Bachelor's degree in one of the basic sciences, plus one year's training or experience in a laboratory specialty; or
At least 90 credits of college study plus a year's training in approved medical technology school or equivalent training and experience; or
Successful completion of HEW exam.
Grandfather provisions apply to those qualifying before July 1971.

Cytotechnologist
At least two years of college study, including specified science courses, plus 12

months in approved cytotechnology training program; or
Prior to January 1969, high school diploma, plus six months' training and two years' experience; or
Successful completion of HEW exam.

Technician
At least 60 credit hours, including study in chemistry, biology, and medical laboratory techniques; or
High school diploma, plus one year's training in approved program, or two year's experience or completion of military medical laboratory procedures course of at least 50 weeks' duration.

NEW MEXICO
No requirements.

NEW YORK
All clinical labs.

Director
Physician, plus certification by the American Board of Pathology, the American Board of Medical Microbiology, or the American Board of Clinical Chemistry; or
Doctor of science or other doctorate, plus certification by ABP, ABMM, or ABCC; or
Licensed physician, veterinarian, or dentist, with certification in a lab procedure or specialty, or four years' postgraduate lab training and experience; or
Doctor of science or doctorate in chemical, physical, or biological science and four years' postgraduate clinical lab training.

Supervisor
Doctorate in chemical, physical, or biological science and two years' experience in a lab specialty acquired in a state-approved lab; or
Master's degree in chemical, physical, or biological science and four years' experience, with two of these years in a specialty acquired in a state-approved lab; or
Qualified clinical lab tech and six years' experience, with two of these years spent in a specialty acquired in a state-approved lab.

Technologist
Bachelor's degree in medical technology; or
Completion of three academic years or 90 semester hours which meet requirements for entrance and completion of an internship of at least 12 months in an approved school of medical technology; or
Bachelor's degree in chemical, physical, or biological science; plus a year of pertinent lab experience and/or training covering the specialty or specialties in which he performs tests, giving him the equivalent in such specialty of the education and training described in the two previous requirements; or

Completion of three years or 90 semester hours in an accredited college or university with the course distribution shown below and not less than one year's experience and/or training in medical technology:
Sixteen semester hours in chemistry, which includes six semester hours in inorganic chemistry acceptable toward a chemistry major; and
Sixteen semester hours in biology pertinent to medical science and acceptable toward a biological science major, plus three semester hours of mathematics.

NORTH CAROLINA
Under hospital licensure law, hospital labs must be directed by a physician.

NORTH DAKOTA
No requirements.

OHIO
No requirements.

OKLAHOMA
No requirements.

OREGON
All clinical labs.

Director
Pathologist; or
A specially qualified physician; or
Doctorate in chemical, physical, or biological science.

Supervisor
Bachelor's degree in medical technology, plus one year's experience; or
Three years of college, plus 12 months' training in a school of medical technology and one year's experience; or
Three years of college, plus three years' experience, one of them in a specialty.

Pennsylvania
All clinical labs and doctors' office labs except those limited to specified routine tests performed for their own patients.

Director
Pathologist; or
A physician, veterinarian, or dentist, plus two years' lab experience; or
Doctorate, with a major in chemical, physical, or biological science, plus two years' lab experience; or
For those employed as a director prior to July 1974, master's degree in chemistry, biology, or bacteriology, plus four years' experience; or

For those employed as a director prior to July 1973, bachelor's degree in one of the basic sciences, plus five years' experience.

Supervisor
Doctorate, plus two years' experience in one or more of the clinical lab specialties; or
Master's degree, with a major in one of the biological or chemical sciences, plus four years' experience in one or more of the clinical specialties; or
Bachelor's or associate degree, plus five year's experience in one or more of the clinical lab specialties; or
Qualified technologist plus six years' experience.
Those employed as supervisors prior to the law's adoption may continue in that capacity.

Technologist
Bachelor's degree in medical technology or chemical, physical, or biological sciences; or
Approved clinical education including one year's experience; or
Successful completion of HEW exam.

RHODE ISLAND
State sets no personnel standards for hospital laboratories. The following apply to independent labs.

Director
Licensed physician, plus two years' lab experience; or
Doctorate, plus two years' lab experience; or
Master's degree, plus four years' experience; or
Bachelor's degree, plus five years' experience.

SOUTH CAROLINA
The following regulations apply to all clinical labs. Observers report that the regulations are not strictly enforced.

Director
Licensed physician, certified in anatomic or clinical pathology or certified by the American Board of Medical Microbiology; or
Doctorate, with a chemical or biology major.

Supervisor
Physician, plus two years' experience in a lab specialty; or
Doctorate, with a major in one of the chemical, physical, or biological sciences, plus two years' experience; or
Master's degree, with a major in one of the chemical, physical, or biological sciences, plus four years' pertinent full-time lab experience, with two of these years spent in the laboratory specialty area; or

Qualified clinical laboratory technologist, with six years' pertinent full-time lab experience, with two of these years in the laboratory specialty area.

Technologist

Bachelor's degree in medical technology; or
Bachelor's degree in one of the chemical, physical, or biological sciences, plus one year's lab experience; or
Three years' academic study and 12 months at a school of medical technology.

Technician

Sixty semester hours in chemistry, biology, and medical laboratory techniques; or
High school diploma, with one year's technical training or two years' laboratory experience.

SOUTH DAKOTA

No requirements.

TENNESSEE

All clinical labs.

Director

Physician certified by the American Board of Pathology, the American Board of Medical Microbiology, or the American Board of Clinical Chemistry; or
Doctorate, certified by ABMM or ABCC.

Supervisor

Doctorate in a chemical, physical, or biological science and one year's pertinent lab experience; or
Master's degree in a chemical, physical, or biological science, plus four years' pertinent lab experience; or; Bachelor's degree in a chemical, physical, or biological science, plus six years' pertinent lab experience; or
Meets medical laboratory technologist qualifications, plus six year's pertinent lab experience.
Applicants must also pass an examination.

Technologist

Meets educational requirements of a school of medical technology approved by the Department of Public Health; or
Bachelor's degree in chemistry, microbiology, or biology, plus one year's training and experience in the lab specialty related to his degree; or
Three years of college and completion of 12 months' training in a school of medical technology.
Applicants must also pass an examination.

Technician

Meets educational requirements of a school of medical laboratory technicians

approved by the Department of Public Health; or
High school diploma, plus completion of a 50-week military medical lab procedures course, plus experience in the military enlisted occupational specialty of medical laboratory specialist.
Applicants must also pass an examination.

TEXAS

Under hospital licensure law, a hospital laboratory must be directed by a physician. If an independent lab serves hospitals, it also must be directed by a physician.

UTAH

Clinical laboratories are subject to the following regulations only under a voluntary program.

Director

Physician; or
Doctorate in either hematology, microbiology, immunology, clinical chemistry, or cytology.

Supervisor

Three years' experience, plus state cytology certification; or
Bachelor's degree in medical technology, plus passing a proficiency exam; or
Bachelor of arts degree, plus passing a proficiency exam.

Technologist

Bachelor's degree in medical technology; or
Bachelor's degree in microbiology; or
State cytology certification.

VERMONT

No requirements.

VIRGINIA

No requirements.

WASHINGTON

No requirements.

WEST VIRGINIA

No requirements.

WISCONSIN

All clinical labs.

Director

Physician certified in anatomical or clinical pathology by the American Board of

Pathology, or board-eligible; or
Physician-director who performs tests for a group of physicians; or
Doctorate, plus three years' training, two of which must be in a specialty; or
Master's degree, plus four years' training in a specialty; or
Bachelor's degree, plus six years' training in a specialty, who was director of a Wisconsin clinical laboratory as of July 1975 and for the previous five years.

WYOMING
No requirements.

XI

LEGISLATION AND REGULATIONS

57

FDA's Blood Labeling Regs

Christopher J. Bale

After an arduous 14 months in the revision mill, the Food and Drug Administration's blood labeling regulations appeared in the Federal Register on Feb. 25, 1977. Blood bankers may not be cheering the results, but given the circumstances, they have some reasons to clap.

First, in retaining its controversial emphasis on distinguishing between "paid" and "volunteer" donors, the agency this time has provided definitions of those terms. Moreover, the definitions conform quite closely with those used and advocated by the American Association of Blood Banks.

Second, the FDA has agreed to drop a contested provision in the original regulations (issued Nov. 14, 1975) calling for blood labels to carry a warning statement. It would have said, in effect, that blood collected from paid donors is associated with a higher risk of transmitting hepatitis than blood from volunteer donors.

Both changes are expected to please the AABB, which by now is resigned to FDA's insistence on more blood labeling.

The new regs bring down the curtain on the hopes of many blood bankers that FDA would pull a philosophical reversal and cease pursuing labeling as a primary tool to implement the National Blood Policy goal of an all-voluntary blood system.

Yet the agency has made some hefty concessions. In line with AABB policy, for instance, it has agreed that a ''paid'' donor will be defined as ''a person who receives monetary payment for a blood donation.'' A ''volunteer'' will be one who ''does not receive monetary payment.''

As for gray areas: ''Benefits, such as time off from work, membership in blood-assurance programs, and cancellation of nonreplacement fees that are not readily convertible to cash do not constitute monetary payment.''

Another reconsideration concerns the regulations' reach. In commenting on the original proposal, the AABB asked why blood components, such as platelets and fresh frozen plasma, were exempt.

This time around, recognizing that ''blood components intended for transfusion . . . carry the same risks as whole blood and red blood cells,'' FDA has expanded the order. It now includes the donor source of platelet concentrate (human), cryoprecipitated antihemophilic factor (human), and single donor plasma.

However, the agency decided not to include source plasma (human) and its derivatives, noting that ''there is no published evidence that final plasma derivative products manufactured from volunteer donor plasma are less likely to produce hepatitis in recipients than similar products manufactured from paid donor plasma.''

In abandoning the warning statement provision, FDA said the simple ''paid'' or ''volunteer'' designation is enough, calling it ''a concise and adequate notification to physicians of the relative risk of hepatitis associated with the blood.'' Because of widespread publicity, FDA said doctors should understand the possible dangers that are implied by a ''paid'' label.

Additionally, the agency acknowledged the validity of arguments that the risk of hepatitis is linked to the population from which paid blood donors usually come, not the act of paying donors per se.

The new document emphasizes that ''the proposed donor classification labeling does not prohibit monetary payment for blood donation.'' Indeed, it adds, ''payment to selected donors, especially those with rare blood groups or with a long history of blood donation without adverse post-transfusion reactions,'' is expected to continue.

One AABB-suggested change not accepted is that imported blood be labeled as to national origin to alert physicians to possible risks. That isn't necessary, says FDA, since the only transfusion-use blood permitted into the U.S. comes from volunteers in western Europe where hepatitis risks are "not known to be greater" than those associated with volunteer blood transfusion here. Nevertheless, FDA adds, the proposed label requirements will apply to all blood and blood components shipped into the U.S.

FDA flatly rejected several other recommended modifications. Among them are these:

Quantitate risk by population. Although this strategy is "scientifically appealing," says FDA, it would postpone for the indefinite future the public benefit of uniform nationwide blood labeling regs. The studies needed would be very time-consuming and expensive, the agency argues.

Let ABC handle it. The FDA points out that it "welcomes" the American Blood Commission's support in implementing the National Blood Policy, and, in fact, discussed in advance with ABC its intentions to develop labeling regs. But FDA says it cannot defer to the ABC and must itself act, being bound by law to insure that drugs and blood are safe and properly labeled.

Testing has eliminated hepatitis risk. The agency thoroughly disagrees with those who make this claim. It points out that the most sensitive, third-generation methods of HB_SAg testing can detect no more than 40 to 60 percent of the blood units containing hepatitis B virus. For that reason, FDA argues, the risk has been reduced, but not eliminated.

Moreover, it notes, studies show post-transfusion hepatitis is also caused by still-unidentified agents for which no practical testing is available. The FDA concludes that "at the present time the best available means for reducing transmission of hepatitis B virus and the unidentified agent(s) is the elimination of blood from paid donors."

Prepare for shortages. The agency says that, contrary to some submitted comments, it has found no evidence that Illinois has had to import large quantities of blood to maintain an all-voluntary supply in the wake of its 1973 paid/volunteer identification law. In fact, says the agency, "Heightened awareness of the public health risk from blood collected from paid donors, resulting from the Illinois blood labeling legislation, appears to have had a strong positive effect on motivating increased numbers of voluntary blood donations."

Therefore, besides being consistent with the National Blood Policy objective of an all-voluntary system, FDA asserts that the proposed regulations are necessary to provide physicians with important information, will not interrupt blood services now provided, will significantly increase the demand for blood from volunteers or from paid donors where paying blood banks demonstrate safety of its donor population, and will reduce the risk of transmitting hepatitis in transfusion therapy.

58

Lab Advertising: The MetPath Case

Christopher J. Bale

Ever since the U.S. Supreme Court's decisions affirming that "commercial" speech is entitled to First Amendment protections, many laboratorians have been watching for the effect of these decisions on the lab field.

They need look no longer. Those who read *Time* magazine may have caught the advertisement in a June 1978 issue from MetPath, the national reference lab chain based in Teterboro, N.J. Others in 11 cities across the country may have seen MetPath ads for specific tests in their local newspapers.

What may have escaped notice, however, is the Federal court decision that seems to have removed the last doubts about a laboratory's right to promote its services not only to its clientele—physicians—but to the public.

The case involved MetPath and a New York City regulation that stipulated: "A clinical laboratory shall not advertise for patronage to the general public by means of bills, posters, circulars, letters, newspapers, magazines, directories, radio, television, or through any other medium."

The reference lab's challenge to this city regulation started with a corporate plan to use avenues it felt the U.S. Supreme Court had opened in two landmark decisions. One, delivered in 1976 and involving the

Virginia State Board of Pharmacy, struck down laws prohibiting advertising by pharmacies. A second, issued in 1977, declared that the Arizona bar could not prevent lawyers from advertising.

"Our reading of those decisions was that the way had been cleared for professionals to advertise, and we wanted to move," explained MetPath counsel Gary Cohan.

Why? "Foremost was the desire to set a tone," he said. "Our concern was that some labs would begin advertising, and perhaps do so inappropriately and precipitate a crackdown that would hurt everyone to follow.

"We also have to contend with a New York billing law," he continued. "Patients' doctors order the tests and supply the results, but patients get the bill out of the blue from some outfit called MetPath. With some institutional advertising, the patients might get to know us, and that would speed up payments."

Nor was it lost on MetPath that patients informed about certain tests might be more inclined to ask for them and, in the event a physician's laboratory didn't offer them, suggest that the doctor use the New Jersey reference lab.

So MetPath prepared two ads. One described its test for HDL. High density lipoprotein, it said, "apparently protects people from heart disease." It went on to describe evidence to that effect and how a diet switch from meat to chicken and fish along with regular exercise can raise HDL levels.

Another ad featured MetPath's glycohemoglobin test, which helps determine glucose levels over a period of time, allowing a physician to prescribe insulin based on an average.

Both of MetPath's promotions added that "even though all laboratory tests must be ordered by a physician, we thought you should know something about us."

Ads in hand, MetPath contacted several states and New York City. Only the latter provided a cool reception.

Dr. Bernard Davidow, the city health department's assistant director, attended the MetPath-city meetings that preceded the challenge. "We understood their arguments about the Supreme Court decisions, but we felt there was a crucial difference. In those cases, the advertising was directed to the clientele. Here, it was to be directed to the public, not MetPath's real customers—physicians."

The city argued in its brief that such advertising creates several problems and much potential for abuses. But in the spring of 1978, the

U.S. District Court for Southern New York disagreed with the city health department at every turn:

Clientele. The court rejected the different-clientele contention. Both MetPath and the public have "significant" First Amendment interests in the free flow of scientific information on the relationship between heart disease and HDL levels, the court ruled. Moreover, this free flow of information is vital to individual economic decisions.

Communicating directly with physicians is not an alternative, the court added, because individuals who don't see a doctor would be deprived of the information, and those who do would hear the information only if the physician chose to disclose it.

Patient insistence. The city health department contended that the ads would place unwarranted pressure on physicians because patients would have preconceived notions about what doctors ought to be prescribing for them.

The court rejected that argument, noting that "the protection of doctors from annoying inquiries by their patients" could not be construed a legitimate interest that would outweigh the public interest protected by the First Amendment.

Costs. New York City also worried that without the regulation in force, health-care costs would climb as patients began demanding the tests being dangled before them in print ads.

Replied the court: "Lifting the advertising ban would neither permit the clinical laboratories to determine what clinical tests to perform on a person nor permit them to perform 'unnecessary and useless tests.' Defendants' [health department] regulatory scheme allows only licensed physicians to authorize clinical laboratory tests; if defendants believe 'unnecessary and useless tests' are being performed, their quarrel lies with the medical profession, not with MetPath."

False promises. The regulation, said the city, protects the public from the "alluring promise of relief and the raising of false hopes" suggested in the ads.

But the court took issue, noting that "insulating the public from 'false hopes' is not at issue in this case. All concede that false, misleading, or deceptive advertising is not protected by the First Amendment, but the defendants maintain they may legitimately prohibit clinical laboratories from disseminating completely accurate information to the public.''

Concluded the court: ''In sum, the public interest served by the regulation causes no perceptible movement when placed on the scales opposite the public interest served by the First Amendment.''

What happens now? MetPath has become a model, but no one knows yet how many clinical labs will follow in its footsteps. Moreover, it's not clear how far clinical lab ads will go. For instance, MetPath has not dealt with specific test prices.

''We've mentioned price only indirectly thus far, referring in the *Time* ad to the myth that independent lab services are more expensive,'' said MetPath's Cohan. ''It seems, though, that mentioning test prices would not be out of bounds since the Supreme Court's Arizona bar decision concerned price advertising particularly.''

As for the future, the district court admitted that while it opened the gates wider for clinical laboratory advertising, it also paved the way for abuses.

''The court is aware that new problems may result from an invalidation of the defendants' ban on advertising to the general public,'' it said. ''Most dangers will be alleviated, however, by the state's power to proscribe false, deceptive, or misleading advertising. And the clinical laboratory's instinct for self-preservation will encourage it to monitor closely its public advertising.

''As to other potential problems, the suppression of information in order to avoid its misuse is a choice not open to defendants or the court. It is precisely this kind of choice the First Amendment makes for us.''

59

HCFA's "Lowest Charge" Reimbursement Plan

Christopher J. Bale

In September 1978, physicians and independent laboratories started to feel how their finances would be affected by the "lowest charge" reimbursement regulations just made final by the Health Care Financing Administration.

The long-anticipated regs specify that Medicare and Medicaid will reimburse 12 commonly ordered diagnostic tests at "the lowest charge level at which the product or service is widely and consistently available in a locality."

The plan is based on HCFA's belief that the services "do not generally vary significantly in quality from one supplier to another."

The lowest charge level is set at the 25th percentile of all charges incurred or submitted to the administrating third-party agency or carrier—in other words, one out of four labs charge that amount or less. It is calculated twice a year, in January and July, and pegged to data accumulated during the second calendar quarter preceding the determination.

In setting the ceiling at the 25th percentile, HCFA explained it was not looking for a figure representing the price of a service available at all times to everyone within a locality. Rather the agency sought a price at which most people needing the service could find it if they did the kind of price-shopping a prudent consumer does.

What impact will the new rule have on Medicare and Medicaid recipients? Based on carrier data, the agency explained, the 25th percentile charge is sometimes the same as the 40th percentile or higher charge. Thus HCFA anticipated that the 25th percentile charge level will probably result in a lower reimbursement than under the current regs, but not so low that people cannot obtain the service at that level.

The 12 tests falling under the regulations account for 50 percent of the total lab fees paid by Medicare. They are: serum cholesterol, complete blood count, hemoglobin, hematocrit, prothrombin time, sedimentation rate, blood sugar (glucose), cytologic study (Papanicolaou type), urinalysis, serum uric acid, serum urea, and leukocyte count.

HCFA emphasized that it will periodically apply the lowest charge formula to other lab services and medical products it believes are of uniform quality.

The lab services ticketed for the reimbursement plan include only those performed by physicians in their offices, by independent labs that meet the coverage requirements, and by hospitals for individuals "who are neither inpatients nor outpatients."

The regulation contains few details that observers who have followed the rule's progress would find surprising. But its preamble sheds important light on the agency's philosophy. Here's a summary of the explanations most pertinent to physicians and lab managers:

Testing quality. Several comments on the proposed regulation suggested that the quality of a laboratory test is not amenable to exact measurement and that within any given locale the listed services could not be considered of uniform quality.

HCFA rejected the argument, noting that valid concerns about lab quality existed and that both HEW and Congress were addressing this issue. The detailed requirements that labs must meet for Medicare certification provided assurance that labs meeting these requirements offered enough uniformity of service to meet the statutory standard for "no significant variation in quality."

Profit and competition. Some comments claimed that the lowest charge level reimbursement could seriously affect the profitability and competitive position of many laboratories.

HCFA responded that one purpose of this regulation is to promote competition by encouraging laboratories with higher charges to improve their efficiency and offer services at a lower price. The agency said that no purpose is served by paying a higher price just to maintain current profit margins.

Other comments noted that high-volume laboratories with sophisticated analytical methods and mass-production techniques would be able to offer services at the lowest rates. They therefore urged HEW to set separate lowest charge limitations, taking into account different supplier capabilities.

HCFA declined, explaining that the law authorizing the new approach requires the government to reap savings from the "competitive forces at work in the market, and from the cost reductions resulting from technological innovations and economies of scale."

Physician services. To those who argued that physician-performed lab services should be exempt from the lowest charge ceiling, HCFA responded that the tests covered by the regs can be competently performed by trained lab personnel and do not require a physician's services. "The fact that a physician performs the service does not change the nature of the service sufficiently to warrant labeling it a physician service [as under Medicare, Part B] rather than a lab service," declared HCFA.

Identification codes. Two state Medicaid agencies asserted that the codes used to identify lab services—the 1964 edition of the California relative value studies—were obsolete and inappropriate.

HCFA replied that it entertained the possibility of employing other codes and systems but decided to use the California values because they were used by the majority of carriers making Medicare payments. The agency said it was looking for a new uniform system of terminology and coding to be used in all Federal systems.

The agency claimed that the 1964 codes were not obsolete for the 12 services on its list. And while some CRVS revisions have redefined earlier codes to reflect new procedures and policies and raise the cost of services, these revisions do not justify the higher charges that would accompany them. It therefore decided to stick with the 1964 codes.

Publicizing the fees. Answering queries about how people would learn of the new policy and where to find the lowest charges, the agency said it would promote consumer enlightenment on a wide scale.

Although this is a final regulation, HCFA seemed open to review and revision. Because this rule represents a significant innovation to the reasonable-charge criteria that Medicare uses, HCFA would closely monitor its first year of experience under it.

The agency said it would then re-evaluate possible alternatives. It would explore the use of market survey techniques to determine lowest charge levels instead of using the 25th percentile. It would also weigh alternatives to updating the lowest charge levels every six months.

60

The Blue Cross Cutback on Lab Test Coverage

Christopher J. Bale

A move that threatens the employment market for medical technologists? An unwarranted slap in the face of pathologists? A cosmetic touch-up that won't produce significant health-dollar savings? A surefire, long-overdue cost-containment measure?

Laboratorians have been searching for answers to these and other questions since the Blue Cross-Blue Shield Associations announced in February 1979 that its 115 member plans will discontinue paying for routine admission profiles on nonsurgical patients.

The controversial policy, which was to take a year to implement fully, provoked a variety of responses from professionals in the lab field. None of the opinions voiced to *MLO,* however, carried the unqualified praise expressed by hospital associations and medical societies, particularly those representing internists.

"I don't know where this policy will lead us, but I doubt it will bring us out with lower hospital costs," said G. William Cole, M.D., who chairs the College of American Pathologists' committee for guidelines for appropriate utilization.

"What's important is not whether a hospital goes with or without admission-test batteries, but the system it uses to control testing and to follow up on interpretation with the ordering physician."

Dennis W. Weissman, then government relations director for the American Society for Medical Technology, said, "We are favorably disposed to Blue Cross's goal, namely to eliminate unnecessary testing. We believe tests should be ordered on the basis of an individual patient's health status rather than an administrative decision to order a predetermined cluster of admission tests for every patient.

"But with the malpractice atmosphere that exists today," he continued, "physicians are still likely to order additional tests, even if they have to do so individually for each patient. I'm not yet convinced that this policy will produce a big reduction in the total number of tests performed."

Blue Cross, of course, anticipated substantial reductions by eliminating reimbursement for test batteries, which include such procedures as complete blood count, urinalysis, blood screens, chest X-rays, and ECGs.

Blue Cross has steadfastly refused to predict the cost savings under the new policy. But President Walter J. McNerney acknowledged, "In the long term, we expect significant savings, although we anticipate some transitional costs in the short term." He speculated that potential savings could amount to $200 million a year.

Nevertheless, the real goal, said McNerney, is to encourage doctors to think about the cost of procedures routinely performed.

Currently, the associations pay a $1.3 billion annual tab for admission batteries performed on some 21 million nonsurgical patients. In 1977, the average Blue Cross subscriber reimbursement for routine diagnostic tests under the Federal Employees Program was $66.

As announced, the policy change applies only to medical (nonsurgical) patients, although Blue Cross indicated that a similar program might be applied in the future to admission batteries for surgical patients.

The policy does not altogether prohibit payment for admission batteries or any individual tests. But for nonsurgical hospital admissions, physicians must explain the "medical necessity" for the tests they order. In some cases, even where a physician justifies his order, a peer-review panel may be asked for an evaluation.

"There may well be occasions in which they [batteries] are justifiable," said a letter of rationale from Blue Cross Chicago headquarters to member plans. "The policy requires that these occasions be identified. Physicians and other professionals have the right to order those tests or perform those procedures which, in their judgment, are beneficial to the patient. It is also important, however, to recognize that plans are obligated to pay for only those services which are medically necessary for treatment and management of the patient's condition.''

The member plans also have been advised to conduct a thorough hospital and physician educational campaign, alerting them to the changes and encouraging adjustments in their procedures well before the new guidelines are implemented and payments stop.

The unanswered question, of course, is how physicians will respond. Both the American Society for Internal Medicine and the College of American Physicians (with 43,000 internists) have wholeheartedly endorsed the change. But it remains to be seen whether an organization's endorsement translates into acceptance by its membership.

Already one ASIM official, speaking personally, has expressed fear that the ''Blue Cross program may be going a little too far. . . . Certain basic blood and urine tests should be done routinely,'' said Hugh Espey, M.D., chief of the ASIM cost-containment task force. ''There are enough people who . . . might have an unsuspected condition that could be discovered through routine testing.''

And, as ASMT's Weissman pointed out, malpractice worries weigh heavily on physicians.

But even if physicians respond as Blue Cross hopes, are big savings assured? David J. LaFond, M.D., president of the American Society of Clinical Pathologists, is skeptical. No one can argue with the goal of eliminating unnecessary tests, he says, but ''the potential cost savings could backfire if patients wind up staying an extra day in the hospital because a physician didn't promptly write orders on admission. . . . I'm just not sure that this program will save all that much money.''

Neither is CAP's Dr. Cole. As director of clinical laboratories at the University of Alabama Medical Center, Dr. Cole oversees a system that utilizes a 30-test admission profile given routinely to medical patients. ''When we started this seven years ago, the medical staff and the administrators wanted us to demonstrate that this system would be no more expensive than the previous method of piecemeal test ordering,'' he explained. ''Our studies show that our package of admission batteries costs less overall. It shortens the average length of stay by eight hours, and the standardization reduced our error rate virtually to zero.''

Did Blue Cross consult Dr. Cole or the CAP about studies on the economics of routine admission batteries? ''No,'' says Dr. Cole. ''Interestingly, they came to us for our views on another subject—reimbursement for outmoded tests. We agreed with them that reimbursement should be disallowed, unless a physician justifies his order.

"But they never mentioned a thing about their plans for a policy revision on admission tests. Instead, they apparently turned to the internists. As a former internist, I find it paradoxical that their society is giving this policy such strong support."

For medical technologists, the Blue Cross move raises a troubling question: If test volume drops dramatically, will the job market suffer?

Weissman, for one, thinks this is not likely. "It's really similar to the issue of computerization and sophisticated technology in the lab," he said. "Advanced technology didn't eliminate jobs so much as create a need to train individuals in areas other than bench work. I believe we'd see the same thing in the event of a significant drop in testing."

And, as others have commented, a departure from the standardization of admission tests means more personnel time and attention will be required for the individualized orders.

But it will be some time before anyone knows for sure.

61

Provisions of the 1978 Medicare Regulations

Christopher J. Bale

After four years in the Federal womb, the ''new'' regulations governing hospital laboratories participating in Medicare/Medicaid came kicking and screaming into the world on Nov. 24, 1978.

Actually, announcement of the effective date came in February 1978, when the by-then hoary proposed regs were published in final form in the Federal Register. In the nine months that led up to the November implementation, however, many laboratorians were the ones doing the kicking and screaming.

Most complaints came during the summer and fall after state health departments, the appointed enforcers of the regs, were directed by the Health Care Financing Administration to ''educate'' hospital labs about the forthcoming rules. Despite the regs' history at that point—they were first proposed in September 1974—HCFA apparently felt many labs would be uninformed or confused, or both.

HCFA, which administers Medicare, was dead right. For many labs, particularly those in smaller, rural hospitals, the education came as a shock. Moreover, the state agencies were not asking opinions but delivering a fait accompli.

Of course, many labs had followed the regs' tortuous trail over the years and knew exactly what to expect (see Chapter 30). Yet even for the majority of these facilities, the current overall picture of laboratory licensure, certification, and inspection contains no more clarity than abstract art does. Here is a summary of the highlights of the new regulations:

The new Medicare/Medicaid regulations require hospital clinical labs, if they seek Medicare reimbursement, to practice specific quality-control procedures and to participate in a proficiency-testing program. These requirements are "new" insofar as they apply to hospital labs. However, they are identical to the conditions that have been in effect for Medicare independent labs. And they are equivalent to the controls in force for all labs engaged in interstate business under the Clinical Laboratory Improvement Act of 1967.

Thus in the quality-control and proficiency-testing realms, the Medicare program has at last attained a long-held goal: uniformity in Federal lab requirements. "The only difference that now remains between rules for Medicare hospital labs and labs licensed under CLIA '67 is in the area of personnel standards, and we're working on those right now," explained HCFA official Martha Chestem.

How will compliance with the new rules be monitored? Agents of the state health departments will conduct the inspections. For several years, the states have carried out inspections of independent labs and hospital labs in interstate commerce for the Center for Disease Control, which is charged with those facilities' compliance with CLIA'67. Now these state agencies, under a contract with HCFA, will be performing the same job—and applying the same standards—for Medicare hospital labs.

However, these state inspectors will visit only those institutions not accredited by the Joint Commission on Accreditation of Hospitals. HCFA estimates there are 1,800 such hospital labs.

HCFA's Chestem explained the reason for the limitation: "In 1978, the JCAH, like Medicare, upgraded its standards for hospital lab quality control and proficiency testing to bring them in line with CLIA '67 requirements. Consequently, Medicare has decided to accept JCAH accreditation as assurance of compliance. The only exception will be CDC's spot checking of labs. That could include as many as 10 percent of the nation's hospitals in a year."

So, to participate in Medicare, JCAH labs will be expected only to pass JCAH inspection standards. For non-JCAH hospitals to qualify for Medicare, they must satisfy the Nov. 24, 1978, regulations, with compliance surveys carried out by state inspectors.

One additional wrinkle should be noted: In September 1978, the College of American Pathologists inked an agreement with JCAH whereby a hospital lab that qualifies for accreditation under the CAP's Accreditation and Inspection Program would not be reinspected by JCAH. HCFA has no problem with that process, Chestem noted, "but that doesn't mean we consider CAP as having 'deemed' status. In our eyes, JCAH is ultimately responsible for a CAP-inspected laboratory's performance."

Most objections to the 1978 rules centered on the adverse cost of implementation for rural hospitals. HCFA felt, though, that the added cost for these facilities would be minimal. Proficiency testing is required for only as many tests as are performed in a facility's lab, the agency said. Similarly, small facilities need only meet the quality-control provisions "applicable to those areas in which the hospital is performing tests," it further stated.

Under the regs, a proficiency testing program must be operated or approved by the state or HEW (now called the Department of Health and Human Services) and cover all clinical laboratory and anatomical pathology specialties and subspecialties performed on lab premises. Labs must accept and analyze specimens "delivered by mail or messenger at such times as designated by the testing service," and maintain records of all proficiency test results and make "results and interpretations routinely available to the state agency."

The quality-control provisions highlight methodologies for all types of analysis a lab performs for verification and assessment of accuracy, precision measurement, and error detection.

"General" quality controls practiced by a lab, under the regs, must provide for:

1. Preventive maintenance, periodic inspection, and testing for proper operation of appropriate equipment and instruments; validation of methods; evaluation of reagents and volumetric equipment; surveillance of results; and remedial action for defects.

2. Adequacy of facilities, instruments, and equipment and of performance methods for test procedures to be certified.

3. Identification labeling of all reagents and solutions and, when significant, titer, strength or concentration, suggested storage requirements, expiration dates, etc.

4. Continuous availability of current instructive lab manuals or other complete written instructions in the immediate bench area where specimen exams and related procedures within a category (e.g., clinical chemistry, hematology, pathology) are performed. Manuals must relate to the analytical methods used by lab personnel, reagents, control and calibration procedures, and pertinent literature references. Textbooks may supplement but not substitute for the manuals.

5. Written approval by the director or supervisor of all changes in lab procedure.

6. Maintenance and availability of records reflecting dates and, where appropriate, the nature of inspection, validation, remedial action, monitoring, evaluation, and changes (with dates) in lab procedures.

7. Solicitation designed to provide for collection, preservation, and transportation of specimens sufficiently stable to yield accurate and precise results.

Lab directors or supervisors unfamiliar with these 1978 Medicare regulations should contact the office of their state health department charged with inspection authority. The state agencies should be able to provide copies of the regulations, published in the Federal Register on Feb. 27, 1978, p. 7984. Pertinent paragraphs: Subpart J, Section 405.1028; Subpart M, Sections 405.1310(c), and 405.1315(a), and 405.1317. Subpart M covers "Conditions of Coverage for Independent Labs," but the designated sections now apply to Medicare hospital labs as well.

62

Federal Agencies' Division of Lab Monitoring

Christopher J. Bale

The word of choice among laboratorians asked to assess their relationship with the Federal monitoring agencies has always been "confused." Now, through two new interagency agreements, the Government believes both regulators and the regulated can clearly see where their responsibilities lie.

The Food and Drug Administration on Oct. 1, 1979, relinquished its inspection duties covering blood-transfusion services in small hospitals. The Health Care Financing Administration, which also monitored these facilities, adopted FDA's standards and is now solely responsible for the once-a-year inspections.

"This advances us toward a major goal, that of eliminating duplicate efforts among Federal agencies," explained HCFA official Martha Chestem.

More important, though, is the broader 1979 accord signed by HCFA and the Center for Disease Control. Through it, both agencies hope to unravel the knots of overlapping responsibilities that have entangled virtually all U.S. clinical laboratories.

For labs, it insures that "the same standards will be applied to all," noted Dr. Roslyn Robinson, director of laboratories at the CDC. "Labs also will have a better idea of whom they are accountable to."

For the Federal agencies, the agreement "will permit us, for the first time, to go about our jobs independently, without worrying about how another organization is doing the same or a similar job," he said.

In the jurisdictional sense, the new pact sorts out the responsibilities of HCFA and CDC (technically, the Public Health Service, CDC's parent agency) under Medicare and the Clinical Laboratory Improvement Act of 1967.

This division of tasks should, according to the agreement, promote streamlined operations and minimize unnecessary burdens on laboratories, the two Federal agencies, and the Medicare state agencies.

Attempts at reorganization have been under way for a decade. Several years ago, in what was then a major realignment, CDC was granted sole inspection authority for labs covered by CLIA '67 and intrastate facilities participating in Medicare.

This served to reduce some duplication of effort, but it didn't go far enough. "Two agencies still had responsibility for monitoring standards, and a lack of understanding remained over who was supposed to do what," Dr. Robinson said. "And even where standards development was concerned, authority wasn't well defined."

Late in 1978, the two agencies sat down to end the confusion once and for all. Finally, in March 1979, they signed a nine-page agreement that assigned responsibilities based on each agency's experience and expertise. "CDC is a scientific organization, and HCFA is in the business of program administration," Dr. Robinson explained. "Dividing the work along these lines was a logical step."

In most respects, the two agencies are to shoulder the same burdens they have been carrying. The most significant changes are the following:

Inspections. HCFA, through Medicare state survey agencies, is responsible for all U.S. lab inspections. Basically, this means HCFA, not the CDC, inspects all the labs subject to CLIA '67.

Licensure. Licenses permitting labs to operate in interstate commerce are no longer being issued by CDC, but by HCFA. In the past, HCFA had certified only labs participating in Medicare, a job it retains.

Proficiency examinations. Exams for clinical laboratory personnel are now developed and administered by CDC, not HCFA. The agreement directs CDC to determine who will be eligible for tests, to decide who qualifies or fails, and to tell HCFA who qualifies and when. HCFA may submit recommendations to CDC and assist in administering the exams "as may be required."

Training and continuing education. CDC, "in coordination with HCFA," is responsible for training HCFA personnel and lab surveyors from state agencies in the technical and scientific standards it develops. Remedial programs for lax clinical labs or unqualified laboratory personnel are also to be developed and implemented by CDC.

Standards. Scientific and technical standards development, and regulations reflecting them, are now unquestionably CDC's domain. The agency will publish its interpretation of its standards for use by clinical labs, the public, HCFA, and Medicare state survey agencies.

Monitoring. CDC personnel will not disappear totally from labs around the country. The pact calls for that agency to spot-check labs through unannounced visits. During these stops, which may cover as many as 10 percent of all U.S. labs each year, CDC will not be inspecting in the traditional sense.

"The purpose is to identify problems in the regulations," said HCFA's Chestem. "CDC will evaluate whether new regulations are needed or whether existing regs are troublesome or inadequate. In this capacity, CDC may also gather statistics for research purposes. But the data will have no bearing on whether a lab gets licensed or certified.

"Additionally, these surveyors will make it a point to cover all types of labs—not just Medicare labs or CLIA labs."

The new agreement has been in force a relatively short time, but both sides already seem convinced that it is proving beneficial to everyone involved.

"We've met with CDC officials several times in recent months about the new division of responsibilities, and nothing has come up that couldn't be resolved right on the spot," said Chestem. "It is working very well."

Meanwhile, HCFA and the FDA have equally high hopes for their own agreement over inspection of transfusion services. Neither agency expects any difficulty in accomplishing their joint objective.

"Our intent is simply to remove FDA from transfusion-service inspections and to leave them completely in HCFA's hands, ending duplication of effort,'' said Joel Solomon, Ph.D., deputy director of the FDA's division of blood and blood products.

This agreement affects approximately 2,400 institutions providing transfusion services that are not part of a total blood bank. (''The more elaborate facilities will be a goal for future divisions of labor,'' Chestem explained.)

When first proposed, the idea sparked instant interest at both HCFA and FDA. ''There were no disagreements,'' Dr. Solomon said. ''It was all very amicable right from the beginning. For our part, inspection of these facilities has always been a drain on our resources. We're really charged with monitoring product preparation and processing, not product administration.''

According to Dr. Solomon, FDA's standards for transfusion were to be incorporated into those used by HCFA, which, he said, ''never had much in the way of standards.'' There is one exception, however. HCFA's more specific personnel standards are retained under the new arrangement, the FDA official added.

In one respect—registration—hospital transfusion services have to maintain contact with FDA. ''These small-hospital operations will still be obliged to register with us,'' Dr. Solomon noted.

63

The Government's Laboratory Personnel Standards

Christopher J. Bale

"Significant changes" in the structure of standards for lab personnel were proposed in late 1979 by the Department of Health, Education, and Welfare (now the Department of Health and Human Services).

The long-awaited regulations would, among other things:

- ease the qualification requirements for laboratory director and eliminate those for general supervisor or chief technologist;
- eliminate all qualification standards for technicians, aides, and other support personnel;
- provide for bench supervisors—on-site each shift and in each specialty—to insure consistent quality in both testing and procedures; and
- end competency exams as one method to qualify as a medical technologist.

Three years in the making, the revamped approach "will be more efficient and effective in assuring the quality of test results," HEW predicted.

But professional associations whose members will be affected by the new regulations contested that point vigorously in their comments to

TABLE 63-1

HEW (HHS) Laboratory Personnel Standards

Specialty	Qualifications for technical supervisor	Qualifications for bench supervisor
Serology	A or B or C or E	F or G or H or I
Microbiology	A or B or D or E	F or G or H or I
Hematology	A or B or C or E	F or G or H or I
Immunohematology (transfusion service)	A or B or E	F or G or H or I
Immunohematology (nontransfusion service)	A or B or C or E	F or G or H or I
Clinical chemistry	A or B or D or E	F or G or H or I
Radiobioassay	A or B or C or E	F or G or H or I
Histopathology	A	A
Cytopathology	A or E	J or K
Oral pathology	A	A
Cytogenetics	B or C	F or G or H or I
Histocompatibility testing	B or C or E	F or G or H or I

A. A person with a doctoral degree in medicine, osteopathy, or dentistry who is board-certified or -eligible.

B. A person with a doctoral degree in medicine or osteopathy with at least four years of clinical laboratory experience in the designated specialty acquired after the doctoral degree was received. (Two years of experience before the doctoral degree was received may be applied against the required four years of experience.)

C. A person with a graduate degree in microbiology, chemistry, immunology, medical technology, or biology, with at least 36 semester hours pertinent to the clinical laboratory sciences; or a person who has completed graduate-level coursework in a specialty and has had at least four years of clinical laboratory experience in the designated specialty after receiving the graduate degree or equivalent coursework. (Two years of experience before the graduate degree was received may be applied against the required four years' experience, and 12 of the 36 semester hours may have been earned in an undergraduate curriculum.)

D. Same as C, except that a graduate degree in microbiology or chemistry or equivalent coursework is required to serve as a technical supervisor in microbiology or clinical chemistry, respectively.

E. A person who previously qualified under HEW regulations as a technical supervisor in the designated specialty.

F. A person with a bachelor's degree in medical technology; or 90 semester hours; or 60 semester hours if received before Sept. 15, 1963. These individuals must also have successfully completed the prescribed curriculum in an accredited school of medical technology and must have at least three years of general clinical laboratory experience in producing test results. A one-year internship included as a part of a medical technology curriculum may be counted as one year of experience.

G. A person with at least 90 semester hours leading to a bachelor's degree in the clinical laboratory sciences, who has completed bachelor's-level coursework in the specialty and who has at least two years of clinical laboratory experience, acquired after the coursework was completed, in producing test results in the specialty. A qualified technical supervisor in the designated specialty shall attest to the experience.

H. A person with at least 10 years of clinical laboratory experience in the designated specialty, provided that at least three of the last five years' experience have been at the supervisory level. A qualified technical supervisor in the designated specialty shall attest to the experience.

I. A person who passes a properly benchmarked and validated competency examination to be developed by or for the Secretary. A person must have three years' experience in a specialty to be eligible to take this examination.

J. A person who has successfully completed at least 60 semester hours and 12 months of training in an accredited school of cytotechnology or six months' formal training plus six months of full-time cytology training under a board-certified pathologist; and who has at least four years of experience as a cytotechnologist.

K. A person who previously qualified under HEW regulations as a supervisory cytotechnologist.

HEW. The College of American Pathologists and the American Society of Clinical Pathologists acknowledged many strong concerns. Both were especially displeased with what they see as an apparent downgrading of the position of laboratory director.

ASCP also worried that the regs, if adopted as proposed, would escalate lab costs considerably without improving patient care. Moreover, the "effect on rural hospitals in terms of costs and staffing requirements would be devastating," one spokesman said.

American Society for Medical Technology President Glenda Price said that her organization found virtually nothing praiseworthy in the proposed regs. "President Carter has suggested we cut back on regulation in this country, and I think these regulations were written in that spirit. But I also believe that those who wrote them seriously misread the interest in standards among lab personnel."

Some of the authors admit that one goal was to streamline regulatory requirements. "But this isn't the Administration's final position on these rules," an official said. "We'll recommend changes wherever there is strong professional sentiment that we should."

At the heart of the regulations is what Center for Disease Control officials refer to as a trade-off—eliminating the paper requirements for the laboratory hierarchy while providing for strengthened bench-level supervision.

The main problem with current rules, said HEW, is that laboratories could meet the letter of the law and still not have adequate supervision in all specialties. The new rules are aimed at remedying that situation. They will require personnel who are technically competent in a given specialty to be in the laboratory on every shift and held personally accountable for quality test results.

The proposals increase the number of regulated specialties from eight to 11 and delineate four areas of technical accountability: selection of appropriate test systems; development or designation of a protocol for on-site validation of each test system; development of a detailed procedure manual; and provision for a technically competent individual—for each specialty and on each shift—to certify that operating test systems are "in control" for each run.

"Theoretically, one individual, such as a pathologist, who is technically competent in all specialties, could carry out all the functions," the proposed regs say. "But in practice, the volume of work in large labs requires a division of labor among the staff."

To that end, the amendments identify two classes of supervisory personnel—the technical supervisor and the bench supervisor—who would qualify to perform the functions.

Since accountability would rest heavily with these two classes, existing standards for qualifying as a lab director would be replaced with a less burdensome requirement, namely, that the director need be qualified as a technical supervisor in only one specialty the lab offers.

The regulations would permit laboratorians to qualify as a technical or bench supervisor in a variety of ways, including education, practical experience, testing, and competency exams. But since competency exams for technical supervisors are costly to develop and administer, HEW said, they will be provided only if the Secretary determines they are needed.

The new personnel rules, which would affect all hospital and independent laboratories under Medicare and the Clinical Laboratory Improvement Act of 1967, contain five major sections. Here is a rundown:

General requirements. These note that laboratories must be in compliance with the standards set forth in the regulations, and their personnel must be appropriately licensed. Academic coursework evaluated under the standards must be earned at an accredited institution or judged equivalent if earned outside the U.S. Part-time work considered in work-experience evaluations would be prorated so that 2,000 hours equals one year of experience.

Staffing. For each specialty in which a lab performs tests, a written policy would specify the minimum amount of time a technical supervisor must spend in the lab during operating hours. This would have to be in accord with the laboratory's workload and needs in each specialty the technical supervisor is responsible for.

For each period or shift during which the lab provides services, a qualified bench supervisor would have to be present at all times for each specialty in which tests are being performed and results recorded.

The technical supervisor would also be responsible for determining the competency of all personnel who work under his or her supervision and for annually attesting, in writing, to their competency. Technical supervisors would also have to confirm in writing that the laboratory's technologists and cytotechnologists meet the personnel qualification requirements.

Technical supervisory personnel. The proposed rules call for "a sufficient number of technical supervisory personnel who are qualified by education, training, and experience to conduct, interpret, and supervise the performance of tests" in each of a lab's specialties.

Standards are established for three positions: laboratory director, technical supervisor, and bench supervisor. A director would have overall responsibility for managing the laboratory and would have to be a qualified technical supervisor in at least one of the specialties handled in the laboratory. He would insure that all technical supervisors conform to requirements for on-site evaluation of accuracy and reliability.

A technical supervisor would be accountable for the overall quality of testing services. His responsibilities would include the selection or endorsement, validation, documentation, and installation of test systems. He would also be responsible for developing comprehensive procedure manuals, for selecting and retaining qualified bench supervisors, and for attesting yearly in writing to their capabilities.

A bench supervisor would be designated for each specialty a lab provides and be held accountable for supervising other support personnel. He would insure that the procedure manual is faithfully followed and that test systems are in control for each run from which results are reported. Technical supervisors would be permitted to serve as bench supervisors in their qualified specialties.

Qualifications of technical supervisory personnel. The proposed rules state that each person who would serve as a technical or bench supervisor must meet at least one of a variety of requirements in each specialty for which he is responsible. Only in histopathology and oral pathology—where supervisors must be board-certified pathologists—are no options available. An explanation of the qualifications is shown in Table 63-1.

Qualifications of technologists and cytotechnologists. Technologists and cytotechnologists could perform tests requiring independent judgment and responsibility only in those laboratory specialties in which they are qualified by experience, education, or training.

The laboratory's technical supervisor must determine that technologists qualify under one of the following provisions:

1. A person with a bachelor's degree in medical technology or 90 semester hours (60 hours if received before Sept. 15, 1963) in an accredited medical technology program may serve as a technologist in any specialty except the pathology specialties.

2. A person with at least 90 semester hours leading to a bachelor's degree in clinical laboratory science, who has completed bachelor's-level coursework in a specialty, may serve as a technologist in that specialty.

3. Persons who qualified as technologists under prior HEW regulations or who passed the HEW exam may continue as technologists.

4. A person with three years' lab experience in a specialty may serve as a technologist in that specialty if the technical supervisor attests in writing to the person's competency. (This provision may be used to qualify a person in any specialty except the pathology specialties.)

And the provisions for cytotechnologists:

1. A person who successfully completed at least 60 semester hours and either 12 months of training at an accredited school of cytotechnology or six months of formal school training and six months of acceptable full-time cytology training under a board-certified pathologist may serve as a cytotechnologist.

2. A person who qualified as a cytotechnologist under HEW standards prior to the effective date of these regulations may continue as a cytotechnologist.

64

HCFA's Plans to Streamline Regulations

Marian Wolfson

In 1979, the Health Care Financing Administration became the Federal government's primary regulator of almost 13,000 clinical laboratories around the nation.

That's quite a responsibility for an outfit so young that its name still prompts people to ask "Who's that?" when it's mentioned. But as administrators, HCFA had the right credentials. It was set up in March 1977 by former Secretary of Health, Education, and Welfare Joseph A. Califano Jr., to run and assure quality of the Medicare and Medicaid programs. And officials seem confident that they will lower the high cost of laboratory regulation by establishing a more efficient regulatory process.

"In surveying costs alone, we expect to save $3 million or $4 million a year on the Federal level," said Ed Kelly, deputy director of HCFA's Health Standards and Quality Bureau. "And individual laboratories should save about $3 million more."

To accomplish this objective, HCFA is using a combination of tactics. It is cutting down on the number of laboratory inspections by combining inspections previously made by several Federal regulatory agencies. Where feasible, it's granting reciprocity to professional organizations whose evaluation standards are at least as high as its own. And in cooperation with the Center for Disease Control, it is setting standards that it considers low enough to be realistic without compromising the patient's right to quality care. We'll consider each of these areas in turn.

Cutting the number of Federal inspections. Two agreements with other agencies have streamlined the laboratory inspection process. The more far-reaching of the two is a formal interagency agreement with CDC, which was signed in March 1979.

Under this agreement, HCFA is taking over CDC's responsibilities for licensing and inspecting labs covered by the Clinical Laboratory Improvement Act of 1967, and it will continue to inspect laboratories for Medicare certification as well.

CDC will remain in the laboratory program as a technical and scientific advisor, responsible for developing minimum technical, scientific, and personnel standards to assure quality care. It will also monitor the effectiveness of the regulatory program with follow-up visits to between 500 and 1,000 laboratories that have already been inspected.

The other agreement, with the Food and Drug Administration, involves about 3,000 transfusion services. Under this agreement—a less formal memorandum of understanding that involves no transfer of funds—FDA has ceased to regulate transfusion services that are not part of a total blood-banking facility. HCFA has always inspected these services anyway and will now incorporate FDA's standards into its own.

If these two agreements work as planned, they should go a long way toward easing the burden of Federal regulation. "Take a laboratory, for example, that participates in the Medicare program, engages in interstate commerce, and has a transfusion program," said Royal Crystal, director of the division of laboratories and ambulatory services at HCFA's Health Standards and Quality Bureau. "In the past, that laboratory was subject to at least three surveys a year—one by HCFA, one by CDC, and one by FDA. Each survey tied up personnel and cost the laboratory money. Now, with one person surveying for all three programs, a huge amount of money will be saved—both by the government and individual laboratories."

Granting reciprocity to professional organizations that inspect laboratories. This is another heartening trend at HCFA. Over the last few years, the Joint Commission on Accreditation of Hospitals has raised its inspection standards for laboratories and added medical technologists to its survey teams. So HCFA accepts JCAH accreditation as assurance of compliance with its own regulations.

JCAH, in turn, has begun to grant reciprocity to the College of American Pathologists, whose standards it considers at least equal to its own. That decision will affect about 1,800 laboratories. HCFA, however, isn't involved in this secondary agreement.

"We hold JCAH responsible," Kelly explains. "But CDC has assured us that CAP's procedures are sound and its standards equivalent to those of the government. So when JCAH certifies a laboratory based on CAP certification, we consider the laboratory clear."

Theoretically, then, aside from a possible state or city inspection, a hospital laboratory accredited by either JCAH or CAP will be subject to only one comprehensive inspection a year, although organizations like the American Association of Blood Banks will continue to evaluate specialties.

Setting standards. CDC, in its role as technical and scientific advisor, writes the standards and is responsible for publishing them in the Federal Register. But since HCFA has overall responsibility for the program, it is in daily conversation with CDC officials as they develop and write the standards. The two agencies shape the standards together, hashing out between them which ones are necessary for quality care.

CDC is also responsible for training HCFA surveyors who work, under contract to HCFA, either out of a state's health department or its bureau of laboratories. In 1979, 185 surveyors completed an intensive, two-week program. Although only about half of the surveyors are from laboratory agencies, they are all medical technologists.

This is a great improvement over the days not so long ago when laboratory supervisors swapped stories about the inspector who fainted at the sight of blood or the one who cut his visit short because he still had to inspect a meat-packing plant. Although HCFA's surveyors have always been medical technologists, FDA's have not. Now all Federal surveyors who go into a laboratory know what to look for.

"Every surveyor is qualified in one or more areas of laboratory work," said HCFA's Royal Crystal. "In addition, each one has practical laboratory experience and attends frequent technical updates."

The surveyors use a checklist developed by HCFA, which is less detailed but more flexible than the CDC's was. Crystal explained: "Let's say the lab has two or three specialties. CDC had a separate checklist for each one. We look at the same items they checked, but instead of having a separate checklist for each specialty, we combine the answers with notes annotated to single items on the list."

HCFA's inspections, Crystal said, generally last about as long as CDC's. And like CDC's, most of its inspections of independent labora-

How Well Are the Interagency Agreements Working?

To answer that question, *MLO* spot-checked some laboratories by phone. So far, arrangements for reciprocity appear to have had little impact on the number of laboratory inspections.

Wesley Medical Center in Wichita, Kan., had undergone a one-day evaluation —which it passed with flying colors—by a five-man team from the CAP just three weeks before *MLO* called, and was in the middle of a three-day JCAH inspection.

MLO noted that JCAH granted reciprocity to CAP and that if a lab had been inspected by CAP, JCAH would accredit it without making its own evaluation.

"That's what we thought," Ted Street, the administrative technologist answered. "In fact, that's why we applied for CAP accreditation. We wanted to avoid a second inspection. But JCAH evidently didn't get the word from CAP."

The lab at Harrisburg Hospital in Harrisburg, Pa., was in the midst of a comprehensive state inspection. *MLO* asked Mary Yelito, administrative director, how many other inspections they had had during the year.

"Just recently we had a CAP inspection," she said. "The FDA was here to inspect the blood bank. And next week the Pennsylvania Association of Blood Banks will be here."

Another lab, at 60-bed D.W. Seidle Memorial Hospital in Mechanicsburg, Pa., underwent a JCAH survey one week, and a week later was singled out for a CDC spot check. Laboratory supervisor Mario Marchi described the experience: "When the JCAH inspector arrived, I was expecting the worst. He called us all together and said that he would go over the lab with a fine-tooth comb and didn't expect to miss a thing. Frankly, I was scared to death.

"The surveyor checked everything exactly as he said he would, following the guidelines word for word. He went through our quality-control and maintenance procedures and made a couple of suggestions about performing certain aspects of my paperwork differently. But he didn't find any deficiencies.

"The CDC inspector was very thorough, too," Marchi said, "and she spent just as much time as JCAH had. The only difference between the two inspectors was that the CDC inspector brought along hematology slides and chemistry specimens for us to do. This one, too, went without a hitch."

tories are unannounced. Its hospital inspections, however, are announced in advance.

As for the standards, one of HCFA's main goals now is to achieve uniformity in Federal laboratory requirements. In the past, Medicare standards in individual states varied all over the map. Some were rigid,

---

Asked whether, as supervisor of a lab in a small rural hospital, he found any regulations difficult to live with, Marchi singled out two problems. First was manpower—having to have a technologist supervise a technician is difficult for them—and the other problem was paperwork. He said that larger laboratories can spread the burden of paperwork among more people, but he is forced to do it all himself.

Supervisors in larger labs don't find paperwork requirements any easier. In fact, Robert Loder, administrative technologist of the lab at 550-bed Loma Linda University Medical Center in Loma Linda, Calif., thinks regulation creates about 20 to 25 percent more paperwork than they would otherwise have.

But the required records become so much a part of laboratory routine that most people we talked to said their labs would keep them even if regulations disappeared tomorrow.

"Yes, we'd still do quality control," Mary Yelito admitted. "It was easier 20 years ago when we came in, did the tests, and gave the physicians the results. But once you've got your record-keeping system in order, your laboratory is prepared for any inspection.

"Most checklists are pretty similar now, and the surveyors are laboratory people who know what they're talking about. We used to teach the inspectors. Now we gain from their expertise."

Ted Street agreed with the necessity for regulations. "Actually, they are minimum standards of quality control, maintenance, and personnel. Laboratories must document what they are doing—not only for government, but for third-party payers and their own administrations."

What laboratories really object to is the overlapping of regulations. In a comment typical of several, Mary Yelito said, "I'm concerned because inspections are becoming so routine they are losing their power to keep us on our toes."

Virtually everyone *MLO* surveyed heartily approved of the new trend toward reciprocity, but they feel it hasn't gone far enough or fast enough. They are looking forward to the day when one inspection will be enough to assure that a laboratory's standards are acceptable to everyone.

and others were nonexistent. Gradually, HCFA has developed uniform standards. It now has uniform quality-control standards that spell out requirements for preventive instrument maintenance, adequate facilities, proper labeling of reagents, procedure manuals, test records, and specimen handling.

But requirements still vary in some areas, such as standards for mail-in proficiency testing. The regulations specify only that a lab participate successfully in a proficiency-testing program approved by the Secretary or the state in all specialties performed in that lab. A laboratory in a state program that consists of a total of three pure cultures a year—as some do—obviously isn't meeting the same challenge that faces a lab in a program like CDC's, which provides at least 20 mixed cultures a year.

"CDC is working on new proficiency-testing regulations now," Crystal said, "and we will eventually develop a program that will standardize the number of challenges in each specialty."

Personnel standards are another matter altogether—and one that has created its fair share of publicity in recent months. CDC published the proposed standards in the Federal Register in October 1979, and agency officials were confident that new, uniform personnel standards would eventually come out of them.

"Certainly there will be modifications based on comments from the public—that's what the period of public comment is for," said Crystal. "If there are a substantial number of negative comments on any proposed regulation, we change it. Almost all regulations go through some modification between the proposed and final versions.

"But basically, we believe these proposed standards are greatly simplified, more realistic, and less costly for labs than existing ones. All labs should be able to meet them without undue hardship."

One thing the proposed regulations make clear is that the old HEW technologist's proficiency exam is out. Few laboratorians should mourn its demise since it routinely caused almost as many problems as it solved. HCFA says the exam was never meant to be anything but a test of minimum competency in laboratory procedures, but technologists who passed it saw it as an alternate route up the career ladder.

But laboratories that employed HEW technologists seldom agreed about what passing the exam meant. Some ignored it. Others granted HEW technologists the same pay raises and promotions they gave technologists with a four-year degree. Whatever the decision, someone was unhappy.

In many ways, these exams symbolize the difficulty of developing regulations that are fair to everyone. Regulations should reflect standards necessary to protect the patient and acceptable to the profession being regulated. But when a profession is as divided on an issue as laboratory medicine is about the whole question of credentialing, it's impossible to develop standards that satisfy everyone.

Personnel requirements still vary from state to state and cause confusion and inconvenience to job-hunting laboratorians who find that their credentials in one state may mean nothing in another.

This problem is outside of HCFA's realm, Kelly said. "It's a state's right to set its own standards. We can't set standards that supersede state regulations."

Nevertheless, some states with no personnel requirements are evidently sitting back to see what Medicare does—and justifying their inaction by pointing out that most laboratories in their state are subject to Medicare regulation.

Kelly accepts the suggestion that Medicare is in a position of leadership. "But Medicare doesn't cover 100 percent of anything," he points out. "It doesn't cover all the hospitals or even all the nursing homes. Those that want to participate must meet the requirements for participation. We have no control over the others."

Nevertheless, since a large majority of the country's labs participate in the Medicare program, Medicare is, in effect, the law of the land.

Of course, HCFA and Medicare aren't the only agencies that regulate the laboratory in one aspect or another. The Occupational Safety and Health Administration sets standards for health and safety in the lab, as does the Nuclear Regulatory Commission where radioactive materials are used. The Environmental Protection Agency has proposed standards for disposing of hazardous wastes. The Department of Labor sets employment standards. And the Bureau of Health Planning oversees the certificate-of-need process. FDA not only regulates blood banks; it now sets standards for medical devices and reagents used in the lab.

But none of these agencies has as much impact on the laboratory's day-to-day business as HCFA. And its decisions are becoming more far-reaching. Nor will all of them ease the impact of regulation. Some will add to it.

For example, besides setting minimum standards for laboratories, HCFA is beginning to look more closely at the medical necessity of laboratory tests. The countrywide network of professional standards review organizations under HCFA's direction determines at the local level whether hospital services are medically necessary and follow recognized standards of quality.

"At this point," Crystal said, "PSROs don't have a direct relationship to laboratory services. But under the law, they can evaluate laboratory services, and in the future, we hope they will."

HCFA is also considering regulations to computer-screen laboratory tests for medical necessity. It has already set a ceiling on payment for the 12 most common laboratory tests under Part B of Medicare. And it may begin to make reimbursements based on what laboratory tests may reasonably be expected in the course of a particular illness rather than on tests that are actually ordered.

In the past, Medicare has been accused of inviting fraud with its lax methods of reimbursement. Former HEW Secretary Califano estimated that $1 billion in ineligible Medicare-Medicaid claims were filed annually. As a result, HCFA is now pushing laboratories toward a leaner operation. But how lean can a laboratory get before its quality is affected? Many laboratory professionals are clearly worried that HCFA may be going too far.

"We're not against government regulation," said Glenda Price, president of the American Society for Medical Technology, an organization that pushes for higher standards in the laboratory. "In fact, history has shown that laboratory professionals cannot agree voluntarily on standards, so government regulation may be what we need to provide the impetus. But regulations should raise standards in the laboratory, not lower them.

"Take the proposed regulations for laboratory personnel, for example. A number of organizations have suggested that if you raise personnel standards, you'll have to pay higher salaries, which will increase the cost of laboratory services. But studies have shown that the cost of service in states with high personnel standards is no greater than the cost in states with none.

"That's because mistakes are costly, and unqualified technicians tend to make mistakes. If tests have to be repeated or patients have to undergo needless therapy, laboratories don't save money. They waste it."

ASMT identified 30 areas of concern in its comments on the proposed personnel standards. If enough organizations agree with its point of view—and can back their concerns with evidence—the regulations will be modified.

In the final analysis, HCFA can go only so far toward streamlining government regulations. "We expect to continue to look for ways to make regulation as efficient as possible," Kelly said. "This is our entire thrust."

But it cannot eliminate all duplication among Federal, state, and city agencies. Someday, perhaps, one inspection will take care of all government regulations affecting the laboratory. But not yet.

65

CDC's New Role in Laboratory Regulation

Marian Wolfson

As a regulator of independent and interstate laboratories, the Center for Disease Control never measured its success by the number of laboratories it put out of business.

Although it carried a big stick, it preferred to use the power of persuasion: If errant labs shaped up, they weren't shut down.

In its new role as technical advisor to the Health Care Financing Administration, CDC still relies on persuasion. But now it has no choice. To develop technical and scientific standards for laboratories enrolled in the Medicare program, it must convince others in and out of government that these standards are necessary. And it is finding that persuasion is much more difficult without a weapon to back it up.

Primarily, it must convince HCFA. That isn't easy, since the two agencies have different philosophies toward regulation.

''Our attitude is that there is always room for improvement in laboratory testing,'' explained Joseph Boutwell, M.D., Ph.D., deputy director of CDC's Bureau of Laboratories. ''During the years we regulated laboratories, our goal was to upgrade them.''

Louis C. LaMotte Jr., Sc.D., CDC's director of licensure and proficiency testing, amplified: ''When we found deficiencies—some 61,000 in the course of six or seven years—we notified laboratories about them.

And almost every one of them corrected those deficiencies without further prompting.

"In only about 4 percent of the cases did we have to resort to muscle by suggesting that their licenses could be revoked. That was usually enough to get the corrections made. We revoked licenses in very few cases. That's successful regulation. We weren't in the business of closing laboratories, but improving them."

HCFA's goal is to set minimum standards for laboratory testing. It is not committed to raising levels—only to maintaining them. HCFA must consider administrative and political factors as well as the scientific and technical, while CDC and its scientists focus narrowly on how to provide the best possible laboratory service.

With their fundamentally different approaches to a joint task, the two agencies are bound to clash on occasion. If CDC says, for example, that a technologist needs 30 academic hours in chemistry to work as a specialist, HCFA is likely to question whether that much is really necessary and counterpropose 15 hours.

Before the two agencies signed an interagency agreement in 1979, HCFA regulated laboratories enrolled in the Medicare program, and CDC evaluated and licensed facilities covered by the Clinical Laboratory Improvement Act of 1967. When the two agencies combined forces to streamline the Federal regulatory process, HCFA was given responsibility for the overall program.

This makes CDC's position awkward. As technical advisor, it finds itself in the position of having to sell its recommendations to HCFA, and the resulting give-and-take between the two agencies is sometimes viewed by the public as a house divided. This troubles CDC, particularly since it is seen as the faultfinding critic that impedes progress.

"But," Boutwell said, "if we weren't pointing out deficiencies, we wouldn't be doing our job. We think of our criticisms as constructive."

Despite the constraints on CDC, officials seem to feel they are gradually winning HCFA over on many important major points—and making progress with the minor ones.

According to the agreement, CDC is responsible for five broad areas of the joint program:

- developing technical and scientific standards;
- developing and administering competency examinations of clinical laboratory personnel;

- monitoring the effectiveness of state and other third-party evaluation programs;
- training Medicare's state surveyors, and offering remedial help to labs with deficiencies; and
- researching more efficient evaluation methods.

A short tour of these functions will show their impact on laboratories.

Developing technical and scientific standards. Specifically, CDC is responsible for developing technical and scientific standards, including personnel standards, for CLIA '67 and Medicare laboratories. It must also develop regulations that reflect those standards and submit them to the Secretary of Health and Human Services (formerly called Health, Education, and Welfare) for approval. And it must interpret those standards, publish them, and make them available to HCFA, Medicare state survey agencies, clinical laboratories, and the general public.

CDC guides these recommendations through a labyrinth of steps. First, they must gain HCFA's approval. Sometimes, since CDC is part of the Public Health Service, the recommendations must also filter through other PHS agencies. Then, after all agencies involved agree on a standard, CDC must get approval from the HHS Secretary. At any of the steps along the way, the proposal can meet with resistance that prompts revision.

Finally, HHS publishes the proposed standards in the Federal Register and invites public comment before making them final. During this period—usually 60 to 90 days—professional organizations whose members will be affected by the standards state their positions, for and against.

After evaluating these comments, CDC will modify the proposed standards to reflect valid objections and send the final version to the Secretary for approval.

CDC relies heavily on the comments. "Professionals in the field often show us that we have overestimated or underestimated—or even misinterpreted—a particular point," noted Dr. LaMotte.

One of CDC's current projects is to push for a single set of proficiency-testing requirements. Current rules for Medicare labs aren't specific about the tests a laboratory must perform, and the state-approved programs vary widely in the degree of challenge they present.

LaMotte said the Special Survey of the College of American Pathologists' proficiency-testing program is excellent, comparable to CDC's own program. The New York state program is also excellent. But the Joint Commission on Accreditation of Hospitals has no proficiency-testing program. And some state programs are so sketchy—sending out as few as three pure cultures a year for identification—that in LaMotte's opinion, they are worse than none at all.

"If the challenge offered for hepatitis, for example, isn't nearly as exacting in one state as it is elsewhere," he pointed out, "Medicare has no basis for knowing whether there's a problem in that state."

LaMotte considers CDC's proficiency testing a good example of a minimum program. Four times a year, it mails out about five sample cultures to participating laboratories, which are expected to enter them into the regular work flow. Over a period of time, the lab has an opportunity to identify many important bacteria. Half the cultures are pure, but in the others the lab must isolate the pathogen from normal flora and identify it correctly.

While recognizing the limitations of mail-distributed proficiency testing—that it reflects special rather than routine effort by the laboratory staff—LaMotte nonetheless endorses the concept strongly. "Don't negate the importance of such testing," he cautioned, "because it detects a significant amount of poor performance.

"And when laboratories are told where their weakness lies, they generally do something about it. They train the individuals who ran the tests. We recommend that laboratories use an internal blind sample program for their people—recycling samples that have already been tested."

CDC would like to see HCFA give priority to uniform proficiency testing requirements, which the center considers just as important as quality control, already part of Medicare regulations.

LaMotte said, "A lab can meet the standard perfectly, particularly when they know an inspection is coming up, and still provide poor results on a routine basis. Unless there's a proficiency-testing program, an inspection won't detect poor work."

But a standardized program would cost money to set up and run—and so far CDC hasn't been able to convince enough people that it would be worth it.

Another current project would revise standards for automated chemistry and hematology procedures. With technology changing rapidly, older guidelines have become outdated. "Before we can propose such regulations," LaMotte said, "we must educate whole layers of people, whose approval we must have, about the need for new standards."

CDC is also responsible for developing standards of quality control for new testing methods, such as the alpha-fetoprotein test for spina bifida.

"We determine what quality-control systems should be in place in laboratories doing such tests," LaMotte said. "We do field testing and then provide standards for a proficiency-testing program. Of course, until standards are published in the Federal Register, no one is obliged to follow them, but they can if they wish. We send out this kind of information on a regular basis."

Developing and administering competency examinations. HEW first offered written exams in 1975 in compliance with the Social Security Amendments of 1972. The stated intent was to insure that independent laboratories applying for Medicare certification had enough "properly qualified technical personnel" for the work they were doing. Anyone who didn't automatically qualify through education, experience, or certification could take the exam to prove competence.

Now under the interagency agreement, CDC is responsible for producing such examinations. But their future is unclear. The last examination under HCFA auspices was given in the spring of 1979. As of this writing, CDC hadn't started to develop a new exam—and had no immediate plans to do so.

"We can't do anything," LaMotte explained, "until the proposed personnel standards become final. We can't develop tests and validation procedures until we know exactly what standards to apply."

No one can yet predict the final form of the regulations. As proposed, they spell out qualifications for laboratory directors, technical supervisors, and bench supervisors, but leave to supervisors' judgment whether or not technical personnel are qualified for the work.

The proposals also say that competency exams may be developed "if and when the Secretary determines that they are needed," pointing out that such exams are costly to develop and administer. Not only that, past exams have caused a great deal of confusion—in part, CDC officials feel, because some people think they should represent a substitute for years of academic training.

"The argument is still going on," Boutwell said. "Every month you see an article on the subject in some professional journal. But we don't think any written examination can completely take the place of classroom exposure. In the laboratory, this is even more true.''

Does this then mean that CDC is opposed to the idea of developing a test that represents an alternate method of climbing the career ladder in a laboratory?

''No,'' LaMotte said. ''But we say that the test should demonstrate competency equivalent to that of a medical technology graduate. We'd like it to show that someone without a degree working in bacteriology, for example, has the knowledge of bacteriology that a qualified medical technologist has.

''The problem with competency exams has been that compromises begin to creep in. Some people say the exam should last only four hours, that the questions can't be too hard, and that a passing grade should be 10 points lower than the lowest grade made by medical technologists.

''Such compromises are a giant step backward. We want to give the person who wasn't fortunate enough to go to school a chance, but lowering standards doesn't do him or anyone else in the lab a favor. We want to develop an examination that will be a reliable predictor of performance for the person who has to depend on it—the laboratory director.''

Monitoring state and surrogate programs. Prior to the interagency agreement, CDC inspected and licensed laboratories subject to CLIA '67, and HCFA certified Medicare laboratories. Now HCFA is doing it all, using the same state survey agencies that, under contract with HCFA, handled Medicare inspection and certification. Almost 13,000 laboratories across the country are involved, including 3,000 transfusion services formerly inspected by the Food and Drug Administration.

CDC's job is twofold: to find out how effective these inspections are in stimulating compliance with regulations, and to evaluate the overall effectiveness of the HCFA and other regulatory programs. In other words, CDC no longer evaluates laboratories; it evaluates the programs that do the evaluating.

To do this, it conducts spot checks of labs already visited by state inspectors. It also spot-checks labs accredited by JCAH and CAP, since HCFA accepts such accreditation as assurance of compliance. In 1978, CDC visited about 380 laboratories, and it projects an annual figure of 1,000. That represents almost a tenth of the total number, which CDC feels will be a good sample.

HCFA inspections are quite different from the CDC's, which were known for their thoroughness. For one thing, HCFA announces its calls. For another, checklists are not as detailed as CDC's were. CDC has strongly recommended surprise visits because it feels they provide a more realistic picture of how things are done in a lab. And detailed checklists, it says, are needed to stimulate a thorough inspection and show a laboratory director exactly where deficiencies lie.

"If a checklist asks the question, 'Do you regularly check each new batch of media with known organisms?'" LaMotte argued, "and the examiner checks No, the laboratory director is left with the problem of finding out which of 150 different media types were not being checked. How can he correct a deficiency if he doesn't know what it is?"

Let's say CDC wants to look at the effectiveness of HCFA's surveyors in Kansas. Within 30 to 45 days after HCFA inspections, CDC sends one of its seven field surveyors into several of the same labs—always without prior notice.

"We have the option of using a complete checklist or part of it, or looking at a single department," said LaMotte. "Any of these ways is appropriate as long as we limit ourselves to looking into the same things the initial surveyor did."

CDC seeks to determine not only how many deficiencies were detected by the state or surrogate agency, but how many were subsequently corrected. What it wants to find out is whether the surrogate inspection program needs technical assistance.

"If we find a laboratory isn't performing reasonably well in chemistry, for example," LaMotte said, "we have a basis for saying something is wrong with the system the state is providing or approving. Then we can sit down with state officials and help them solve the problem."

Training state surveyors. Since signing the interagency agreement, CDC has conducted four or five courses for the laboratory specialists in HCFA's 10 regional offices around the country and for state examiners under contract to HCFA.

During these two-week sessions in Atlanta, CDC gives participants a thorough rundown on current Federal laboratory standards, with particular emphasis on interpretation.

"Unfortunately," admitted LaMotte, "there's a tendency on every level of government to obfuscate rather than clarify regulations, and the training is meant to clarify the intent of the regulation. After training, an examiner knows that the legal jargon about quality-control standards in bacteriology, for example, means simply, 'Be sure to check every batch of media with known organisms.' ''

Researching evaluation methods. Another CDC responsibility is to look for more efficient ways of evaluating individual laboratories.

''We know there are more efficient ways than what we are doing now,'' LaMotte said. ''For example, instead of having yearly inspections, we could go around and collect a certain number of patient specimens that have been reported and tested and bring them back here for retesting.

''We need an opportunity to field-test a few such nontraditional systems before we can recommend them. But I know we can come up with some cost-effective alternatives.

''We need to put more effort into detecting problems and then working to help laboratories improve. It's not enough just to find the problem; we need to help the laboratory solve it.''

Dr. Boutwell summed up this way: ''The effectiveness of a regulatory system rests on how well that mechanism stimulates professionals to put their house in order and agree about what standards should be applied to the laboratory.''

But he seems optimistic about the outcome: ''We think standards will be maintained because of the intense professional pride among clinical laboratorians. From pathologists on down to the person who stains Pap smears.''

66

Hazardous Waste Disposal: A Regulatory Headache

Christopher J. Bale

Independent clinical labs and hospital pathology departments with less than fastidious waste disposal procedures could wind up mired in a $1 billion swamp of capital expenses, courtesy of the Environmental Protection Agency.

Such is the risk envisioned by the American Hospital Association from the EPA's proposed rules for identifying, labeling, and disposing of chemical and infectious waste.

The proposed regulations not only touched off a fiery reaction from hospitals, but confused and angered related organizations, such as the Health Industry Manufacturers Association. "It is unreasonable and excessive to require that all waste from surgical, obstetric, and pediatric patients' rooms be treated as hazardous," HIMA observed. "The waste paper from a pathologist's desk . . . [is] not hazardous and need not be handled as such."

But administrative waste is not what the EPA is after, insists Claire Welty, an official in the agency's Hazardous Waste Disposal Division. "I'll admit that the regulations left room for assumptions like that," she said, "but that's not what we want. Rather, it's things like bags of body fluids that are left in loading-dock dumpsters, then get punctured and drain all over parking lots."

Both hospitals and independent labs are included among the estimated 270,000 waste-generating facilities under the EPA's plan to manage the country's hazardous waste from generation to disposal.

Hazardous wastes, within the regulations, fall under two categories: chemical or infectious. For chemicals, "hazardous" is defined by degrees of toxicity, corrosiveness, ignitability, and reactivity, as determined by established test methods.

For infectious materials, "hazardous" is defined by source rather than a quantifiable test measure. "We decided we couldn't realistically and reliably use numerical criteria like 'x' number of bacteria per gram," Welty said.

So the EPA took the Center for Disease Control's list of Etiologic Agents and designated Classes 2 through 5 as hazardous waste sources. The agency then matched these with hospital areas where they would be likely to crop up. Thus, these hospital departments are targeted under the rules: emergency room; obstetrics, including patient rooms; surgery, including patient rooms; morgue; pathology; autopsy; isolation rooms; intensive care; and pediatrics.

Under the regulations, hazardous waste would have to be placed in a waste management system, either on-site or in an approved off-site location. The latter alternative would require labs, hospitals, and other waste generators to maintain packaging, labeling, shipment, delivery, and disposal records for all hazardous materials leaving their premises.

Most pathology departments and labs won't face the extra work that other hospital departments could confront under the new rules, notes Dr. Roger Splinter, of the University of Iowa Hygienic Lab, which is affiliated with the state health department.

"Most labs disinfect their infectious materials before disposing of them," he said.

Indeed, explained EPA's Welty, "any facility that renders its own wastes noninfectious automatically falls outside the system" and is not subject to the documentation requirements.

"It's my impression that most labs already fall into that category, although they should take steps to be sure they're in compliance," she suggested. The EPA intends to seek stiff penalties—$25,000 a day for violations.

Facilities that produce less than 100 kilograms (220 pounds) of hazardous waste a month would not be subject to the paperwork if they employ off-site disposal. "It's quite likely that a lab won't have that much chemical hazardous waste in a month,'' Welty explained. ''But what we found is that labs often let their chemical materials build up over a period of months before having them hauled away. If they do that when the regs are in force, and the waste weighs over 100 kilograms, they'd be subject to the rules.''

While labs are likely to find themselves in compliance, other hospital departments may not be so blessed. And the AHA is clearly concerned. In comments to the EPA, the hospital association contended that there have been no significant, documented public health problems arising from hospital waste and labeled the extent of response demanded by the regs ''unwarranted.''

Moreover, the rules would destroy hospitals' cost-containment efforts, the AHA argued. Ultimately, the regs ''will dramatically increase hospital solid-waste disposal costs without any appreciable . . . benefit to public health,'' the AHA said.

Approximately 4 percent of hospital waste is considered hazardous, the AHA maintained. This material is handled through double-bag procedures, autoclaving, on-site incineration, or hauling to a landfill.

But under the EPA's new strategy, approximately 40 percent of hospital waste—100 percent in the case of some of the specialty hospitals —would have to receive special and expensive disposal treatment, the AHA contended.

Although the EPA would permit disposal through gas sterilization, incineration, autoclaving, and off-site dumping, hospitals would have to autoclave most of this additional waste, according to the AHA.

Reason: In the face of tougher clean-air laws, hospital capacity for incineration has decreased. At the same time, the availability of sanitary landfill sites has also decreased, making hauling an unattractive option. Gas sterilization would not suffice, the association noted, because of the ''massive quantity of trash that would be classified as hazardous.''

But autoclaving could cost the nation as much as $1 billion in capital equipment and installation costs alone, the AHA insisted. Furthermore, autoclave manufacturers have indicated that most of their equipment now on the market could not meet the sterilization requirements and that, in any case, they would have trouble supplying the necessary volume.

At the very least, the EPA should exempt obstetrics, emergency, surgery, intensive care, and pediatrics departments from the regs, the AHA argued, noting that including isolation rooms would adequately provide for wastes from those areas.

But the AHA also recommended that the EPA:

- accept as adequate the waste-disposal standards of the Joint Commission on Accreditation of Hospitals;
- permit states to administer their own waste programs since "most are already providing excellent direction"; and
- consider in their deliberations "the absolute need for hospitals to contain costs."

According to the EPA, the hazardous waste regulations were to be finalized by December 1979 and become effective in June 1980.

67

Product Regulation: A Growing Influence

Richard Conniff

The FDA's Bureau of Medical Devices has inched ahead in certain directions with all the glacial slowness of a bureaucracy, while powering by with startling speed elsewhere. Either way, the result has been the same for laboratorians—hardly noticeable.

Six years after it opened its doors and almost four years since Congress greatly expanded its authority to evaluate, regulate, and even ban diagnostic products, the agency has wrought no dramatic changes in the practice of laboratory medicine.

But for better or worse, the impact of the Bureau of Medical Devices will become more apparent over the next few years. And the bureau will not concern itself solely with manufacturers; laboratorians and clinicians will also find themselves under its scrutiny.

The direct influence will, of course, continue to fall mainly on device manufacturers—through Good Manufacturing Practices regulations, performance standards, and product evaluations. Laboratorians will feel the resulting changes indirectly: They may find that instruments and reagents work better, but that new and useful products take much longer to become available; that products may increase in price; and that, in a few cases, products they depend on may be withdrawn from the market altogether.

Laboratories will also feel some direct effects. Indications are that in certain unusual cases, such as alpha-fetoprotein testing of pregnant women, the bureau will determine not just how well a product works, but which laboratories are competent to use it. That means a laboratory may have to pass a proficiency test and be capable of performing a specific volume of alpha-fetoprotein assays and a careful sequence of follow-up tests before it receives permission to use the assay. Moreover, the laboratory's results may be subject to postmarketing surveillance, possibly by the FDA.

Product standards. Let's look at the bureau's slow side first: the development of product performance standards. Under the Medical Device Amendments of 1976, all clinical laboratory products must be placed in one of three categories: Class I, requiring conformance to general controls such as labeling and registration; Class II, requiring establishment of performance standards; and Class III, requiring premarket approval. New products not equivalent to those already on the market automatically go into Class III.

Expert FDA panels placed the great majority of clinical laboratory products in Class II. That was a mistake, manufacturers say, because few lab products are hazardous enough to require performance standards. Richard G. Nadeau, Ph.D., president of Ortho Diagnostics, served as industry representative to the clinical chemistry classification panel. In a 1978 letter to the FDA, he said: "The panel wanted the manufacturer to guarantee a high level of accuracy and precision, whether or not the medical situation warranted it."

The imposition of performance standards would be unnecessary and enormously costly. Not only that, Nadeau told us, the resulting proliferation of standards could obscure the few cases in which standards are really appropriate.

Manufacturers would be driven to invest in "overly sophisticated manufacturing and testing systems." Laboratories would have to pay for Cadillacs where Fords would have sufficed.

So far, those dire predictions have not come to pass. Theodore Peters Jr., Ph.D., former chairman of the chemistry classification panel, explains: Though the different panels put almost 300 groups of clinical lab products in Class II, "the bureau has yet to come out with a single performance standard. They've been working on glucose for at least four years, and the last I knew it was still in the hands of lawyers at the FDA."

A research biochemist at the Mary Imogene Bassett Hospital in Cooperstown, N.Y., Peters allows that performance standards may help laboratories. Even the long-awaited glucose standard "would make calibrator values and instrument performance somewhat better," he says. "But they would also up the costs because it means a lot of extra effort for manufacturers." Is that trade-off worth it? "I think the situation would probably get better without the FDA."

The bureau hoped to make its glucose standard available in 1980. Beyond that, the schedule is open. Richard S. Stimson, Ph.D., associate director for standards, working from a high-priority list of 90 products, is now overseeing preparation of a high high-priority list that will include about 40 devices. This list was to be published in the Federal Register in early 1980. But when asked if standards will have been developed for all those devices within five years or even 10, Stimson replies, "We haven't set any targets yet."

Nevertheless, the glacier is beginning to move less slowly. Rather than develop all performance standards itself, the bureau has opted to endorse suitable standards developed by outside "consensus" groups, notably the National Committee for Clinical Laboratory Standards, which has almost 50 standards already prepared (though not all are performance standards) and plans to add another 30 this year.

Standards endorsed by the FDA would be voluntary. The bureau will encourage manufacturers to note conformance on their labeling, and it will promote use of endorsed standards in laboratory purchasing decisions. Private accrediting groups may require that laboratory products meet the standards, but there will be no Federal enforcement mechanism. The bureau hopes to develop mandatory standards only where no adequate voluntary ones exist or where industry conformance is inadequate and stronger regulatory control is needed.

Even some of the bureau's critics are optimistic about what that will mean for laboratories. "Voluntary standards are more likely to work," says Nelson Alpert, Ph.D., a clinical instrument consultant to manufacturers and laboratories. "Anything is better than something prepared by a bureaucrat sitting in an office completely removed from the lab."

More positively, John McConnell, executive director of NCCLS, says his group's standards "are at the forward edge of things, helping people develop laboratory tests that are medically useful and clinically relevant." FDA endorsement, he says, "will help focus manufacturers' efforts on the critical product performance criteria."

Eloise Eavenson, Ph.D., the bureau's acting director for in-vitro diagnostic standards, contends that FDA endorsement of standards will not just make laboratory purchasing decisions easier, but may actually help reduce costs. "For example," she says, "suppose we had a standard that described the minimum performance required for thyroxine determinations used in neonatal screening for hypothyroidism. If the laboratories performing these tests agreed with such a standard and used it in purchasing and evaluating products, the manufacturers would no longer have to deal separately with each laboratory's performance requirements. They could still, however, provide their products in very different forms to meet the needs of the various types of laboratories, so long as the products met the minimum performance standards. We're not talking about changing the practice of medicine; we're talking about setting norms for products based on current good practices."

Some observers worry that FDA-endorsed standards, even though voluntary, may reduce competition and discourage innovation by locking the field into one method of doing a specific test. Eavenson answers that the bureau will specifically look for anticompetitive tendencies before it endorses a standard. And she says that the makeup of consensus groups like NCCLS, drawing together laboratorians, researchers, physicians, and manufacturers, will discourage development of a standard that favors any one manufacturer or method.

Finally, David M. Link, director of the Bureau of Medical Devices, notes that the voluntary character of the standards will make for flexibility: "We're not saying this is the only way an analyte can be tested or a product must perform. If somebody can think of a better way or a different way that doesn't meet the standard, that's O.K. On the other hand, I think *mandatory* standards could involve high costs and long delays and could very easily deter people from developing certain laboratory products."

Unfortunately, the possible effect of performance standards, whether suggested or dictated, remains a subject for speculation. The bureau is only now publishing its voluntary standards policy.

Product evaluation. Laboratorians may doubt that any regulatory body has ever been able to do anything fast. But the speed of new product evaluations at the Bureau of Medical Devices is the second reason the bureau has not affected laboratories more. That speed, like the bureau's preference for voluntary standards, reflects David Link's managerial philosophy, which emphasizes minimum delay in product review and the least possible Federal intervention. ''We try to review information expeditiously,'' says Link, an engineer who has an industrial background. ''If you agree we have an obligation to get good products onto the market, as much as to keep bad ones off, you can't condone needless delay.''

Makers of laboratory products generally agree that Link has minimized delay. The Pharmaceutical Manufacturers Association says some of its members have gotten diagnostic products through the so-called ''510(k)'' premarket notification process in as little as a month, though the law allows the government 90 days to determine whether a product is ''substantially equivalent'' to existing products.

''I haven't heard many complaints of delay,'' says Larry Pilot, special counsel to the Scientific Apparatus Makers Association and formerly Link's associate director for compliance. ''The bureau has handled thousands of 510(k) notifications on schedule. It has also handled a number of premarket approval applications [for nonequivalent products] within the 180 days stipulated by law.''

''I'd suggest that we cause no unnecessary delay in the great majority of cases,'' says Link. ''If a manufacturer notifies us 90 days prior to marketing and we make the judgment that his product is 'substantially equivalent' [and thus requires no further Federal action] well within 90 days, we haven't held up his schedule at all.''

But that may be changing, according to Nelson Alpert. ''What's happening—and I've heard this from several companies—is that the response now takes the full 90 days and then comes back with a question. And when you answer the question, it starts your 90 days again. The number of incidents has increased as the bureau has taken on additional personnel who ask more questions. This has delayed some 510(k) procedures.''

One manufacturer, Wien Laboratories, is especially bitter about a 15-month struggle to market its new radioimmunoassay for tricyclic antidepressants. Wien applied in July 1978 for reclassification of its product from Class III, where it was awaiting premarket approval, to Class II. The bureau's panel asked for additional studies detailing possible problems and comparing the test with existing methods. Answering the questions cost the 12-employee company more than $14,000, boosting Wien's total investment in the product to $100,000. At this writing, six months after the experts recommended reclassification in July 1979, the company is still waiting for the bureau to publish the reclassification notice in the Federal Register.

Meanwhile, says company President George Wien, many labs that are not equipped for gas chromatography, and that *could* use the radioimmunoassay, instead continue to send such tests to reference labs. "And the only question was proving to the panel that what we said on our label was true."

If such delays become common, says Nelson Alpert, it could mean not just that laboratories will have to wait longer for new products, but that some useful products may simply never come to market at all:

"Companies considering something clearly innovative now look ahead and say, 'If I get stuck in Class III, I'm going to have to go through a procedure very much like the procedure for a new drug, and that's going to take a year or two years and a lot of money, in addition to the time I spend developing the product.' The result is that we are already seeing a proliferation of me-too products rather than innovations. The trend has been to discourage innovation. It's usually smaller companies that go off in a new direction, and they're the ones who can least afford a Class III process."

David Link maintains that the bureau attempts to avoid delay and needless expense and to speed useful new products to the market. Thus, to reduce paperwork and bypass unnecessary premarket approval or needless reclassification hearings, the bureau has adopted criteria for evaluating the equivalency of new laboratory products: If a test measures a known analyte by an old procedure or by a new but accepted procedure, it can now go straight onto the market.

Link's industry critics naturally applaud such measures, believing that less government is better government. They regard most FDA standards and evaluations as useless wheel spinning, particularly because laboratory test results usually pass through two professionals before reaching the patient and are seldom the sole basis for diagnosis or treatment.

Outside observers have similar doubts about the need for this regulation. "If a firm establishes a reputation for giving bad results, it'll go out of business," says economist Daniel Benjamin, Ph.D., an assistant professor at the University of Washington, who served briefly as an FDA consultant. "That's the discipline of the market. With medications, the way a firm may be put out of business is by killing a few people. Well, that's a lot less plausible for devices that are going to be used by professionals who know what they're doing."

In contrast to those who think the FDA moves too slowly or should not be involved at all, there are critics who think the Bureau of Medical Devices under David Link has moved too fast. Ralph Nader's Health Research Group has attacked Link for concentrating on technical questions to the exclusion of larger public health concerns. Others say the bureau sometimes cuts corners because of Link's concentration on moving products along.

Says Link: "I see it not only as not being wrong, but as being responsible that we try to conduct expeditious reviews. The important thing is to ask the right questions before you let a product loose. We're not asking *every* question we could ask. That would take manufacturers months or years to answer and could keep products from ever going to market. You'd avoid the hazards associated with a product. You'd also avoid the benefits."

As for his concentration on technical values, Link says consumerists too often want the bureau to go "well beyond the basic properties of a test, to restrict devices in a way that recognizes what they see as deficiencies in the whole health-care system.

"The professional user ought to have available the best products people can think of," adds Link. "But he still has an obligation to critically examine products before he buys, because the Government isn't going to make the judgment for him in every case. We can't tell what the laboratorian wants."

The AFP case. But critics who say Link goes too fast and is too easy on manufacturers have already proved themselves influential in the alpha-fetoprotein case. Their efforts raise questions about how the bureau, regardless of its director's philosophy, may handle—or be forced to handle—controversial products in the future.

More than 20 groups, including the American College of Obstetricians and Gynecologists, the American Academy of Pediatrics, the Spina Bifida Association, and the Center for Disease Control, have combined to delay and dramatically restrict the marketing of alpha-fetoprotein reagents. Outside pressure has caused the bureau to recommend tentatively that the test be limited to facilities with such backup procedures as additional AFP testing, ultrasonography, amniocentesis, and genetic counseling; that participating laboratories pass a proficiency exam, possibly administered by CDC, CAP, or FDA; and that manufacturers conduct postmarketing surveillance of laboratories and physicians. In addition, it now appears the FDA may adopt a Health Research Group proposal to limit the test to laboratories performing a minimum number (possibly 50) AFP tests weekly.

Link had originally proposed to approve the alpha-fetoprotein reagents for unrestricted marketing, but with extensive labeling information for the laboratory, the physician, and the patient. The apparent benefits were great: Accurate screening of maternal serum alpha-fetoprotein levels would help detect pregnancies that might end in stillbirths or in offspring severely handicapped by spina bifida, a neural tube defect. But the Health Research Group charges that Link's emphasis on marketing rather than medical concerns caused a "scandalous underestimate of the risks associated with AFP testing."

In the proposed nationwide screening program, the American College of Obstetricians and Gynecologists estimates that 10 to 15 normal fetuses would have been aborted *for every abnormal one*.

The problem, says Ervin Nichols, M.D., the college's director for practice activities, is the test's high potential for false positives; both incorrect estimation of fetal age or a double pregnancy can make normal values seem abnormal. Moreover, because techniques and equipment differ and incidence of neural tube defects varies from region to region, each laboratory has to set up its own curve of normal and abnormal values—with additional potential for false positives.

Finally, quality control is difficult. "In expert hands, some AFP assays perform with excellent precision," says James Macri, Ph.D., director of a large pilot AFP screening program. "But if the assay is not handled in the most critical way, the degree of intra-assay drift can be staggering." If a routine clinical laboratory failed to monitor the test with the greatest care, he adds, it could encounter extreme difficulties.

Dr. Nichols, the Health Research Group, and others believe the unrestricted release of alpha-fetoprotein reagents originally contemplated by Link would have created havoc. In their view, panic abortions of normal fetuses would have occurred where genetic counseling was lacking or where facilities were inadequate for a rapid, carefully orchestrated sequence of follow-up tests. In addition to false positives, the test's potential for false negatives might have resulted in emotional backlash among mothers who had been assured that they were carrying normal children.

At the same time, suggests Robert Leflar of the Health Research Group, the potentially valuable alpha-fetoprotein assay would have been discredited, the professional reputation of laboratories would have suffered, and malpractice suits against laboratorians would have resulted. Expert users of AFP assays report no malpractice complaints so far, but it may be worth noting that a Chicago hospital was recently party to a $1.3 million settlement for a missed diagnosis of phenylketonuria; the case raised the question of whether small labs should be doing such tests.

The Pharmaceutical Manufacturers Association claims the bureau's proposed restrictions amount to needless interference with the work of laboratorians and an assertion that physicians are unable to interpret the test properly. Dr. Nichols counters that the bureau will be saving mothers, physicians, laboratorians, and perhaps even the manufacturers much grief.

The cost of regulation. What about costs entailed by the bureau's work? Have Good Manufacturing Practices requirements and the expense associated with product evaluation boosted the prices laboratories must pay for instruments and tests? Almost everyone in the field says "Yes, but . . ."

The laboratory eventually pays for the studies and data summaries needed to answer the bureau's questions. "But it's worthwhile having the data," says research biochemist Peters, who had earlier questioned the value of performance standards. "The expense here is work that they really should have done anyway, to see if the product is worthwhile." But he dislikes the related expenses—the paperwork, the lawyers, the government representatives. "It's too bad it has to involve all this, all the regulation."

The bureau's Good Manufacturing Practices, which set forth quality-assurance guidelines, would seem to be the single most likely cause of cost increases. The FDA shut down one manufacturer of microbiological media for GMP violations. After suffering what it called terrific losses, the company reopened on a much smaller scale under a consent order to upgrade its facilities. Such cases will probably become more common, especially for small manufacturers of media, and could affect prices "significantly," according to a lawyer in the field.

"GMPs may or may not involve extra cost, depending on how sophisticated the manufacturer is to start with," Link says. "And GMPs tend to be a good investment because the product is more consistent, and there is less waste and fewer returns and defects. I think you can also say GMPs lower the likelihood of product-liability claims."

Former FDA consultant and economist Daniel Benjamin, who spent four months studying the economic impact of device regulation, argues that the bureau's estimates of cost savings from the GMPs seem "preposterously high relative to the potential cost additions."

And he concludes: "What bothers me about this is that the FDA thinks it knows how to manufacture stuff better than the guys who make a living at it."

But Nelson Alpert, hardly an admirer of the bureau, says, "I've heard manufacturers grouse a lot less about GMPs than about other aspects of device regulation. By not complaining very much, that's saying something good."

Where does that leave laboratories? Probably with bigger equipment and supply bills, and possibly with additional headaches from performance standards, delays, proficiency tests, and other effects of device regulation.

It may be some small comfort to look beyond the short-term costs to long-term benefits: Products may tend to work better and to conform more closely to their labeling claims; device delays may yield answers to important questions; laboratory results, as in the alpha-fetoprotein case, may be used more carefully; and when something goes wrong with a diagnostic product, there will be a mechanism for correcting it before bad results damage laboratory credibility and patient health.

For laboratorians and for David Link and his successors in device regulation, the struggle will be to balance the costs and the benefits.

68

Laboratory Law in the Year 2000: More Regulation; Some Malpractice Relief

Michael X. Morrell, J.D.

Efforts to predict the fate of the second Clinical Laboratory Improvement Act (CLIA) over the past few years have all failed. Unforeseen political events and other variables combined to preclude enactment of CLIA, despite the conventional wisdom of the experts that passage was imminent.

In light of this experience, it seems somewhat foolhardy to predict the evolution of the legal and regulatory environment for clinical laboratories over the rest of the century.

Fortunately, we have a good idea what fundamental issues and beliefs will underlie public-policy debates on health care during that time. As the framework for legal and regulatory decisions affecting the health-care system, these factors will be more important than any one law or regulation. They point the direction government will take in dealing with problems of the clinical laboratory.

1. The American people believe that health care is as much a right as "life, liberty, and the pursuit of happiness." No elected official, of whatever political stripe, will challenge this "right" directly; vested interests would unite to defeat any such effort. Thus the Carter Administration, responding to pressure from interest groups, has exempted almost 40 percent of the nation's hospitals—and labor costs at *all* hospitals—from its proposed cost-containment legislation. But politicians will continue to attack the health-care industry superficially, through exposure of fraud and abuse.

2. The debate over three competing goals—health-care quality, availability, and cost control—will continue to influence health policy fundamentally. Debate on any specific health-policy issue tends to reflect philosophical disagreement on how to reconcile these goals. The philosophical preferences of those exercising the decision-making power will directly affect the course of regulation and legislation. But the trend for the last 30 years has been toward increasing quality, accessibility, *and* cost, despite the efforts of different administrations to emphasize one goal over the others. The Carter Administration's emphasis on cost control will probably not alter this trend.

3. The movement to deregulate airlines and other industries is not likely to extend to the health-care industry. Federal and state governments pay more each year for health-care services, particularly through reimbursement. That precludes any chance of eliminating or even reducing government control. In fact, the opposite is much more probable. In all government-funded programs, increasingly complex, detailed, and restrictive requirements come with the funds.

Over the next 20 years, changes in the legal environment for laboratories will be concentrated in several areas.

Professional liability. Even with the advent of the regulatory era in medicine, malpractice litigation still looms as the most feared and unsettling legal experience for health professionals. An increasingly demanding and knowledgeable public not only goes to court often, it also chooses defendants by the "shotgun" approach, naming all members of the health-care team, including clinical laboratorians.

This trend will continue, for both legal and medical reasons. Lawyers like to name several defendants to protect themselves by including all possibly culpable parties, and in the hope that one defendant, in attempting to clear himself, will implicate another. At the same time, doctors are ordering a greater number and variety of laboratory tests, both to meet the obligations of patient care and to insure that their defensive medicine precludes malpractice claims. The result: more laboratorians as malpractice defendants.

Like workmen's compensation litigation in the past, malpractice litigation ties up our courts and wastes valuable resources. Moreover, though only a small percentage of patients and doctors are actually involved in suits, the trend is detrimental to the physician-patient relationship generally. I believe state governments will begin to resolve these problems with a setup like that now used to handle workmen's compensation cases.

The states first established workmen's compensation boards when suits for work-related injuries were similarly clogging the courts and damaging the employer-employee relationship. The boards removed such cases from the courts and soon demonstrated their effectiveness in processing claims efficiently and in making awards consistent with well-defined, equitable overall standards.

I see each of the 50 states establishing a comparable agency to deal with malpractice claims. At least 10 states have already established administrative procedures to screen malpractice claims and decide whether the facts warrant trial in court.

Under a 1976 Massachusetts law, tribunals consisting of a lawyer, a physician, and a judge have found that half the malpractice cases were "not sufficient" to merit trial. A plaintiff can still go to court after such a finding, but must first post a $2,000 bond; most plaintiffs have decided not to. Top courts in Massachusetts and Michigan have found malpractice screening to be constitutional. Legislatures in other states will probably note their example.

Health-care facilities regulation. Accreditation of clinical laboratories will remain the responsibility of nongovernment organizations such as the College of American Pathologists and the Joint Commission on Accreditation of Hospitals. But government will continue to influence the standards and procedures used in the accreditation process. In particular, the Federal Trade Commission will increasingly look at professional associations as they would at any trade association, with an eye to unfair competitive practices.

Accreditation will remain voluntary, but more clinical laboratories will participate because of external pressures, including Federal reimbursement, consumer demands, and medical technologists' insistence on affiliation only with accredited labs.

In the future, clinical laboratories will be subject to more pervasive government control through certificate-of-need laws regulating capital expenditures and changes in service. The states are already expanding their jurisdiction under these laws to encompass virtually every type of health-care facility, including the laboratory. Some have reduced to $10,000 the minimum capital expenditure necessary to invoke their authority; others have required government approval for any new service, regardless of its cost.

Laboratorians can expect further certificate-of-need controls limiting their power to make decisions on equipment, tests, and services without first obtaining government approval.

Health-products regulation. The Medical Device Amendments of 1976 charged the Food and Drug Administration with regulating all medical devices—from the tongue depressor to the most sophisticated CAT scanner. So far, because of such administrative start-up problems as inadequate staffing, the impact of this law is only beginning to be felt. That moratorium won't last much longer.

It is safe to predict that the FDA's course of action will parallel its regulation of the drug industry, at least to the extent that all devices, including in-vitro diagnostics, will be subject to more numerous, more restrictive, and more complex regulation. Studies have shown that it takes about eight years from the time a law is enacted before the affected industry really feels its impact. So we can expect a dramatic increase in regulation of devices up to the end of the century.

Device regulation will affect clinical laboratories in several ways, and not just through delay of new in-vitro diagnostic kits and other devices that need FDA approval before marketing. The FDA will also promulgate good laboratory practices regulations (stipulating, for instance, that bench techs should not perform quality-control checks on their own test results), stringent investigational requirements, and reporting and record-keeping standards. These regulations will force laboratories to expend substantial resources on compliance.

The Health Care Financing Administration will probably also exercise an increasing influence on the availability and use of medical devices. In judging the eligibility of devices for Federal reimbursement, the HCFA may go beyond the FDA's traditional twofold safety-and-efficacy test. Now under consideration is a requirement that a product also be cost-effective.

In contrast to the FDA, which must judge an individual product without reference to others, HCFA could limit availability of a safe and effective drug or device purely on comparative economic grounds. This could mean significant intrusion on the laboratorian's ability to function according to his professional judgment. Moreover, it could prevent gathering data on clinical experience with a new product, even though such data are vital to a definitive appraisal of the effects, intended or otherwise, of any product.

It is difficult to predict if HCFA will adopt this approach. But if it does, the result could be to limit the development of medical technology.

Health-professions regulation. I believe virtually every state will adopt licensing requirements for clinical laboratorians, probably down to the level of the medical technologist. It is ironic that states have long licensed barbers and other "professionals" who have far less impact than laboratorians on public health. But 32 states now require licensure for laboratory directors, 18 of them also license supervisors, 14 license technologists, and 11 license technicians. This trend will continue.

Certification of clinical laboratorians will remain voluntary, but the professional and economic advantages of certification will grow stronger, resulting in almost universal participation. Certification should still be provided by private organizations, since both the professions and the Federal government prefer to keep that function in private hands.

The Department of Health and Human Services (formerly HEW) may include some form of proficiency exam for laboratorians in its personnel-qualification standards, now being rewritten, for laboratories delivering Federally reimbursable services. No such exams are now being offered. But even if they were, they would not, as is commonly supposed, constitute licensing or certification. From the beginning, HEW intended them as an alternative to education and experience requirements in meeting personnel standards for the Medicare-Medicaid laboratory.

As the level of professionalism rises and as government pressure for cost control increases, laboratory peer-review organizations will be established. The problems associated with peer review are well known, but it represents a legitimate compromise that allows review of individual decision making without bringing in bureaucrats.

Legislation. In the short run, prospects for passage of the Clinical Laboratory Improvement Act are dim because of the Carter Administration's wavering support, because of higher priority being given to other health legislation, and because of the lack of Congressional leadership on the issue. But many of CLIA's goals will probably be achieved anyway through administrative measures under existing statutory authority.

Notably, it would be to the advantage of all affected parties to end the current jurisdictional conflicts involving the CDC, the FDA, and the HCFA and to place full regulatory control over clinical laboratories in a single agency. Thus CLIA or its equivalent will gradually come to be a fixture of clinical laboratory practice by the year 2000.

The prospects for national health insurance are more difficult to predict. The budget for the next several years will not permit implementation of a full-scale national health insurance program such as that proposed by Senator Edward Kennedy (D.-Mass.). Even a gradual phase-in, the compromise announced by President Carter at the start of his Administration, would probably cost too much. It appears likely that instead of a full national health-insurance system, we will achieve many of the same objectives with piecemeal legislation, particularly enactment of some type of catastrophic coverage. The Federal government will probably implement other key aspects of national health insurance with a carrot-and-stick approach, requiring laboratories to comply with minimum standards or risk losing Federal money. Increased coverage and regulation thus appear inevitable.

The challenge for health professionals, including clinical laboratorians, will be to keep added regulation from adversely affecting their care of patients. It won't be easy, especially if state and Federal governments become so attracted to the short-term benefits of cost control that, in the long run, they impair the quality and accessibility of laboratory medicine.

INDEX

Index

Other Titles of Related Interest From Medical Economics Books

Sharpening Laboratory Management Skills
Compiled and edited by Edward M. Friedman
516 pp., 6 × 9, ISBN 0-87489-204-X, hardcover.

Laboratory Communication: Getting Your Message Through
By Arthur F. Krieg, M.D., et al.
192 pp., 6 × 9, illustrated, ISBN 0-87489-185-X, hardcover.

Managing the Patient-Focused Laboratory
By George D. Lundberg, M.D., et al.
396 pp., 6 × 9, ISBN 0-87489-065-9, hardcover.

A Practical Guide to Financial Management of the Clinical Laboratory
By Janiece Sattler
152 pp., 8½ × 11, ISBN 0-87489-235-X, softcover.

Job Plodd, Pathologist—Satirical Sketches
By Alvan G. Foraker, M.D.
204 pp., 6 × 9, ISBN 0-87489-095-0, hardcover.

For information, write to: